THE SPINSTER
THE PROPHET

THE SPINSTER
THE PROPHET

H.G.Wells, Florence Deeks,
and the Case of the Plagiarized Text

A.B. McKILLOP

Four Walls Eight Windows
New York/London

Published in the United States by
Four Walls Eight Windows
39 West 14th Street
New York, NY 10011
http://www.4w8w.com

UK offices:
Four Walls Eight Windows/Turnaround
Unit 3 Olympia Trading Estate
Coburg Road, Wood Green
London N22 6TZ

First published in Canada by Macfarlane Walter & Ross
First U.S. printing August 2002

Library of Congress Cataloging-in-Publication Data:

McKillop, A. B.
    The spinster and the prophet : H.G. Wells, Florence Deeks, and the
mystery of the plagiarized text / by A.B. McKillop.
        p. cm.
    Includes bibliographical references and index.
    ISBN 1-56858-236-6
    I. Title.

D21 .M248 2002
941.08'092--dc21

                                                    2002071292

Printed in Canada

10   9   8   7   6   5   4   3   2   1

To
Jeannie Grant Ritchie McKillop
(1921–1998)

In Memoriam

"I'm writing a history of the world," she says. And the hands of the nurse are arrested for a moment; she looks down at this old woman, this old ill woman. "Well, my goodness," the nurse says. "That's quite a thing to be doing, isn't it?"

Penelope Lively, Moon Tiger (1987)

"Always easier to believe in a gaga older woman, than in a man's perfidy. I've seen it many times."

Amanda Cross, Sweet Death, Kind Death (1984)

Contents

Preface

"Alas, we historians have so little scandal. We are
not palaeontologists to display our Piltdowns."

Angus Wilson, *Anglo-Saxon Attitudes* (1956)

THE SPINSTER CAME INTO MY LIFE with a foot-
note. I had been doing some research involving a Canadian historian,
Frank H. Underhill, who had been a prominent and controversial
public figure. I thought I knew his lengthy and distinguished career
well, but halfway through the only biography of him, *Frank H.
Underhill: Intellectual Provocateur*, by R. Douglas Francis, I was
stumped.[1] In 1930, he had played an important part in a sensational international legal and literary controversy involving one of
the most famous authors in the world, some leading publishers on
both sides of the Atlantic, and an unknown Toronto woman. The
woman's name was Florence Deeks. The author was H.G. Wells.

This was news to me. Wells, of course, I had heard of. Who had
not? He was a founder of modern science fiction, a great social
prophet, and the author of *The Outline of History*, one of the most
popular works of history in the twentieth century. But who on earth
was Florence Deeks? What was this curious business all about? The

xiii

Underhill biography said little about the controversy and even less about Miss Deeks.

This is where the footnote came in. It mentioned a collection of "Deeks versus Wells Papers" and pointed in the direction of the Toronto Public Library. I resolved to visit it when an opportunity arose. Meanwhile, some preliminary digging in my university library was in order. Soon I knew a little more, for the journalists Donald Jones and Robert Fulford had written briefly about the story of Deeks and Wells.[2] Works of reference indicated that corporate papers of one of Wells's publishers, Macmillan & Company, Limited, were preserved in the British Library in London, and that those of Macmillan of Canada were at McMaster University in Hamilton, Ontario.

In his several guises – as writer of science fiction, as advocate of progressive causes such as the liberation of women, and as social prophet – Wells has inspired a very large body of writings about him, scholarly and otherwise. A quick check in the university library suggested that study of the various threads of his life had become almost an industry unto itself, and much of it was easily accessible. Fortunately, Wells's voluminous papers were in North America, at the University of Illinois. The private papers of some of his friends and correspondents could be found in archives at Oxford, Brighton, and elsewhere.

Doing history can be fun, especially when a subject promises a compelling story or an unresolved mystery, and early in my career it had been my good fortune to discover a long-suppressed biography of the Upper Canadian radical William Lyon Mackenzie languishing in a dusty archive, and to have it published.[3] I therefore felt twice blessed. No historian who has had such good luck can forget the thrill of discovery it entails. The curious encounter between the spinster and the prophet piqued my interest in just such a way, as if its details sought release from an unbidden past. An unknown spinster. A famous author. Literary theft. Scandal and intrigue. Courtroom drama. Above all, the spinster. Who was she? And had she really written her own history of the world?

The conventions of scholarship are my stock-in-trade, and this was a story that would require the careful layering of circumstantial detail in order to convince. But fidelity to the factual record alone, I sensed, could not entirely get at the deeper truths of some characters central to the story I wished to tell. Much of it is about silences, about things said and done in the interstices of private life. The conventions of the academic monograph lend themselves poorly to the reconstruction of this kind of world. This was a story, it seemed, that needed to be informed by scholarship on a variety of subjects; but it was also clear to me that the apparatus of scholarship by itself could not adequately address the particular silences of more than one of its main characters.

In *Dead Certainties (Unwarranted Speculations)*, Simon Schama quotes from *The Sense of the Past*, an unfinished novel by Henry James. A historian named Ralph Pendrel wants desperately to communicate with the dead, but the conventional practice of history denies him this. "He wanted the unimaginable accidents, the little notes of truth for which the common lens of history, however the scowling muse might bury her nose, was not sufficiently fine. He wanted evidence of a sort for which there had never been documents enough or for which documents mainly, however multiplied, would never *be* enough."[4] Exactly.

In *The Spinster and the Prophet*, the inner life of characters is at times suggested, but only if empirical evidence points to the likelihood of the interior monologue or of the private act. If, then, I portray Miss Deeks sitting alone in her parlour, or Mrs. Wells taking tea, again alone, in an armchair in her garden, and if I suggest that these women may have been thinking about something, I hope readers will forgive these and other small inventions. For they are inventions only when measured against the empirical, which affords itself certain privileges even as it excludes. The great irony is that most working historians recognize that the seemingly objective order of event-driven history dissolves into the realm of the interpretive in the actual practice of their craft. They, too, largely work within the framework of inferred probability.

This is a story that hinges on likelihood. As a legal mystery, its resolution is constructed of circumstantial evidence, and considered as a whole it is powerful stuff. As a domestic drama, the story has come to involve two women, and their voices are often silent just when we want them to speak their minds. But Florence Deeks and Catherine Wells did spend time alone in their parlours and their gardens, just as they ate lunch and combed their hair; and at times they were lonely even when surrounded by others. Often they left only indirect testimony of such mundane details of their lives, but it is testimony of such implicit resonance that not to address it would be tantamount to suppression of a vital element of likely truth.

In his March 1999 keynote address, "The Great War and the Historical Imagination," given to the annual Frank H. Underhill Colloquium in Carleton University's Department of History, the eminent historian Modris Eksteins reminded his audience, "For facts to become memorable, an element of fiction [is] essential." If at times I violate convention, I do so in order to reconstitute likely occurrence. Such passages, fully consistent with the facts as I know them, are invoked as angels of a deeper truth.

The great American historian Carl Lotus Becker once reflected on his experience in writing. His work might not be history, he wrote to a friend; maybe it was moonshine. But Becker wrote in the only manner he could in order to tell his tale. Similarly, my story, history or moonshine, is told in the only way I have thought might do justice to the remarkable entanglement of Miss Deeks and Mr. Wells, who met but once, and to the little-known inner life of Catherine Wells. Besides, moonshine casts its own illumination and it, too, can reveal shadows of hidden figures lurking behind bushes.

A.B. McKillop
Ottawa, Ontario / Messines, Quebec
May 2000

I   *Lace Curtains*

> History keeps memorials of the great, the saintly or
> the victorious, but we may pine for the chance to hear
> about men and women more like ourselves: common
> folk . . . Reading the documents . . . , we hear the
> ancient equivalent of lace curtains being moved aside.
>
> Anne Wroe, *A Fool & His Money* (1996)

INSIDE THE PARLOUR WINDOW on a cold weekend
evening a week before Christmas, 1920, a woman settles into her
favourite chair to read the latest issue of *Saturday Night* magazine.
Each week the masthead of this Toronto magazine of politics and
culture, founded in 1887 to capture the interest of the nation's
middle class, reminds its readers that it is "The Paper Worth
While." Middle-class citizens of the city – known for years as
"Toronto the Good" and renowned for its profusion of churches
and its evangelical Protestant ethos – turn to *Saturday Night* for
serious commentary on politics, society, and the arts.[1] The Deeks
women are among them, and it is Florence, not her widowed
mother or her sisters Annie and Mabel, who has picked up the
magazine this winter's night. Like Annie and Mabel, Florence
Deeks is a spinster.

As usual, the first section of the December 18 edition details the
political and financial affairs of men. Two issues earlier, the politician and statesman Sir George E. Foster had been the subject; then
came the turn of D.B. Hanna, president of the Canadian National

Railway Company. This week a large photograph and profile of Sir Lomer Gouin, former premier of Quebec, commands the front page. Editorials surround the picture. They preach the harsh competitive doctrines of the day, dismissing the Toronto school board as a "spendthrift organization," condemning trade unions, and applauding the United States government for its imminent repeal of a tax on excess profits. "Let's get back to business," the editor urges.

And for the ladies? The lead page of the women's section is about a woman in Walkerville, Ontario, who uses corn husks and scissors to fashion fairy figures in various poses – "The Little People of the Cornfields." There are photographs of them. The author of the piece, Frances Fenwick Williams, has spotted a lesson in the artist's fey art: "The Little People are potent emancipators. They free us for the time being from the sordid world of commerce and economics and monotonous toil." Frees them, the "Society" section seems to say, for dinner dances, debutante balls, and lavish society weddings.[2]

Florence Deeks is well into middle age. Slightly taller than average, she had maintained a trim figure even into her forties, but no longer. Like her waist, her face has filled out with the passing years until now it is round and fleshy. Her jaw seems permanently set in a look of stern determination, as if to ward off any hint of life's caprice. Once a warm brown, her hair is turning grey. She seldom wears a smile, although her younger sister, Mabel, tries her best to provoke one. Florence is like her mother, for whom not much in life is a source of amusement. Woman's lot is a hard one. The house at 140 Farnham Avenue is made of bricks and mortar, but it is held together by earnestness.

This evening, Florence seems impatient with *Saturday Night*. The crassness of the business and political commentary, centred on the cash nexus, offends her moral sensibility although she has no objection to fortunes won by dint of self-help and hard work if applied to worthy ends. The women's pages are no better, merely the reverse. They are too given over to frivolity to appeal to her sense of romance, merely insulting her intelligence. With more than the hint of a frown, she flips pages in search of something to stimulate an intelligent woman's mind, eyes scanning the "Music and

Drama" section, its reviewer full of praise for the Massey Hall concert performance by the contralto Marguerite D'Alvarez. The singer possesses, it is said, a "divine lust of song" surpassing "even the impulse of Caruso." No doubt it is the Methodist in Miss Deeks that accounts for her glower at the sensational photograph of the actress Helene Sinnott, with her sultry and seductive eyes and telling décolletage. Sinnott is to play the lead role in *East Is West* at the Royal Alexandra Theatre.

The books profiled in *Saturday Night*'s "Bookshelf" section – a biography of a former premier of Greece and two holiday season offerings aimed at pubescent boys – do not particularly interest her. *The Trail Makers Boys' Annual*, edited by R.G. MacBeth, M.A., and available from the Macmillan Company of Canada, Toronto, for a price of $2.50, promises its youthful readers outdoor tales of famous fur traders, the Royal Canadian Mounted Police, and the Prince of Wales in Canada. Floyd Dell's novel *Moon-Calf* holds more promise, for the reviewer assures his readers that the theme of a young man growing up amidst poverty, helped by a "toil-worn" mother exhausted and old before her age, is noble as well as tragic.[3]

The book that is about to change the life of Florence Deeks is much more important than these, and *Saturday Night*'s assistant managing editor has singled it out for his personal attention. His weekly column, entitled "Reflections," is headed as always with the drawing of a handsome man comfortably seated in a plush arm-chair in a book-lined den. Dog at feet, newspaper in lap, and sherry decanter on the side table, the man in the illustration draws at his pipe while gazing thoughtfully into the blazing fireplace before him. In look, in tone, in content, the image perfectly reflects the self-satisfied author of the column. Hector Charlesworth is a man whose place in the world is secure, and he holds firm opinions on any topic at hand.

In a nation of self-made men, Hector Willoughby Charlesworth had forged himself into a member of its aristocracy of merit. A Hamilton-born Canadian whose paternal forebears had come to Quebec just after the Conquest in 1759 and whose maternal ones had arrived in 1812 at Red River with Lord Selkirk, Charlesworth had lived in Toronto since shortly after his birth in 1872. He went to the city's public schools and, while not following directly in his father's footsteps as a shoe manufacturer, went far enough along this path to article at fifteen as a chartered accountant.

Then, at seventeen, he began to submit poems and prose sketches anonymously to *Saturday Night*, using the *nom de plume* "Touchstone." So impressed and intrigued was its founder and editor, Edmund E. Sheppard, that in 1891 he used his column to invite "Touchstone" to disclose his identity. Charlesworth replied, and Sheppard immediately offered him a position. He had found his calling. After a year at *Saturday Night* he left to gain broader experience as a reporter. For the next eighteen years he worked for Toronto daily newspapers, including the *World*, the *News*, and the *Mail and Empire*.

By the time he rejoined *Saturday Night* in 1910, he had been city editor of the *Mail and Empire* for a half-dozen years and had done much else. He was widely known as an editor, but he had made his reputation as a musical and dramatic critic. He also enjoyed the worlds of politics and finance, and nothing delighted him more than writing about the patriarchs of Canada, especially the captains of industry and the great politicians he knew and admired.[4]

In 1919, Charlesworth approached the pinnacle of a career by no means near its end. He had been chosen as the editor of *A Cyclopedia of Canadian Biography*, published in that year. From this position, he presided over the writing of almost 500 entries on "Representative Canadians." Not one was a woman. The entry on himself, its prose bearing a distinct resemblance to his own style, was a third longer than that on the premier of New Brunswick.[5] Sporting a beard carefully trimmed to resemble that of the late King Edward VII, Hector Charlesworth was the very embodiment of the Edwardian patriarch.

The book Charlesworth had settled down with in December 1920, and for which he now offers his considered reflections, is *The Outline of History*, by the novelist and social prophet H.G. Wells. Whatever else this edition of *Saturday Night* magazine may contain, this item certainly gets Florence Deeks's full attention – not for the fame of the author but for the subject he has chosen.

Charlesworth has found *The Outline of History* almost beyond praise. What better New Year's resolution can there be, he begins, than to read it? But by no means should it be "raced through in a hurry," for the book is so monumental in size and scope that even he, a professional reviewer, cannot "yet pretend to have exhausted its many phases." Charlesworth stands in awe of what Wells has accomplished. "To anyone professionally familiar with the business of writing," he says, "contemplation of the task that Mr. Wells undertook, and accomplished within a comparatively brief period, is almost appalling – nothing short of compressing into two volumes, each about the length of 'David Copperfield,' all history from the evolution of the earth out of space to the international events of the present year. Such a synthesis, such an interpretation of life as a cognate whole has never been attempted single-handed by any other man."[6]

As she reads these words, Florence Deeks begins to feel light-headed, with a sinking feeling in the pit of the stomach. With a pencil, she begins to capture some of Charlesworth's passages within parentheses; others she highlights with harsh vertical lines scored in margins. Later, she will scissor the Charlesworth review from the magazine – hastily, raggedly, angrily.

Her pencil falls harshly on Charlesworth's second paragraph, setting its first sentence apart from the body of the text by parenthetical marks. The task of writing such a massive work of history, just published in North America, "has in a mechanical sense been accomplished since the armistice," Charlesworth says; yet "it is necessarily the fruit of a lifetime of thought and mental discipline." The marked passage hints at Florence's exercise in simple arithmetic. Since the armistice? Since November 1918? If Charlesworth is correct, Wells has not only seen his two-volume work of more than a thousand pages through the press but has also written it in less than two years. Even if the book does reflect a "lifetime of thought and mental discipline," is such a feat possible in a work of history as massive as this?

Charlesworth has tried his best to explain this superhuman achievement by pointing to the help Wells had received from others. Wells "does not claim exclusive credit for the achievement," he notes with a sigh of relief that is almost audible. "On his title page he acknowledges 'advice and editorial help' from Mr. Ernest Barker, Sir H.H. Johnston, Sir E. Ray Lankester, and Professor Gilbert Murray. In his preface, he also speaks of assistance from forty other more or less noted specialists. In addition his volumes are documented with citations from many renowned authorities, living and dead, but it is certain that none of these could have accomplished what Mr. Wells has done in marshalling every essential fact, scientific and historical, since the beginning of things." These words, too, draw the attention of Florence Deeks's furious pencil.

Wells's book on the evolution of human civilizations begins before the caveman and ends with the catastrophe of the Great War of 1914–18. His argument is that war is not an inevitable element of human existence but is brought about by "militaristic thinking born of the old desire to seize the property of others." The rest of Charlesworth's review, which ends with the words "A great book – one of the greatest of all time!" reinforces Miss Deeks's growing sense of alarm. She resolves to obtain a copy of *The Outline of History* as soon as possible.

Saturday Night is not available each week until late Saturday afternoon – it is intended, after all, for leisurely reading on a weekend evening. So she will need to wait, for the stores are closed and they will remain so until Monday, when she will go to the T. Eaton department store and buy a copy of *The Outline of History*.

A vivid image springs to mind: Florence, first thing Monday the 20th, stepping down from the streetcar at Yonge and Queen Streets, the heart of the retail district, head burrowed into collar against the harsh west wind and the temperature hovering around the freezing point, eyes wary of darting pedestrians and glancing quickly to the discreet gilt-bordered "T. Eaton Co." sign between the second and third storeys. It is a bustling intersection in December, crowded with Christmas shoppers. Eaton's main floor is even more boisterous than Yonge Street; floors sloppy with slush from outside, scurrying citizens, now customers, energized by the prospect of bargains for which Eaton's has become famous.

To people originally from rural or small-town Ontario, like Florence, the sheer range of goods available for purchase is almost overpowering, dizzying. Boudoir lamps reduced from $9.00 to $6.75, embroidered luncheon napkins at $2.50 a dozen, beautiful cedar chests for $18.50. Watercolours and oil paintings, varnish and stains, Wilton hearth rugs, English tapestry table covers, velvet rugs, and hand-embroidered pillow cases. At $12.00, the two volumes of Wells's *Outline of History* are a considerable investment for Florence when $4.90 will get a Buster Brown box camera for a nephew and $3.75 will bring home a lovely cut-glass bonbon dish for a deserving sister. But for her fear that the book might sell out before she can obtain a copy, she would have waited until the new year. Yet there she is, walking briskly in her winter cloth coat, with purpose as always, oblivious to the racks of women's laced boots finished in black gunmetal or the men's wool pullovers, special at $2.95, or the vast displays of fabrics – black chiffon, black messaline, coloured or black silk chiffon taffetas – all around her.[7]

And then, still on the main floor, she reaches her *sanctum sanctorum*, the Eaton's book department. It lacks the warm atmosphere of Albert Britnell's store further north on Yonge Street, but it carries a broader selection of popular titles, often at discount prices. Compared with the swirl in other Eaton's departments this is an island of repose, one of the few havens where lingering remains a virtue. A man may not be able to purchase his pipe fixings, cigars, or cigarettes at Eaton's, for sales of tobacco products and alcohol have been strictly forbidden by the Methodist Eaton family; but he can take home the latest in popular fiction like the cowboy novels of Zane Grey or William MacLeod Raine, the Tarzan books of Edgar Rice Burroughs, or the combination of western adventure and muscular Christianity that Ralph Connor, Oliver Curwood, and Harold Bell Wright have honed to perfection. For the young lady of the family, there is a vast selection of sentimental romances such as L.M. Montgomery's *Anne's House of Dreams* and *Anne of Avonlea*, Jean Webster's *Daddy Longlegs*, and for her mother and aunts Mrs. Humphry Ward's *Missing* and Eleanor H. Porter's *The Road to Understanding*.

At last, amidst the panoply of gift books, she finds the two thick volumes of *The Outline of History*, by H.G. Wells, published by Macmillan of New York and bound in handsome wine-coloured cloth. Miss Deeks surrenders her cash, her native reluctance over-come by curiosity. She carefully tucks the change into her leather change purse and is soon seated on the streetcar heading north to her modest home on Farnham Avenue, the two volumes in a paper bag, firmly secured to her lap with gloved hands. The return seems longer, but not once is she tempted to open the package to see whether Charlesworth's portrait is true. Not yet, not in a public conveyance.

So she waits until she is home, and even then the parcel sits unopened on the front hall table until she has had her midday meal, as if she is teaching it a lesson in forbearance. Only later, in the parlour, does she begin to examine *The Outline of History* for herself. By the time she has finished the preface, her worst fears are confirmed. From the opening paragraphs of *The Outline*, she begins to recognize words and phrases that are distinctly familiar. Its author makes an argument against the follies of war very similar to the one that she herself has taken such pains to articulate. Something is not quite right, and has not been since she submitted the manuscript of her own history of the world – the labour that occupied her all the long years of the war – to the Canadian branch of the same company that has just published *The Outline of History* by the great H.G. Wells.

2   *Formations*

Most lives have their core, their kernel, the vital
centre. We will get to mine in due course, when I'm
ready. At the moment I'm dealing with strata.

Penelope Lively, Moon Tiger (1987)

Until her dying days, Florence Deeks believed
that the history of Dundas County, Ontario, was near the centre of
the history of Canada. Several times late in life she sought to recapture her sense of this part of eastern Ontario, where the family had
settled and she had been born, by attempting to write novels about
its early years. Whether in "The Homestead by the River," "The
County by the River," or "How Changed the Scene," the setting
was always the same: the area around the town of Morrisburg in
the decades after the arrival of the United Empire Loyalists, fleeing
their former neighbours in Albany and the Mohawk Valley during
and after the American Revolution. "There are many descendants
of those United Empire Loyalists now living on these homesteads
throughout the country and along the beautiful river, with the traditions of early United Empire Loyalists still clear in their minds,"
one of her novels begins.[1]

For a woman with a strong sense of history, Florence Deeks left
remarkably few details about herself or her family. The deepest strata
of her life, the earliest and the most important in her development as

a woman, went unrecorded, alive only in her memory. The only document in which she provided details about her family background states briefly what can be gleaned from her unpublished novels: that she was born in Morrisburg, a picturesque town on the north side of the St. Lawrence River about ninety miles west of Montreal and only a short distance from Crysler's Farm, where British and Canadian troops had repulsed an American attack during the War of 1812. "My parents," she declared proudly, "were descendants of English and United Empire Loyalist ancestors."[2]

Indeed they were. Her grandfather, John Deeks of St. Edmunds in England, had served under Wellington during the Peninsular Campaign and was one of the British "Redcoats" wounded on Canadian soil in 1813 at the Battle of Crysler's Farm. Taken to the home of Major Henry Merkley, a wealthy local landowner, to recuperate, the twenty-five-year-old soldier met Merkley's daughter Catherine, not yet seventeen. Their courtship quickened with the pace of John's recovery. The regimental colonel performed the marriage ceremony, and soon they returned with the regiment to France, where their first child was born.

They remained in France for two years, until the final defeat of Napoleon at Waterloo. John purchased his discharge from the army and returned with Catherine to the Williamsburg area of Upper Canada, settling in 1817 on a tract of land given to them by her father. Eleven more children were born to them, three girls and eight boys. One of the boys was Florence's father, George, born in 1830.

Catherine Melinda Reid, Florence's mother, was seven years younger than her husband and went by her middle name.[3] She was Melinda, a young woman with a mind of her own, and at nineteen she determined that a farmer from Williamsburg, George Deeks, was the man for her. They married in 1856 and took up residence in the nearby town of Morrisburg. Six children followed over the years, and each survived the harsh Upper Canadian winters into adulthood. In the spring of 1871, a government agent recorded the family's ages when gathering information for the first post-Confederation national census. George was forty-one and Melinda thirty-four. Annie Elizabeth, their first-born, was fourteen; George

Samuel and Charles Alexander were twelve and ten, respectively. Florence Amelia, born on September 4, 1864, was seven, followed by her younger brother, John Frederick, who was three years old. Mabel Caroline Louisa would not be born until January 1875 during a family vacation in Europe.[4]

The family of George and Melinda Deeks was a devout one, listed in the census as Evangelical Lutheran.[5] Beginning in 1784, much of the Morrisburg area had been settled by Loyalists with a German Protestant background, bringing with them the founding families of the district, like the Merkleys and the Meikles. One of the first Protestant churches built in Upper Canada was Lutheran, erected in 1789 at Riverside, three miles east.[6] By the 1860s, the family had the choice of several local Protestant churches to attend, including Church of England, Presbyterian, and Methodist.

Later in the century the Deeks family would gravitate to the Methodist church, largest and most successful of the Protestant denominations, for its members were as evangelical as they were Lutheran and, like Victorian Methodism itself, they strove for middle-class respectability. But at least into the 1870s the family appears to have worshipped with the Lutherans. It was probably at Melinda's insistence that the family went to the local Lutheran church, for when asked about her origins by the census-taker she gave "German" as her answer. In matters of religion, the German Protestant side of her parental background prevailed (her mother's maiden name was Weegar). Florence remembered her childhood as one "spent in a home characterised by Christian teaching and a strong incentive to learning and culture."[7]

Amateur histories of Dundas County and of the town of Morrisburg, otherwise so devoted to listing the names of founding families and local boosters, are silent about George Deeks. If he was at all like the son to whom he gave his Christian name he was a thoughtful but quiet man, a person who shunned the glare of public attention and who lived to work. Family lore has it that, in contrast, Melinda was a woman of great force of personality and opinion. It seems, clearly, that this was a family that honoured its patriarchal head but was driven by the energy and will of its matriarch.[8] The hand that rocked the Deeks family cradle appears truly to have ruled its world, and would do so for the better part of a century. George inspired his children by dint of example, but it was Melinda who gave direction as well as shape to this Victorian family's values.

Melinda Deeks had high expectations of her children, and she believed that, while piety led to sanctification, education was the key to success and respectability. She wanted her children to rise in the world. She instructed the children at home and enrolled them in the local school as soon as they were of age. In the year of the 1871 census, all but John, who was only three years old, were pupils. Seven-year-old Florence walked with her brothers and sisters to Morrisburg's school on Colin Street, a five-classroom brick building with the main floor used as a common school, the second floor as a grammar school (secondary school), and the large basement as a town hall.

Families who sent one or several of their children to provincial grammar schools rather than private schools or academies were usually, like the family of George Deeks, large ones. For them, grammar schools provided an inexpensive and ready means to a good education. This was especially the case in small communities such as Morrisburg, which lacked a variety of educational alternatives. In the mid-nineteenth century, however, few families assumed that their children would be schooled for any prolonged period, and farmers and merchants sent fewer of their children to grammar schools than did the professional classes. Girls attended less frequently than boys.[9]

Parents like George and Melinda may have wanted all their children to obtain a grammar school education, but very often practical necessities gave boys priority over their sisters. Boys entered the grammar schools at a young age in order to get a quick start on the classics, and they stayed in school longer. In contrast, if they entered grammar school at all, girls enrolled at a later age and for a shorter period of time, usually no more than five years. In fact, daughters of those who saw themselves among the "gentleman" class stayed in school for a shorter period than those of labourers, since they had more opportunities and less need of an education for vocational purposes.[10]

By the time Florence was old enough to qualify for secondary education, a handsome new building for the upper school had been built on the corner of Second and McKenzie Streets.[11] Now designated the Morrisburg Collegiate Institute, it was to prepare students academically for college or university. Provincial regulations instituted in 1865 tied school funding to the number of students studying Latin and Greek, and excluded students not studying the ancient languages from attending grammar schools at all. This largely meant girls. Educational authorities clearly wished to restrict a classical education (and therefore entrance into university) to boys. Girls, it was thought, should attend their own schools and "be taught a curriculum appropriate to woman's peculiar nature and duties in life."[12]

A fire in 1925 destroyed many of the Morrisburg Collegiate Institute's records, but some survived in private hands. Among them is its *Calendar* for the year 1910–11, which includes a list of past graduates. Florence Deeks's name appears in the list of "Senior Leaving Graduates" for 1894. She graduated at the unusual age of thirty.[13]

Florence Deeks and her sisters, like so many other girls and young women of the day, were very likely required at different points in their youth to interrupt their schooling. Perhaps the fortunes of the Deeks household fluctuated with the harvests and market conditions for produce, and at times the family found it difficult to make ends meet, thereby making it necessary for the Deeks girls to secure paid employment outside the home. It is possible that the educational advancement of Annie, Florence, and Mabel was a sacrifice deemed necessary if the Deeks boys were to succeed in life. Moreover, when Florence was in her mid-teens, around 1880, the acquisition of a secondary school diploma was not a pressing matter for girls unless they were intent on obtaining a teacher's licence, for Ontario universities had yet to accept a woman student and public attitudes in the province scarcely favoured the idea.

For whatever reasons, Florence postponed completion of her high school education. Besides, she was not seen to be the scholar in the Deeks family. This distinction belonged to her brother

George Samuel. Of all their children, it was in his future that the parents of Florence Deeks were to place their heaviest investments.

Victorian Ontario was thousands of miles from the imperial heartland, but the Victorian self-made man, whose moral attributes Samuel Smiles gave definitive expression in his book *Self-Help*, was a contemporary social type found in abundance on both sides of the Atlantic. Born in 1859, the year Smiles's book appeared, George Samuel Deeks was to become one of them. Another, in England, was born seven years later. His name was Herbert George Wells.

By the 1880s, Herbert Wells had come a long way in life from his early years in Bromley, a small market town not far south of London. Born on December 21, 1866, he was the third son of a loveless marriage. His father, Joseph, was from a family of gardeners and loved the outdoor life, gardening, and cricket; his mother, Sarah Neal, daughter of an innkeeper, worked as a lady's maid. The two had met and courted at Up Park, the estate in Sussex where she worked. The maid and the gardener married in 1853, but from the start the match proved a difficult one. Sarah was soon unemployed because she was pregnant; he lost his job through indifference to his work. She recognized that she had fallen beneath her station, and she resented it bitterly. They quarrelled; they considered emigrating to Australia; they lived with relatives of Joseph in Gloucester and Kent. In 1855 they managed to borrow enough money to purchase Atlas House, a small china and dinnerware shop with living quarters, in Bromley. It came with old stock and little trade. It gave Joseph a sense of freedom and Sarah one more source of resentment.[14]

At home, the father was companionable enough to the children, although he disliked the constrictions placed on his life by Sarah's pregnancies. They seemed to come so rapidly, one on the heels of another. The mother was constantly depressed and given to self-pity, her energy laid up for her role as domineering matriarch. As an adult, her son Herbert remembered her as a nag, given to "slaps and scoldings," a woman embittered by her lot. Her "moral harshness,"

Wells later wrote, "overshadowed and embittered our adolescence," and "her passionate mothering . . . sheltered our childhood."[15] This was not a happy home. Joseph spent as much time as possible away from the atmosphere of Atlas House, often over pints at the Bell parlour or the White Hart.

Bertie Wells was a sickly but precocious child, his mother's favourite, a little boy who resented attention paid to his older brothers, especially when it came at his expense. His moods ranged from petulance to aggression. Frequent tantrums were the result. His older brother Frank remembered: "Woe betide if toys his highness wanted were denied him." He would throw objects at his brothers even as he warned them that they had better be easy on him because he was of frail health. As one biography concludes: "At an early age he was learning how to have it both ways."[16]

Bertie Wells fell in love with the world of words at the age of seven, when he broke his leg and discovered the joy of reading during the long recuperation that followed. This was one positive contribution his mother made to his life, for early on she taught him his alphabet and encouraged him to read. So, for that matter, had his father, who often brought home books on any manner of subjects from the local lending library. Shortly after Bertie recovered, he was sent to the Bromley Academy on High Street, not far from Atlas House. There he assimilated the attributes of gentility and book learning in equal measure, and he flourished.

By the late 1870s, however, life at Atlas House had reached a point of disintegration. Joseph Wells injured his leg by falling off a ladder, and a life of real poverty, not just of the genteel sort, lay on the horizon. Sarah had had enough. When an unexpected offer of employment as housekeeper to the lady of Up Park arose in 1880, she jumped at it. Joseph remained in Bromley, to rattle around in Atlas House. Fourteen-year-old Bertie would need to leave school and make a life of his own.

Sarah was intent that each of her boys should learn a trade. "Almost as unquestioning as her belief in Our Father and Our Saviour," Wells later noted, "was her belief in drapers."[17] For Sarah, to work in the textile trade, making fine curtains and clothing, meant to live a respectable life; so she had arranged for Bertie to be apprenticed to one, as his older brothers had been. In this way, his adolescence took Dickensian twists – an apprenticeship at thirteen in Windsor, seventy-hour weeks working for sixpence, sleeping four to a room. But he was an indifferent worker, unrefined in appearance and careless in balancing his accounts. He was soon let go. Adrift, he returned for the winter to his mother and Up Park.

In the stately house he could enjoy the orderly atmosphere of fixed stations in life, a social world without ambiguity – "a complete authentic microcosm . . . a little working model . . . of the whole world" as he wanted it to be.[18] His mother's senior rank gave him free range of the estate and access to its library. He took full advantage, reading promiscuously, especially about politics and philosophy. The stately home's atmosphere of security and books like Paine's *Common Sense* and Swift's *Gulliver's Travels* more than compensated for his small attic room.

Early in 1881, his mother found Bertie employment at a chemist's shop in a nearby town; but he knew little Latin, a necessity for dispensing chemicals. So with help from the headmaster of the local grammar school, he began to acquire the language. Since he had little desire to be a purveyor of patent and other medicines, he managed to convince his mother to help support his enrolment as a full-time student. The headmaster, Horace Byatt, quickly recognized this boy's voracious appetite for learning, and soon Bertie Wells was hard at work at physiology and mathematics, clearly the most promising of the thirty-three students in the school.

Bertie's hopes were dashed once more when his mother again arranged for him to be apprenticed to a draper, this time in Southsea. To his mind, he was enslaved, condemned to thirteen-hour workdays of mind-numbing drudgery. He spent the next two years there, reading books on the conflict of science and religion and visiting Up Park whenever he could escape. In letters to his mother, he begged to be allowed to break his indentures. At last, near a state of emotional breakdown, he simply walked away from his servitude. He confronted his mother and threatened suicide unless he was allowed to return to school so that he could become a teacher. In the end, his parents capitulated to his demands and his father promised to pay the school's tuition fees.

Back with Byatt, he flourished as a student-teacher, earning a modest wage while learning. He discovered Plato, read *Progress and Poverty* by the controversial American land reformer Henry George, and helped other students. All the while, he scrambled to catch up for lost time in his own studies. Before the year was out he had earned several first-class grades and was offered the right to apply for a government scholarship to the Normal School of Science, in Kensington, near the heart of London. He grasped the opportunity and was overjoyed after learning he had won the award. " 'Gloria in excelsis mei!' " he wrote to his brother Frank. "I have now become a holy, a respectable person entitled to wear a gown . . . and to call myself an undergraduate of London University."[19]

Wells was joyous for more reasons than this. The Normal School of Science in Kensington was the institution inspired and led by T.H. Huxley, popularizer of Darwin's ideas. By the 1880s, with the age of industry near its apogee, Huxley had become renowned as the "high priest of evolution," the most energetic advocate of the unlimited possibilities of science. Wells encountered him in a year when Huxley was particularly overburdened with work, tired and in black depression. Still, the great man inspired, and the precocious eighteen-year-old worshipped him, purchasing his most recent writings and attending his lectures on biology and zoology with an eagerness that caught the attention of others and with a mind that appeared to absorb everything around it. During the time he studied under Huxley, Wells caught the master's essential message. This year, 1885, Wells later wrote, was "beyond all question, the most educational year of my life."[20]

After his months under Huxley's tutelage, however, everything about Wells's studies seemed anti-climactic. He made a few friends, most notably a fellow student, Richard Gregory, who came from a background even more impoverished than his own. Both young men had caught the progressive spirit of Huxley's view of modern science and its potential, but Wells's attention drifted away from academic science and his grades suffered. Physics taught by Professor F. Guthrie paled in comparison to lessons by Huxley, for Guthrie was no Huxley and the discomfort caused by his undiagnosed cancer made him an ineffective teacher. Within the year Wells, by his own

recollection, was no longer an "extravagantly greedy and industrious learner" but a "facetious, discontented, restless and tiresome
rebel."[21] Depressed and confused, this young man, who had witnessed the polarities of British class structure first-hand at Up Park,
found himself drawn to socialism and its politics of class, and to
expressions of power in history through the ages.

In sexual matters, his life was no less confused. Like other ado-
lescents, he was given to sexual fantasies about idealized females,
and he was ill at ease with the few girls of his own age he met. His
parents' loveless relationship, marked by acrimony and mutual
accusation, helped him little in understanding the nature of intimacy. His first physical encounter with a woman, the sister of the
owner of his boarding house, was brief and unsatisfying. He left
that place to live with his aunt Mary, and there he met her attractive daughter, Isabel Wells. His cousin became the first love of his
life, the first woman who took him seriously. She was "the one
human being who was conceivable as an actual lover" to this short,
underweight, and shabbily dressed young man. Before long the
couple became, in Wells's later words, "passionate allies who would
conquer the world together." Isabel was also a final distraction
from his studies, and after failing his examinations in 1887 he left
the Normal School of Science.[22] His academic career was over, and
the unsettled lover soon left for a teaching position at Holt
Academy in northern Wales.

The relationship between the immature Wells (still "Bertie" to
friends and family) and the naive, trusting Isabel continued during
his time at Holt Academy. Yet neither she nor his position met his
needs. He detested the academic attitude and the physical surroundings at Holt, and soon became infatuated with the daughter
of a local clergyman, Annie Meredith, a schoolteacher with whom,
as he put it, he "carried on a brisk and spirited flirtation."[23] Isabel
began to drift from his thoughts, as needs overcame commitment –
understandable enough, perhaps, in a young and immature man.
But in the case of H.G. Wells, this was the first hint at a lifetime of
betrayal of those he loved.

In 1880, the year Florence turned sixteen, she bid farewell to her twenty-year-old brother, George. Always an excellent student, he left home for the town of Cobourg, Ontario, and Victoria College, where he entered the bachelor of arts program of the Methodist institution, founded in the 1840s. There he became a brilliant student, excelling especially in mathematics. More than seventy years later, the historian of Victoria College recalled that his scholarly achievement had equalled that of his classmate Lewis Emerson Horning, subsequently appointed to Victoria's faculty as professor of Germanic languages. At their convocation in 1884 the two young scholars were joint recipients of the Prince of Wales Gold Medal.[24]

For a time after his graduation, George turned to teaching, quite successfully it appears, although it is not known where or at what level.[25] But he had set his sights on a more adventurous future. His ambition, like his energy and his intelligence, refused to accept the restrictive boundaries of the classroom. In the 1880s the future of Canada seemed boundless. Its industrial revolution was well and truly under way, and so was its revolution in transportation. A year after George graduated from university, the Canadian Pacific Railway reached the west coast, and with it came unlimited prospects for success in commerce and industry. Financiers and entrepreneurs made vast fortunes. This was no time for the timid, so George S. Deeks moved west to work in the railway industry. Always good at mathematics, he would try his hand at engineering.

Within a decade after graduation, his combination of ambition and skill was much in demand, for he had developed ingenious techniques for laying trackbed in the most inhospitable terrain. As one writer observed, "He went west and in turn conquered the stony crags of the Rockies for the C.P.R. and elsewhere."[26] Deeks proved able to accomplish feats of engineering where other men failed. He became invaluable to railway companies in his role as master of the muskeg, which seemed to be without solid foundation for everyone's rails but his. Many railways sought his services, and the North American northwest and all of the Canadian north became his terrain. Soon he commanded hefty fees and commissions. He was constantly on the move. Early in the new century, his ambitions not fully met, he began to think about ventures beyond engineering, such as real estate and construction.

Everything that is known about George S. Deeks, particularly in his later life, indicates that he was a dutiful son, dedicated to supporting his family and generous to a fault in the financial help he provided to them. There can be little doubt that as soon as he was in a position to do so, he began to send some of his savings home to Morrisburg. By the 1890s, the elder George Deeks was in his sixties, his strength drained by farm work. Enough money appears to have been sent, and on a regular enough basis, to allow the aging farmer to retire and to take on less onerous work as a clerk in the Fifth Division Court of Dundas County.[27]

George's contribution to the family economy, which may well have begun in the 1880s, would also have taken pressure off his sisters to finish their formal education in the local schools. It would have allowed them to pursue their dedication to cultivation and refinement in their own ways and at their own paces. When discussing her early years, Florence spoke of going to a boarding school for girls, although she does not say when or where. "Besides academic work," she added, "I devoted considerable attention to the study of art and music, and also travelled in Europe and America."[28] Perhaps her generous brother's new-found affluence made such luxuries possible, delaying the need for a secondary school certificate.

In 1894, at thirty, Florence completed the final courses and examinations necessary to graduate from the Morrisburg Collegiate Institute. After receiving her certificate she took leave of her family at the multicoloured stone Morrisburg railway station, with its two chimneys and its Romanesque windows, and boarded the Grand Trunk train heading west to Toronto. Like her brilliant older brother, she too would enrol in Victoria College. By then it had federated with the University of Toronto, having relocated in 1892 from Cobourg to Toronto and to an imposing new stone building on the northeast edge of Queen's Park, location of the provincial legislature.

The mid-nineties were an exciting time for most of the students at Victoria College. Fresh breezes filled the air. Everyone had adjusted, after the initial disruption of the move from Cobourg.

New faculty and staff appeared, offering new courses of study. Students announced student clubs and associations in almost every issue of *Acta Victoriana*, their venerable magazine. They created a missionary society in 1894, joining Victoria's men and women formally in a common activity for the first time since 1880, when Nellie Greenwood arrived in Cobourg as the first female student.[29]

At Victoria, in the autumn of 1894, Florence enrolled for an arts degree as a "Specialist in Arts – French and German," a four-year program.[30] In addition to her interest in modern languages, including English, she was also drawn to the study of history. Her professor of German was L.E. Horning, George's rival as Victoria's gold medallist a decade before and now the college's distinguished professor of Germanic languages. The affiliation of Victoria with the University of Toronto also made it possible for Florence to study with professors – Maurice Hutton in classics and W.J. Alexander in English, for example – who later became the stuff of academic legend at the University of Toronto.

Hutton and Alexander were proponents of a distinctive fusion of Christian idealism and Arnoldian humanism in the approaches they took to their subjects. Both men taught at the University of Toronto's "secular" arm, University College, a quarter-mile or so west of Victoria College on the other side of Queen's Park. W.S. Milner, a professor of classics, taught ancient history there. Modern history was covered by the thirty-four-year-old ecclesiastical historian George M. Wrong, whose remarkable promotion from lecturer to the chair of Canadian history in 1894 would within a year help precipitate an undergraduate student strike that shook the university to its foundations. Professor Wrong, the strike leaders claimed, had received the appointment only because his brother-in-law, Edward Blake, a former premier of Ontario, was the chancellor of the university.

Florence continued her studies for two or more years, but she did not finish her degree. No doubt she admired George's achievements, but how could she possibly have hoped to equal much less surpass them? From the moment she set foot in the Victoria College building, with the Biblical injunction "The Truth Shall Set You Free" etched in stone over its entrance, she probably felt inadequate, prisoner to her brother's reputation. To Professor Horning especially, would she ever be other than "George's sister"?

She loved languages and learning, culture and history, and did her best to meet the demands of her courses and her professors. A decade older than most other students, she must however have felt alienated from the mix of student life – the juvenile initiations of freshmen, the boisterous annual student parties named "the Bob" by college tradition, the crude college songs, the frivolous undergraduate chatter, the scurrying around to classes, the polite but constant joustings in the tug-of-war between the sexes. The Reverend Nathanael Burwash, head of the college, distrusted anything – like the new tennis courts north of the main building – that distracted students from their studies. Florence probably held a similar attitude.

Formal studies at Victoria College served as only part of her higher education. There was much in the burgeoning city of Toronto to attract the approval of a person of genteel British-Canadian upbringing, imbued from childhood with the Victorian values of hard work and earnestness. In every direction, church spires of many religious denominations competed for attention. The city was overwhelmingly drawn from the best racial stock, as it saw itself. More than ninety per cent came from an Anglo-Celtic background. Every day hundreds of new immigrants poured out of the Grand Trunk Railway Station near the waterfront, most from Great Britain although southern and central European faces were increasingly common. Work was plentiful, for by the mid-1890s Toronto had recovered from the end of the transatlantic economic downturn of the past two decades.

The good times had begun. New factories opened daily. Real estate boomed. Builders could scarcely keep up with the demand for new factories and office buildings. Land north of Bloor Street, such as Seaton Village, the Annex, and Yorkville, absorbed by the city in the 1880s, teemed with workmen building handsome brick homes for the swelling middle class. Electric streetcars, introduced in 1894, carried workers to the stores and offices on Yonge, Bay, Queen, and King Streets. Florence Deeks now lived in a world that had been beyond her ken in Morrisburg. However much she loved her hometown and her parents and her brothers and sisters, she needed to expand – her mind, her interests, her vistas, her expectations. Morrisburg held the past she so prized, but Toronto bore the secret to her future.

Florence's name is absent from the Toronto city directories for the years 1894 through 1896, when she was an undergraduate student at Victoria College. But this is simply an indication of the transient nature of student life. The college did not yet have residences for students, so like other undergraduates she probably lived in one of the city's many boarding houses for single young men and women. Some of these were indescribably filthy, as the moral reformer C.S. Clark revealed in his lurid 1898 exposé of social conditions and underclasses, *Of Toronto the Good*.[31] Many others, however, like those along the quiet streets of Yorkville, just north of Bloor Street near Yonge Street, offered perfectly respectable rooms for single men and women. She did not live in one for long, for at the end of her second year at university she took up a teaching position with an opportunity to live in residence.

One day in the spring or summer of 1896, Florence walked the short distance north from Victoria College to the handsome new three-storey building that housed the Presbyterian Ladies' College. The address was 151 Bloor Street West, just off the intersection of Bloor and Avenue Road. Undeveloped fields lay adjacent to the occasional government or university building – the provincial parliament at Queen's Park to the south, University College in the distance to the southwest with the Anglican Wycliffe College just north of it, the red-stone McMaster University building bulking large on the south side of Bloor, not far to the west. Looking northward from Bloor Street and Avenue Road, the corners punctuated by tall stone columns that served as the base of ornate gas lamps, one could see trees lining the boulevards. A few minutes' walk north lay open land stretching away for a mile or so to Upper Canada College, the private school catering to the sons of the city's elite. It, too, was coming within the city's grasp, for paved and well-lit streets had begun to appear and the area was busy with the din of carpenters' hammers and horse-drawn supply wagons. City residents were moving north.

Florence had learned that a position was open at the Presbyterian Ladies' College for an instructor in modern languages. She applied for it and was offered the position, so in the autumn of 1896, although still enrolled as a university student, she became a member of the college staff. It is at this point, apart from the lone appearance of her name in the census of 1871, that she begins to be part of the historical record, to be part of "history." Her name appears in the 1896–97 *Calendar* of the college as an instructor in German languages and literature, with "Honour Undergraduate, Toronto University," listed as her honorific.[32] In 1897 her name is listed for the first time in the *Toronto City Directory*, her address that of the college.

In the summer of 1888, in poor health and separated from Isabel, Herbert Wells left Wales for Up Park, where he spent several months recuperating. Then he returned to London. He was nearly penniless. Over the next year or so he tried tutoring, began to contribute modest pieces to London mass-circulation magazines, took a position teaching in a school in Kilburn, and, with an initial reluctance, renewed his relationship with Isabel. Any future with her meant putting his domestic economy on a firm footing, and with new resolve he completed the courses for his degree in zoology and secured a position as a biology instructor in a tutorial college run by the educator William Briggs that had recently opened in an alley near the Strand. He and Isabel married at the end of October 1891.

The union was doomed from the start, for it was one between a woman Wells deemed to be too unresponsive physically, and too little interested in the life of the mind, and a man fuelled by the power of ideas but incapable of commitment. He was divided and confused in his sense of obligation, and so he came to think of her as "the gently firm champion" of all that he felt was suppressing him.[33] Romantic love turned to polite endearment, his attention turned to other women, and soon he had again betrayed her, this time with her friend from the photographer's shop where she worked. He did so in a manner decidedly more calculated than he had in Wales. As he put it later, "I embarked as soon as I was married, upon an enterprising promiscuity. The old love wasn't at all dead, but I meant now to get in all the minor and incidental love adventures I could."[34] Thus began his career as a serial adulterer.

By the autumn of 1892, his eyes were fixed on one of his students from the college, Amy Catherine Robbins, whose "fragile figure, . . . very delicate features, very fair hair and very brown eyes" he found alluring. She soon came to symbolize for him the "better companionship" that might be possible in a life without Isabel.[35] He believed he loved his wife, but he came to think that he had found a soulmate. In December 1893, he convinced Isabel to accompany him on a weekend trip with Miss Robbins and her mother, and it became obvious – at least to Isabel – that the marriage was seriously compromised.

Perhaps forced to do so by his wife, Wells chose between the two women. He opted for the soulmate, although not before securing counsel and support from Richard Gregory. The two had kept in touch since their student days together at the Normal School of Science, and they remained close friends. Years later, Gregory reminded Wells of the occasion: "You asked me to come to 4 Cumnor Place to see you, and you told me in a walk towards Banstead what you intended to do. I remember very well seeing your trunk in the front room ready . . . to take with you the following morning."[36] In January 1894, Bertie and Catherine eloped, against the strong objections of Mrs. Robbins, to begin a life together. They married the next year, not long after his divorce from Isabel on the grounds of adultery.

Wells's career as a writer flourished after his marriage to Catherine in 1894. Life with this self-confident young woman, much more intellectually inclined than Isabel, gave him renewed confidence and energy. He knew that a career as a teacher was not for him. He was too impatient, and it paid too poorly to sustain family life and help support Isabel. The vibrant world of journalism appealed to his restive nature, and he resolved to earn a good living as a freelance writer. Soon he was a regular contributor to the *Pall Mall Gazette* and Frank Harris's *Saturday Review*.

It was a beginning, but freelance work was notoriously unreliable as a basis for family life. Would it be sufficient to sustain him and meet his obligations? He began to write fantastic stories drawn from his interest in science and fuelled by an unbounded imagination. Encouraged by William E. Henley, editor of the *New Review*, he soon expanded some of these stories to book length.

The immediate result was receipt of a cheque from Henley in the tidy sum of £100 for a story about time travel. It was published as a book by William Heinemann in the summer of 1895. *The Time Machine*, with its generous press run and promise of a twenty-five per cent royalty, gave the twenty-nine-year-old author a foothold on a secure future. He felt liberated, and his imagination reacted accordingly. Comfortably at ease with Catherine in a small town in Kent, his pen flew furiously across the page and his publishers could scarcely keep up with his pace. By the turn of the century he found himself heralded as a man of genius, an original thinker, the author of a group of highly successful scientific romances that others might be proud to claim as the achievement of a lifetime. *The Time Machine* was followed in rapid-fire succession by a remarkable series of books: *The Stolen Bacillus and Other Incidents* (1895), *The Island of Dr. Moreau* (1896), *The Wheels of Chance* (1896), *The Invisible Man* (1897), *The War of the Worlds* (1898), *Thirty Strange Stories* (1898), *Tales of Space and Time* (1899), *When the Sleeper Awakes* (1899), and other works.

It was an extraordinary feat for a man still in his early thirties. He was an author readers were coming to know as possessing an impressive mind and an astonishing imagination. The books were hugely popular and met with critical acclaim. But his furious pace had taken a heavy toll. In 1897 alone his health failed on at least three occasions. But he was now famous and on the road to financial security.

On the eve of Queen Victoria's diamond jubilee in 1897, Florence Deeks must have been enormously pleased at the turn her life had taken. The position at the ladies' college was everything the thirty-three-year-old teacher could have hoped for. Her work would be challenging yet rewarding. She could help shape the academic and moral development of young Christian women not only in the classroom but also, by living in residence, in their private lives. Financial independence meant she was mistress of her own destiny.

The Presbyterian Ladies' College had opened in 1889 and was incorporated six years later with an advisory council that included Principal William Caven of Knox College as well as other luminaries of the Presbyterian community in the Toronto area. "It had long been felt," said its *Calendar*, "that such an institution for the higher education of young women, aiming at thorough intellectual culture, and surrounded by healthy social and religious influences, was urgently needed in the city of Toronto." The college offered the best of facilities, its "Bloor Street façade being one of the finest in the city from an architectural point of view." Its grounds were "capacious, extending from Bloor Street to Cumberland Street, and so laid out as to afford ample opportunities for physical recreation."

The college curriculum offered courses in literature and science that prepared girls for matriculation at standards set by the University of Toronto and for the Junior Leaving High School Examination, the non-professional qualification for second-class public school teachers. In general, its academic course aspired to provide an education equivalent to a good high school or collegiate institute and to separate intellectual culture from mere memory work. Perhaps more important, it reflected the intentions of the founders by seeking "to provide for young women a thorough, practical, and liberal education under the safeguard of pure evangelical Christian principles."[37] The family back home was no doubt pleased that Florence seemed to have found her niche in life, and at such a respectable institution too.

In her first year of teaching at the college, the curriculum was offered by a faculty of eight, led by its principal, the Reverend J.A. Macdonald, who taught English literature, history, and composition. Most courses were taught by women – English, French, Latin, and German language and literature; music; sciences such as anatomy, botany, geology, and chemistry; physiology and hygiene. Some possessed an undergraduate degree; invariably, like Miss F.A. Deeks, they were unmarried. Florence taught German language and literature courses that addressed grammatical questions on prose extracts and translations of English into German and of German into English from texts by various authors. The work was demanding, but since she taught only a handful of the ninety-three students enrolled in the college, there was time enough to continue her own university studies. Then, in late winter of the 1896–97 academic year, her father died.

The death notice for George Deeks was brief, appearing in the *Globe* on March 5, 1897, probably placed on behalf of the family by Florence herself. He had died suddenly three days earlier, of "apoplexy," at the age of sixty-seven. The newspaper's understated words captured the quiet dignity of the man and his family. "The deceased," went the copy, "was a very much respected citizen of Morrisburg."[38] This was all that needed to be said. The grieving family conferred about its future, and one of the possibilities seems to have been for the family matriarch, Melinda Deeks, to move to Toronto.

Florence continued to teach at the Presbyterian Ladies' College and to live in residence. By the 1898–99 academic year she had shifted her field of specialty. In that year, still listed as an "Honour Undergraduate, Toronto University," she was made responsible for offering British, Canadian, and ancient history. She felt more comfortable teaching history than the German language, and she had more students with whom she could share her enthusiasm for the glories of the past.

In 1899 the *Toronto City Directory* noted for the first time that "Melinda Deeks, widow of George," had taken up residence in Toronto at 15 Washington Avenue. The new home of Florence's mother was a two-storey brick attached townhouse on a block-long street on the northern fringes of the University of Toronto campus immediately south of Bloor, running west into Spadina Avenue. Perhaps the faithful and prosperous son George made the move and the purchase of the home possible, but it is just as feasible that the estate of Melinda's husband met the necessary expenses.

Florence's brothers Charles and John made their own ways in life, but Annie and Mabel appear to have moved to Toronto when their sixty-two-year-old mother did. Annie was then forty-two, Mabel twenty-four. Their unmarried status meant that a successful brother's generosity was their sole means to a secure future. The *Toronto City Directory* is silent about them until the new century, and even then their names appear in some years only to disappear in others. Most likely, the directory simply failed to find them, just as it said nothing about so many others who neither owned property nor paid formal rent.

Early in the new century, for reasons that remain unknown, Florence lost or resigned from her position at the Presbyterian Ladies' College. By 1903 she too lived with her mother and sisters on Washington Avenue. She was almost forty. Yet there is no evidence that this was a family of diminished means, forced to close ranks in order to economize. In fact the opposite seems to be the case, for in the years after Melinda moved to Toronto, Florence's circles of acquaintance and her social and cultural activity broadened. Her earliest days in Morrisburg aside, the decade and a half before the Great War of 1914–18 appear to have been the happiest years of her life – a personal renaissance before the encounter with Wells in the pages of *Saturday Night* magazine would dictate her future.

Her interests were broad, ranging from history through art to music, and she needed to give them expression. "I took up journalistic work," she wrote years later, "writing chiefly along the lines of art, music, travel, biography and historical sketches."[39] She joined and was very active in a variety of women's clubs, including the Alumnae Society of Victoria University and the Toronto Women's Liberal Club, and served as honorary corresponding secretary for the latter. One of her favourite clubs was the Women's Art Association of Canada.

3   *Labour and Constancy*

"For ten years and more I worked as hard as any
man; I shall never regret it, for it has given me a
feeling of liberty and opportunity such as I should
not have known if I had always lived at my ease. It
taught me a great deal, too; supplemented my so-
called education as nothing else could have done."

George Gissing, *The Odd Women* (1893)

LITTLE ABOUT FLORENCE DEEKS suggests that she
possessed noteworthy artistic talent. No dainty watercolour, no
still-life or landscape is to be found in her surviving effects.
Membership in the Women's Art Association of Canada was nevertheless very important to her because it played a part in shaping her
as a historian. It also helped mould her into a feminist.

The art club Florence joined had very much been the creation of
Mary Ella Dignam. This highly independent young woman had left
Toronto for Europe in 1880, at the age of twenty, shortly after mar-
rying and giving birth to her first child. For the next six years, based
in Paris, she studied art, supporting herself by organizing art tours
for young ladies and travelling with them to Italy and Holland to
view works of the Old Masters.[1]

On her return to Toronto she joined the staff of the Associated
Artists' School of Art and Design, founded in 1884 by Miss E.K.
Westmacott and dedicated to the education of women in handicrafts. Soon, under Mrs. Dignam's tutelage, the group offered classes
in drawing, painting, and modelling in its studio on the second floor

of the Yonge Street Arcade, between Adelaide and Richmond Streets. A tireless worker in the causes of women, art, and citizenship, Mrs. Dignam created in 1887 an organization of young women artists that ran parallel to the one led by Miss Westmacott.

Miss Westmacott soon fell ill, and before two years had passed Mrs. Dignam had taken her place as president, announcing her intention "to create a taste for a higher standard of art in all its phases" and "to make art a patriotic and educative force in the community."[2] The two groups shared space in the Yonge Street Arcade, but it was this second group that in 1890 was incorporated as the Women's Art Club. Two years later it became the Women's Art Association of Canada.

The records of the Women's Art Association do not show Florence Deeks joining it until 1903,[3] but it is likely that she took in its functions almost as soon as she arrived in Toronto in the mid-1890s. Certainly she was familiar with its early history, for in 1912, on the occasion of its twenty-fifth anniversary, she prepared a detailed "historical sketch" of the association that was read to members as part of the celebrations.

In it, the association's first historian took pleasure in noting that the group had been founded as a "self-governing, mutually helpful society." She noted the innovation in women's art studies marked by use of the "living model" in addition to sketching from still life. She described the activities of the association over the years: its art exhibitions; its expansion to the national level through the creation of local branches throughout the country; its Out-Door Sketch Club; its affiliation with the Women's Institute of London; its role in reviving and developing Canadian handicrafts. These, she insisted, were important elements of national development.

One of the signs of the association's acknowledged role as champion of the active involvement of Canadian women in national affairs was its affiliation late in 1893 with the National Council of Women of Canada. It was the first women's organization to do so. Ishbel Gordon, Countess of Aberdeen, wife of the governor general and a leading catalyst in the movement for moral reform, had been instrumental in the founding of the National Council of Women. The Women's Art Association elected Lady Aberdeen its patron.

The members of the Toronto branch of the art association found edification in studio work, but they were also part of a larger and expanding network of women's groups dedicated to moral and social improvement. For the most part, Florence confined her sketch to a straightforward account of the art association's broadening range of progressive activities, but by the end of her address she could not maintain her silence or contain her enthusiasm for the association's objectives. "While the Association is doing pioneer work in art education in Canada," she wrote, "it has always manifested a spirit in sympathy with the advanced thought and movement of the age, which is in some degree indicated by its affiliation with the National Council of Women of Canada. [Its] aim is to stir artistic impulse, educate artistic ability, promote artistic growth and produce artistic accomplishment, a condition which is surely being attained by the united and persevering efforts of its members, 'By Labor and Constancy.'"[4]

Labore et Constantia. Whatever talent Florence Deeks may have had with brush and canvas, she could certainly identify with her group's motto, borrowed from the Plantin Printers of Antwerp. Dedication to work and steadfastness of purpose were among her greatest strengths and, as if to emphasize that members who found it difficult to make art could at least aspire to it and toil at it, she managed to linger over the phrase no fewer than three times in her historical sketch. Members of the Women's Art Association seem to have recognized that Florence embodied the club's maxim, for she served for several years in the early twentieth century as its recording secretary, no doubt as hard-working as she was faithful in carrying out her duties.

One of the Women's Art Association's activities of particular interest to her, and one she may have helped to develop, was the study of art history. The occasional guest lecture, characteristic of the association's earlier days, had given way to organized groups of lectures and reading courses on different schools of art and their development, from classical antiquity to the nineteenth century. Experts from the Toronto intellectual community were asked to offer their expertise, including Chancellor O.C.S. Wallace of McMaster University and Canon J.H. Cody of St. Paul's Anglican

Church. Prominent members of the University of Toronto faculty such as the political economist James Mavor, the classicist Maurice Hutton, and the historian George Wrong frequently spoke on cultural subjects. Occasionally, members of the Arts and Letters Club, an association for men only, would visit the Women's Art Association's studios or come to its exhibitions.

It is difficult to think of Florence as other than active in organizing and encouraging this more academic study of art and its history. But it is also difficult not to conclude that in drawing upon the knowledge of such local experts – all men – a degree of tension, and perhaps silently nursed resentment, had also been introduced to the affairs of the Women's Art Association. Its very existence testified to the effective exclusion of women from other groups in the community, such as the Arts and Letters Club, the Ontario Society of Artists, and the Royal Canadian Academy.

Nothing must have irked the members of the Women's Art Association more than the treatment accorded to their esteemed president, Mary Ella Dignam. Although she had exhibited her work with the Royal Canadian Academy often since 1883 (and would continue to do so until 1924), and was frequently proposed for full membership, she was always rejected. Forty-seven of her paintings eventually featured in RCA annual exhibitions, but she could not gain acceptance as anything but a dabbler in art. The conclusion drawn by a later historian of the art association is that this refusal "was not based on the quality of her work; but rather on her well-known strong feminist stance as an advocate for women artists."[5]

Since the 1870s, Ontario women had sought a measure of equality in provincial political and social life. The Toronto Women's Literary Club, founded in 1877 by Dr. Emily Stowe, had evolved by 1883 into the overtly political Canadian Women's Suffrage Association. Its members had championed the coeducation of women at the University of Toronto, and in 1884 they had gained victory when the Ontario legislature opened University College, the provincial university's teaching arm, to women. (It would take until the years of the Great War for women to win the right to vote in provincial and federal elections.) On another front, the poet, dramatist, essayist, and historian Sarah Anne Curzon argued for the equality of women by encouraging women to write history. Local and provincial historical associations, like those of artists, were overwhelmingly a male preserve. One who insisted that the loyal Laura Secord had been a heroic central figure during the War of 1812, Curzon wished to place such women into the historical record. Like Dignam and the female artistic community, Curzon was refused full membership in historical societies such as the York Pioneers of Toronto and the Lundy's Lane Historical Society, except in an honorary or auxiliary capacity. Her response was to form the Women's Canadian Historical Society of Toronto in 1895.[6] The writing of history could be a political act; it took political and moral courage to reappropriate the past.

Inspired and led by such impressive figures as the writer and reformer Emily Murphy, Sarah Curzon, and later the radical feminist Flora MacDonald Denison, Ontario women became increasingly vocal in their desire to participate fully in political and professional life. Often spurred to action by their dedication to evangelical culture, they joined a host of social and moral reform associations, including those aimed at furthering temperance, female suffrage, child welfare, the eradication of prostitution, and the improvement of working conditions. Membership flourished in the Young Women's Christian Association, the Women's Christian Temperance Union, the Women's Missionary Aid Society, and kindred groups. The National Council of Women was founded largely to link such groups and to help coordinate their crusade for moral improvement.

The members of the more staid and seemingly less political Women's Art Association no doubt differed in their degrees of commitment to such causes, but they clearly saw themselves as part of the larger movement to empower women in a world whose ills were the consequence of the decisions of men. They too would do their part to meet reform goals, and while they may not have been in the forefront of the crusade, they knew that by labour and constancy they could remain engaged in reform work in their own ways.

Women involved in the Toronto art scene often found themselves reminded of the need to remain active in the cause of women's equality. All they needed to do was read newspapers or magazines to learn what men thought of them, their capacities, and their abilities. Every year, local art critics scrutinized their exhibitions, invariably to write patronizing reviews. "In previous years' exhibitions by the club studies of flowers were so numerous as to give reason for the poetic remark that women see the world through flowers," observed the *Globe* in 1892. "This year . . . they are not in number out of proportion . . . Miss Daisy Clark's studies of vegetables are noticeably clever, especially her carrots."[7]

Not to be outdone by the dailies, *Saturday Night* delighted in lampooning the Women's Art Association's chosen genres, for example devoting much of a front page in 1897 to one artist's parody of the women's work that year. In his inversion of their chosen subjects – whether landscapes, still-lifes, or portraits – the artist's caricatures transformed these "women's subjects" into objects of masculine ridicule.[8] Two years later, the sarcasm continued unabated. "There were many delightful bits treated daintily and modestly," said *Saturday Night* of the ceramics of Miss Grace D. Kerr, "and we know it will not be at all necessary in the interests of art to do as Miss Kerr thinks inevitable, 'to die and so become famous.' Most of us will be forced, we fear, to resort to that extremity, but not Miss Kerr."[9] If the reading room of the Women's Art Association of Canada subscribed to *Saturday Night*, the irritation of its members over such relentless jibes can be well imagined.

There were several pathways to feminism, and one lay in the necessity to come to grips at a personal level with assaults on a woman's dignity. At the very least, the need to articulate a personal response to these insults helped create the conditions in which otherwise conservative and reserved women like Florence Deeks might come to embrace the feminist cause.

Almost nothing is known about the inner life of Catherine Wells, at least in a direct sense. The perspective history provides of this marriage is almost entirely that of the husband, the provider, the patriarch. What little we know of the life of Mrs. H.G. Wells is almost entirely his creation, her persona another product of his inventive mind.

Glimpsed from outside, the marital homes of Mr. and Mrs. Wells can only impress. Near the end of 1900, the couple were preparing to take possession of Spade House, the large home they were having built in Kent at Sandgate, near the seashore and not far from Folkestone. Complete with buttresses, a low-eaved roof, iron casements, leaded lights, and spacious grounds, it became what Henry James called their "treasure house on the sea shore."[10] Away from the bustle of London, it was to be their haven for almost a decade, the place where their sons were born and spent their infancy. In some ways, Catherine must have looked back on these early years of her marriage as productive and fulfilling ones. George Philip, her first-born, came along in 1901, followed by Frank Richard in 1903.

Judged only by the building and grounds, the Wells home bears all the marks of success and stability. An observer would assume a world of comfort, order, and happiness inside its walls, a world of servants and nursery maids, of lavish dinner parties and witty repartee. One imagines the famous writer at his desk, scribbling furiously while Mrs. Wells superintends the smooth running of the household – providing the staff their orders at one moment, seeing to the children's needs at another, helping whenever possible with her husband's correspondence, and typing his chaotic manuscripts. Indeed, at a certain level this was the rhythm of their daily life.

Wherever H.G. Wells and Catherine lived, it was she who made certain the household was efficiently managed, comfortable for her husband and children, and inviting to guests. But at the centre of each place was Wells himself. Everything revolved around the man, his work, and his needs. He was often at his desk before dawn, and from the first days of his marriage would call out from his study for "tea and toast, tea and toast," to whoever was within hailing distance, scarcely interrupting his train of thought.[11] His habit was to write well into the afternoon, leaving the evening free for family, entertaining, visiting friends, or going to the theatre. To the extent that he was settled at his work, everything remained on an even keel. But he was notoriously mercurial, and when his needs were unmet, everyone about him adjusted to help fulfill them.

As the new century unfolded, Wells found himself with an ever-widening circle of friendship and acquaintance. London book, newspaper, and magazine publishers knew him well and sought his work. He was a vital element in literary London, a man of letters, a much-sought-after guest at dinner parties and clubs. He numbered among his friends the novelists George Gissing, Joseph Conrad, and Ford Madox Ford and the American poet Hart Crane. He took pleasure in the company of the literary lions Edmund Gosse, J.M. Barrie, and Henry James. He hosted lavish literary parties on weekends, where the fledgling and the famous played games often of Wells's own invention. Host and guests discussed all manner of subjects, competed and flirted with one another, and had a jolly good time. Life, for H.G. Wells, should have been good at the dawn of the twentieth century.

In the language of addiction therapy, a "geographical cure," a move from one place to another in the hope things will get better, is no cure at all. It is merely a form of avoidance, while the problem remains unresolved. So it was with Wells. Each time he decided it was time to move, as to Spade House, it was a sign that something momentous was happening in his life.[12] Catherine may well have reflected on her own circumstances along such lines. The move from London to Spade House took place at a time when her husband was having great difficulty as a writer. In spite of the immense success of his scientific romances, and the financial security it afforded, he was determined to write a novel that was a work of art worthy of a James or a Conrad. At once flattered and annoyed at being heralded as a second Jules Verne or a latter-day Jonathan Swift, he had begun by 1896 to craft a very different kind of book.[13] His new subject was one in which science and the future played only a secondary role. It was to be a story about himself, about the rise of a young man from an impoverished background who becomes a student with the promise of a successful career in science, only to find his hopes dashed by marriage to Ethel – his first wife, Isabel, in thin disguise.

That book, *Love and Mr. Lewisham*, appeared in 1900. As a former science student herself, Catherine had taken an interest in her husband's scientific romances, but this novel was different, one with which she could identify at an entirely new and personal level. It was an experiment as much in technique as in content for Wells, so he took pains to read it to her, chapter by chapter, in order to get it right. In January 1899 he even drew one of the pen sketches he dubbed "picshuas," of a bespectacled Catherine, manuscript in hand, looking sternly at her anxious husband, who sits in an armchair, stiffly cross-legged, as if his very manhood is at risk. Wells called the sketch "Waiting for the Verdict."[14]

After four years of hard work and no little agony for its author, the novel was published to great acclaim by readers and critics alike. But what lessons did the second Mrs. Wells derive from this book, so transparently about her husband's earlier life and innermost thoughts, this personal story taken to the point at which his fictional self was just about to meet the real Catherine? What does it feel like to know that you are on the horizon of a plot by your novelist husband?

Love and Mr. Lewisham is the story of a young man who becomes snared by the trap of domesticity. Lewisham sacrifices a promising future as a scholar for the sake of maintaining his marriage to Ethel. Wells would later write: "At the time of writing it I did not consciously apply the story of Mr. Lewisham to my own circumstances, but down below the threshold of my consciousness the phobia must have been there."[15] But the fear must also have been present in a conscious and direct way during the intimate and perhaps animated conversations between Wells and Catherine about the drift of the book and the motivations of its main character.

The lengthy discussions with his wife about the sad fate of Mr. Lewisham allowed Wells to introduce Catherine to the notion that if their own marriage was to last, it must not repeat the experience either of Wells with Isabel or of Lewisham with Ethel. And he let it be known that in their own marriage there was more than a little of Isabel and Ethel in Catherine herself. The Catherine he had pursued earlier had been a scholar and a woman of independent mind, strong-willed enough to face the ire of her mother in leaving home for a married man and the ostracism involved in being named as co-respondent in a divorce on the grounds of adultery.

But to what end? As discussion over Lewisham's predicament evolved, it no doubt became abundantly clear that this was not merely talk about a novel. It was also about their own marriage – and about her. Worldly success made possible for Wells the freedom of individual choice and action his fictional hero Lewisham craved but did not achieve. It also allowed him to reshape his marriage in ways he could only have dreamed about a few years earlier, and for purposes dictated by uncontrollable desires. Sexual restlessness nagged at him still.

"So long as we were in the opening phase of our struggle for a position and worldly freedom," he later wrote, the question of his sexual needs "was hardly a practical issue between us. There was neither time nor energy to indulge in any form of wanderlust. But with the coming of success, increasing leisure and facility of movement, the rapid enlargement of our circle of acquaintance, and contact with unconventional people, there was no further necessity for the same rigid self-restraint. The craving, in a body that was gathering health and strength, for a complete loveliness of bodily response, was creeping up into my imagination and growing more and more powerful."[16] He was determined to let Catherine know that these cravings had to be satisfied, but he needed to do so in a way that did not put his marriage at risk. The irony was that he found himself propelled into a life of sexual adventure only if he could be confident of the stability of his family life.

The discussion over Lewisham continued in such a vein, Lewisham's thwarted desires resolving variously into Wells's own drives and back to the novel's frustrated protagonist. Four years of such talk, by the end of which the confident Catherine of 1894 was no more. "A very explicit understanding," as he put it, had been reached. He had managed to convince her that he had physical and other wants different from hers, and greater. He argued and ultimately he persuaded. Surely she would not force on him the failed life of poor Lewisham, or, for that matter, his own near-fate in the unsatisfying marriage to Isabel? As Wells's old friend Richard Gregory wrote when telling him how much he liked the novel: "I cannot get that poor devil Lewisham out of my head, and I wish he had an address, for I would go to him and rescue him from the miserable life in which you leave him."[17] Poor Lewisham, poor Wells.

At some point in the slow settling of this marriage, the couple came to an acceptance of his condition, and he chose to conceive it as mutual agreement. But there is a difference between a willingness to accept a proposal and welcoming the conditions of acceptance. The pact was scarcely one between equals, for there was little true reciprocity. In Wells's view, he was the one with sexual needs, she the one whose "delicacy" could not satisfy them. He gave little if any thought to Catherine's desires but took satisfaction in her self-effacing compliance, which the wordsmith chose to interpret as willingness. Later, he took comfort in the rationalization that it was she who "realized perhaps sooner than I" how little their alliance "demanded a monopoly of passionate intimacy."[18]

But was this so? Catherine's submission to his will convinced him that the agreement was one of mutual benefit. Had he not consistently argued with her that his anticipated sexual exploits were to be, to use his term, mere *passades* – not real or enduring love affairs, and certainly of no risk to their marriage? Her "delicacy" required no such release. That, at least, was his theory, as it had been earlier with Isabel. He needed a wife as his helpmate in life, if not in the physical aspects of love. He needed the security of marriage but let it be known that domesticity was "claustrophobic."[19]

The *passades* likely began earlier than Catherine knew. As early as 1888 Wells had confided to one of his friends from the days at the Normal School of Science that he was "one of those human beings who with the simplest and purest of lives, have the most shocking scale of morals believable."[20] If the later claims of Ivy Litvinov, a daughter of Wells's friend Walter Low, are to be believed, he began to demonstrate them in the 1890s. Low was Wells's colleague at the tutorial college, and Wells socialized with Low's family. In Litvinov's recollection, the family friend soon made a pass at her mother and possibly at her aunt, and made suggestive overtures to herself and her daughter.[21]

Enjoying every moment of his new-found fame, Wells seemed to absorb women as he absorbed plots and ideas – as so much raw material to be manipulated to his own ends. In his furious pursuit of literary success, he thought little of ransacking any source at hand for a good storyline. He drew freely on his own experience but had become expert at making the thoughts of other writers his own. According to Wells, ideas and words existed as the common possession of humanity, so when another work offered suitable ones to him, he freely conscripted them for his own purposes.[22]

This was a pattern of behaviour no less portentous than the one that existed in his relationships with women. Although he did not recognize it as such, it was another form of betrayal, trust violated by personal need and for personal gain.

The attraction between Wells and the women he approached was usually mutual, and he struck different women in different ways. The Swiss governess he later employed remembered him as "a young-looking man of medium height, slight, with a large forehead, a heavy moustache, bushy eyebrows, and small hands and feet . . . His eyes under the bushy eyebrows twinkled with boyish gaiety." "He perpetually twinkles," the novelist Berta Ruck wrote, "as though he were catching the eye of the Universe over some cosmic yoke, and he is of what men call a 'useful build.'"[23]

Shortly after her mother's death by suicide in 1895, Dorothy Richardson, a young woman with glowing blond hair and a petite frame that made her look younger than her twenty-two years, came at Catherine's invitation to visit with Mr. and Mrs. Wells. Catherine's close friend from school days in Putney, Dorothy was at first struck by Wells's ordinary looks. But she soon noticed his quick mind, and then the grey-blue eyes and the voice, at once rough yet curiously fragile. She returned often, drawn not to the school chum she had known as "Perky" but to the charisma of the man. She devoured his books and was introduced to his friends, like George Gissing and Grant Allen and Frank Harris, and she attempted to share with Wells her views on the great issues of the day. As often as not, he reacted with impatience and sarcasm, his Cockney voice squeaking with agitation.

With the eye for detail of the extraordinary novelist she was to become, Dorothy Richardson marked this couple closely. Her friend Catherine was now, for some reason, called Jane. In her fiction, Richardson would have her own name for Catherine: Alma, wife of the writer and social thinker Hypo Wilson. "Alma, sitting behind the tea-tray in a green Alma dress with small muslin cuffs and collars." Alma, who "agreed with this man" but "told him nothing, or only things in the clever way he would admire."[24]

Like others, Richardson witnessed the domineering side of Wells, with vitriolic comments aimed at his compliant wife even in public or surrounded by company in his home.[25] "The little man began making statements about Alma. Sitting back in his high-backed chair, with his head bent and his fine hands clasping his large handkerchief, he made little short statements, each improving on the one before it . . . But how could he speak so of her?"[26] Many years later, Wells acknowledged the accuracy of Richardson's portrait: "Her 'Pilgrimage' books are a very curious essay in autobiography; and in one of them, The Tunnel, she has described our Worcester Park life with astonishing accuracy."[27]

Richardson was captivated by this man who "grabbed what he could, revered nothing, felt inferior to no one, and pronounced all this pontifically." The lonely and vulnerable young woman worshipped him. He became, in the words of Richardson's biographer, "the vital center of her life" because every once in a while the famous man would make her think he was interested in her.[28] She was thrilled.

Catherine Wells gradually acquiesced, slowly and reluctantly at first, repressing her own needs and subordinating her desires. In their place, her husband later recalled, she put "the practicalities of life." She took refuge in the arena where he allowed her freedom, that of the home. And as his life enlarged, hers seemed to diminish. Gone were the nicknames for each other from the first flush of marriage. She was no longer "Bits," or "Miss Bitts," or "Snitch-It," with their hints at sexual attraction.[29] She had always liked her name, but he had long insisted on calling her Jane, and that is what she became – just plain Jane to their expanding social circle. His was the roving eye; hers the one to watch the children and order his home. His energies were to be directed outward, to the women he attracted; hers inward, to family finances, domestic routine, the children, the servants, and the garden. For Catherine, labour and constancy became the method of keeping her marriage intact. Whatever else the lengthy discussions of Love and Mr. Lewisham had taught, they could not have served better to put Mrs. Wells in her place, not an unusual feat in the Edwardian years when the monarch was well known for the mistresses he kept.

The vivacious Catherine Wells, in 1894 the very model of the "new woman" who would usher in the new century, found herself transformed into the reserved and controlled Jane that her husband's circle came to know, a model of discretion where his worldly life was concerned. An acquaintance captured this newly refashioned woman in 1902: "His wife is a pretty little person with a strong will, mediocre intelligence and somewhat small nature. She has carefully moulded herself in dress, manners and even accent to take her place in any society her husband's talents may lead them into. But it is all rather artificial, from the sweetness of her smile to her interest in public affairs. However, she provides him with a charming, well-ordered home, though I imagine her constant companionship was somewhat stifling."[30]

This crabbed judgment reflected outward appearance, not the inner woman. For inside "Jane," Catherine still existed, her longings guarded and repressed, but emerging unbidden when the loneliness and isolation became unbearable. "Dearest, dearest, dearest, dearest," wrote the woman within, when her husband was away from her in 1901, "do not forget me – do not fail me. My dear love do not doubt. Do believe in me a little – till I make you quite believe – till I can show you. Oh, but I love you and I am just longing, longing for the time to come. My very very dear. Your (shameless) wife in love." Beneath the calm exterior lay swells of unfulfilled desire and more than a hint of humiliation and desperation. A year later, Catherine again reached out: "I was all silly and crying when you went. I didn't feel a bit dismal, only somehow I think you reduce me to a sort of dewpoint – and the foolish thing is always being tearful and doesn't want to be."[31] The husband's response, as one of Wells's biographers noted, was to counsel "moderation in her approach to him," and in a manner that befitted a father or an older brother: "Don't think me an outrageous squasher of hopes. But what we want before all things is a household we can leave with a tranquil mind at any time."[32] Mrs. Wells wrote to her husband as Catherine; he responded to a wife called Jane.

Florence's circumstances continued to change in the first flush of the new century. Brother George was once more the catalyst, for her fortunes ran in train with his. Now in his forties, George S. Deeks had become a man of means, and in 1904 he married very well. His bride was thirty-year-old Helen Ethel Campbell, a university-educated young woman from the small Ontario town of Morpeth. She had moved with her family to Toronto in 1893 when her father, a prominent member of the federal Liberal Party, founded the Campbell Flour Mills there.[33]

As if to consolidate his new social and marital status, George settled with Helen in Toronto and invested his considerable energy in the flourishing industrial construction business. By 1906 he was the founder and president of the Toronto Construction Company, Limited, with offices at 70 Victoria Street. He and Helen took up residence the next year in the solidly bourgeois Annex district, at 84 Walmer Road. The grand, semi-detached red-brick house stood only a few short blocks north of his mother's home on Washington Avenue.

Perhaps the proximity to Melinda proved too much, for like her mother-in-law, Helen Deeks was a woman of independent mind and strong will. By 1908, George had purchased a new home for his mother and sisters, a mile or so north of Bloor Street, past the ravines of Ramsden Park, at the crest of the rising slope of Avenue Road. The district was now a true suburb of Edwardian Toronto. From the second-floor rear bedroom of the spanking-new brick home on Farnham Avenue, Melinda Deeks and her three daughters could see the clock tower of Upper Canada College to the north, for little lay between them and the college except the vacant grasslands bordering Avenue Road.

George's business went from strength to strength. Possibly the connections of his father-in-law helped; for Archibald Campbell had for several years been chairman of the Banking and Commerce Committee of the House of Commons. The Toronto Construction Company outgrew its original premises during the years when, newly appointed to the Senate, Campbell became chairman of the parliamentary Railway Committee.[34] The firm moved to a larger office on Wellington Street just east of Yonge, the centre of the business district. In 1909, with Helen expecting her second child, George and his wife moved again, this time to the place where they would settle in for good and raise their children.

The new home of George S. Deeks and family at 77 Admiral Road was one worthy of a captain of industry. With an entrance framed by Greek columns, and with six second-storey windows facing the street and four dormers jutting forward from its tiled roof, the brick and stone mansion easily commanded the street. On Sundays, George and his family could hear the bells of the Presbyterian Ladies' College in the distance, for they were only two blocks or so away from the college grounds.

At the time of her move to the new house that George had provided on Farnham Avenue, Florence was at the height of her involvement in the Women's Art Association and the other clubs to which she belonged. Fortunately, the streetcar lines on Yonge Street and Avenue Road made the trips to and from the art association building brief and enjoyable. Her new sister-in-law and her sister Mabel became art association members. Yet for all her outward appearance of independence and economic security, the reality, as Florence well knew, was much different. Her station in life and her ability to pursue her varied interests depended almost entirely on the continuing good fortune of her brother. The entire second Deeks household, the one on Farnham, was in a state of ongoing uncertainty. Only George's generosity, his business acumen, and the state of his health stood between a life of quiet comfort and genteel poverty for Melinda Deeks and her three spinster daughters.

The reality of spinsterhood was probably another factor that helped lead Florence towards feminism. When she stepped out onto Farnham Avenue she entered and could draw sustenance from circles of acquaintance at the Women's Art Association, the Toronto Women's Liberal Club, and the Alumnae Society at Victoria College. But what became of her when she returned home and closed the front door, leaving that world behind?

During her unrelenting journey into middle age, more than once she must have dwelt on her marital status and the possibility of a life without a mate or children of her own. She believed in the centrality and the transforming power of love, rooted in home, family, and motherhood; but as long as she continued to do so it was difficult for her to accept fully the late-nineteenth-century view of some unmarried women, that spinsterhood offered liberation from forms of subordination imposed by married life. Like other women of her generation, she believed that men and women existed in separate social and political "spheres," distinguished by power and aggression and love and nurturing. It was easy to see herself as fully equal to men in the abstract, perhaps even morally superior to them. But the equality existed only as an unrealized ideal.[35]

Florence Deeks's sense of herself as a spinster comes across as a complex one, layered in ambiguity, and it probably appeared to her as a decidedly mixed blessing. As an avid reader, she would have received contrary messages from the many articles of debate about women, marriage, and spinsterhood that appeared in the novels, periodical press, and newspapers of the late nineteenth and early twentieth centuries. And the arguments were changing. When she was a child, the dominant attitude towards spinsterhood had been one of scorn or even hostility. Fearful of the threat posed to social morality and order by the perception of a vast body of single – "surplus" – females, Victorian observers viewed them as "odd women."[36] They were often depicted as having physical "deformities," such as thinning hair or flat chests or big feet.[37]

The very thought that a woman might choose not to marry was seen as a threat to the institution of marriage itself, so the mid-Victorian spinster had tended to be either demonized or shamed into her senses. So the nineteenth-century English novelist Anthony Trollope portrayed the unmarried Georgina Longestaff in *The Way We Live Now*: "At nineteen and twenty and twenty-one she had thought that all the world was before her . . . But now she was aware that hitherto she had always fixed her price a little too high."[38] The stereotype would by no means disappear, but by the late nineteenth century it had competition.

With the gradual improvement of women's condition in the Anglo-American world because of reform of property and divorce laws, greater opportunities for a higher education, and the expanding range of employment and careers, spinsterhood came to be seen in a rather more positive light. For an increasing number of unmarried women, to be single was to be engaged in their own form of revolt. Their decision to remain single allowed them to be part of the cause of women's equality, and they consciously rejected the restrictive and unequal nature of a marital relationship. The image of the "new spinster" became linked to that of the "new woman" in the many articles written on the subject between the 1870s and 1920. The "new spinster" travelled, was self-confident, and viewed marriage as an option rather than a necessity. "I've chosen my life as deliberately as my sisters and brothers have chosen theirs," wrote one woman to *Scribner's Magazine* in 1917. "I want to be a spinster and I want to be a good one."[39]

Florence was trapped between these two extremes. She shared the commitment of the "new woman" to higher education, a career, and an independent life. She had seized what opportunities life had afforded her, and had made the best of them. She had broadened her mental horizons, forged a life for herself. But she never surrendered the emotional core of the belief in "separate spheres" for men and women. Whatever her own personal ambitions, she believed in the sanctity of home and motherhood. Yet to what form of new life could she, at forty-five, possibly give issue?

These ambiguous and even conflicting assumptions were invisible strands of the snare in which Florence became caught after she left the Presbyterian Ladies' College. Not many positions were open to a single middle-class woman in her mid-forties. No positions arose for women in the English or history department of the University of Toronto, nor did she have the necessary qualifications if one came open. She was too old, and perhaps too fixed in her ways, to take courses in teacher training. Perhaps in her own mind, she was not of a "marriageable" age. Her family's social station made it awkward if not impossible to accept menial clerical work, and her occasional forays into journalism did not bring in enough money to maintain an independent existence. So she had returned to the home of her mother.

The house on Farnham Avenue, isolated from the blend of Town and Gown on Bloor Street, was at once a sign of security and a symbol of her new isolation. Florence may have seen herself as a "new spinster," committed to personal freedom and the fundamental equality of women and men, but she could not have escaped noticing the way her life seemed to exist on separate yet dissonant planes. Here she was, free in the abstract and part of the social geography of the urban middle class and dressing as well as most others around her; all the same, she was unable to escape fully from the abasing daily entrapments of economic dependence. As much as she sought to expand her mind and her experience, her personal fate always seemed to spring back to her brother George.

It must have occurred to Florence that she remained in middle age a dependent daughter of a wilful mother. Many years later, the family's recollection was that the daughters of George Deeks did not marry because no suitor proved of sufficient merit to meet the standards and expectations of their mother, "a very matriarchal lady."[40] A variation on Lady Bracknell's admonition to Mr. Worthing, another suitor, in Oscar Wilde's play *The Importance of Being Earnest* comes to mind: to have one daughter lose a suitor is an accident; to have two daughters lose suitors suggests carelessness; but to have three daughters lose them smacks of the worst excesses of a mother's expectations.[41]

Resentment is no stranger to love. How much of this did Florence come to harbour, and how corrosive the mixture? Florence and her sisters remained free from matrimony, but what price freedom? In 1909 an American woman published a work called *The Spinster Book*. In it she wrote: "The chains of love may be sweet bondage, but freedom is hardly less dear."[42] The words spoke only in part to loneliness; they spoke also to freedom from want. Florence would not have forgotten the stinging words from Jane Austen's *Emma*, that "it is poverty only which makes celibacy contemptible to a generous public! A single woman, with a very narrow income, must be a ridiculous, disagreeable, old maid! . . . But a single woman, of good fortune, is always respectable."[43]

Loneliness has less to do with isolation from people than with a lack of connectedness to the world outside the self, with the constrictions, the devaluations, the silences, the unsaid. Another spinster perhaps captured the mood behind the curtains of homes such as theirs a few years earlier: "Even after the crucial moment has passed and the single woman has drifted from girlhood to spinsterhood, a cold climate, raw winds, chill rains, and snow tend to increase the loneliness of it . . . The nights are long in the North, and the wind has a way of howling through the trees and slamming shutters and rousing weird echoes which are not enlivening companions for a lonely woman with a memory."[44]

Four women, when the whim struck, glanced discreetly out the front-room window at 140 Farnham Avenue during winter's long days, and often the weather outside was hostile and kept them inside. But what was it like in the home of these aging women? Did they occupy themselves with chores, taking comfort in the daily rhythm of domestic routine? Did they speak much among themselves, or did invisible fences protect their private space? Did their thoughts radiate outward from themselves, in the direction of George's growing family on Admiral Road, and the social flux beyond it, or did they draw inward towards sour reflection on lives not fully lived? Did the lines of interaction run from each towards the others, or in straight lines outward from the mother? Was it love or duty that forced the rhythm of daily life in this house on this street?

If Florence nursed resentments, she bore them silently or acknowledged them in whispered confidences between sisters. It may have struck her that the family patriarch had not really been buried after her father died in 1897, but instead lived on at 77 Admiral Road. In some ways, her brother was less a sibling than a surrogate for the archetypal father-provider. The flesh of patriarchs decayed, but the structure of patriarchy endured beyond the span of generations.

In textile work, the weft is the cross-thread; only when it is laid in does the act of weaving take place, allowing a pattern to appear. Patriarchy was an invisible thread, Florence was beginning to see, the weft in the fabric of history as surely as economic power was its warp. Both had woven themselves through her own life, but they had existed also as far back in time as her limited knowledge of history allowed her to see. The first glimmerings of a pattern had dawned.

4 The Great Reserve

"So many *odd* women – no making a pair with them. The pessimists call them useless, lost, futile lives. I, naturally – being one of them myself – take another view. I look upon them as a great reserve. When one woman vanishes in matrimony, the reserve offers a substitute for the world's work."

George Gissing, *The Odd Women* (1893)

WELLS NEEDED TO MOVE AGAIN, for by 1909 his life had become unmanageable on all fronts. Spade House, with its distance from London but promise of the order he needed, no longer served its purpose. Perhaps it never had. It was a place he escaped to, leaving his emotional and public lives behind him, wherever he had just been. This was a building whose architect's trademark was the integration of small hearts into door panels and windows, but Wells had vetoed this. He wanted the hearts inverted, so they became spades. From the beginning, it had been clear that there would be no needless sentimentality in this house.

With the publication of *Love and Mr. Lewisham* in 1900, and its attack on the suffocating nature of conventional morality, Wells had turned his back on the nineteenth century and looked towards the future. The following year he published *Anticipation*s, a distillation of his view of what the world might look like in the year 2000. Old institutions must go, whether old-style liberalism, the ruling class, or conventional religion and social relations. Overcome by the inexorable weight of historical forces, these would be swept away and replaced by a world order where social engineering, not old-fashioned patriotism, prevailed.

The new state of Wells's anticipation was to be a world-state, led by "beautiful and strong bodies, clear and powerful minds," one in which "the procreation of base and servile types" would be held in check. It is as if he now sought a purgation of everything he detested about his early life and background: "For a multitude of contemptible and silly creatures, fear-driven and helpless and useless, unhappy or hatefully happy in the midst of squalid dishonour, feeble, ugly, inefficient, born of unrestrained lusts, and increasing and multiplying through sheer incontinence and stupidity, the men of the New Republic will have little and less benevolence."[1]

Anticipations met with decidedly mixed, and extreme, views. Some people, like the young G.K. Chesterton, thought it a detestable work; others, like Wells's friend the novelist Arnold Bennett, were overwhelmed at its daring. Among those who approved of its emphasis on eugenics were the socialists Sidney and Beatrice Webb. This, and Wells's earlier sympathetic portrayal of the plight of the working-class Lewisham, convinced the Webbs to open the Fabian Society to him.

In this way, Wells was drawn increasingly away from Spade House, to London and the Fabian socialists. Some of them, like the political reformer Graham Wallas and the critic and playwright George Bernard Shaw, he had encountered earlier. But now he began to consort with the broader circle of socialist acquaintance. The group formally accepted him for membership in 1903, and before long he and the Fabians began to circle each other, each vying to make their own ideas prevail. It was an uneasy alliance from the outset. His first lecture, delivered poorly in his high-pitched voice, was an unmitigated disaster. He was desperate to be taken seriously, like Shaw. But he remained an outsider. Within a year he had threatened to resign, and he remained a member only after others convinced him of his importance to the Fabian cause. He continued, however, to criticize the society's elitism and its methods of organization. There was much in this working-class man from Bromley that did not harmonize with these middle-class progressive reformers, and it nettled him. In 1906 his behind-the-scene criticisms became public ones when he read to the group a paper called "Faults of the Fabians." It divided them, and alienated him from the Webbs – but he had become the centre of attention.

The controversy within the Fabians and his success as novelist and prophet kept him, however, a much-sought-after guest of some of them. Among these was the family of Hubert Bland and his wife, Edith, who under the name "E. Nesbit" was well known as a writer of the children's books that provided much of the Bland family's income. One of the "founding fathers" of the Fabians, Hubert Bland was the Victorian hypocrite in purest form. To outside observers, he appeared to be the Victorian gentleman, complete with high collar, frock coat, and monocle, accompanied with the platitudes of High Victorian morality; to those who knew him better, he was a philandering roué who had been engaged to a pregnant woman at the time of his marriage to Edith, herself seven months along. Edith, scarcely conventional herself, took the woman, Alice Hoatson, into her home; after she discovered that her husband was the father-to-be, she agreed to adopt the baby. The child was a girl, and they named her Rosamund. Later, Hubert and Alice had another child. Edith carried on as if nothing of consequence had happened.

Wells first frequented the Bland home to bathe in its bohemian goings-on when Rosamund was a young girl, but by 1905 she was in her teens and was a founding leader of the group of reformers' children known variously as the Fabian "Nursery" or "Kindergarten." He started visiting the Blands more often. Rosamund was precocious and available, open to his overtures and willing to meet his desires. These were satisfied when the two spent a few nights alone in Dymchurch, a short distance from Spade House.[2] According to Wells, he was doing the girl a favour, rescuing her from the lecherous intentions of her father. "I conceived a great disapproval of incest," he wrote, "and an urgent desire to put Rosamund beyond its reach in the most effective manner possible, by absorbing her myself."[3] Once again, his principles followed in the wake of his actions.

The Fabians, with their calculated flaunting of convention, were a rich sexual hunting ground for Wells. The aura of fame that surrounded him drew women of all ages, and memoirs of these Edwardians suggest that several of the Fabian wives, possibly Edith

Bland herself, succumbed to his allure.[4] He brought with him the promise of sexual freedom, and he practised what he preached. When his next book, *In the Days of the Comet*, appeared in 1906, it was evident that he was in earnest in his commitment to sexual licence. It articulated a doctrine of sexual freedom in the extreme, and met with savage denunciation from newspapers and pulpits. As the public campaign against Wells gained momentum, it also secured sympathetic support for the besieged author from his Fabian friends. The Webbs and the Shaws went out of their way to comfort him.

The air of scandal surrounding Wells heightened his appeal. Here was an author who did not write books suitable for display in polite company. If the conclusion of *Comet* was to be believed, it took a ménage à trois, or even à quatre, to build the new world order. Wells defended himself by saying that free love was sordid only because women remained a form of property, captive to convention: "To experiment you must be base; hence to experiment starts with being damned."[5] Free love became an issue in the 1907 election campaign in Bromley, and the ever-compliant Jane signed a letter sent out to defend her husband's good name. But a further complication lay ahead, and its name was Amber Reeves.

The Reeveses were a Fabian couple of long standing. William Pember Reeves was director of the London School of Economics, a wealthy gentleman socialist for the likes of whom the phrase "stuffed shirt" seems to have been coined. His wife, Maude, shared his political sympathies, and she became smitten by H.G. Wells. So did her beautiful nineteen-year-old daughter, Amber, a child of the Fabian Kindergarten and easily as forward in her views and actions as Rosamund Bland. At the time she and Wells were introduced, she was a student at Cambridge, with the looks of a Pre-Raphaelite and a brilliant academic future ahead of her. By all accounts, she set out in pursuit of Wells, with the complicity of her mother, and he proved to be more than willing to be chased and cornered.

It was Wells, however, who made the first decisive move when he visited Amber's Cambridge rooms in May 1908. The relationship soon became a public one, observed for example by the poet Rupert Brooke, and the mutual infatuation was all too evident.

Beatrice Webb confided to her diary about Amber Reeves: "A some-what dangerous friendship is springing up between her and H.G. Wells. I think they are both too soundly self-interested to do more than cause poor Jane Wells some fearful feelings – but if Amber were my child I should be anxious."[6]

Meanwhile, Wells and Dorothy Richardson had renewed their friendship, for he had suggested earlier that they become lovers.[7] She had decided it was time to take up the offer.[8] In 1907, she mis-carried with Wells's child. The same year, Wells attempted to elope to the continent with Rosamund. Fabian rumour had it that the couple were stopped only at the train station by Rosamund's furious father, who punched the forty-year-old Bromley Lothario in the nose and removed his daughter from the coach.[9] "And damn the Blands!" Wells confided to Bernard Shaw. "All through it's been . . . lies that has tainted this affair & put me off my game."[10]

Matters were clearly out of control, even for Wells, for the ongoing affair with Amber was now a serious one. While Pember Reeves put up with his daughter's too-public flirtation with Wells, her mother, a member of the Fabian executive and a leading advo-cate of women's suffrage, clearly encouraged the liaison.[11] Wells invited Amber to Spade House to meet his wife, who remained backstage while the little Edwardian drama unfolded in full light. Amber returned frequently, sometimes for weeks on end, for she and H.G. had fallen in love, coupling in London flats whenever the mood suited them.[12] They went arm in arm to dinner parties and the theatre. Amber, proud of her catch, began to boast of the affair. Wells's love life remained at the centre of Fabian gossip. But this time he seemed to have crossed a boundary that even Fabians could not accept.

Amber Reeves became pregnant in April 1909. This was no *passade*. For the first time Wells thought seriously about divorcing Jane, and he announced to his friends that he intended to do so and to sell Spade House. Amber was pressing him to marry her. Wells resisted at first, but before the spring was out he and Amber departed from Victoria Station for Le Tourquet and a furnished chateau in France. Wells began making arrangements to sell Spade

House. It had become one more symbol of "domestic claustrophobia." His intention was to experiment in polygamy.

A telling photograph, taken when H.G. and Jane lived in Spade House, sets the domestic scene – one not of convivial life with a partying smart set but of the husband and wife, alone with their young children in the nursery. Frank and George (nicknamed "Gip") kneel, annoyed that the camera has interrupted their play with the train set that surrounds them. Gip looks unhappily into the camera lens, a hint of suspicion in his eyes. Jane, seated in a high-backed spindled chair, hands clasped on her lap, looks vacantly down towards the children. Wells stands uncomfortably, hands in pockets, also looking down. But his eyes seem directed towards the miniature railroad tracks, not his boys. He is the one nearest the door. A few years later, Gip would write to his mother: "When is Daddy coming to have a look at me?"[13]

During the summer of 1909, Wells abruptly took a house in Catherine's name on Church Row in Hampstead. The entrance of the comfortable three-storey Georgian terrace was protected from the street by wrought-iron railing, its brickwork softened by a cover of ivy. Here was a place most people would covet, an easy stroll to the peacefulness of Hampstead Heath or the countryside, yet close enough to the heart of London that friends would not be inconvenienced when visiting for dinner or for parties. Wells made the move so he could be near the cottage he had rented for Amber at Woldingham in Surrey.

The relationship had deteriorated while they were on the Continent. Wells was torn between Jane and an orderly home, and Amber and adventure. Where provision of creature comforts was concerned, Amber was no Jane and she made it plain that she did not intend to become one. Wells returned to England and Jane, and then he played his ace in the hole. It took the form of Rivers Blanco-White, a barrister who had declared his desire to marry Amber in spite of her relationship and her condition. Wells now dared her to marry Blanco-White; shocked at the suggestion, she responded by saying that the next thing would be that he would recommend prostitution. But she knew now that she could not compete with Jane and win. She telegraphed Blanco-White and left for England. Wells wired his wife to join him for a family holiday in France.[14]

The affair was by no means over. At the end of July 1909, after she and Wells had discussed their predicament with Jane, Amber and Blanco-White married, and in Wells's interpretation she refused to let her husband touch her until her child was born. The baby arrived on New Year's Eve, 1909, a girl she named Anna Jane. Officially, Amber lived in her Woldingham cottage, but Wells continued to visit her regularly. Fury among the Fabians now knew no bounds. "The blackguardism of Wells is every day more apparent," Beatrice Webb wrote in her diary near the end of September. "He seduced Amber within the very walls of Newnham, having been permitted as an old friend to go to her room . . . Anyway, the position now is that Amber is living in a cottage that has been taken by Wells, and is receiving frequent visits from him while her husband lives in his chambers in London. And poor Reeves is contributing £300 a year to keep up this extraordinary *ménage!*"[15]

Wells was trapped in "a web of affections and memories" that bound him to two women, and it was one he had spun himself.[16] He was in love with a woman half his age, he admitted to his friend Violet Paget (known to readers of her essays and novels as Vernon Lee). But he was adamant now that he would not leave his wife. Paget was sympathetic but saw through the moral pretence. "What grieves me," she wrote to him, "is not that those who have eaten the cake or drunk the wine should pay the price of it, but that the price should be paid by others who have not their share." Had Wells given a whit of real thought to the emotional cost to Catherine of his misadventure? And what about the essential inequality of the relationship between Wells and Amber itself? "My experience as a woman and a friend of women," Paget told Wells, is "that a girl, however much she may have read and thought and talked, however willing she may think herself to assume certain responsibilities, cannot know what she is about as a married or older woman would, and that the unwritten code is right when it considers, that an experienced man owes her protection from himself – from herself."[17]

It is highly unlikely that Florence Deeks read the *Toronto World* on weekdays. She would instinctively have disliked the newspaper's sensational style of journalism, its chatty prose, its irreverent outlook. Yet she liked its commitment to social reform, and each Sunday the self-proclaimed "people's paper" carried Flora MacDonald Denison's "Under the Pines" column, a wide-ranging discussion of women's issues. Florence often bought the Sunday *World*. On December 14, 1909, she almost certainly did. That day, after she had finished reading Denison's column, she clipped it out. She kept it for the rest of her life.[18]

Flora Denison was one of the great and most radical advocates of feminism in Canada, and Florence had come to see in her something of a kindred spirit. They were about the same age (Florence was three years older) and both had been born and raised in small towns in eastern Ontario – in Denison's case, Belleville and later Picton. Like Florence, Denison had attended the local collegiate institute, followed by a move to Toronto. Flora had married, but the marriage had failed and she managed to support herself as journalist, businesswoman, and (since 1906) secretary of the Dominion Women's Enfranchisement Association.[19]

Denison's subject that Sunday was "What Women are Doing for the Advancement of Civilization." In it, she brought her readers up to date on the women's suffrage movement in Toronto. "Many encouraging happenings are piling up each day," she wrote, "and the careful ones who thought it unwise to introduce a Militant Suffrage to a conservative Toronto audience, are finding out that Toronto has been doing a lot more thinking on the suffrage question than appeared on the surfaces."

Of all Toronto suffragists, Flora Denison was among the most militant, especially, as she demonstrated this day, in arguing that only by direct political action would women be able to improve their condition. "In order to make homes safe," she declared, "women must not only help to make the homes but they must help make the laws that govern the homes. They must evolve a social soul." They must resist the argument that politics is degrading, or that by engaging in political activity women became "unwomanly."[20] More immediately, Denison suggested, Toronto's women should go to Massey Hall the following Saturday night to judge for themselves whether radical suffragists had abandoned their womanhood. They should go there to see Mrs. Pankhurst.

For the past month, Emmeline Pankhurst of England, founder and leader of the Social and Political Union and the most militant suffragette in the world, had been on a North American tour, speaking to huge crowds in Boston, New York, and elsewhere. Toronto was one of her final stops before returning home, and the prospect of her visit had made quite a stir in the provincial capital. This was the woman at the centre of the gathering of thousands of women in London's Hyde Park only a year earlier. Her supporters, intent on winning the suffrage, had paraded on Downing Street, heckled politicians, spent time in jail, starved themselves, disrupted the House of Commons, and made powerful cabinet ministers cower.[21]

In the "Saturday Magazine" section on November 20, 1909, the *Globe* announced Mrs. Pankhurst's arrival in town. In an act of perhaps deliberate irony, on facing pages it juxtaposed her photograph with one of Goldwin Smith, formerly Regius professor of history at Oxford and Canada's most prominent social critic and best-known anti-feminist. There was the wizened eighty-six-year-old Smith, sitting at his desk in his downtown mansion, the Grange, formally dressed in black tie and skullcap, gazing sombrely at his papers. He had just announced his retirement from journalism after a Canadian career of more than thirty years, and the watch and fob that hung from his waistcoat seemed to serve as a glum reminder that his day was past. Mrs. Pankhurst, on the next page, wearing middle age well, looked firmly beyond the camera lens, her hair parted in the middle and a scarf wrapped tightly around her neck. That very day she was to bring her "campaign of martyrdom" to the city.[22]

Massey Hall that night held an audience its founders had not anticipated. The Masseys had built their fortune on the production and sale of farm machinery, and by the 1890s the family mix of Methodism and money was helping turn them into Toronto's most prominent philanthropists. The concert hall that bore their name had opened in 1894, and it was there that patrons of the arts listened to concerts performed by the Toronto Philharmonic Society and its symphony orchestra, the Toronto Choral Society, and the Toronto Mendelssohn Choir. On the evening of November 20, 1909, its program was very different.

A few people began to mill around the entrance to the imposing but severe red-brick building on Shuter Street just off Yonge, in the middle of the retail district, very early in the evening. More soon arrived. Many came alone, others in small groups. Suddenly the hall was surrounded by an animated throng waiting for the front doors to open. Late arrivals stood in ragged lines for a block east down Shuter. Others, it seemed in the thousands, snaked out onto the Yonge Street sidewalk, blocking pedestrian traffic attempting to move north or south. The corner was a slow swirl of dark, ankle-length dresses protruding from overcoats protecting their wearers from the evening chill. Almost every person in this anxious yet polite crowd was a woman.

They arrived from all walks of life and in all manner of dress. Society matrons stepped from their private coaches in expensive hats and shawls; shopgirls and sales clerks, ill clad against the evening, scurried straight from their shifts at Eaton's or Simpson's. Teachers, struggling on meagre wages to present a respectable public face, walked from their rooming houses. Members of the Women's Christian Temperance Union arrived fresh from Willard Hall a short distance away, handing out pledge cards to anyone who would take one. Undergraduate students came in groups from their cramped rooms and boisterous university residences. Together they clustered in common cause against the wall of the concert hall, seeking shelter from the November wind.

Finally, the ushers unlocked the doors and the sea of women began slowly to be swallowed up by Massey Hall. Those fortunate enough to gain entrance waited quietly in the plush seats or spoke in hushed whispers to their neighbours. The auditorium was crammed to the rafters, and overcoats shrouded the balcony rails and backs of seats. Many more women stood impatiently outside in the cold. They would not get in that night, and an official's announcement at the entrance that the keynote speaker would be prevailed upon to speak again the next day at the Princess Theatre failed to dissolve their disappointment. Slowly they disappeared into the night.

It is very likely that Florence Deeks was one of the lucky entrants that night, sitting patiently in her seat, waiting for a sign of movement towards the podium at centre stage. At last a stirring of the curtains, and Joseph Oliver, in his second year as mayor and wearing his chain of office, took the stage, along with several local dignitaries and the band of the Grenadiers. Oliver offered a few words of welcome to the assembled audience, then introduced the guests – the physicians Dr. Margaret Gordon and Dr. Augusta Stowe-Gullen and the educationalist James L. Hughes, champions of the cause of social reform and women's rights. Then the Grenadier band took over. The acoustics of the hall were superb, and the brassy martial air of the Sousa marches seemed surprisingly appropriate.

Then Mayor Oliver took the podium, and with the first mention of Emmeline Pankhurst's name, utter silence. The occasion was already remarkable. Here was the mayor of the city introducing a woman and a cause that (as the *Globe* was to put it the following Monday) only a few years earlier had been discussed "with cheap sneers and smoke-room jokes."[23]

Suddenly there she was, peering over the lectern. How tiny this enemy of orthodoxy seemed! Every eye in the house was on Mrs. Pankhurst now. What a contrast between the ferocious reputation and the ladylike looks! She was beautiful. A historian would later write: "She resembled a virgin rather than a virago. With her svelte pre-Raphaelite figure borne majestically erect, with her clear, olive complexion and full, rosy cheeks, with her raven-black hair, with her delicately pencilled eye-brows and deep violet-blue eyes, above all with her entrancingly melodious voice, she was the very antithesis of the frustrated spinster and the soured old maid of popular mythology."[24]

She spoke softly at first. "It seems like one of the great audiences we are in the habit of addressing at home," she began. But as she warmed to her theme, her voice grew tense and her slender nostrils contracted. Her eyes flared whenever she sought to drive an important point home.[25]

A *Globe* reporter in the audience began to take notes. It was not the first time that day he had heard her speak, for she had addressed the local chapter of the Canadian Club, all men, at noon. "A slight, intellectual-looking woman," he had scribbled, "of splendid voice, and possessing remarkable power as a speaker." As she reached full voice, she again made clear how far she and her supporters would go, and had already gone, to secure votes for women. They had been to jail, and by refusing to take food in prison they had helped force their cause to the forefront of British politics.

For the next hour and a half she told the assemblage of women the story of the suffrage movement in England. As she had earlier in the day, she spoke about the earliest struggles for the male franchise. Men themselves, she pointed out repeatedly, had widened the range of voters only by committing acts of violence. Now they had won the vote and possessed the full powers of citizenship. Women had not, and their interests were different from those of men. It was time women took control of their destinies.

Pankhurst was in full flight now, her clear, strong voice easily reaching the balcony. Woman needed and wanted power in order to protect their interests. Politicians had finally been forced to listen and take heed. Pankhurst finished her speech with a flourish. "You haven't got men big enough, strong enough or intelligent enough to continue the empire, and that is our business." Women want to improve the conditions of life. Women are the future, she proclaimed, and the future is theirs to shape. It would be woman who made "healthy mothers of healthy men," she "who would be the backbone of the empire."

She was done. The house was silent. First a ripple, then a wave of applause rising in volume and intensity filled the auditorium. As a single body, the full house stood in tribute. It was in high spirits and it wanted more, but Pankhurst, exhausted, waved in reply, politely shook hands with Mayor Oliver and the podium guests, and disappeared beyond the curtains. Still the audience clapped, and only gradually did it allow Dr. Gordon, Dr. Stowe-Gullen, and Mr. Hughes to give the short addresses they had prepared.

It is just possible that on Farnham Avenue, later that night, the three Deeks sisters gave voice to the inherent zeal of their evangelical heritage. In the flush of enthusiasm for the evening's message, they gather at the piano in the parlour, around Mabel, who now puts her studies at the Royal Conservatory of Music to good use.

Florence's clipping of Mrs. Denison's "Under the Pines" column is propped against the piano's music rest. It is the one that had announced the coming of Mrs. Pankhurst, and it contains the words to "The Woman's Marseillaise." One can almost hear the three sisters singing once again the French anthem with which the gathering at Massey Hall had ended, revised now for the purpose of their own liberation:

> Arise, ye daughters of the land
>   That vaunts its liberty,
> Make reckless rulers understand
>   That women must be free,
>   That women will be free,
> Hark! hark! The trumpet's calling,
>   Who'd be a laggard in the fight?
> With victory even now in sight,
>   And stubborn foremen backward falling.

Mabel, improvising furiously at the piano, is in full voice as her fingers reach the chorus, and Annie lends vocal support. Even usually reserved Florence has caught the spirit as the trio issues its musical challenge, singing of "freedom's call," their voices rising with each stanza, until the final chorus: "March on, march on, / Face to the dawn / The dawn of liberty."

The sisters have collapsed in a fit of half-embarrassed laughter. What had gotten into them? What if Mother had been roused by the noise? What giddiness has this been?

Not quite giddiness. Florence picks up her clipping and puts it into her handbag for safekeeping. Denison's message, like Pankhurst's, has become important to her. She will treasure this piece of paper. The sisters go quietly up the stairs to their rooms, but for Florence some disparate strands of thought seem to have come together.

Emmeline Pankhurst left Toronto for England at the end of November 1909, soon after her Massey Hall address, but not before she paid a polite visit to Professor Goldwin Smith at his home in the Grange.[26] Back home, she and her supporters used increasingly militant and spectacular means to win victory for the suffragists' cause. Over the next few years, Florence Deeks kept abreast of her activities, for they often appeared on the front page of the *Globe*, the *Mail and Empire*, and the *World*. In 1912 Pankhurst was arrested and imprisoned, winning release only after she went on a hunger strike. The next year she was again arrested, refused to eat, and was released – only to be confined again under the newly passed "Prisoners, Temporary Discharge for Health Act." The cycle repeated itself a dozen times in as many months. But this kind of militant radicalism was foreign to Florence's disposition, as it was to most Canadian women.

She much preferred the more cerebral and broader radicalism of Flora Denison, whose articles in the *World* continued to develop a brand of militant feminism more congruent with her own view of life. Denison consistently preached that economic independence was central to any true emancipation for women. "Women's sphere," she wrote, "should only be limited by her capabilities and I believe there is no sex in the human brain. Women are at last in the commercial arena and each day becoming more independent. Their final salvation will be achieved when they become the financial equals of men."[27] Everything in Florence's life pointed to the truth of Denison's assertion, and she knew it.

The Toronto feminist leader did not argue against home or marriage as such; she believed instead that, by romanticizing these institutions, social observers ignored the way the dependence they entailed transformed them into prisons of domesticity for women. "Now we all know there is a great deal of maudlin sentiment written about the home," Denison wrote in 1909, "for we see on all sides, women whose lives are dull and monotonous if not tragic, just on account of this wonderful talk of the sacredness of the home." This was a refrain Denison repeated constantly. When Florence picked up her copy of the *World* on the morning after Pankhurst's speech at Massey Hall and turned to Denison's column, the message was there: "The homemakers have been the workers with too often neither freedom, hours or wages."[28]

What could Florence Deeks do to serve the cause of women? She did not know; she needed to learn much more, especially about the origins of the injustices under which women everywhere suffered.

"Nobody will ever know what Jane thought," one of Wells's many biographers once wrote.[29] Perhaps, but an informed guess can be made at her state of mind during the chilly autumn of 1909. The past few years had been the most stressful ones of her marriage. She had done so much to make it work, taking Spade House from an empty shell and transforming it into a haven as comfortable and happy as her husband's unpredictable moods would allow. Life there had been memorable: guests every weekend, spilling out from the house onto the grounds; servants offering tea and biscuits on the terrace; games of every sort; lively wine-coloured and wit-laced talk in the parlour every evening; Wells, as always, at centre stage, taking everything in even as he held forth.

It is doubtful that Catherine had ever enjoyed her husband's little anecdote about how he had made the architect change the decoration for the front-door letter plate from a heart to a spade because he did not want "to wear his heart so conspicuously outside."[30] But as time passed, she no doubt came to appreciate just how symbolic the decision was. Every glance at it would have reminded her that the house near the sea had never been a place where the heart could find a true place, outside or inside, except with the children. From the first it had been somewhere to help hide emotions, at least of the kind she needed from her husband. And at the end, in the haste and confusion of the move to Hampstead in May, she was probably glad to leave it all behind. She had made her pact with her husband during the many talks over *Lewisham*, and had come to live with his petty deceits and larger betrayals – the flirtations with Dorothy Richardson years ago, the dalliances with the writer Violet Hunt in the tool shed, the trysts with Rosamund Bland in Dymchurch.

She could handle all this only by refraction, by letting each of these rebukes of Catherine deflect towards her persona as Jane. Catherine knew the common perception of her other self: "poor

Jane," "foolish Jane," Jane, the woman who could satisfy her man in efficient domestic management but not in bed. But she knew this man her husband well enough to know that something in him, perhaps the disorder of his early life, required the order and stability that Jane alone could give him. And with each affair, while a little more of Catherine faded into the English mists, Jane grew in strength.

H.G.'s affair with Amber Reeves had thrown all this into doubt. For the first time the pact had been threatened, and divorce became a real possibility.[31] Hampstead was the only possible means of salvaging the situation. Perhaps this, too, would pass. Once he gained his possessions and controlled them, he soon tired of them. He needed his work as much as his women, and for that Jane was his most precious asset wherever they lived. When the business with Amber was at its height and everyone else seemed in a panic, had it not been she, Jane, who had quietly gone out to buy the baby clothes?[32]

It could only have amazed Catherine that in spite of whatever chaotic directions his uncontrolled passions took him in, he never stopped writing. In the early autumn, and throughout his battles with the Fabians, he had been hard at work drafting another novel, and as she read it, chapter by chapter, she would have recognized that it had brought out the best in him. In its vast panorama of Victorian and Edwardian life, it was the work he hoped would give him the recognition as a serious novelist he so coveted. It was his *Tristram Shandy*, his "condition of England" novel, and it was worthy of a Sterne or a Dickens.

The book once more followed the trajectory of her husband's own life. Its main character, George Ponderevo, is H.G. Wells in all but name. The portrait of Bladesover House and his mother in the first chapter are extraordinary, detailed, and poignant portraits of Up Park and Sarah Wells. Ponderevo, like Wells, is a divided man – divided by a commitment to dispassionate and skeptical science and research, yet given over also to the emotional demands of his romantic and sentimental side. Again, the autobiographical elements: the housekeeper mother, the ne'er-do-well father, the stately home's great library, unhappy apprenticeship, attendance at a

London college of science, association with Fabians. A quick love affair, marriage, divorce. But this novel was so much more than *Lewisham*. Far beyond anything else he had written, it revealed the complexity, the aspirations, the deep discontent of this man.

There was much Catherine would have admired in the book, not least its emotional honesty. But there was so much else. It was also his indictment of the ways the old England he idealized had come to be corrupted – by crass materialism, imperialist adventurers, and a venal capitalism. As George travels through life, from Victorian Bladesover to Edwardian London, England seems to collapse around him under the weight of its own corruption. In this England, there are no certainties or enduring values.[33] Eventually Wells had settled on the title "Tono-Bungay" for the novel, the name of a patent medicine invented by George's uncle. It is at once the source of the family's wealth and a phony panacea for the ills of society.

Tono-Bungay appeared early in 1909 and met with a lukewarm reception. But his next book was taking a more troubling direction. True, *Tono-Bungay* had used many aspects of his past life to flesh out the bankruptcy and decline of a civilization. In it, he had written about his past. But now, in the new book, his daily private life threatened to become his art.

During the first half of 1908, while the scandal over his *passade* with Rosamund Bland had Fabian London gossiping, Wells had steadily worked on the new novel, *Ann Veronica*. As Catherine read, typed, and retyped the first chapters, the story of an intelligent and independent-minded young woman who chafes under the restraints of a suburban life and an authoritarian father, she no doubt recognized a good deal of herself from the days before her marriage. After leaving home against the will of her father, Ann becomes involved with a middle-aged married philanderer, Ramage. Helped by a loan from this man, she enters a Kensington college of science, where she meets and falls in love with her teacher, Capes. She continues to socialize with the benefactor, Ramage; but after she rebuffs his attempt to assault her sexually in the private room of a restaurant, she is enraged and resolves to throw herself into the cause of the movement for women's liberation.

In May 1908 the real world of the suffrage movement had exploded in an assault by suffragettes on the House of Commons in Westminster, and Wells made Ann Veronica one of them. She is sent to prison a restless and discontented young woman, and she emerges hardened in her determination to let nothing get in the way of obtaining what she wants from life. Fully herself now, she is a model of the newly liberated woman; but in the writing the thinly disguised portrait of Catherine is transformed into a character who distinctly resembles Amber Reeves.

Catherine must easily have recognized the transmogrification of her earlier self into her husband's new love as the novel advanced. Ann Veronica has become a woman with an active sexual appetite and a determination to have it satisfied. She spurns convention by breaking her half-hearted engagement with her suitor, Manning, in order to run off with Capes on an illicit "honeymoon" in the Alps. The Catherine of the first half of the novel had failed to be enough; for her creator, nothing less than Amber would do, and that is what Ann Veronica becomes. In the final chapter of the novel, which takes place four years after the affair in the Alps, Capes is a famous dramatist; Ann Veronica is pregnant and thoroughly domesticated. Wells the novelist had transformed her back into a variation of Jane.

In *Ann Veronica*, Wells acted as the voice of women liberated from the bonds of marriage and sexual custom, but only when this served his own purposes and those of his fictional self, Capes. Both had gone with their young women to the Continent for an illicit affair. But Wells showed himself to be no champion of actions taken by the suffragettes to achieve their end. In the novel he pilloried them unmercifully, making one, Miss Miniver, into a ridiculous caricature of neurotic and sex-fearing zealotry. Some among his readers may have taken Ann Veronica as their guide to a life without inhibition; but if so they would have to turn a blind eye to the fact that in the end she is fulfilled only after Capes has had his will and his way with her.

Publication of *Ann Veronica* in October 1909 renewed the scandal that surrounded Wells's private life. His Fabian friends were embarrassed that he should have made so public his private affairs, and his enemies found a new reason to damn the immoral life he led. Even his usual publisher balked at the implications of his storyline. Wells had promised the book to Macmillan, which had published several of his previous books; but once he had read it, Sir Frederick Macmillan refused to publish the novel. Knighted just that year and in charge of the firm since 1903, he was no Victorian prude. The urbane, cigar-smoking publisher, whose bushy grey moustache rivalled his bow tie in size, was a master at his trade, and he knew well the likes and dislikes of Macmillan readers.

Sir Frederick recognized that the reading public would take offence at this latest offering by Wells, and he informed the author of this fact. Everything about the novel, he said, was fine until the episode of the suffragettes. "When, however, Ann Veronica begins her pursuit of the Professor at the International College, offers herself to him as a mistress and almost forces herself into his arms, the story ceases to be amusing and is certainly not edifying."[34] Negotiations between publisher and novelist went nowhere. Wells pleaded with him, to no avail, and when the book appeared, it was under the imprint of the less seasoned publisher Fisher Unwin.

Sir Frederick Macmillan's estimation proved correct. Press and pulpit vilified the book and its author. The private scandal that had once been more or less confined to literary London became a very public affair. The earlier campaign against Wells gained new force, and a life of its own, energized by the way Wells seemed to have written against the grain of the entire contemporary movement for moral reform. On November 20, an anonymous reviewer for the *Spectator* described *Ann Veronica* as a "poisonous book" with "pernicious teaching." "The Wellsian world," he declared, "consists of this and nothing more: If an animal yearning or lust is only sufficiently absorbing it is to be obeyed. Self-sacrifice is a dream and self-restraint a delusion. Such things have no place in the muddy world of Mr. Wells's imagining. His is a community of scuffling stoats and ferrets, unenlightened by a view of duty or abnegation."[35]

Leaders of the YWCA and the Girls' Friendly Society declared their outrage. Lending libraries refused to stock the book. Throughout London, "Clubland" was abuzz at Wells's latest outrage. It was one thing to sneak away with some young thing not one's wife, but quite another to parade the affair on the printed page. In the men's clubs of the city, whether the Athenaeum or White's or Wells's own Reform, eyebrows were raised and brows furrowed. If the man was so willing to reveal the grossest details of his own love life, what would prevent him from turning his savage pen on the politicians, statesmen, clerics, and men of letters he had also come to know?

From the street everything looked normal at 17 Church Row, Hampstead. Servants left in the morning for the market or the stores, the postman delivered mail several times each day, and the occasional guest arrived in the early evening. H.G. and Jane seldom went out, and their parties were fewer, often confined to lunchtime – pale affairs compared with the times at Spade House. Their social circle had noticeably shrunk in the face of the campaign against the immoral author. Wells avoided his clubs. Some of his friends believed he had undertaken not to see Amber for a year or two. When he left Church Row, however, he was often headed in the direction of Woldingham and Amber, sometimes for weeks at a time – but just until the baby was born, he promised Jane. Only whispered confidences with Arnold Bennett over lunch and letters from the ever-faithful Richard Gregory, the favourite family "uncle," seemed to cheer Wells. "The worst of reading a book like this," Gregory wrote to his old friend after finishing *Ann Veronica*, "is the desire to experience a woman like V. It was the same with Beatrice in *Tono-Bungay* and others back to Weena in *The Time Machine*. In spirit I am a polygamist with the lot."[36]

During the bitter winter months of 1909–10, Catherine Wells had come so very close to losing her husband. He had been willing to throw up everything for Amber Reeves, and had been stopped in the end not by anything Jane represented but by Amber's own decisions and by her pregnancy. She had seen the signs in his attitude towards their sons. H.G. was pleasant enough around them, but he seemed curiously disengaged, without the parental will to connect. From his point of view, for example, the child he had fathered with Amber was "an extraordinary irrelevance."[37]

As the November winds swept up and over Church Row, only to descend and gather dust in swirling eddies from the graveyard across the street, Catherine may well have taken comfort in the thought that the furor caused by *Ann Veronica* might at last end her husband's adulteries. Perhaps he would settle down to prove the greatness as a novelist that *Tono-Bungay* had promised. But she never knew what was really on his mind until, as Jane, she carried away his rough drafts to type.

On March 20, 1910, Beatrice Webb recorded in her diary that H.G. Wells seemed to have been "frightened into better behaviour" by the way in which one friend after another was sheering off and by the damning review of his book in the *Spectator*.[38] His first novel of that year seemed to bear this judgment out. *The History of Mr. Polly* was a funny book, his Alfred Polly a fully realized Dickensian character with an eccentric but amusing vocabulary and a hapless life. The characteristic thefts from the author's own life were there – the indifferent education, the apprentice draper, the marriage to a cousin, the walking out of the marriage – but Polly was a figure of fun and the book offered pleasant resolutions. None of the opprobrium levelled against *Ann Veronica* could be repeated with *Mr. Polly*.

For Wells, such a consoling thought was little more than a bucket of water thrown in the direction of encroaching flames. The harmless nature of the book encouraged him to renew his adventurous social life and hold forth once again at the Reform Club. Many among his social circle greeted *Mr. Polly* with relief, although some, like Shaw and the Webbs, were aware that he continued to see Amber Reeves and seemed heedless of the wreckage the relationship had left in its wake.

Wells was already at work on a very different kind of book, *The New Machiavelli*. Whatever contrition he harboured had turned to anger at the charge that his books were immoral. He continued to resent Sir Frederick Macmillan's rejection of *Ann Veronica*. In February 1910, when he got Jane to send *The New Machiavelli* to Sir Frederick for publication, it was as much as anything an act of defiance. The book, he told the publisher, would be a political one.

Catherine could see the telltale signs – the restlessness, the irritability, the need for constant movement that in the past had meant another affair, either in progress or just over the horizon. As she had prepared the new book for presentation to a publisher she could tell from it, too, that nothing had really changed since the scandal with

Amber Reeves. In fact, *The New Machiavelli* enlarged on the central themes of *Ann Veronica*. Once again, her husband ransacked the stuff of his own past. The central character, Richard Remington, writes from exile in Italy, where he is with his young mistress, Isabel Rivers. He has tried to write his own version of *The Prince*, but has failed. In frustration, he decides to tell the story of his own life, and of the way his private passions have defeated his hopes for a life in public service.

From his early life in Bromstead, a suburb of London, Remington manages to get to Cambridge, where he flirts with socialism and studies political economy. Later he moves to London and manages to forge a successful career as a journalist. While there, he becomes acquainted with Oscar and Altiora Bailey, two leading Fabians whose home is a gathering place for political reformers. He also renews his friendship with Margaret Seddon, a former Cambridge science student of progressive political views whom he had met several years earlier through relatives. Torn between his aspiration to public service and his sexual longings, he sees in Margaret a means of satisfying both needs.

They marry, but it is a marriage without passion from the outset, a life of "generous-spirited insincerities." Richard wins a seat as a Liberal MP. But while campaigning he meets Isabel Rivers, the young daughter of a constituent. Remington is restless but now feels energized even as he is "beset" by sex. Embracing the suffragette cause, he renews his friendship with Isabel, visiting her in Oxford, and they become lovers. They try to avoid scandal and talk about the moral implications of their illicit affair and the possibility of having an illegitimate child. He discusses his problems with Margaret, who proves to be an understanding soul. Remington is touched by her compassion. He is torn between his commitment to Margaret and his longing for Isabel. Disenchanted with politics, he meets with Isabel in St. James's Park, and they decide to leave everything behind. The novel ends where it had begun, with Remington and Isabel alone in Italy, where he will write his memoirs and help raise their child.

As Catherine read through the novel, she must have noted the irony. In real life, as Jane, hers was a life lived in the background, always at the periphery of the action, apart from the centre of attention. But in her husband's novels, she often played a leading role. For here she was again, easily recognizable as Margaret, the ever-understanding, loyal wife. Even her private thoughts were now on display, as when Margaret sends her husband a letter as he is about to leave England: "I've always hidden my tears from you – and what was in my heart. It's my nature to hide – and you, you want things brought to you to see."[39] These were her thoughts, all right, but filtered through his needs. For Catherine, reading this passage, one thing must have been clear: they would soon be moving again.

Assured by Wells's promise that *The New Machiavelli* would be a "large and outspoken" political book, and would not revisit the themes of *Ann Veronica*, Sir Frederick Macmillan had purchased the rights to it sight unseen. Despite his rejection of *Ann Veronica*, he was nothing if not a good businessman, and he wanted this successful author back. For his part, Wells wanted their relationship to continue. The book was to be published in monthly parts in the *English Review*, beginning in May. Macmillan could publish it any time after September.[40]

The publisher was shocked at what he now read. Politics there may have been in the novel, but at its heart was the story of Wells's relationship with Amber Reeves, now fully fleshed out. Defiant and obviously unrepentant, Wells was, in effect, daring society to tell him that what he had done was truly wrong. But there was also much more than this. Some of the leading lights of London were subject to his acid pen. Not only the Webbs, as the Baileys – "two active self-centred people, excessively devoted to the public service"[41] – but, more alarming to Sir Frederick, a good number of its most important politicians in thin disguise.

Edwardian London was a very large city, but in some ways its circles of social influence and association were decidedly circumscribed. Important men gathered information, formed alliances, and made decisions in the private dining rooms and lounges of its men's clubs. The centre of influence and Empire was a cloud of cigar smoke, dinner jackets, and decanters of fine wine. In the new novel, much of this was placed on open display for public scrutiny. The situation was intolerable. How could Wells's publisher hold his head up at the Athenaeum if he published this book? As one of Wells's biographers puts it: "The scene was crowded with living portraits, and Sir Frederick would have none of it."[42]

On June 21, 1910, Sir Frederick sent Wells a letter of rejection. The finished book, he said, was not of the sort they had agreed to. "It is unnecessary for me to particularise," he went on, "but I feel sure you will agree that the kind of thing we objected to in *Ann Veronica* is here intensified, and that if we had good reason for rejecting *Ann Veronica*, there is twice as much reason why we should not publish *The New Machiavelli*."[43] Their contract had been broken. Wells responded with an angry letter, but Sir Frederick remained adamant, even after seeing revised proofs. He would not publish a book that made adultery some sort of perverted moral virtue.

The nominal theme of *The New Machiavelli* was the way one must capitulate to convention or take flight in the trains of passion. But behind it lay an attitude of defiance and a motive for revenge. At Sir Frederick's initiative, the book went the rounds of several of London's leading publishing houses, but none would touch it. Finally it appeared in 1911 under the imprint of John Lane, who was someone for whom Wells had acquired an intense dislike. As with *Ann Veronica*, the circulating libraries refused to carry *The New Machiavelli*. The *Spectator* declined to advertise it; Edinburgh booksellers sought to return their copies; the Birmingham city council banned it. Wells even held a press conference to deny that it offended against decency. The book sold well, but those whose good opinion, like Henry James, Wells so coveted denied it the acclaim he thought it deserved. "There is, to my vision, no authentic, and no really interesting and no *beautiful* report of things" in the book, James wrote to him.[44]

From this point on in his career, H.G. would no longer attempt to be the "man of letters" he was not. His was the voice of prophecy, he realized, not of literary illumination. His private battle was against a world without vision, one that lacked his moral courage. He would continue to go his own way. And he would sell the place on Church Row.

5   *Loves and Wars*

Suffice it that now I conceive of the task before
mankind as a task essentially of rearrangement, as a
problem in relationships, extremely complex and
difficult indeed, but credibly solvable.

H.G. Wells, *The Passionate Friends* (1913)

A TRAIN RIDE OF ABOUT AN HOUR out of London
leads to the place where H.G. Wells and his wife spent the rest of
their married life. In Essex, nestled in mildly rolling countryside
near the town of Dunmow, a visitor finds himself near land once
owned by Frances, Lady Warwick, an attractive and eccentric
woman, for many years mistress of the Prince of Wales.[1]

Wells found the place in 1911, while spending a weekend with
R.D. Blumenfeld, editor of the *Daily Express*. Charmed by the area
and intrigued by Lady Warwick, he soon arranged through
Blumenfeld to rent the Old Rectory on her estate at Little Easton.
She was delighted to let the house to him, and by the spring of 1912
Wells and his family had settled comfortably into the red-brick
Georgian house, although they decided to maintain their London
house for a year to ease the transition. From its windows, one could
look out over the spacious lawns towards cornfields trimmed with
dogwood hedges and see the woods and the unkempt pastures, and
beyond them the village nestled between the soft waves of the hills.[2]

The prospect of leaving Hampstead came as a relief to husband

and wife. Wells had never really warmed to the place, and once the affair with Amber had cooled there was little reason for remaining, except that it provided a possible locale for dalliances. Catherine lived in the hope that perhaps H.G.'s constant restlessness would diminish with the move, that perhaps, at the age of forty-five, he might find his need for affairs a phase through which he had finally passed.

Now that the scandal surrounding Amber Reeves had faded, and she was safely married, friends and acquaintances vied once again for visits. On weekends the rectory was seldom without guests, and Wells noted with approval and relief the enthusiasm with which Jane threw herself into making it into a comfortable, permanent home. But if the outward circumstances of his life had changed, little was different within the man. Even before the decision to leave Hampstead, he had found a new paramour in Elizabeth von Arnim, the Australian-born widow of a Prussian count who had died the previous year. A novelist and playwright of Wells's own age, the wealthy woman had long wanted to meet him. In November 1910, she wrote him an effusive letter praising "the aching, desolating truth" told by *The New Machiavelli*.[3]

Wells was once again enmeshed. When Catherine was away from Church Row, he entertained Elizabeth there. "She's a nice little friend to have," he wrote to his wife, reassuring her that the morals of the countess were strict and that "sad experience" had "taught her that if she so much as *thinks* of anything she has a baby."[4] The reality was rather different. In her 1914 novel, *The Pastor's Wife*, Elizabeth wrote of her relationship with Wells. At one point the Wells character, Ingram, tells his paramour that she is "a perfect seething vessel of independent happiness." "Teach me to seethe," she replies.[5]

The escapade with Elizabeth began, like so many of them, with quiet walks and the great man's excited chatter. But Elizabeth was an elusive quarry, animated and outgoing yet with an aristocratic scorn that ensured the kind of distance that attracts. Throughout 1911 and 1912, they accompanied each other frequently in London. Later she rented a flat near him, and on occasion she used Lady Warwick's home as her "weekend house." On one occasion, if Wells is to be believed, they made love in the woods on a copy of *The Times* featuring an outraged letter from Mrs. Humphry Ward denouncing the moral standards of modern youth.[6]

He began to urge that they spend time together in Ireland. She resisted his suggestion, but later they did travel together to Italy. She maintained her independence, and it made him a jealous man. He continued to pursue her, and they carried on their affair, as he put it, "with an impudent impunity. We flitted off abroad and had amusing times in Amsterdam, Bruges, Ypres, Arras, Paris, Locarno, Orta, Florence – and no one was a bit the wiser." He wrote beseeching letters, once even arriving unannounced at her Swiss home. Eventually she made her one big mistake: she began to demand "depth of feeling" from him, and it was not in him to offer it. Elizabeth wanted a serious relationship, and he wanted fun. She began to ridicule Jane, and told him he was but "half a lover." The affair had run its course, and the relationship slowly matured into an enduring friendship but nothing more.[7]

Catherine let the affair with the countess expend itself, as she knew it would, pouring her energies instead into Little Easton. But it was clear that her husband remained dissatisfied with his lot. At Hampstead, and now at Little Easton, he had been hard at work examining his life anew in his next book, entitled *Marriage*, to be released in the fall of 1912. Jane took particular care with this novel, correcting the proofs and seeing it through the press.[8] But no doubt Catherine read it with a different purpose altogether. What wife would not want to know the goings-on in the deepest recesses of her husband's mind, particularly when relations with other women affected his view of marriage – his own as well as the institution in general?

Predictably enough, the book was about the frustrations of wedlock. Catherine could take some comfort in the fact that in it a husband and wife work through their difficulties, even though it took a visit to freezing Labrador to sort them out. Told almost entirely from the man's point of view, the early part of the novel recounted Wells's experiences with Isabel. But Catherine was there. She was now Marjorie, a woman who could not comprehend any meaning in life beyond the material possessions that made for a comfortable existence. "She was dreaming, and in a sense she was thinking of beautiful things. But only mediately. She was thinking how very much she would enjoy spending freely and vigorously, quite a considerable amount of money, – heaps of money."[9] Could H.G. not see that she truly dreamt of beautiful things, and ones that were not mere objects or baubles? Or that it had been he who kept insisting that their marriage could not survive unless they lived in a manner that ensured him his creature comforts?

In the end, once more the husband of a Wells novel gave up a promising future in science for the sake of domestic peace – another Wells protagonist who truly commits himself to no one. When the book appeared, some readers were relieved at the author's retreat from his earlier apostasy, in life and in fiction. Sir Frederick Macmillan was one of these, for he published *Marriage* with evident relief, thereby bringing Wells back into his stable.

Not all readers reacted to the book in this way. There was little civility and a lot of scorn for *Marriage* in a review that appeared in the *Freewoman*, a feminist publication, in September. In the lengthy essay, a critic named Rebecca West tore the book apart. She ridiculed Wells's feminism and the falseness of the married couple's intellectualized affectations. Wells, she said, was "the old maid of novelists," uttering the platitudes of a phony feminism. What happens to Marjorie, the wife, for the sake of the marriage? She broods on her own worthlessness, and the author uses this "as the basis of a generalisation as to the worthlessness of all woman."[10] Miss Rebecca West would have none of this.

The review was devastating, but it had been pulled off with such wit, such cleverness, and with such clarity of insight into the false values of the book that it piqued Wells's interest in the reviewer. Just who was this impertinent but penetrating woman?

Catherine Wells had every right to be intrigued by the writer when she learned of her review. This unknown woman seemed to have looked through the windows of all her homes and seen the purpose for which Jane had come into existence. It must have startled her to read that "one knows at once that Marjorie is speaking in a crisis of wedded chastity when she says at regular intervals, 'Oh, my dear! . . . Oh, my *dear*!' or at moments of ecstasy, 'oh, my *dear*! My *dear*!' For Mr. Wells's heroines who are living under legal difficulties say, 'My man!' or 'Master!'" The word "master" was not for Catherine, even as the compliant Jane; but how many times had she caught herself saying "My dear" in moments of embarrassment or self-doubt? Was there something in Catherine that wanted to cheer when this West woman pilloried life in the "great, beautiful house," filled with expensive belongings and "creatures of genius and silly, chattering people"?[11] Often, she would later write, she felt she was "only a part of the wallpaper against which those more brilliant lives were played out." While the glamorous people around her played cards, she remained "alone and unnoted as in the company of clockwork toys."[12]

She and her husband knew that in important ways their married life was an elaborate sham, and Rebecca West had managed uncannily to see through it. Catherine acquiesced to H.G.'s suggestion that the writer be invited to Little Easton for a weekend to explain what she had meant by calling Wells "pseudo-scientific" in her review. Both were more than a little curious. When they greeted her at the train station in Dunmow, they were surprised to discover that "Rebecca West" was the *nom de plume* of a mere slip of a girl. She was nineteen years old, and her name was actually Cicily Fairfield.

Before the weekend was over, Catherine may well have recognized that her husband was smitten by the young house guest. He was attracted by the broad brow, the dark and expressive but troubled eyes, the soft mouth and small chin.[13] But what struck husband and wife alike was the way this child-woman assumed from the outset that she was Wells's equal, refusing to be intimidated by the force of his opinion and backing up her own views with broad reading and a superb memory. "I had never met anything like her before," he later recalled, "and I doubt if there ever was anything like her before. Or ever will be again."[14]

Inevitably, the encounter blossomed into a full-scale romance. His fame mingled with her literary ambition. She appeared to soak up the glamour of the association with him, while not worrying about his reputation as – to use his words – "a promiscuous lover." Soon, when they were alone together in the house on Church Row, a conversation about weighty affairs in front of his bookshelves turned to a kiss, and along with it the thralls of passion. Wells continued as he had from the start, captivated by the "curious mixture of maturity and infantilism about her." To her mind, the kiss had implied a promise.[15] He was still involved with Elizabeth von Arnim, however much they now quarrelled, and Rebecca did not want to risk alienating her mother and sisters, so the affair remained a furtive one, often conducted at the spacious flat Wells took after he finally left the Hampstead house. His London base was now St. James's Court, a stone's throw from the grounds of Buckingham Palace. There, the lovers could consort whenever they pleased, taking pleasure in quiet walks in the luxurious gardens of the majestic building's large inner courtyard. It was at St. James's Court in December 1913 that Rebecca West became pregnant with Wells's child. It would be several months yet before she was to turn twenty-one.

The move to Little Easton had cured none of H.G.'s errant ways. Catherine knew this from the first and saw that his latest affair threatened to become just as scandalous, and more of a threat to her marriage, than the earlier one with Amber Reeves. Wells had arranged for Rebecca to live in a house at Braughing, a small village no more than a dozen miles from Dunmow, and he now spent much of his time there. But what could Catherine do? As Jane, she had thrown herself fully into domestic concerns, just like Marjorie in *Marriage*. H.G. had broached the possibility of giving up the rectory, but this time she had resisted strenuously.

This was Catherine speaking, and H.G. knew it. She would not move again. She was tired of his juvenile ways – the petulance, the waves of ennui that rolled over him so frequently, the sense he conveyed that even when home he longed to escape. So she had insisted on a long lease for the Old Rectory and a major transformation of the place. Jane would take care of all this: adding more bedrooms and bathrooms, modernizing the heating, and installing a large window overlooking the valley.

During the renovations Wells spent much of his time away. When he did write to her, it was to blame the upset of domestic routine for his discontent. "My irritability at home is due to the unsettled feeling due to rebuilding," she read. "I do not think you understand what a torment it is to an impatient man to feel the phantom future home failing to realize itself. I *hate* things unfinished & out of place. I want things *settled*[.] I want a home to live in & have people into – people one can talk with. At present home is a noisy, unsympathetic, uninteresting muddle."

So it was she who was to blame for his difficulty in settling down, was it? And of course it was also she who bore the responsibility for his other restlessness: "When I have been at the Rectory for a few days," he went on, "I get into a state of irritability because of sexual exasperation . . . I want a healthy woman handy to steady my nerves & leave my mind free for real things. I love you very warmly, you are in so many things, bone of my bone, & flesh of my flesh & my making. I must keep you. I like your company . . . But the other thing is a physical necessity. That's the real hitch."[16]

This was their moment in Labrador, together but apart, settling things but resolving nothing, all the conditions set as usual from the vantage point of Wells's own wants and needs. He would spare no expense to help her fix up the rectory; but he must also be allowed to live his triple life – in London with his circle, in different places with Rebecca, and at home whenever the mood suited him. Nothing less would keep him happy.

There would be few if any outward signs of Catherine in the remaining years of this marriage. A critical point had been reached in the twenty-year-old relationship. She could not withstand further assaults on her dignity, and she knew that some of their friends wondered how she had been able to take them. But they should have understood her better than this, for they were English and generally of good stock. They, above all, knew from birth that the best manner of confronting an indignity was to meet it with a politesse that disarmed and humbled the accuser. In this, Catherine's greatest ally was Jane.

Discussing this situation, one of Wells's biographies notes that Jane was able to cope with this latest instance of her husband's gross misbehaviour "because 'Catherine' was not touched."[17] Catherine managed to maintain her dignity, and a presence, because she allowed her persona as Jane to emerge and take over. As Jane, she had other advantages that, as Catherine, she lacked.

Her husband needed security as much as he needed sex, and Jane could provide that in spades. The Jane inside her would become the very model of domestic perfection he expected. Catherine knew that the more he carried on, the greater became his need for a safe and comfortable refuge, and Jane would ensure it was ready for him. There was a certain power in servitude.

Catherine was well aware that Jane brought domestic security for herself as well as for her husband. Catherine Wells sought a refuge within the inner recesses of this marriage, and Jane Wells could help ease the pain of the retreat. And the advantages in life made possible by H.G.'s inventive mind – wealth, comfortable surroundings, a wide and interesting social circle, holidays on the Continent – these were not to be discounted. All this and more would be lost should she ever leave this less than perfect marriage. As Catherine, she had other ways of alleviating the pain. Listening to Chopin helped, as did writing short stories and poems, often in secret.

In the years to come, Jane would prevail, but Catherine would remain intact. Jane would do everything she could to maintain her peace with this man and with herself. She would continue to help him with his work in whatever ways possible, and spend freely and fill with guests the place they had renamed Easton Glebe. Catherine, meanwhile, found other ways to express her loneliness and her longings.

Overnight, it seemed, it was August 1914 and war. The news had stunned Florence Deeks. It had all come so suddenly, over a holiday weekend. All of Toronto had been abuzz, and great crowds had gathered around the newspaper offices eager to find out what was happening. The Bloor Street Methodist Church that Sunday had been filled with Christians anxious to learn whether Great Britain would declare war, and she had seen in the men's eyes that they fully approved of the minister's insistence that every Christian's duty was to serve the noble cause of God, King, and Empire.

Like other Canadians, Florence learned that England was at war with Germany when she opened the newspaper on the morning of

Wednesday the 5th. Its editors seemed eager for Canadians to be part of the action, and two days later, when Prime Minister Robert Borden announced that the country had joined the effort in support of the Empire, everyone seemed ecstatic at the prospect of a good scrap with the Germans. Thousands had marched down Yonge Street with Union Jacks and drums, singing choruses of "Rule Britannia," "God Save the King," and "The Maple Leaf Forever," afterwards scattering in groups looking for the nearest recruiting office.[18]

Florence had been at loose ends for the past year. The clubs to which she belonged kept her occupied – "beguiled the time," as she put it – but she seemed simply to be drifting. What had she done with her life? What had she accomplished? A stint at teaching, some journalistic work, but what else? She recalled "the supreme elation" of the family back in the 1880s, when brother George had won the gold medal at Victoria College. Each member of her family had possessed "some righteous ambition," but what was hers? It had always been to write a book, but as yet she had done nothing to realize her dream.[19]

One day, quite by chance, she ran across an acquaintance in the publishing industry and asked him about a subject that might be suitable for a short book. He was kind enough to give her a scrap of paper with four or five ideas on it, including one on women, but when she next looked she could not find it anywhere.[20] She remembered, however, that one of the suggested subjects had been something like "women's share in Canada's development." That was as good a subject as any to work on, so she gathered her resources and took herself to the public library. But the subject seemed intractable. She could scarcely find any material on the topic. Perhaps, she thought, she should write a short history of Canadian life and incorporate women's work and influence into it. So far as she knew, history had recorded little of the life of women and the home, whether in Canada or elsewhere.

Back on Farnham, she broached the idea to her sisters. Annie was excited about the possibilities. "Yes," she told Florence. But why think small? "What could be more fascinating than the whole story of mankind with its love episodes woven into the narrative? I

know," Annie said, "so far as I am concerned I should be delighted
to have the romance of mankind in a nutshell." Florence was
intrigued by the thought. Love episodes. Points in history when the
power of love showed through and made a difference. The romance
of mankind. A new kind of history of the world. A history with
women in it. A history where women mattered. The theme was
wonderful.[21] For the rest of the summer and well into the fall she
began to think seriously about writing something along these lines.

By November of the first year of the Great War, men in khaki
gave the city a truly autumnal hue, and lads in their teens paraded
in ragged formations on the university grounds, mock rifles shoul-
dered at every angle. Only a few weeks earlier, the first contingent
of volunteers from across the country had left for England and the
front. What had become of the brotherhood of man and the Biblical
counsel to "love thy neighbour as thyself"?

North winds gathered force as they swept in off Avenue Road
onto Farnham Avenue, bringing with them a draft from the
fireplace and a chill Florence could not shake. The house was especially silent these days. Her sisters and mother seemed stricken with
foreboding. What of George? Would he enlist? Would they let him,
a man of fifty-five? Perhaps his engineering skills would be seen as
essential to the war effort, but was this enough to keep him from
the front? Night after night the sisters and the mother sat mute,
bidding such thoughts away by force of will. Such notions brought
bleak prospects, for them as for George.

Given such domestic circumstances, exactly what prompted
Florence Deeks to go to the Toronto Public Library and commence
work on a history of the world, a history with women in it, remains
a matter of conjecture. It may have been Annie's suggestion, turning
over in Florence's mind. Perhaps it was the war itself, its carnage
all too evident by the late autumn of 1914. Or just possibly it was
something else, something she read. Florence admired Flora
MacDonald Denison and liked her writing; she may well have
encountered a little pamphlet written by Denison for the Canadian
Women's Suffrage Association in the first months of the war. The
title of the tract was *War and Women*.[22]

Reading the new polemic, Florence would for once have been disappointed. Denison's argument was murky, her logic convoluted, and the tract raised as many questions as it answered. She talked much about the evolution of war but said little about love's own evolution. "The Peace idea," said Denison, "had been tried and not found wanting." Then why, Florence may well have asked, was the world at war?

She would have been puzzled by the silences, the lack of background in the pamphlet. Denison asked whether altruists had "lived and worked and thought for nothing?" But she did not reflect historically on the matter. What were the actual origins of altruism, and why was it so easily sacrificed at the altar of war? When the suffragist leader stated, "It is only yesterday that a social conscience was born," was she correct? How could this be, if the nurturing and protective instinct was part of a woman's very nature and had presumably been so since the dawn of time? Was it true, as Denison claimed, that "the human, and especially the male, has thought in terms of combat and dominance through force"? The human? Women too? Surely not.

The world war spoke to the truth of this consequence of human evolution, but what of the redemptive power of love? Where was the mother, the woman, in all this? Denison's answers took the form of assertion, not explanation. How little she actually said about women's place in history! Much had been written about war; Florence knew that much. Men caused war. Men wrote history. Men *were* history. That was the problem. But what was the history of women? What was the past of love and the history of the bonds of affection and commitment and selflessness that knitted people together as mates, as families, as whole communities?

Love and War. This was surely the heart, the starting point, of any attempt to discover the origins of war and its relation to women. However Florence Deeks came to think along such lines, the fact is that she did. She resolved to learn much more about women, the family, and love, precisely because the world was at war.

A different kind of history, a history of the world, now began to take shape. Women and love were central to the past, but they remained exempt from it. Yet they constituted the warp of history, their lives intertwined with the weft of men and aggression, caught together in the web of humanity.

The day the war broke out, Wells was at home at Easton Glebe, taking in a local flower show with friends. A short distance away, his mistress gave birth to a son, to whom she gave the name Anthony West. During the months of Rebecca West's pregnancy, the father-to-be continued in his split existence. He had assured Jane that the marriage was not threatened by his relationship with Rebecca, but he had also written to the expectant mother on several occasions that he was devoted entirely to her. He divided his time between the two women. Bound to their separate dwellings, they viewed each other with suspicion and more than a hint of animosity, particularly on Rebecca's part. Wells tried his best to bring about a suspension of hostilities in these domestic skirmishes, separated by a no man's land of only twelve miles.

A few months earlier, he had placed a book with Sir Frederick Macmillan about war. He called it *The World Set Free*, and it proved to be his most prophetic work, for in it he anticipated a future invasion of France by Germany, through Belgium. To an extent, the book marked something of a return to scientific fantasy. It posited a not too distant future in which the atom had been split, making atomic warfare a possibility – and a deterrent for combatants. But international economic collapse in 1956 would precipitate a nuclear holocaust. Wells's portrait of the destruction of civilization and its structures allowed him to speculate about its reconstruction as a world-state unfettered by decaying institutions and ruled by enlightened and superior beings rather like himself.[23]

On August 4, 1914, however, the prophet was genuinely "taken by surprise" by the outbreak of hostilities. He took some comfort in the possibility that the war would take public attention away from his latest escapade and its bawling progeny. His campaign began in earnest with a widely circulated work called *The War That Will End War* – a tract whose title gave the twentieth century one of its most enduring phrases. Its title essay urged that everything possible be done to ensure that this war would be the last one. From the outset, Wells devoted his energy to clarifying the Allies' war aims and creating the means of a settlement that would be a just one for all concerned. As summer faded into autumn, all his hatred of traditional patriotism vanished, and he became a mainstay of the jingoism of the newspapers controlled by Alfred Harmsworth (shortly to become Viscount Northcliffe), alienating him from his Liberal friends and acquaintances.

The private war of Mr. Wells was fought, however, on more fronts than this. Another was literary. In March and April 1914, Henry James had made public his view of the inferiority of Wells's fiction in two essays published in the *Times Literary Supplement*. Wells was furious, and in June 1915 he exacted revenge in a novel called *Boon*, published by T. Fisher Unwin under the pseudonym "Reginald Bliss," with Wells purportedly writing only the introduction. The ruse fooled no one. The book's bitter satirical sketch entitled "Of Art, of Literature, of Mr. Henry James" mercilessly attacked the grand old man of Anglo-American letters. To sharpen his barb, Wells personally delivered a copy of the book to the Reform Club, where he knew it would find its way to James. He did not bother to enclose the customary covering note of greetings.

The calculated insult hurt James deeply and alienated many within the London literary community from Wells. That James was very ill and going blind was well known in those circles, and their anger at H.G. was fuelled by pride that James was in the process of renouncing his American citizenship in order to ally himself with the British cause.[24]

The domestic front was scarcely peaceful. While Jane occupied herself with Easton Glebe and the garden she tended so lovingly, Wells found his relationship with Rebecca growing tense. Rebecca had come to hate her situation, moving from one cramped cottage to another. It had not taken long for the tiny village of Braughing to learn her identity and her unenviable situation as an unmarried pregnant woman. She detested the contemptuous looks of villagers and servants, and could all but hear their gossip, so she made little effort to get along with any of them. Moreover, she resented the fact that Wells refused to leave his wife, that perfect but bloodless little factotum. But she did gain some satisfaction in working on an impudent but appreciative study of Henry James at the same time as Wells did his best to destroy the author's reputation by writing *Boon*.[25]

After the birth of Anthony, it became clear that the relationship between Wells and West had reached an impasse. Both knew that he would not leave Jane, and Rebecca could not stand her role as a social outcast. Amber Reeves had solved her own problem with Wells by opting for a loveless marriage. For Rebecca, this was not an option. She was in love but confused. As her son grew, she found herself making concessions to family pressures and telling him she was "Aunty Panther." Wells at first resisted the subterfuge but later continued it by giving the child the impression that, as "Mr. West," he was a kind of concerned uncle.[26] The experience scarred the boy for life.

Florence sat at the far end of "her" table. Like the others, it was a long one. The College Street branch of the Toronto Public Library had become her second home, and she loved it; loved the spacious reading room with its many large windows, and the rows of potted plants on the bookshelves below them. She loved the majestic Romanesque arches at the room's ends and the intricacy of carved detail on the heavy wooden ceiling beams. She had even got used to the hard wooden chairs with the round backs and the spindles that dug into her spine.[27] She knew each nook and cranny of this place and felt like one of its fixtures. She treasured the thought, for she belonged here. She liked being surrounded by other people, each in a private world, intensely occupied with the books in front of them. Finally she felt truly part of something, connected to a community of the curious, to people with intellectual purpose.

At first her work had been hard going, for she scarcely knew where to begin. She had studied history at the university under Professor Wrong, but she did not regard herself as by any means a real historian. Only four years older than herself, Wrong had nevertheless been an enthusiastic and engaging professor, if a little pompous. But he had been a good teacher of history. Through him, Florence had been introduced to the works of some of the major historical works of the nineteenth century, including Francis

Parkman's romantic narratives and John Richard Green's comprehensive account of the progress of England in his *Short History of the English People*.[28] Green's work, in particular, had stuck with her because he had not been entirely preoccupied with politics and war.[29] But there had been very few women, if any, in the books used by Professor Wrong, or for that matter in the lectures Wrong gave on European or colonial history.

Early in her research, she had discovered how little had been written about women, at least as revealed by the library's card catalogues. Among the books she did find was one by Jane Johnstone Christie, called *The Advance of Woman from the Earliest Times to the Present*, published in 1912, and it pointed to further sources.[30] She began reading books on Europe. This led to studies of the Middle East and Asia. Frustrated with this lack of focus and direction in her research, she decided to write her account of "woman's work and influence" with the help of such published histories. She knew that her book would not be a work of original scholarship, but she did not intend it to be one.[31] For her purposes, she did not need to document her sources, and she did not initially think to keep a list of those she consulted. She wanted to write a book that would be read by a wide audience, especially by women interested in learning about woman's past. No footnotes were necessary. She intended to provide a synthesis of a subject that nowhere, to her knowledge, existed between two covers.[32]

The idea was certainly an audacious one. She knew she could write decent enough prose, and she had studied history at university, but she scarcely held an adequate command over the millennia of recorded human experience. "Before I could achieve my purpose," she wrote later, "I had to work out for myself an outline of history."[33]

In short, although she intended to use her own words and her own ideas in her book, she needed to gain an overview of the past as previous historians had conceived it. "The only short history of the world to be found," she wrote, "was an old one written by Duruy about 1850." The book that suited her purpose was Victor Duruy's *General History of the World*, first published in English early in the twentieth century.[34] Its 967 pages provided her with an account of the vast stretches of history she wanted to treat. For the later period, so did Green's *Short History*, which she enjoyed revisiting. It pleased her that she was now using it for very different reasons than either Green or Wrong had ever had in mind.[35]

The public library was well stocked with works of history. They were almost always by men, and at first glance each book seemed concerned only with the lives and doings of men. But they helped increase her stock of general knowledge. She found a helpful essay by James Harvey Robinson on history in a volume called *Source Book of Social Origins*, and *Chambers' Encyclopedia* filled many gaps. As her research progressed, it seemed constantly to regress to an earlier decade, an earlier century, an earlier age. She resolved to begin at the beginning – the very beginning – with accounts of the earliest humans by anthropologists and historians of the ancient world. Here she found herself thankful for Professor Wrong's lectures on ethnology, and to Professor Daniel Wilson, Wrong's predecessor, for making ethnology part of the history curriculum.

Eventually she found that if she took enough of these books from the shelves and examined them carefully enough, the occasional and offhand references to women were surprisingly suggestive. In this way, she combed the catalogues for further works, and the fruits of these, too, she incorporated into her ever-expanding "plan."

A very serious game had begun – her private game, one that saw her ransack scholarly and general works of history, daring them to mention women and teasing the smallest bit of evidence about her own sex from the text, anything at all that spoke to woman's place in history. To her delight, she even found more works specifically on women, such Guglielmo Ferrero's *The Women of the Caesars* and Gidoro del Lungo's *The Women of Florence*. She felt alive.

The peacefulness inside the library on College Street in the fall of 1916 belied the reality outside. The Great War, as people were now calling it, had been raging in Europe for two long years. Gone was the earlier enthusiasm for a few weeks of adventure on the continent. Battles such as those at Ypres in the spring a year earlier, where the Germans had used deadly gas, and at the Somme this summer and fall had done away with that. Everyone was shocked to learn that in the battle of the Somme alone there had been almost twenty-five thousand Canadian casualties and over a million from other countries. The mood in the streets outside the library was sombre, even sorrowful.[36]

In March 1916, Ontario's premier, William Hearst, had said that the war had changed everything, and he was correct. The government and military had just warned that enlistment had fallen to dangerous levels, and that the horrific losses at the Somme had to be made up. There was open talk of conscription. Recruitment officers seemed to be everywhere – at concerts, in churches, and at meetings of associations of every type. Lady Aberdeen was a forceful voice in encouraging enlistment, as was Mrs. Pankhurst, who had recently completed a cross-Canada tour. The women at the art association, like so many others, had dropped their paintbrushes for knitting needles, and schoolchildren everywhere had been enlisted to do tasks like rolling bandages or sewing uniforms.[37]

Little doubt there were moments at her table in the library when Florence wondered whether she should put aside her history and do volunteer work for the Canadian Patriotic Fund or the Red Cross. But eventually she summoned the courage to put her first words to paper: "In the beginning!! There floated in the immensity of space a speck."[38]

She had made good progress after penning those words early in the war; sixteen chapters and she had only reached the Renaissance. There was so much more to be done, yet she was pleased. The book was certainly about women in history, but it had become much more than this, almost as if it had a will of its own.

As she now saw history, from the beginning of human life women had been the constructive influence, taking care of the children, protecting and nurturing them while men went in search of food. Women had been responsible for the slow growth of the habit of staying in one place. Woman was "the architect and builder" of the first home; she also controlled the food supply. The violent and aggressive activities of men led them to acts of "selfish domination and destruction," but these had been mitigated by the natural instincts of woman towards cooperation. Woman, not man, was the progenitor of communal life.[39]

It was woman who inaugurated art, initially by imitating "the

forms and colorings of nature" and weaving twines and threads and
sinews into ever more intricate and precise patterns. In this way,
she laid the foundations for arithmetic and geometry, just as her
use of plants as herbal remedies served as the basis for therapeutics.
Woman, not necessity, was the mother of invention.[40] Florence
readily acknowledged that these ideas had not been her own.

One of Florence's central themes was women's struggle for independence. Egyptian women, for example, often possessed more
wealth than their husbands. "Descent," she wrote, "was in the
female line, and property was still inherited by daughters instead of
sons, men were not polygamous, nor was the wife the subject to
her husband."[41]

It was because relative equality existed between the sexes in
Egypt and Babylon that they had achieved greatness as civilizations.
Only later, when women became subject to capture and sale, and
love was made secondary to male aggression, did they lose their
independence. In this way, Florence argued, "as the covetous militarist hesitated at no depredation to gain a desired possession, crime
increased and misery followed in proportion, and for this cause
alone – the personal possession of property – untold crimes began to
deluge the world with inconceivable miseries." This was so whether
she looked at the history of the Middle East, India, or China.[42]

For a long time, the women of Greece held positions of authority and influence. Had not five of the eight Greek deities been
female and many Greek cities been named after women? Woman
was also supreme among the Latins and especially the Etruscans. In
ancient Rome, Florence had written, "descent was in the female
line, woman had full freedom, husband and wife were friends and
companions, and citizens were on a footing of equality." But even
within these civilizations, woman eventually became subject to the
dictates of man. In Greece, woman lost the franchise and citizenship, and descent changed to the male line. This did not end
woman's influence, for "although the supremacy of might and of
patriarchal authority was now established, the old habits still
clung to the nation, and in many districts the old order continued
to prevail, and woman remained the centre and inspiration of
society."[43] Eventually, militarism prevailed and women became

mere chattels, to be disposed of at will or whim. From the Greek god Dionysus came the idea of "the divinity of fatherhood."

At the same time, however, Florence stressed the ways in which women resisted such subordination. She devoted attention to the free women of Athens and noted that within Rome there had existed "a kind of women's club" consisting of members of the great families, women who demonstrated in the forum and other public places "to obtain laws and other provisions from the magistrates." They persisted in the face of opposition and succeeded in acquiring a degree of freedom, Florence declared. In property relations, only the dower, not all of a woman's possessions, became the property of her husband. The unmarried woman was also independent, "the lifelong male guardianship appointed by her father" passing away to such an extent that she was allowed to make a will.[44]

For Florence, the example of Greece provided the most striking illustration of "woman's high position" at a certain stage of history; but it also demonstrated her consequent dethronement by forces that led to "war, slavery, massacre, internal strife and the final annihilation of the state taking the race down with it." Even Greece proved unable to control "the demon of war." The possibility of a civilization driven by love and beauty was lost, for the triumph of physical force led instead to "degeneracy and misery."[45]

Even so, Florence continued to emphasize the beneficial influence of women, whether through the wife of Pontius Pilate or Mary the mother of Jesus. "Mary," she wrote, "was keenly alive to the terrible wrongs under which her nation had so long suffered, and she at once beheld in her infant son the long-looked-for Messiah through whom God was to save the world – not by militarism but – by Love." It was the women who were with Christ who first recognized his divinity and accepted his plan of salvation.[46] The Christian church, however, served the cause of woman's subjugation. During the early Middle Ages the different church councils removed woman from ministry and the altar, banned her from the diaconate, and forbade her to receive the Eucharist in her bare hands "because of her impurity, or to sing in church because of her inherent wickedness." In 595 AD, the Council of Macon even discussed whether woman possessed a soul.[47]

One institution governed by woman persisted: the home. Italian matrons, exemplified by Portia, Livia, Antonia, and Agrippina, continued to be its strong protectors. The women of northern Europe, while not allowed to sit at the same table as their husbands, nevertheless turned the home into "a field of action" aimed at undermining "the dash and clash of militarism" and "the psychological dominance of ecclesiasticism, with its imposing but empty and deceptive ritualism." It had been at the castle of Matilda of Canosse that Emperor Henry IV had met Pope Gregory VII, a meeting that eventually led to Henry's capture of Rome and his appointment of the bishop of Ravenna as the antipope Clement III.[48]

In these and in many other ways, sitting day after day in the Toronto Public Library, Florence Deeks developed the main themes of her life's work: the initial equality of woman and man at the dawn of time; her gradual subordination – physically, legally, and economically – to him; yet her continuing, beneficent influence on the course of history in the face of all odds. During the horrifying months of the slaughter on the Somme, Florence wrote about Dante, about the way Beatrice mourned Dante's suffering on earth. It was Beatrice, his beloved, who awakened in him the awareness that he had strayed from his high ideals, and who drew his eyes once more towards Heaven. "Observe me well; I am, in sooth, I am *Beatrice*."[49]

At Easton Glebe, Catherine was in her usual spot on a cool, late-August morning in 1916, in the white chair of cast-iron filigree. From where she sat in the garden, taking her tea, she could look out past the sprawling lawn towards the village and the hills beyond. The place was eerily quiet these days, the silence punctuated only by the chirping of finches and the occasional bellowing of cattle in the meadows below. At times she swore she could hear a distant, rolling thunder.

H.G. was in Flanders, touring the battlefields. Harmsworth had asked him to do so earlier in the year, but only in the summer had he accepted. Wells could not have found a worse – or for him was it a better? – time to have gone across the channel. A ferocious battle had been taking place along the Somme since the beginning of July, and the casualty lists were staggering. Like some kind of slow-growing malignancy, the war had penetrated all aspects of life in Britain. Everyone Catherine knew seemed to have lost someone. Dunmow seemed in an ongoing state of mourning now. Her heart went out to Cynthia Asquith, grieving over the loss of her youngest son, Yvo. Her husband's friend Sir Ray Lankester, sitting in his London flat at the age of sixty-nine, had written her a letter in which he had worried himself silly about the possibility of Zeppelin raids.[50] Arnold Bennett, the friend of her husband to whom she felt closest, scarcely came around these days, consumed as he was with war work at Wellington House, headquarters of the Ministry of Information, and for the Wounded Allies Relief Committee. Like the other literary lions of the day, whether Galsworthy or Conrad, Yeats or Masefield, Bennett had published little in a literary vein this year. Like the nation itself, they all seemed to have lost momentum, satisfied enough simply to survive into another day.

All, that is, except H.G. Wells. This rogue of hers had managed not only to carry on, but in his own way to flourish despite the demons in his life. His latest novel, *Mr. Britling Sees It Through*, was about to be released, and she was certain it would be a huge success. She remembered the aggressive nature of his early writings on the war, and how his tone had turned to despondency once the prospect of a lengthy war hit home and the long lists of war dead began to appear in local newspapers.

She picked up the letter that had arrived from him in the morning post and unfolded it. "Dear Mummy," it began. She could feel his angry mood as she read his views of the French generals he had met. "I doubt if they will affect history very profoundly. They are all so sure . . . that it will be over in six or eight months . . . It's an imbecile expedition." He signed the letter "Poor bored Daddy," but she knew he was anything but bored. The letter exuded an exasperation born of a sadness so deep it was almost too painful to bear. His infantile regression made him resemble nothing so much as a lost child traipsing around the battlefields of Europe.[51]

Perhaps *Britling* would help make up for the indifferent success of his last few books, once again refractions of H.G.'s life and affairs. In *The Passionate Friends*, published the year before the war, he had cast himself as Stephen Stratton, a man with a keen interest in the politics of Empire, and had explored the frustrations of his involvement with Rebecca West. Lady Jane, the object of the married protagonist's obsessive attention, was a combination of West and Lady Warwick. Jane Wells had her own part to play, as Rachel, the self-sacrificing and supportive wife and mother. Later Rebecca West would describe Rachel in a review of the novel: she was "a phantom doormat."[52] By the novel's end, Lady Jane is destroyed by the mutual jealousies and suspicions of her husband and her lover, and Stratton lives on in despair with his faithful and compliant wife, to whose position he gives no thought at all.[53]

The Wife of Sir Isaac Harman (1914) had continued such themes. Ellen – who resembles the mother of Amber Reeves – suffers under an abusive husband who treats her like so much property. She chafes at her subjection and finds a measure of release through involvement with suffragette friends. Catherine Wells would have noticed that the real villain of the book was not the nasty Sir Isaac, who dies, but marriage and the bondage it entailed. The widowed Lady Harman is now free, and she expresses her liberation by refusing to marry her friend and possible suitor, Mr. Brumley – a character not unlike H.G. – who discovers that he is as guilty of jealousy as Sir Isaac had been.

True freedom and happiness, the two novels said, are found only outside matrimony and only in a world released from jealousy. The husbands in H.G.'s novels were often blackguards, but at the same time there was scarcely a single woman in them who did not ultimately cause a man's ruin and prevent him from reaching his potential. The theme was getting time-worn, like Catherine's marriage. As sales indicated, the reading public had grown tired of H.G.'s self-justifying revelations.

But *Britling* was different. Written in the midst of all his other war work, it captured the changing mood of Britain and the pain and confusion of the home front like no other novel of the day. In fact, *Britling* read like a social history of the past two years, from its lovingly painted details of life at Matching's Easy (Easton Glebe by a truly Wellsian name) at the outset of the war to its anguished portrayal of a citizen and father who has suffered grievously and wants to understand its meaning. *Boon* had spoken of the war but had done so in a tone of mocking sarcasm. The liberal press had pilloried him, first for his war-mongering and anti-German views and then for the derision Wells heaped on others in *Boon*. *Mr. Britling Sees It Through* was bound to help them understand his anguish.

H.G. is Britling, and Britling is England – carrying on, somehow, in the face of catastrophe. Britling is a philanderer, all right, but above all he is human. He is in love, but with a son and with England. The book is also a poignant love song for a generation of lost youth, German as well as English.[54] It begins with belligerent Mr. Britling wanting to arm the Boy Scouts and arrives at the recognition that the war had become "like any other of the mobbing, many-aimed cataclysms that have shattered empires and devastated the world; it is a war without point, a war that has lost its soul." At its conclusion, words fail, and the reader is left only with the claim that "our sons . . . have shown us God" and the image of a sunrise. It is the story of a change of mind – in a man, in a people.[55]

Catherine's mind drifted to this unfathomable man and to the front, and then she quietly folded her letter, reached for her teacup, and made her way back up to the house.

Mabel Deeks stood at the window in the late spring of 1917. She was worried about Florence, now heading east down Farnham to the Yonge Street streetcar. For two long years her older sister had left the house each weekday, and some Saturdays, for the public library on College Street. It must be taking a toll on her health although there were no obvious signs. At fifty, she should be relaxing more, but that had never been Florence's way. Early each morning she set out, no matter the weather, lugging her canvas bookbag; each evening she returned at six, new books under her arm.

Every afternoon when Mabel returned after giving her piano lessons at the Toronto Academy of Music,[56] she waited anxiously for her sister, for Florence's historical work had brought new life to 140 Farnham. Florence's enthusiasm often now overcame her natural reticence, and every night seemed to bring another interesting story from the past. Mabel and Annie could scarcely believe there was so much history to tell, so many stories about people they had never heard of. One evening it would be Pericles's mistress – Aspasia, was it? The next, it might be the Roman matron Cornelia or Anne of Constantinople or the English Queen Matilda.

The growing pile of neat typescript on the dining room table testified to the importance of this history. The whole family had become interested in what Florence was doing. It made Mabel recall table talk back in Morrisburg about the Loyalists and their grandfather and Wellington. Her father had always taken a special interest in history.[57] Even Mother and George now asked about Florence's book, questioning her when she was not busy with her "plan."

It had often been difficult to carry on much of a family conversation while George's children were around. And what a handful they were: ten-year-old George – called by his middle name, Campbell – was reserved, like his father; but Douglas, eight, and little Edward, six, seemed cut from a bolder and less predictable pattern.[58] Once the little ones were put to bed, however, conversation shifted from the news of the recent Canadian victory at Vimy, and they all turned to Florence and the tales she had gleaned from the past. It had been difficult for the others to keep a straight face when she told them about how Frederick William of Brandenburg – or was it Prussia? – would approach women he met in the streets, brandishing his cane and ordering them back into their houses and telling them that decent women should keep indoors. And they had been shocked when she informed them indignantly that George Jeffreys, chief justice under the Stuarts, known as the "hanging judge," had sentenced women to be burned to death merely for giving food and shelter to the Puritan rebels.[59] Florence had acquired such a stock of these stories!

Everyone marvelled at Florence's single-minded dedication and the sacrifices she had made, even Helen, who usually remained detached from her sister-in-law's enthusiasm. Shortly after she started going to the library Florence had given up almost all her other activities. She had resigned as recording secretary of the Toronto Women's Liberal Club, much to Mother's initial chagrin, and had even stopped going to the Women's Art Association. The history consumed all her energy, and Mabel was amazed that, with the drain of war, her sister still had so much of it in reserve.

Sometimes Annie helped with the typing, for she had clerical skills. Usually, though, it was Florence at the Remington, pounding each day's writing into presentable text.[60] And when not doing that, she was often at the small desk in her upstairs bedroom, sorting through her piles of books and sheaves of notes, adding to her "plan." It occurred to Mabel that her sister was engaged in her own private war – one of ideas and words fought against the attitudes and deeds of men through the ages. It tickled Mabel's fancy: a little war fought in a public library and in a woman's modest home on Farnham Avenue.

6   *History and Humanity*

"Now *you* will tell us. How does one know the truth
about something? Do we know it in a flash – So! –
or does it come to us very slowly like a tortoise? Is it
a big thing or is it little things? There you are. A
difficult question . . ."

"A difficult question?" he said. "I should have
thought it was quite simple, if you know all the
facts. It's just a matter of getting every detail in its
right place, isn't it? Making the right pattern."

Angus Wilson, *Anglo-Saxon Attitudes* (1956)

IN 1916, H.G. WELLS EXPERIENCED a moment of
epiphany. He was taking his usual noonday walk from the flat in
St. James's Court to lunch at the Reform Club. It was one of life's
more pleasant city ambles, north on Buckingham Palace Road,
past the palace grounds, through St. James's Park and onto the
Mall, heading towards the club on nearby Pall Mall. Just beyond
Clarence House and St. James's Palace, he reached Marlborough
House. As he walked alongside it, he noticed a large poster on the
courtyard wall. It was a royal proclamation, a message from the
King to his people. The message itself was unimportant: what
struck Wells was the language George V used. He spoke of "my
people." Suddenly Wells realized that what he had believed about
the war and its disruption of civilization had been a delusion.[1]

Much of what Wells had written during the first two years of the
war had reflected his view that the conflict in Europe meant the
breakdown and destruction of the old order he so detested. He
believed that the common sense of people would recognize this and
would help sweep away existing political systems and outmoded

reactionary beliefs. In its place, he thought, a new international and "confederated system of socialist republics" would arise. The King's appeal to "his" people disabused Wells of this naive optimism. As he made his way to the Reform Club, the monarch's words echoed in his mind. "My people." Wells had long been a firm republican, but his reaction went well beyond the institution of monarchy. "'*My* people,'" he muttered, "– me and my sort were *his* people!"[2]

It struck him that the "war to end war" was not "a war for civilization"; this was merely a "consoling fantasy." It was instead, as reflected in the King's words, a reassertion of already established "policies, interests, treaties and secret understandings after the accepted manner of history." These policies continued to be directed by "duly constituted military authorities, engaged in war with the allied central powers." Under such a state of affairs, "no other war was possible." He could not get this thought out of his mind.[3]

Unless there was a revolution in human consciousness through a new understanding of history, he now believed, nothing fundamental would change. He resolved to do his part to bring this change about. *Britling* had gone some way along these lines, but by the novel's end Britling has found God, not the way to a socialist future. Wells held no faith in traditional forms of Christianity – especially the Anglican church – so for a time during the war he turned his idea of a New Republic into a divine monarchy. As earlier in *Britling*, it was an attempt "to deify human courage." The year 1917 saw the publication of further attempts at the personification of progressiveness and the deification of humanity in *God the Invisible King* and *The Soul of a Bishop*.[4]

No work better exemplified Wells's discontent than his novel *Joan and Peter*, to which he gave the subtitle *The Story of an Education*. Written in the latter half of 1917 and early 1918, it was nominally the story of the upbringing of two cousins whose parents die, leaving their lives and education initially in the hands of a cantankerous aunt, Lady Charlotte, the very personification of hidebound Victorian Tory and Anglican England, and two spinster aunts, Phyllis and Phoebe. When the imperious Charlotte and the maiden aunts threaten litigation over control of the children, a fourth guardian is called in to take care of them. He is their uncle, Oswald Sydenham, a figure more reminiscent of Richard Remington in *The New Machiavelli* than of Mr. Britling. An imperial adventurer with a background in science and an interest in education, and also a Victoria Cross winner whose face has been severely disfigured in war, Oswald is the vehicle in *Joan and Peter* for Wells's acerbic views on all manner of subjects: Tory England, the Anglican church, the army and its generals, the universities, schoolteachers, socialists and other misguided progressives, pacifists, and politicians.

Covering the years between 1893 and 1918, *Joan and Peter* allowed Wells to castigate all the groups that, collectively, had helped bring the world to the hopeless impasse of the Great War. In many ways, it was one more failure as art, at least to those such as Henry James and his admirers. Its overriding didacticism – severe even for a Wells novel – was offputting and the book was not well received, although it sold well enough on the strength of *Britling*. But the novel is a remarkable key to H.G.'s state of mind during the latter half of the war. Above all, Oswald concludes, education in the broadest sense is the only solution to the problems of humanity. Reform of institutions is impossible without this.

As Wells put his thoughts onto paper and into Oswald's mind, he provided his protagonist with lengthy meditations on the historical forces at work in the evolution of human culture and society. The shock of war is the beginning of the real education of Joan and Peter, as Wells thought it should also be for humanity. Their previous schooling had been a sham. They had learned the official version of history, a history of kings and queens and other great people, but what did this tell them of the social forces hidden in the historical record? What did it tell them of power or imperialism or the origins of war?[5]

Oswald does his best to re-educate his charges to face the world as it really is. Gradually, the shades begin to fall from Peter's eyes. Unsettled, he ruminates about war, Empire, God, and life in general. But it is, of course, Oswald to whom Wells affords the last word – in truth, many of them – in a lengthy final chapter that constitutes his "valediction" to Joan and Peter.

Oswald pontificates in "broad generalisations" on the foolish-ness of the generals, the mendacity of the politicians, and the plight of the world. Again and again he returns to the idea of history – not that of great men, of kings and queens, but of something else entirely. "All history," he comes to see, "is the record of an effort in man to form communities" and of the constant failures to realize that ideal – failures that lead to war and disaster.[6]

Oswald, like Wells, begins to think along another line: the idea of a League of Free Nations, of a world-state or world republic. This is "the rediscovered outline, the proper teaching of all real education, the necessary outline now of human life." Historians, like the universities, should be "working to a common end, drawing together all the best minds and the finest wills, a myriad of multi-coloured threads, into one common web of a world civilization." History as kings and queens and empires and nations did a dis-service to humanity. It failed to address the will of the species, to recognize the reality and the power of human passion. That is why, for Oswald and for Wells, attention always returned to the idea of a League of Free Nations, an idea that has come, thinks Oswald, "with the effect of a personal and preferential call."[7]

February 1918: Florence's history was complete. It had taken her the better part of four years, four long years during the most senseless and tragic of all wars. She had laboured hard and been constant to her task and to the interwoven threads of her argu-ment. Reflecting on her efforts many years later, Florence was to write: "The basic theme of this outline was 'Man's struggle for social values,' including woman's share in that struggle. Thus I endeavoured to weave in chronological order a fabric composed of facts, . . . the story of the world essential to a historical perspective from 'the beginning' down to to-day . . . In it was featured the work and influence of woman in weaving up the story of the human race – the web of human history."[8]

"The web." She had noted recurring images drawn from weaving while she had drafted her manuscript. Then one day, quite "accidentally," she said, those two words took on heightened resonance. The image of a web linked human progress to woman's place and predicament, and that was exactly her argument. Her book had at last found its title: "The Web of the World's Romance."

Her struggle to express her view of the history of humanity was her own peaceful counterpoint to war, fought in a library and in a home. Four years of a battle against conventional historical interpretation, against the snare of history told as the story of man alone, and she had prevailed. She had written her "Web" as a war against all wars, her own quiet act of sacrifice in the service of love.

The western front was going badly. The military desperately needed bodies. The first conscripts under the Military Service Act had already been called up. Throughout Canada, farms were without workers and thousands of schoolboys now served as "Soldiers of the Soil." Food was scarce, fuel in short supply. Churches held services in common, and schools remained closed for weeks on end. Offices, shops, and warehouses lacked heat.[9] Even in the library reading room people kept their overcoats on. The streetcar rides from the library north to Farnham Avenue seemed to Florence longer than ever, and her fellow passengers looked tired and tense. She could not for the life of her tell whether it was stoic resolve or quiet desperation she glimpsed in their eyes. Perhaps it was just winter, which, like the war, seemed to have no end in sight.

At home, she had spent endless nights typing her manuscript into finished form, making two copies in addition to the original. This was no easy matter. In an age before the photocopier made reproduction of a limitless number of perfect copies of typescript a simple and painless matter, preparation for this purpose remained laborious and time-consuming. The typing of each page involved the lining up and insertion of sheets of carbon paper between the pages of bond paper, in this case involving five pieces of paper for each page typed; and after each error in the typing came the task of removing the sheets, making erasures by hand to the original and two copy pages, rearranging and reinserting them beneath the typewriter's platen, aligning the paper accurately, and typing the correct character. All this for the prospect of carbon copies that often lacked sharpness and that faded badly with each copy made. Little wonder that few literary manuscripts other than the original existed for the purpose of circulation.

This making of precious extra copies was necessary but hard-won. Florence stuck to it as she had stuck to the research and writing. She was well aware of the many ways her book failed to do full justice to the majesty of history, but even so she was pleased with what she had accomplished. In a way, it was her only child, the only progeny to which she would give issue. At the age of fifty-four, she had at last given birth. And for this blessing, at least, she could give thanks.

She had written eighteen more chapters since reaching the Renaissance in 1916, and her final chapter – the thirty-fourth – had taken her story to the Great War.[10] Wherever possible, she had taken pains to stress the ongoing influence of women in history, an influence that had continued even as patriarchy endured and grew, placing women in a position of subjection. She had delighted in pointing to Lucrezia de Medici's influence on the education of her son Lorenzo. It was she who "really ruled Florence." Columbus had learned his map-making skills with the help of his wife, Philippa, daughter of Perestrello, one of the foremost Portuguese navigators.

Again and again, Florence placed women at the centre of attention: Isabella of Aragón, the power behind the throne of late-fifteenth-century Spain; Marguerite de Roberval, who helped establish domestic life in sixteenth-century New France; Marguerite Luther, who had been so instrumental in forming the character and beliefs of her son Martin. "The family home," Florence insisted, "– not the Renaissance – made Luther what he was." Talented women, not only men, helped make the Renaissance: Vittoria Calonna, the marchioness of Pescara; Veronica Gambara, countess of Corregio; Constanza d'Avalos, duchess of Amalfi; Laura Ferracina, Laura Battiferra, Gaspera Stampa, and others. In her treatment of women during the Reformation, she evoked the lives of Florentine of Upper Weimar, who escaped from an unhappy life as a nun, and of Elizabeth, wife of Joachim I (elector of Brandenburg), who was menaced by her husband after he discovered her Protestant faith. Successful in evading his threat to "wall her up," she became instrumental in bringing the people of Brandenburg to Protestantism.[11]

Florence regaled her mother and sisters with the stories of such women, and there were so many to talk about: Luther's wife, Catharine von Bora, of whom he said, "I would not part from my Kathe, no, not to gain all Florence and Venice"; Mary, daughter of Henry VIII and Catherine of Aragon, who "spoke fluently all the modern languages," who "could hold her own in controversy with the most subtle diplomat," and who "was accomplished in music and was practically educated in the New Learning." And of course Elizabeth I, for whom Florence's admiration knew few bounds. Elizabeth had secured to herself an absolute power equal to any European despot, yet "she had so judiciously used that power as to promote a peace within her border through which her people became wildly ebullient in the joy of living, of union, of prosperity, of learning and of liberty."[12]

As one might guess from a historical work that depended on the long view of history already mapped out by nineteenth-century liberal historians such as Victor Duruy and John Richard Green, "The Web" was written within the general interpretive framework known to later twentieth-century historians as "Whig history." This approach to the past assumed progress to be inevitable and located the signs of that progress in the gradual triumph of constitutional democracy over various forms of autocratic government. It was history written with the democratic present in mind, a history fundamentally Protestant in bias and with representative government and parliamentary supremacy assumed to be the desirable and almost necessary outcome.[13] Florence showed her pleasure when the past moved towards democracy and equality, and her scorn when institutions impeded their advent or when civilizations or cultures spurned them.

Florence Deeks was no philosopher of history, and she had little knowledge of contemporary schools of historical interpretation. She preferred the English Whigs to the Tories during the Restoration and the Glorious Revolution, and she saw parliamentary supremacy as a better system than rule by crown alone, however "enlightened" it might be. For her, this was not a matter of historical interpretation: it was plain common sense. Who, after all, would prefer enlightened despotism to democracy and equality? So she provided the only interpretation of the past that made sense to her and to the generation in which the British Empire had reached its zenith.

Yet hers was a Whig history with a difference, one that set it apart from other accounts of the day. The impediment to progress in politics and society remained for Florence the perpetuation of patriarchy and the incessant aggression of men in power, and she took pains to point this out. Earlier forms of subjection through the sale of women and the gradual triumph of patriarchal lineage had merely been transformed into more sophisticated forms of subjection through the possession and inheritance of property. Women continued over the ages to maintain bonds of family and cooperation, but were usually thwarted in their efforts to gain control over their own lives. The power of loving kindness inevitably, therefore, was too often sacrificed to the interests of aggression and private gain, usually by means of war.

To Florence's way of thinking, woman was the "infallible index of a nation's status." But in order to demonstrate this, it was not sufficient simply to portray the great women of history, whether Aspasia or Florence Nightingale. It was necessary also to remind her readers of the ways in which women's interests had been sacrificed to those of men, whether in ancient Israel or India or in the modern world. In the case of Restoration England, she was particularly harsh in judgment. "Woman now suffered," she wrote, "perhaps, the deepest degradation that the country had ever known . . . Everything that belonged to her, real or personal even her clothes as well as anything that she might inherit after marriage, became the possession of her husband . . . She had no power to sell any of her landed property, and even her household property went to her husband . . . He would will away all her property . . . And even their children belonged wholly to the father. Thus a woman owned nothing – scarcely body or soul."[14]

Women remained influential, she insisted, but as individuals, not as a group. Poor women remained uneducated. They were indoctrinated to believe that woman's capabilities were inferior to those of man – for example, that a girl who ceases to blush has lost her most powerful charm and that she should seek to influence men not by reason but by caress. Pioneering women educators such as Mary Anstell sought a proper education for women, but they worked in the face of extraordinary obstacles. The French Revolution may have advanced the cause of liberty, but it was not extended to women. Women of France lost more than they gained by the revolution, and the struggles of the women of Germany "for independence and equality" became more difficult, since the introduction of conscriptive military service took men away from what Florence thought of as "useful and productive work" in order to train them for war.[15]

The history of woman was that of courage and perseverance in the face of such adversity. Often her initiatives had not improved her own circumstances, but, like the women of the French Revolution and the writings of Mary Wollstonecraft, they left an enduring legacy. They inspired others, such as Elizabeth Gurney Fry, to persist in their efforts to alleviate human suffering. Such women in nineteenth-century England, Florence wrote, "were peacefully exercising an active, beneficent and vital influence upon the development of constitutional liberty which the democracy of England had succeeded in establishing and maintaining, and whose principles therefore became so deeply rooted in the life of the nation that no militaristic power has been strong enough or subtle enough to eradicate them." Women as well as men campaigned for the suffrage, and women as well as men were bayoneted or trampled upon by troops at Manchester in 1819 when they attempted to listen to the great radical orator Henry Hunt.[16]

In Florence's view, the accession of Victoria to the English throne was "the fairest day" since "the close of the matriarchate" at the dawn of history. Hers was a reign governed by the principles of "domestic virtue," learning, "nobility of purpose," and "intelligent activity." A Victorian herself, Florence had nothing but praise for the ethos invoked by the example of the English queen whose name became that of the age. "The sovereign power of Victoria," she wrote, "was exercised with a loving and judicious firmness that worked wonders. It produced a silent and humane revolution which force could never accomplish, and which tended to subdue violence, refine manners, and to awaken in woman a realization of her superior endowments . . . And in proportion as force gave place to gentleness and justice and mental superiority, woman's position rose and peace settled down upon the spirit of the nation, and steady advance was made in both political and social reforms."[17]

The polarities of Florence Deeks's history of the world were oppression and liberty. Liberty, she believed, "had its origin in no particular country and in no particular creed." It was born, instead, "in the home." In this respect, her perspective was that of the maternal feminism of her day. The legislation that enlarged the sphere of freedom may have been initiated by men, but its seeds had been laid throughout the ages near the family hearth and at the cradle. Genuine liberty became possible, she insisted, only as a result of "the altruistic, insinuating, beneficent, subtle persistent influence and effort of normal woman" in the face of "indescribable sufferings imposed by the physical force of the warrior."[18] If history embodied progress, it was in large part because ordinary people did extraordinary things in acts of nurturing, kindness, cooperation, and benevolence, thereby making improvement in the human condition possible. Florence had one word to capture the source of such acts of selflessness. It was "love." Before aggression, before war, before kings and despots and tyrants and generals, before patriarchy and armies and laws – before all these things there had been love, and love had somehow endured.

As the Great War reached the middle of its fourth horrific year, Wells found himself near the seat of imperial power, yet he maintained his critical stance. After his tour of the Italian, French, and German fronts in the late summer of 1916, he had written of his experiences and projected his thoughts forward in a book called *War and the Future*, published early the next year. In it, he had complained about the "ineffectiveness" of British and other organizations in explaining the meaning of the war. Much of the propaganda, he said, was nonsense. This war would not end war: in this belief he had been deluded. The experience of the war was "like something in a dream"; the world, he said in proclaiming his pacifism, was "not really awake." The war was nothing but "waste, disorder, disaster," a brutal mixture of flags and nationalities and "irrational creeds and ceremonies." Only when people awoke from their dream-like state would they turn from their Babel-like nationalities to the "one God of mankind."[19]

This was a man whose energies needed to be harnessed to the Allied cause, for from the perspective of British leaders his ideas were at best unhelpful, and at worst dangerous. He had declared that the war might well go on into 1918 or 1919 and was critical of the "peace at any price" campaign. His insistence that the Allies be absolutely clear about their war aims and devote attention to the shape of peace after the war took attention away from the desperate need for victory. Worse, he argued that to be effective the postwar peace treaty must control munitions throughout the world and that the United States must take the lead in proposing the peace settlement.[20]

During the spring of 1918, Lord Northcliffe, the press baron who had become director of enemy propaganda, asked Wells to chair an advisory committee aimed at spreading propaganda in enemy territory.[21] He liked what Wells had written for him in the early stages of the war, and the writer's collections of essays such as *An Englishman Looks at the World*, published in 1914, and *What Is Coming?*, which appeared two years later, had provided further proof of the continuing fertility of his prophetic imagination. Northcliffe now sought to harness it once again to the cause of patriotism by enlisting Wells for service at Crewe House.

Wells joined the advisory committee because he believed he could harness official propaganda to his League of Free Nations idea. It did not work; he experienced nothing but frustration. At St. James's Court he spent sleepless nights annoyed that his imagination had not been called upon to help develop effective tanks (after all, it was he who had dreamt up the notion of Land Ironclads in a *Strand Magazine* piece back in 1903), and at Crewe House he did little more than superintend the manufacture of leaflets to be distributed by secret agents and the forging of "pseudo-German newspapers with depressing suggestions." This was nothing compared with what he believed the ministry should be doing. All day long he helped manufacture lies, and he wanted desperately to tell the world the truth. Above all, the combatant powers must somehow reach a common understanding of the mechanisms of a lasting peace.[22]

To Wells, the war effort was in the hands of small-minded men, men of "limited outlooks and limited motives." He continued to press within Crewe House for a clear declaration of Allied war aims, and he was instrumental in drafting a memorandum by the advisory committee insisting on the development and implementation of his idea of a League of Free Nations, led by a security council of the great powers, that would limit the Allies' sovereignty, territorial possessions, and subject peoples "in the common interest of mankind." The document was duly sent from Northcliffe to Arthur Balfour and the Foreign Office. Wells initially assumed that the principles outlined in it had been accepted, and continued in his propaganda effort. He soon concluded, however, that he and his Crewe House colleagues were merely being used as "decoys" by Foreign Office officials who had no intention of acting upon the advisory committee's recommendations and who had put Northcliffe in charge of propaganda only to keep him from knowing too much about Foreign Office initiatives. Even more frustrating for Wells, Northcliffe himself was two-faced. As master of Crewe House, he had sent out the League of Free Nations memorandum under his signature, but as the press baron of Printing House Square, he sanctioned the ongoing "rant" of newspapers such as the *Times*, the *Daily Mail*, and the *Evening News* over the perfidy of the Germans.[23] Wells complained to Northcliffe, to no avail, and by the end of June he was on the verge of resignation from the propaganda work.

Increasingly he devoted his energies to the League of Free Nations, helping consolidate several groups into a single League of Nations Union with a research committee consisting of the major figures of the movement. Along with Wells, Viscount Grey of Fallodon, Lionel Curtis, J.A. Spender, and Leonard Woolf, the research committee included the prominent scholars G. Lowes Dickinson, Gilbert Murray, and Ernest Barker. Collectively they put together two pamphlets, *The Idea of a League of Nations* and

The Way to the League of Nations. "It is clear," said the former, "that if a world league is to be living and enduring, the idea of it and the need and righteousness of its service must be taught by every educational system in the world." In this way, the research committee repeated the central message of *Joan and Peter*: that world peace was fundamentally a matter of an education in humanity.[24]

Once again, however, Wells's efforts were thwarted. In 1917, acting on his belief that the Americans must lead the way to peace, he had sent a lengthy outline of his League of Free Nations idea to President Woodrow Wilson by means of a letter delivered through an American intermediary. Early in January 1918, in an address to both houses of Congress, Wilson introduced his "Fourteen Points" for a peace settlement. It included a proposal to establish a League of Nations. The winds of initiative had been taken right out of the British sails. Wells faced the prospect of endless committee meetings, all of which now had necessarily to respond to policies emanating from across the Atlantic.

This proved too much for him to bear. He hated committee work, and while the Fourteen Points led generally in a direction of which he approved, it held out little prospect for the broader ideal of a new world confederation of socialist states.[25] In early July, he presided over a Reform Club dinner attended by British and American champions of the League of Free Nations. During it, he spoke at length of the need for a new understanding of history. By midsummer Wells had announced his resignation from the propaganda committee. He continued with League work, but his attention had drifted to other matters.

Whatever course the remainder of the war would take, one thing was clear to Wells the prophet: that the peace must usher in a new world order. He was determined that the world would learn of his vision of the future. In order to secure a foothold on that future, humanity would need first to heed the lessons of its past. It was time to act on this conviction. The moment had come to set aside fiction and to embark on his own history of the world, however long it might take.

At the end of July 1918, Florence Deeks stepped off the streetcar at Yonge and Dundas Streets, carrying a bulky package under her arm. A short block east on Dundas, she turned south. Bond Street was pleasant – only a few blocks long, and shaded on both sides by large trees, a pocket of repose that almost kept the din of Yonge Street at bay. Florence could see St. Michael's Cathedral at the first intersection, not far from Massey Hall.

The building she wanted was number 70, and she found it standing proudly between the offices of Presbyterian Publications and a house once lived in by the fiery Upper Canadian rebel William Lyon Mackenzie. It was an impressive structure in its own right, five storeys high, mainly of brick but with a first storey of Ohio blue-stone.[26] Number 70 Bond Street was the headquarters of the Macmillan Company of Canada.

The interior was just as striking. Florence passed through a vestibule of marble panels into a bright inner hall with a mullioned window of leaded cathedral glass. Just past the spacious staircase and the passenger elevator, she found the waiting room and educational office. Settled in one of the wooden chairs, her parcel on her lap, she took in the surroundings. The room seemed perfectly suited for the Canadian headquarters of a great publishing firm – wall panels and bookcases in dark stained wood, complemented by a wallpaper of deep green. The atmosphere seemed just right, dignified but not sombre. From where she sat, she could see the office of the president and directors off to the side, and the president's secretary busy at her desk.

Shortly after putting the final touches on "The Web" she had written to the education editor of Macmillan's Canadian branch, John C. Saul. Florence had been worried that perhaps she had drawn too heavily on Green's *Short History of the English People*, both in paraphrase and in quoted extracts. Since she understood that Macmillan, publisher of the book, held copyright, she felt obliged to ask the company whether any exception might be taken to her use of Green. In a letter to Saul of February 22, she had explained her problem, mentioning in passing that her manuscript was a short history of the world and that she would conform to the publisher's wishes in every way. Saul had responded around the middle of March, saying that it would be best if she left the manuscript with him so he could examine it. "Of course," he wrote, "you are quite aware that if your book was very much like Greene's [*sic*] 'Short History of the English People,' our English House would probably not sanction its publication."[27] He suggested that she telephone him to arrange for an appointment.

Florence had not acted immediately on the invitation. Macmillan was one of the largest and most prestigious publishing firms in the world, and its imprint was seen on books by famous authors such as Tennyson and Kipling and H.G. Wells. She had been reluctant to subject her work to the scrutiny of its editors, even if only to check passages from Green. But she did need to have some professional eyes examine it, so she had gone first to the Methodist Book and Publishing House in the Wesley Building at the corner of Queen and John Streets and left her manuscript with a Mr. E.J. Moore to look over and provide advice. She also left a copy with J.M. Dent and Sons.

The act of surrendering "The Web" to strange men's eyes required more courage than Florence felt she possessed, and she could not bring herself to give her own name as its author. Instead, she chose a pseudonym that combined humour and self-deprecation in equal measure, as if to distance herself from potential criticism. The title page of "The Web" indicated only that it had been written by "Adul Weaver." By whatever name, its author remained taut with worry about its fate. After a couple of weeks without word from Moore, she had become so nervous that she asked him to return it. He did so, along with a letter that declined to publish because of economies forced on the firm by the war.[28] Dent reacted in a similar way.

Sitting in the Macmillan waiting room, fingers nervously tapping the wrapped copy of her manuscript, she wondered whether she had made a mistake in asking Mr. Saul for an interview. Suddenly he was in front of her, hand outstretched in welcome, a tall, amiable-looking man about fifty years old, with a slight stoop, dishevelled hair, and a wild moustache that badly needed a trim. Judging by his looks, he could just as easily have been a scholar or a bohemian as a respected publisher.[29]

Like the man, Saul's office bore little resemblance to the dignified atmosphere of the waiting room. His desk was strewn with
bulky files. A pile of manuscripts and folders threatened to topple
from it. Books lay in disarray on shelves, organized in no obvious
order. They were on all manner of subjects, from nineteenth-
century poetry to histories of Russia. A pile of detective stories sat
near the edge of the desk. Even before Florence was able to unwrap
her copy of "The Web," a cloud of smoke from Saul's pipe threatened to engulf the room.

The meeting was brief. She told Saul hesitantly about her history
of the world, mentioned that she was seeking advice with a view to
eventual publication, and repeated to him her fear that she had used
Green too much. Then she gave him her manuscript, and he sat
back in his chair and, puffing away, flipped through it at random,
reading portions as he went along. Somehow, she observed, the
unruly hair and moustache did not jibe with the high, stiff stand-up
collar and straight tie he wore. After a few minutes, he put the manuscript down and asked to keep it for a while. Summoning her
remaining courage, she took a few poems from her handbag and
offered them to him. He shook his head. "We are not interested in
poetry, we do not buy," he said.[30] So she put them back. The interview was over. She thanked him for his consideration, took her
leave, and left the building for Farnham Avenue and home.

A couple of weeks later, on August 14, she received a letter from
Saul, apologizing for the fact that he had not yet been able to give
any detailed attention to her manuscript and asking her permission
to allow it "to remain where it is" until he returned in a couple of
weeks from a business trip. She did not mind at all, for she was
about to leave Toronto herself for a brief vacation.[31]

7   *Shadows*

> "Lying and deceit! That's not the colour of *those*
> days. It's the present that is a perjurer, not the past."
>   "It's to clear the past of a lie that may have been
> laid upon it that I am asking these questions . . ."
>
> Angus Wilson, *Anglo-Saxon Attitudes* (1956)

O N THE DAY THAT FLORENCE DEEKS met John
Saul and presented him with a copy of "The Web," Frank Wise,
president of Macmillan of Canada, was very probably at work in
his Bond Street office, adjacent to the room where sales agents and
prospective authors sat, waiting for their meetings with the publisher or his editors. A photographer captured him at his desk,
probably during the war, leaning forward towards a desktop so
high that the top of his pen seemed level with his neck. Some
natural light filtered into the room through the leaded glass window
behind him, but for the most part the desk was lit from the electric
light attached to the richly wood-panelled office wall.[1] At work in
his office, Wise looked every bit the successful Canadian publisher
he was. In fact, by 1918 he was acknowledged by all to be a pillar
of the nation's literary establishment.

At fifty years of age, Frank Wise had reached the summit of his
career. Born in 1868 in Boston, Lincolnshire, England, he had emigrated to the western United States as a young man, working first
as a bank clerk and cashier. But his education at the Boston

Grammar School had stood him in good stead, for it had cultivated literary interests in him. From the bank he moved to the Kansas City *Times*, where he worked on advertising accounts and did some reporting. Finally, in the mid-1890s, came his big break: a position with the American branch of Macmillan in New York.

Wise remained fiercely proud of his British heritage and counted himself fortunate in the extreme to have joined a company that in an important way was part of British imperial expansion. Founded in 1843 by the Scottish brothers Daniel and Alexander Macmillan, of the Isle of Arran, the firm had from the outset combined financial acumen and literary prescience. By the late nineteenth century, its list was central to the British literary canon. The company had published Charles Kingsley's *Westward Ho!*, Thomas Hughes's *Tom Brown's School Days*, E.T. Palgrave's *The Golden Treasury*, Lewis Carroll's *Alice's Adventures in Wonderland*, Sir J.G. Fraser's *The Golden Bough*, and Rudyard Kipling's *The Jungle Book*. Its authors also included Alfred, Lord Tennyson, Henry James, and Thomas Hardy. If Empire involved the dissemination of culture as well as commerce and political administration, the London-based house of Macmillan was as much an agent of Empire as any advocate of formal imperial federation.

Wise took pride in being part of the Macmillan empire in North America. Moreover, the moment of his employment by Macmillan's New York branch had been a propitious one. In 1896, following the death of Alexander Macmillan, the English parent firm reorganized itself into a limited company, Macmillan & Company, Limited, and the American branch was incorporated separately as the Macmillan Company, New York.[2] Daniel's sons Frederick and Maurice Macmillan and Alexander's son George Macmillan were on its board of directors, and George P. Brett was named president.

Born in London in 1858, George Platt Brett had lived in the United States since the age of eleven, when his father, George Edward Brett, had been appointed to set up an agency for the sale of Macmillan titles in North America. After the family emigrated, the son had gone to the City College of New York, but publishing ran in his blood and he joined the firm at the age of sixteen as its first travelling salesman.

In 1890, George Edward Brett died and the son took over his father's publishing concerns. At the age of thirty-two, the young man had already led a full life. Fear of tuberculosis had forced him to leave his sales position years earlier. Married at twenty-three to a Toronto woman, George and his bride abandoned the eastern seaboard for the American west and a ranch he had purchased with a partner. But his wife died from complications arising out of giving birth, and while he was away from the ranch searching for domestic help the partner disappeared with Brett's savings and "everything else of value."[3] He returned to New York to work for his ailing father.

At the time George P. Brett formally took over his father's business, members of the Macmillan family continued to hold the majority of the American company's shares and to take a close interest in its activities.[4] Relations between the American and British branches of Macmillan were close but at times tense. From the perspective of the English firm, the new American branch needed close supervision in order to ensure adequate profit margins, and it was Frederick Macmillan's responsibility to safeguard his family's interests in America.[5] George Brett wished to take advantage of the publicity generated by successful titles of the English branch by republishing them under the New York imprint for sales in North America.

At the same time, the ambitious Brett wanted to take the American company in directions of his own making. The 1896 reorganization allowed him to move his company towards autonomy. He expected the departments of the firm to operate independently and outdistance their competition, and soon they did. A publisher, Brett said, should "keep his ears to the ground and interpret through books the sounds that he hears." And he practised what he preached. He scoured periodicals to discover promising new writers. He began to publish titles of his own choosing, American authors like Jack London, Owen Wister, and the novelist Winston Churchill. Churchill's historical romance, *Richard Carvel*, sold 250,000 copies in 1899, only to be outdone three years later by the sale of 750,000 copies of Wister's *The Virginian*.[6]

This short, stocky "bantam rooster of a man," with the rimless spectacles, the dark moustache, and the "thrusting chin" and its pert little grey goatee, superintended every facet of his business, from the choice of authors to the condition of the basement boilers. He hired thoroughly competent people and dominated them through sheer force of personality. By 1918, George P. Brett not only had a large number of best-sellers to his credit but had almost cornered the highly profitable national textbook market. His fully stocked branch offices in major cities helped revolutionize methods of wholesale distribution of books. Plans existed for agencies throughout the world. In 1918, he was well on his way to presiding over one of the largest and most successful publishing firms in the world.[7]

Frank Wise occupied an uneasy place in the transatlantic Macmillan enterprise. As an employee of the American firm, he was expected to take George Brett's lead, and he did. Over the ten years in which he worked out of the New York office, he had met with authors, school boards, and members of the academic and college communities, and attended any number of conventions. Eventually he was placed in charge of the company's educational division, helping build sales of textbooks to New York public schools.[8] Yet in spite of his initiative and enthusiasm, as an English expatriate who was not shy in making his British loyalties evident, he may have been seen by Brett and others in the New York office as a possible conduit of confidential information about the New York operation to the parent firm. In any event, when it was decided in 1905 to establish a branch of Macmillan in Canada, Brett recommended Wise to Frederick Macmillan as the person to start up the operation.

Wise arrived in Toronto late in the year, bringing with him his new wife, Gertrude (whom he had married less than a year before), and his young daughter, Margaret. It was his second marriage, for his first wife, Hilda Johnson, had died in 1899, not long after giving birth. He had a family to support, and the powerful lists of the London and New York branches of Macmillan were his main assets.

Under Wise's direction, Macmillan of Canada began operations at the beginning of January 1906, with $20,000 capital, rented offices on Richmond Street West, a staff of three or four, and a stock of books supplied by London and New York. No sooner had he settled in than a fire devastated the building, requiring renovation to the offices but leaving the piles of Kipling and Tennyson, Hamlin Garland, and other authors intact. Undeterred by the near-disaster, Wise went about selling his books.

Dapper in appearance, Frank Wise was a balding man of white shirts, dark suits, and tie pins. His short eyebrows, light eyelashes, and hooded eyes gave him a dignified but at times melancholic look.[9] Yet the calm exterior belied aggressive instincts and a gruff manner. A man of unbridled ambition, he would go to great lengths to secure what he wanted. Soon he was negotiating prospective titles and Canadian prices with the English and American branches, arranging a distribution deal with the Canadian News Company, and attempting to secure Canadian copyright on volumes by Tennyson and Kipling.[10]

Wise was no diplomat, and he spoke his mind in ways not known for understatement. Although he could report to Frederick Macmillan in June 1906 that "business is looking very bright," he also felt obliged to complain of "the disgraceful piratical methods" of the Canadian News Company, which threatened to steal the Canadian market from Macmillan by importing both copyright and non-copyright books from its own New York house. By the end of 1907 he had "ruffled the feathers" of at least one prominent New York publisher, Doubleday, and George Brett took him to task for the indiscretion.[11]

To outside observers, the world of publishing was one of culture and civility; but to those who knew it from the inside it was one of cutthroat competition by men who used every means at their disposal to secure an advantage. Pirated and competing editions and deeply discounted retail prices were the greatest threats Wise faced in these years, and he did his best to wage war with rival firms on these and other issues. When Rudyard Kipling and his wife, Caroline, made a cross-country tour in 1907, the year he won the Nobel Prize for literature, Wise made certain that he spoke privately to them to ensure that they continued to publish in Canada exclusively through Macmillan. He was annoyed when he learned that the Kiplings had arranged to publish with Methuen also. He made his views known, and the Kiplings took offence, in part because, in Mrs. Kipling's judgment, Wise had not sufficiently pushed sales of her husband's works. She informed Frederick Macmillan of the unacceptable behaviour of Macmillan of Canada's president. In defending his actions, which included making arrangements with Canadian authorities to confiscate pirated Kipling works, Wise wrote, with an air of exasperation: "It may be that your relations with these persons are of a more rapturous character [than] we seem to be able to maintain with the Atlantic between us."[12]

The problems Wise faced as a Canadian publisher were not only ones of strained relations with authors and other publishers; they also involved the changing tastes of Canadian readers. Try as he did to maximize sales of British authors in Canada, he soon discovered that Canadians wanted to read books about Canada and by Canadians. He found sales of Macmillan's "Colonial Library" slow, and he chafed when London insisted that the Canadian market must surely be capable of taking up more of the volumes. Similarly, he found himself explaining to the British firm, rather crankily, that there was scarcely any "private schools" market in Canada suitable for purchasing Latin texts, nor was there much public interest in the Colonial Library.[13]

Wise remained a proud advocate of British imperial achievement, but as his years in Canada lengthened, his sense of it broadened to include its Canadian variant. Imperialism was in fact one contemporary form of Canadian national commitment, and Wise attempted to build on this sense of vicarious participation in world affairs. So he began to publish books by Canadian authors, including Colonel George T. Denison's *The Struggle for Imperial Unity* in 1909 and his own work, *The Empire Day by Day*, in 1910. He was determined, like George Brett in New York after 1896, to establish his own distinctive list. "If you remember," he had written to Brett early in 1909, "at the time of our establishment here, I suggested, in a fit of banter, that the motto for the Canadian house should be 'Canada pro Canadienses,' and I think that it would have been a most appropriate one." This went against the views of Frederick Macmillan and George Brett, both of whom believed that the main purpose of establishing the Canadian house was "to sell the publications of the New York and London houses."[14]

Handsome profits could be made in publishing, but in the Canadian context they came about less through sales of general-interest books for the small but highly competitive national retail trade market than through adoption of textbooks by provincial boards of education. And the pursuit of such adoptions was something that Macmillan and Brett had encouraged from the outset of Canadian operations. But competition was fierce. For years, Macmillan's Toronto competitors, W.J. Gage, Copp Clark, and the Canada Publishing Company, had enjoyed exclusive contracts with the provincial government of Ontario for the production of readers. Major American publishing firms offered established texts at low prices because of their large print runs. Even the T. Eaton Co., with its enormous advertising capacity, had gotten into the textbook business when it began to produce school readers on a break-even basis. Not to be outdone, the Ontario government produced its own speller and offered it to the Ministry of Education at virtually no profit.[15]

In a province where major publishing contracts were often let without tender, on the basis of a handshake between gentlemen, personal influence was everything. To possess it, one needed contacts; and to secure them a significant public profile was essential. Frank Wise did everything in his power to build one. He joined the Board of Trade and chaired its publishers' section for three years. He met with university presidents and faculty. He cultivated contacts with the press across the country. He helped organize the Bureau of Municipal Research and served on its board and council, as he also did with the Citizens' Research Institution of Canada. He joined the Navy League and became a Fellow of the Royal Colonial Institute.

By 1918, Frank Wise was well known throughout the country. For a dozen years he had spoken to groups large and small about a wide range of subjects and had published a steady stream of articles in Canadian, American, and English newspapers. Wise held strong opinions on just about everything, and he was not afraid to tell anyone who cared to listen just what they were.[16] At the end of the war, however, Wise was perhaps best known to the Canadian public as an organizer and leading spokesman of the Imperial Home-Reunion Association.

The organization had come into existence in 1912, as a nation-wide effort run by influential business and professional men to support British-born skilled workers. It was both a charitable and a business initiative, championed by prominent Canadian men of finance such as Sir Edmund Osler and Sir Edmund Walker. As a charity, it advanced money to workers so that they might bring their families to Canada from Britain; as a business venture, it ensured that remittances back home were no longer required. Wages paid in Canada stayed in Canada. By 1913, thirty branches of the Imperial Home-Reunion Association existed throughout the Dominion, and Wise had been personally responsible for establishing twelve of them in Ontario and Montreal. He was president of the Toronto branch.[17]

Wise claimed in newspaper interviews that his involvement in the Home-Reunion Association put him out of pocket, but this is doubtful. In July 1913, he had privately established his own labour bureau, the British Employment Association, on Simcoe Street in Toronto. In return for a one-dollar fee, the association found employment for British-born men; cheap transportation to job sites was provided for them by means of arrangements with railways.[18]

Macmillan of Canada had also grown in size and influence, as if swept up in the wake of Wise's rising reputation within the publishing and business communities. By 1910, the company had outgrown its Richmond Street offices, and by sheer persistence he managed to overcome the reluctance of Sir Frederick and George Brett and convinced them to help finance the acquisition of land and the construction of a new building on Bond Street, in the heart of downtown Toronto.[19] The company moved into its impressive new headquarters later that year.

Perhaps the greatest achievement of Frank Wise, however, was the 1912 acquisition of the Morang Educational Company. When it took place, *Publishers' Weekly* described it as "probably the most important deal in the history of publishing in Canada." George N. Morang had been in business since 1899 and had established a solid reputation as publisher of a large number of textbooks and the Alexandra Readers widely in use in the rapidly expanding western provinces. But by 1910 Morang was overextended and in debt. Wise was of the view that Morang had established "the best Canadian list of school books" in the country and, knowing of the man's difficulties, he determined to secure control of his ailing company. Shrewd negotiations, helped by Morang's worsening financial condition and backing from Sir Frederick and George Brett, enabled Wise to purchase the company for his original offer of $115,000, only half of what Morang originally wanted. With the purchase came Morang's backlist, including public school and high school history textbooks and readers. Wise had found a way of establishing the basis of a substantial educational division intended to serve as the profit base of the company. As he sat in his office in the summer of 1918, he could reflect on the fact that, during the years of his presidency, on average the company had managed to pay a seven per cent annual dividend to its shareholders on a yearly turnover of nearly $400,000; the company now held assets of almost a quarter of a million dollars.[20]

At a *pension* in Pimlico with Rebecca West during the summer of 1918, H.G. Wells tried to think about what shape his projected history might take, but nothing more consequential could be done there. Writing history was fundamentally different from writing a novel: it required evidence, facts, a comprehensive sense of the sweep of the past. Imagination alone, however powerful, could not bring it into existence. Much of his thinking over the past half-dozen years had run along historical lines, but what he needed now was close access to a library, and his library was at Easton Glebe. Still, Rebecca continued to want him to spend time with her, and the ongoing League of Free Nations work required him to spend time in London, working out of St. James's Court. He continued to work on his plan for the book into the autumn.

Late in October, he exchanged letters across the Atlantic. The first, undated but written around the 20th of the month, was from Wells to George Brett, who had published several American editions of his books.

Dear Mr. Brett;

Every book can't be a Britling. I know you will do all you can to keep my end up over there.

I'm very much taken up with work for the League of Nations Movement over here, and I have been writing very little. But there is an idea I have in hand that I wish I could talk over with you. We think here that the time draws near when instead of the History of England and the History of the U.S.A., and the History of France and so on, children all over the world ought to learn the History of mankind and I believe that it is up to me to plan to write the first School "History of Mankind."

It will have to be an illustrated book, and I see it as a book of about two hundred thousand words and about one thousand maps, illustrations, full page or smaller. What do you think of the project? It might be produced, first of all as the sort of book that is given to a boy as a prize, and then, if opportunity arose, inserted it [sic] in schools in a cheaper edition. I want you to think it over, something of the sort I feel I must do, because it is one of the things in which I can show the way to well qualified but less broadly imaginative men.

On November 8, Wells received Brett's reply.

Dear Mr. Wells,

I have just received your letter in regard to the book which you think of writing to be called the History of Mankind, or some such title . . .

There is no doubt in my mind that your plan for the book on the History of Mankind is a very feasible one, and I should think that the book would interest young and old readers alike, although at first it might be difficult to have the book studied in schools, as part of the regular course, yet I should not be afraid to venture that in the long run the book itself, or some modification of it might find use in this way. At any rate, I make no doubt the book would be recommended for school reading, and this might itself result in a considerable sale.

Your letter tells me nothing of the way in which you intend

to write the book, and of course, it might be prepared from the standpoint of Social History of Mankind. The Material History of Mankind, or the purely natural development of Mankind from its physical standpoint.

Naturally one would suppose that you would be more likely to trace the history of mankind from the standpoint of its social development, but I should much like to have from you, if you have time for it, a little outline of just what your book is to be so that one might perhaps consult one or more of the well known educational authorities on this side and see as to whether such a book could perchance be actually used in the schools themselves.

In any case, however, whether this be so or not, I think that the book should be written, and I earnestly hope that you will undertake it for a valuable and constantly increasing public must be found, it seems to me, for a work of this character.

Hoping that you will give me, by and by, a few more details about the book, and awaiting these anxiously . . .

These letters constituted Wells's first written exchange with a publisher concerning *The Outline of History*, and it is clear that he was only about to begin serious work on it.[21] By this stage in his career as a novelist, it was no longer obligatory (if it ever had been) for him to provide prospective publishers with a plot summary. Offered a Wells novel, most would take it sight unseen. George Brett had published several of his novels and collections of essays before, and could have had little doubt that any work by the author would be likely to return a handsome profit. But this new offer was different. It was to be a work of history, and, while Wells had a fine sense of the past, nothing he had so far written indicated that he had acquired the skills or depth of knowledge of a historian – certainly not those required of the enormous project he now had in mind. Besides, the writing of history had undergone a renaissance of sorts since the 1890s. How different would Wells's book be from those of James Harvey Robinson and the other Progressive historians?

As Brett suggested, the author had not helped him much. Apart from a few generalizations, he had said nothing about the nature of the proposed book. No overview, no chapter outline, no prospective table of contents that historians searching for a publisher normally provided. Wells said nothing of his approach to his subject, and little of its magnitude. Had he already drafted even a few early chapters by late October of 1918, he would have had a more accurate sense of the number of words that lay ahead. As it was, all he could do was guess. Work on his outline of history remained in the future, still "something of the sort I feel I must do."

During the following weeks, Wells turned his attention to British publishers. In November, he wrote to Sir Frederick Macmillan about "a project I have in hand," a "Universal History." What he had to say about it took only four sentences, and the only useful information that Sir Frederick could have gleaned from the proposal was that the book might run from 200,000 to 300,000 words and that it would be useful as "a prize book & for reading." Of all publishers, profit-conscious Sir Frederick, publisher of the wildly successful *Britling*, knew what a best-selling Wells book could do for a firm. And he had long since made his peace with the author after the scandals of *Ann Veronica* and *The New Machiavelli*. But the paragraph from Wells gave him no confidence in the novelist's capacity as a historian. His reply of November 22 was brief: "I am much obliged to you for letting me know of your project for 'A School History of Mankind' and for the implication contained in your letter that you would consider an offer from us to act as your publishers. I fear however that this is not an occasion on which we can be of any assistance to you."[22]

Wells had mentioned something about the project to another London publisher, Sir Frank Newnes, in August 1918, when the two had met in the Reform Club. He wanted the book published in cheap monthly parts, and Sir Frank thought it would be of sufficient length to merit publication in serial form; but not until mid-November did he write to Wells that his directors liked the idea "very much" and that the two men should now "put the whole thing in a more concrete form." Like Sir Frederick Macmillan, he had been given only the most general idea of what Wells had in mind.[23]

It is clear that Wells had done very little on his outline of history, either in research or writing, until after the November armistice that brought an end to the Great War. At the end of the month, he replied at some length to the letter in which George Brett had asked for "a few more details" about the book. Even then, instead of describing the work he had done, he simply directed the New York publisher to James Henry Breasted's volume on ancient history and those of James Harvey Robinson on the medieval and modern periods, pointing them out as works that covered the ground but were "badly done." He could still not speak substantively of his own work, except to say that it would have "more unity of presentation" and lots of maps and illustrations. "I've never been so interested by any book as I have by this one. For the time I have put aside a novel I have in hand about a Schoolmaster, who like Job holds his faith and bitter affliction. But the history is going to be a big undertaking . . . The history must not be hurried. It goes on well but it seems [to require] not only thought and planning but masses of reading."[24]

Then again, perhaps the history was not going as well as Wells let on. The next month he wrote to Brett again. "The unusual History is going to be a long business." Meanwhile, he had decided to "push" the work on his Book of Job novel, to be called *The Undying Fire*. About half of it was written, he claimed; but he hoped to have it ready for publication in May or June of the next year.[25] In the crucial first six months of 1919, when by all accounts much of *The Outline of History* was researched and written, Wells wrote 30,000 words of a different book.[26]

Florence was now becoming anxious. More than six months had passed since she had left "The Web" with John Saul. The war had ended, Christmas had come and gone, and the New Year had been ushered in. Things were getting back to normal. Yet still no word from the Macmillan editor about the status of her manuscript. At first she had been encouraged, because the delay suggested that it "was receiving proper attention." But as time went by, encouragement turned to unease. One day she spoke to her brother George about it. Later she recreated the conversation:

"Hasn't the Macmillan Company returned your manuscript?" he asked.

"No, not yet," I replied.

"Aren't you uneasy about it?"

"Yes, I am somewhat. I did not want to hurry them with it but I did not expect they were going to keep it forever."[27]

She was now concerned on two counts – anxious to get some information about her manuscript but even more so "not to spoil any chance of success by over haste." So she did nothing until mid-January, when she wrote to Saul. Surely, she thought, "the answer from Macmillan and Company, London, ought to be ready." She was losing confidence in her work. Having read it over again, she recognized that it needed revision – so much, she wrote, that "I think I have been unwarranted in asking you to read it in its present condition." She expressed her willingness to rewrite it along the lines of "the rise and development of democracy as the World's civilizing influence," and of "militarism as a degenerating influence." If necessary, she added, she would eliminate much of her material on women; she now feared it was "unreliable." Torn between her desire to place women in history and to publish a possibly more timely book on the origins of war, she opted for the latter. Such a revision, she noted, would reduce the size of the manuscript by half from its current 185,000 words; then she asked for the name of a "reliable collaborator to help in the work of revision."[28]

Still no reply, not until the end of the month. Then in the mail came a short letter from John Saul. He had read portions of "The Web" and had concluded that it should be "materially condensed," so he was "glad indeed" that she was willing to cut out "the woman idea." She was startled to learn that as of the next day, January 31, he would no longer be with Macmillan and that he was at that moment "cleaning up everything before leaving." He remained quite willing to discuss a revised version of the manuscript with her; meanwhile, he concluded, he was leaving the manuscript at her disposal.[29]

Florence was puzzled. "If Mr. Saul was clearing everything up before leaving and if the manuscript were there with the answers from Macmillan Co. London, why did he not return it with those answers?"[30] Why had he not simply sent the manuscript to her, with his letter, in the post?

Annie and Florence Deeks (in a photo taken around 1880) spent their formative years in the Loyalist town of Morrisburg, in eastern Ontario. Like their sister, Mabel, they were young women with high expectations.

Florence Deeks was an early member and the first historian of the Women's Art Association of Canada. At a reception for musical festival artists in Toronto around 1909, she is the sixth from the left in the back row.

A rare photograph of the Deeks sisters together, taken at the wedding of their brother George to Helen Campbell in 1904. Left to right: Florence, Annie, and Mabel Deeks, Helen, her mother, and her sisters Mabel and Maud.

Family life and loyalty were important to George S. Deeks, seen here with (left to right) his sons Douglas, Edward, and Campbell. Financial support from George for his sister Florence made *Deeks v. Wells* possible.

H.G. Wells and his second wife, Catherine, on a rowing excursion in the 1890s. From the first, her eyes sought his attention but his were looking elsewhere.

Florence Deeks spent much of the Great War of 1914–18 in the reading room of the Toronto Central Library, on College Street (above, about 1920), researching and writing "The Web," her feminist history of the world.

Wells sketched this 1899 "picshua" during the many months of talk between husband and wife about *Love and Mr. Lewisham*. The artist depicts the anxious author "Waiting for the Verdict."

Wells insisted on calling Catherine "Jane," for him the embodiment of wifely duty and compliance. For Catherine, "Jane" served to preserve a marriage in any way possible. "Without her constant help," said H.G., completion of *The Outline of History* "would have been impossible."

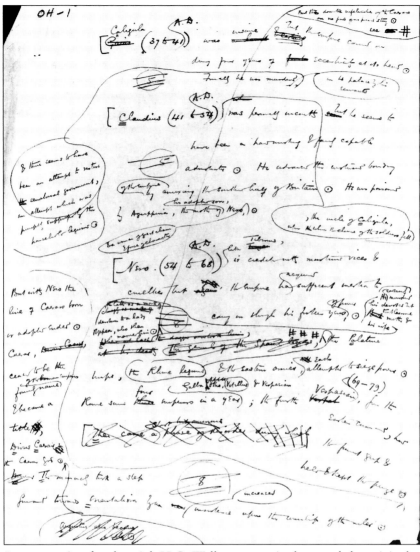

In preparation for the trial, H.G. Wells was required to send the original draft of *The Outline* to Toronto for examination. Wells drafted the work in his typically chaotic hand, but it was the version typed by Jane that the plaintiff scrutinized at Osgoode Hall. Why would he not produce the handwritten original?

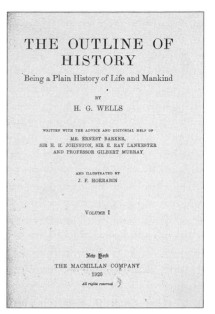

THE OUTLINE OF
HISTORY

Being a Plain History of Life and Mankind

BY

H. G. WELLS

WRITTEN WITH THE ADVICE AND EDITORIAL HELP OF
MR. ERNEST BARKER,
SIR H. H. JOHNSTON, SIR E. RAY LANKESTER
AND PROFESSOR GILBERT MURRAY

AND ILLUSTRATED BY
J. F. HORRABIN

VOLUME I

New York
THE MACMILLAN COMPANY
1920
All rights reserved

For the Toronto journalist and critic Hector Charlesworth, the expertise and authority suggested by the scholarly collaborators named on *The Outline*'s title page helped explain how Wells had researched and written his two volumes within a year. Florence Deeks, reading Charlesworth's review, thought otherwise.

Frank Wise, seen here in his Macmillan of Canada office, enjoyed the power of his position as founding president. How deep was the involvement of this man, later convicted of forgery and imprisoned, in the apparent disappearance of "The Web" from his company's vault?

mass of matter, not yet concentrated into a compact centre of
heat and light, considerably larger than it is now, and spinning
very much faster, and that as it whirled, a series of fragments
detached themselves from it, which became the planets. Our
earth is one of these planets. The flaring mass that was the material of the earth broke as it spun into two masses, a larger, the
earth itself, and a smaller, which is now the dead, still moon.
Astronomers give us convincing reasons for supposing that sun
and earth and moon and all that system were then whirling about
at a speed much greater than the speed at which they are moving
to-day, and that at first our earth was a flaming thing upon which
no life could live. The way in which they have reached these
conclusions is by a very beautiful and interesting series of observations and reasoning, too long and elaborate for us to deal with here.
But they oblige us to believe that the sun, incandescent though it
is, is now much cooler than it was, and that it spins more slowly
now than it did, and that it continues to cool and slow down. And
they also show that the rate at which the earth spins is diminish-
ing and continues to diminish — that is to say, that our day is
growing longer and longer, and that the heat at the centre of the
earth wastes slowly. There was a time when the day was not a
half and not a third of what it is to-day; when a blazing hot sun,
much greater than it is now, must have moved visibly — had
there been an eye to mark it — from its rise to its setting across
the skies. There will be a time when the day will be as long as a
year is now, and the cooling sun, shorn of its beams, will hang
motionless in the heavens.

It must have been in days of a much hotter sun, a far swifter
day and night, high tides, great heat, tremendous storms and
earthquakes, that life, of which we are a part, began upon the
world. The moon also was nearer and brighter in those days and
had a changing face.[1]

[1] For a convenient recent discussion of the origin of the earth and its early history
before the seas were precipitated and sedimentation began, the student should
consult Professor Burrell's contribution to the Yale lectures, *The Evolution of the
Earth and Its Inhabitants* (1918), edited by President Lull.

At the top of this key page of Florence Deeks's annotated copy of *The
Outline*, she underlined unacknowledged words of the French historian
Victor Duruy. Wells said he had not used Duruy as a source, but in "The
Web" Deeks had.

—Photograph by Ashley and Crippen

In 1925, the news that a Toronto woman was suing H.G. Wells stunned the literary community. Publishers and writers wondered who this Miss Deeks was and whether such a figure as Wells could really have committed "literary piracy."

Norman Tilley, Ontario's finest litigator, had taken on Miss Deeks's seemingly outrageous case. Was it, as some hinted, the wealth of her brother that persuaded him to support her cause? Or was Tilley convinced that her evidence was strong enough to win?

She wrote back at once, asking for the immediate return of "The Web." Again no reply, and her attention turned elsewhere. Finally, at the end of March, came a letter. It was from a new editor at Macmillan of Canada, a Montrose W. Liston. He had glanced through the pages of her manuscript and wished to set her straight about publication. He was brutally frank about her audacity. She had embarked "upon a sea of past, present and future," and on a subject that "stretches from the beginning to now. It is evolutionary, psychological, metaphysical, speculative." The manuscript was far too ambitious. Either such a work had to be one of "encyclopedic lengths" or it must be a mere "skeleton index of what you want to say." Liston recommended the latter. In its present state, the plan of "The Web" was "impracticable." Perhaps she should content herself with producing a brief pamphlet on some such subject as "Love and War."[31]

Florence was devastated. All that work for nothing? And what about the basic question she had asked of Saul? Had Macmillan in London accepted her use of passages from Green's *Short History of the English People* as fair? She still had no answer.

Following Liston's suggestion, she went to Macmillan's Bond Street office early in April and spoke with him. He offered her suggestions about a new work, written along different lines, and use of the office library. Then he called his secretary to bring "The Web" to the library, where they stood. A few moments later, it was once again in her arms, "securely wrapped." She was thoroughly dispirited. "I carried it away feeling that all hope of revising the manuscript into a good book successful for publication was at an end. In this mood of dejection, I laid it away without even unwrapping it."[32]

In the months that followed, "The Web" remained untouched in her Farnham Avenue bedroom. She managed to summon enough energy to write the pamphlet-length essay Liston had suggested, "Love and War," which she sent to him in May or June. But he rejected it and returned the modest typescript in mid-July.[33] Another failure. She was fifty-five years old, and her only child had been stillborn.

When Frank Wise set up the British Employment Association as a private venture, taken on in addition to his publishing activities and with himself as its chairman, he assigned to it the cable address "Otherwise."[34] It was a private little joke, too clever by half. His employment agency was but one of several "other" business affairs during these years. In 1918, he was to the public eye a man of impeccable character and reputation. Others knew better.

To begin with, his work finding employment for British emigrants to Canada was not exactly born of philanthropic motives. It was a plain business venture. He sought contract work from companies like the Canadian Northern Railway, provided inexpensive transportation to job sites, and charged for the service. In order to be effective, he had built up since 1908 a large list of contacts ranging from politicians such as Sir George Foster in Canada to representatives of the Central Emigration Board in London, whose president was the Duke of Sutherland, K.C.[35] Words he used when corresponding with Foster betray the absence of charitable sentiment. "My wish," he wrote, "is only that capital and labor shall be made to kiss each other properly. I could wish to God that someone would make those devils in the north of England and Scotland get to work or get shot."[36]

Wise did not find it easy, however, to keep these and other private activities separate from his work at the Bond Street offices of Macmillan. In fact, the company had become downright convenient. The official address of the Toronto branch of the Imperial Home-Reunion Association was 70 Bond Street, and he used the facilities of the firm to further this work.[37] He had a sizable staff and ample room in the Macmillan building. Why should he not use them for worthwhile pursuits? Similarly, when he learned that the *Times* of London was in the process of compiling a history of the Great War, it occurred to him that here was one more opportunity, and it was not to be missed. He set up a private company, Sales Unlimited, in the hope of obtaining Canadian rights and gave it, too, space in the Bond Street offices. Few people, except those who worked in the building, knew about it.

Some members of his staff had become quite concerned about their president's willingness to mix the business of Macmillan of Canada with his own private affairs. In October 1917, Wise wrote to Sir Frederick Macmillan informing him that he had decided to dismiss the Canadian company's founding secretary. It was a clerical position but an important one, for the secretary needed to keep abreast of issues related to finance, personnel, and general management. For reasons left unstated, Wise wished to replace him with "Mr. Purver, our finance man and subscription Manager."[38] The transition in personnel went forward without a hitch, and the secretary with twelve years' service, William Whitney, left Macmillan. H.W. Purver took his place.

Sir Frederick Macmillan and George Brett, unaware of the unusual activities in the Canadian office, knew only that its finances left much to be desired. Sir Frederick had written to Wise in June about the previous year's balance sheet. While the overall performance of the Canadian branch was "highly satisfactory," yielding a gross profit of thirty per cent, company expenses were so high that the net profit was only six per cent.[39] Wise should seek means of reducing his expenditures. The New York office also noticed the problem. In May 1918, Brett reported to Sir Frederick that while Canadian sales had increased, profits were down. Turnover during the past year had been $250,000, but net profits somehow amounted to less than a thousand dollars. Brett noted that he had suggested to Wise various ways of transforming the situation, but at the time neither he nor Sir Frederick thought the problem sufficiently worrying to look further into why such a "gratifying increase" in sales had yielded such poor results.[40]

Meanwhile, Wise had other problems. In January 1919, three days before Florence Deeks wrote to John Saul inquiring about her manuscript, Wise reported to Brett that it was likely the company would lose him. The senior editor, Wise claimed, had been offered a position at a rival firm with a substantial increase in salary and a staff of three editors under him. Saul did not wish to leave Macmillan, Wise stated, but he had said that if he left he would do nothing to "pull down what he has built up." The Macmillan of

Canada president hinted darkly that he was not certain about this, for Saul had refused to tell him the name of the company to which he might move.[41]

Saul had been perhaps the most valuable asset obtained by Macmillan of Canada in the purchase of Morang. Editor-in-chief at Morang since 1902, he had come to Macmillan with the other property in 1912 and assumed the same position under Wise. As such, he had been responsible for the firm's educational division during a period of rapid expansion.

Born in Ottawa in 1869, John Cameron Saul had moved to Winnipeg in 1880. There he attended the University of Manitoba, where he won the university silver medal in modern languages in 1887. He was restive. First he read law with the firm of Munson and Allan, then he spent eight years teaching English in a Winnipeg collegiate institute. Literature was his first love, and he was a compulsive collector of books on nineteenth-century poets. In the mid-1890s, he had begun collecting any volumes with references to Tennyson he could lay his hands on, and soon he possessed hundreds. When an opportunity to enter the publishing business with Morang arose early in the new century, he had jumped at it.[42] By 1918, Macmillan possessed one of the most experienced editors in the country. Saul had edited the *Canada Education Monthly*, had contributed to the *Westminster* and other periodicals, had compiled a volume of selections from Morang's "Makers of Canada" series, and had edited Morang's Alexandra Readers and some forty textbooks, at all school levels, in geography, history, and literature.[43]

Saul was widely read, and he seemed to know every potential author, sales representative, librarian, provincial education department bureaucrat, and deputy minister of education in the country. His affable manner made otherwise reserved people open up to him. Saul possessed a knowledge of what was going on that others in the Canadian publishing industry could scarcely hope to approach, much less to surpass.

On the last day of January 1919, Saul left Macmillan of Canada for Gage, one of Macmillan's major competitors in the field of textbooks. Wise's attitude towards him now shifted dramatically. His letters to Brett and Sir Frederick vilified the departed editor. "I know

you are aware of a number of disgraceful episodes in the past,"
began his letter to Brett, "but I think the manner of his leaving really
transcended everything. He just slunk out like a scullery maid who
is offered a half-a-crown more by somebody round the corner . . .
Of the tangles he left; of the definite promises given to writers; of
the abstraction and destruction of papers; . . . of his absolute
neglect of work for the past month, . . . and of many other things
which wring the heart I shall wait to tell you when I see you."

Whatever problems existed on Bond Street, Wise was making
certain that they did not rest with him. He went on to catalogue
other complaints. His head traveller was constantly complaining,
and he was about to "get rid of him." His staff was depleted from
the epidemic of influenza ravaging the city. Saul was at that moment
in New York, presumably "to gather to himself and Gages the
Canadian market" for the public schools list. "I think I shall shortly
feel the necessity of getting a lot of this stuff off my chest," Wise
told Brett, "and come and pour it into your ever friendly ears."[44]

Seen as the disappointed reaction of an employer at the sudden
departure of an invaluable employee to a rival firm, the hostility of
Wise to Saul is understandable. But their correspondence over the
previous two years, particularly during Saul's sales trips to the
western provinces, presents instead a picture of Saul as a loyal
employee who enjoyed a very close working relationship with his
employer. He warned Wise when he learned that a disgruntled business partner had made a "bitter personal attack" on the Macmillan
head in a letter sent to the London office. He had gone out of his
way to provide intelligence about the man and his complaints and
provided Wise with the basis of an informed response and with
advice on how to defuse the animosity.[45] He wrote to his boss when
he found out that "an old friend of yours" from another publishing
firm was about to give Wise trouble over the geography market in
the west by importing plates from the United States.[46]

Letter after letter sent from Saul to Wise between June 1917 and
August 1918 testifies to the closeness of their relationship and to
the lengths to which they would go to maintain supremacy in the
publishing field. "Every traveller who has come up here," Saul
warned Wise in July 1917, "has made a dead set on the Macmillan

Company, and some of them have plainly indicated that there is a nigger somewhere in connection with us. And a lot of this is sticking." He urged Wise to be more discreet, for people took his inflated rhetoric at face value, and it threatened the reputations of Wise and Macmillan alike.[47]

February 1918 had found Saul in Winnipeg. Writing from the Canadian Pacific Railway's Royal Alexandra Hotel, he reported on the shift in the province's schools from Canadian to general history. The problem was that no existing book was fully suitable. Macmillan needed its own text in the field, and quickly.[48] It was an almost passing reference to a pressing need. Saul's attention soon turned to a "double cross" on algebra texts and someone "raising Hades" over chemistry in Alberta.[49] In the letters that followed, the history textbook issue remained unresolved. But it was not forgotten.

The matter arose again in July, towards the end of Saul's summer trip to the west. He had found out that British Columbia was about to replace its high school history texts and was searching for a new one in general history. The chosen textbook would go into the schools in about 1920, a year after the choice was made. "Please remember," Saul wrote to Wise, "that in addition to the Gage campaign . . . , both Dent and Oxford are showing their Canadian histories hard."[50] Macmillan did have a Canadian history text on its list, but the B.C. competition served as a reminder to Saul and Wise that the Macmillan list remained weak in that subject.

Saul returned from the west early in August, spent a week or two in his Bond Street office, and by August 20 was back west, in Regina. He was furious, and more than a little frustrated, and he let his emotions show in a letter to Wise. He had learned that the British Columbia government had decided on a textbook for its general history course, one in several volumes by the American historians James Harvey Robinson, Charles Beard, and James Henry Breasted. Ginn had won the lucrative contract.

Only a couple of weeks earlier, back in Toronto, Saul had met with Florence Deeks about her history of the world, and had read parts of the manuscript – as patriotic a story of liberty and freedom and democracy as could be written, when it had not gone on about women. This could not have escaped his memory as he fulminated at British Columbia's choice, a book co-authored by a radical American Progressive historian, Charles Beard. "That History," he wrote to Wise, "is as beautiful a piece of German propaganda as I have ever seen and Beard wrote the modern history. It will be absolutely necessary to slam the said Mr. Beard in connection with his pro-Germanism." Saul was outraged at the "damnable" reasons Beard had given for Great Britain's entry into the war. Not only was the American historian unpatriotic, he seemed also to be "a confirmed socialist of the rankest sort." "It would be a damned disgrace to allow that Ginn book, with its lovely Germanism, to go into a Canadian province."[51] What Macmillan needed was a good book of its own on the subject.

8   *Outlines*

Fools make researches and wise men exploit them.
H.G. Wells, *A Modern Utopia* (1905)

Exactly when H.G. Wells turned from think-
ing about the problem of re-educating people about history in
general to doing the actual work on the narrative history of the
world that was to become his most successful and lucrative book
has been something of a mystery. Biographies are curiously silent
about the period from the fall of 1918 until the summer of 1919,
when much of the research and writing of *The Outline of History*
was completed. Wells himself is of no more help in his *Experiment
in Autobiography*, for he says virtually nothing about the months
in which he wrote what the literary historian Samuel Hynes was
later to call "the most important history in English in the twentieth century."[1]

Biographers invariably point to Wells's preoccupation with
history by 1918 and imply that he was able to research and write
his massive tome so quickly because he was a prolific author. And
massive it was. At first, he had estimated that the book would run
to about 200,000 words, long enough. But the North American
first edition contained well over 400,000 words in 1,324 pages

(including the 48-page index) that required publication in two volumes.[2] In some unspecified way, biographers hint, Wells had been preparing it most of his life. Besides, if he could write at such confident length about an unknown future, would it not be easy for him to do so about a known past?[3]

Above all, the conventional explanation goes, he had surrounded himself with an impeccable team of learned collaborators, named on the title page of *The Outline*: Ernest Barker, Oxford classical scholar and student of political thought; Sir Harry Johnston, African explorer and expert on its languages and cultures; Sir E. Ray Lankester, zoologist; and Gilbert Murray, the Oxford classical scholar with whom Wells worked on the research committee promoting a League of Free Nations.

Wells himself came to date his first discussions of *The Outline of History* to his meeting with League of Free Nations advocates over dinner at the Reform Club in mid-July 1918. Among the party was the American scholar Henry Seidel Canby, who solicited an article from Wells soon afterwards for the *Yale Review*. Although the article was to cover "How American History Should be Taught," Canby made no mention of any interest in world history that he might have heard Wells express at the dinner.[4] It seems clear that Wells had only begun to map out his book that summer, when he was with Rebecca West. While she worked on what eventually became her novel *The Judge*, he began to sketch *The Outline*, much to her annoyance. "She came to hate *The Outline of History*," he later wrote, "almost as much as she hated Jane." He wanted to write history as "a picture of developing inter-communications"; she wanted him to devote his imagination to more creative work.[5]

It is one thing for an author with a keen interest in history, a fertile imagination, and a fluid pen to gain an overall sense of the past, but quite another to do the research necessary to execute the subject. For this, a great deal of reading is necessary if only to discover where to look and what subjects to include or exclude. Rebecca's *pension* held few, if any, of the necessary resources for the task at hand. He needed help from people deeply familiar with history as a formal subject of study. He needed expert advice.

Wells's wide circle of acquaintance gave him many such people from whom to seek guidance. The men he chose had extraordinary reputations. When they allowed their names to accompany that of the author on the title page of *The Outline*, they provided an implicit explanation of how he was able to write such a lengthy and detailed work of history in a very short time when it was his first venture into the subject. Michael Coren, Wells's most critical biographer, refers to these men as "a gifted think-tank."[6]

The first member of the "think-tank" was Sir E. Ray Lankester, an eminent zoologist. Son of a physician and coroner, Lankester had met Darwin and Huxley as a boy and had gained a first-class degree in the honour school of natural sciences at Christ Church, Oxford, in 1868, at the age of twenty-one. A series of prized academic appointments soon followed. By 1898 he held the Fullerian professorship of physiology and comparative anatomy in the Royal Institution and was also director of the natural history departments and keeper of zoology in the British Museum, South Kensington.

On his retirement in 1907, Lankester was knighted. He had written some two hundred scientific papers, journal articles, and encyclopedia entries. General editor of the multivolume *Treatise on Zoology* (1900–9), he had also published several books of popular science, including *Extinct Animals* (1905) and *The Kingdom of Man* (1907). Who could possibly question Sir Ray Lankester's place as a major contributor to H.G. Wells's *Outline of History?*[7]

Lankester had long been an admirer of Wells's work, and corresponded regularly with him or with Jane from early in the century. When others attacked or ostracized Wells after the publication of *Ann Veronica*, he had stood by his friend.[8] But by 1918 he was an irascible old man of seventy-one, as often as not complaining from his Kensington flat about how depressed and debilitated he was because of the war. "I returned on Monday night last," he wrote Wells in October 1917, "& heard horrible accounts of the bombing & the panic amongst the people. I confess I can't stand it. I can't work. I sit here alone in a constant state of apprehension – & I don't see exactly what to do. I never bargained (so to speak) for a recurrent bombardment of London & it gets on my nerves. At any moment they may be at it again – & every sound . . . startles me."

Two months later he felt no better. Perhaps to soothe the frayed nerves of their old friend, the Wellses dined with him in London and invited him on occasion to spend weekends at Easton Glebe.[9]

Sir Ray had no written contact with Wells from July through September 1918, and when the correspondence began again it was not about *The Outline* but about *Joan and Peter*, which had just been released. "It is splendid," Sir Ray wrote, "& seems as all your books do as they follow one another – to be just what my own latest thoughts amount to." He went on to talk about Wells's views on God but made no mention of *The Outline*. His friend clearly replied to these kind words, for nine days later Sir Ray wrote Wells again, thanking him for an invitation to visit the Wellses at Easton Glebe later in the month. There is no doubt that by now Wells had broached the subject of his projected history. "I like your idea of a history of Man," wrote the zoologist. "It should include all the present romance of mixed races and nationalities and savages and a sort of traveller's geography."[10]

Early in November, more than a month after staying with the Wellses, Sir Ray wrote a letter giving Wells advice about his history. It concerned cavemen and their drawings. After he had finished complaining about being cold, wet, and alone, he offered his first written suggestions about books Wells ought to consult. A few days later, he was at it again. Addressing Wells as "Beloved pup," he began, "We know nothing of the Heidelberg chap except his jaw-bone," expressing his skepticism about the recent discovery of Piltdown Man. Other advice about toes and thumbs of chimpanzees, lemurs, and humans followed in the letter, but that was it. These were his only written contributions to *The Outline of History* during the months when Wells did most of his research, apart from a letter of November 24 to Jane Wells. Any other help he provided must have taken place through conversation.[11]

A second member of the "think-tank" was Sir Harry Johnston, in his own way as noteworthy as Sir Ray Lankester. Born in 1858, Johnston was a man small in size but large in stature, the very embodiment of the Victorian "all-rounder." From an early age, his interests were language and art, animals and adventure. After a grammar school education, he moved in 1875 to London, where he began to study modern languages at King's College, painting at the Royal Academy Schools, zoology in Regent's Park, and anatomy in the museum of the Royal College of Surgeons. His thirst for adventure unslaked, Johnston also undertook a sketching tour of Majorca, Spain, and France.[12]

At the end of the 1870s, Johnston began an association with the African continent that was to last for the rest of his life. It started with his role as artist, journalist, and adventurer. In addition to collecting scientific evidence along the Congo basin and in the shadow of Mount Kilimanjaro, he also negotiated a number of treaties with tribal chieftains, thereby laying the basis for the later formation of the British East Africa Protectorate in 1895. He received a knighthood the following year.

His skills as a diplomat discovered by the Foreign Office, Sir Harry acted on its behalf in Cameroon and the Niger delta, mollifying local tribes and opening up the region for British trade. As the imperial powers negotiated over the partition of Africa, he was often at the table or in the field. Sir Harry Johnston, the special commissioner to Uganda, pacified the region; Sir Harry the scientist-adventurer explored Mount Rowenzori, recorded flora and fauna, discovered unknown animals, and studied the pygmies of the Congo forest.

Wells first met Sir Harry in 1915 at a meeting organized by Sir Ray Lankester and others concerning the conduct of the war. Sir Ray had come to be "astounded" at the blunders of the British high command and drew together a large gathering of those connected with science at the headquarters of a scientific society in Burlington House, London. Sir Harry may have been an imperial adventurer, but he was no warmonger. He had long been a critic of imperial excess, having made an enemy of Cecil Rhodes in the 1890s when he refused to cooperate with Rhodes in an attack on the Portuguese. Now he found himself allied with Sir Ray and Wells in their mounting criticism of war leadership. Before very long, Sir Harry was an occasional visitor to Easton Glebe, where the two men swapped stories – the adventurer of his African experiences and the writer of his visit to the Italian front. Sir Harry must have been pleased when he read Wells's *Joan and Peter* upon its release in September 1918, for there he was in its pages, cast as himself but playing the role of Oswald's anti-imperialist African mentor.[13]

Sir Harry Johnston's reputation as a master of African tribal dialects and of the anthropology, zoology, and botany of the "Dark Continent" made him an obvious choice as an expert source of help for Wells's *Outline*, particularly its early chapters. But in 1918 the health of the sixty-year-old man had broken down. In 1917, while lecturing to troops at the front under the sponsorship of the YMCA, he had suffered from an attack of mustard gas; now he faced prostate surgery and two quite serious liver-related operations.[14] In several chatty letters to Wells written between 1916 and 1919, he provided details on the intricacies of operations on the prostate gland, talked about a novel he was writing, commented on Wells's own novels, and expressed his disgust with the politicians' and generals' conduct of the war. He talked about many things in his letters to Wells between 1916 and the end of summer 1918, but not about *The Outline of History*.[15]

Early in September 1918, Sir Harry wrote to Jane Wells, confirming his intention to stay with the Wellses at Easton Glebe during the latter half of the month. This was a good time in which to talk directly about *The Outline*, and to point Wells in fruitful directions. Given the phenomenal subsequent success of the book, the exchange between expert and author should have been a memorable one, worth recording. But when Sir Harry wrote his memoirs, all he could remember was that "in between my medical consultations I paid him a visit at Easton in September 1918. We talked about the War, about Hubert Parry, and this, that, and the other thing, whilst the other week-end guests were there." Of the nine letters he subsequently wrote to Wells between October 1918 and August 1919, not one mentioned *The Outline*.[16]

This was probably because Sir Harry Johnston had more things to worry about by then than the history of the world. His health was getting worse, to the point that he looked forward to surgery. His heart was weak, and he spent much of his time in a nursing chair in Poling, more or less an invalid. He had the operation late in 1918 and spent the following months recuperating. He did not return to Poling from his nursing home until April 1919. Whenever he could muster enough energy, he used his time to complete his novel, *The Gay-Dombeys*, which appeared under the Macmillan imprint in 1919, thanks to Wells's sponsorship.[17] After he felt sufficiently recovered, he worked towards the completion of his two-volume study of the Bantu language. In the summer of 1919 he undertook a journey up and down the Rhine Valley and gave lectures for the War Office to the army of occupation in the French and American sectors.[18]

When Wells later commented on Sir Harry's contribution to *The Outline of History*, it was not to thank him for his contributions but instead to complain that "his weakness, or rather, his excessive strength, lay in the abnormal though no doubt righteous, spelling of well-known historical names."[19] In their conversations, Wells no doubt learned much from Sir Harry's store of arcane knowledge about Africa. The question, as with the similar contribution of Sir Ray Lankester, is whether it constituted anything remotely resembling the degree of knowledge or research into the sweep of history necessary to write *The Outline*. These men knew much about zoology, botany, and anthropology, but what could they tell Wells about Pericles or Alexander the Great that he may not already have had at hand in his library at Easton Glebe?

The remaining two members of the "gifted think-tank" thought to have contributed so much to the making of *The Outline of History* were Gilbert Murray and Ernest Barker. Here, perhaps, was the true font of the kind of historical knowledge required to provide the detailed research for the book. These men were Oxford-educated scholars of classical antiquity but with broad-ranging historical and political interests. Certainly, no one could possibly take exception to their right to a place on the title page of *The Outline*.

Born in Australia in 1866, Gilbert Murray had excelled in Greek and Latin composition while at St. John's College, Oxford. But from the outset of his studies he had expressed his dissatisfaction at the narrowness of the conventional approach to the classics, seeking instead to breathe imaginative life into the subject. Study of the classics, he believed, was about culture and civilization, not only language and literature. When he married Lady Mary Howard in 1889, Murray also assumed the chair of Greek at Glasgow. In

1905, he returned to Oxford as a Fellow of New College, followed three years later by appointment as Regius professor of Greek.[20]

Wells and Murray began to correspond in 1917, by which time Murray was well known as the author of *Rise of the Greek Epic* (1907), *Four Stages of Greek Religion* (1912), and *Euripides and His Age* (1913). In that year, Wells sent him a copy of *God the Invisible King*, in which Murray had been quoted. More serious acquaintance took place, however, when the two men became involved in the campaign for a League of Free Nations and began to work together to bring it to fruition. At one level, they had much in common, for both held strong internationalist beliefs. But the relationship was not without tension, since Murray believed Wells would ruin the idea with his too-broad notion of a world federation, while Wells was convinced that people like Murray, however well intentioned, were of too limited a vision.[21]

Murray was as indefatigable as Wells. By July 1918, he was director of the League of Free Nations Association, and over the next year he spent much of his time attempting to unite the League of Nations Society and the League of Free Nations Association. Throughout the autumn Murray was deeply involved with other writers in government work intended to find ways of counteracting German propaganda among neutral countries. He came to call the Ministry of Information at Wellington House the "Mendacity Bureau," but he gave it his full attention. By early 1919 he had agreed to serve on a committee to discuss the Foreign Office draft for the League of Nations covenant. Throughout the last half of 1918 and well into 1919, then, Gilbert Murray was even more involved than Wells in League and war work.[22]

The archival papers of Murray and Wells say next to nothing about any collaboration. The two men wrote to each other infrequently between July 1918 and July 1919. Not until Wells wrote Murray an undated letter from Easton Glebe, most likely in 1919, does the subject of *The Outline* arise. In it, Wells complains that he is physically unable to continue League work. He has grown disenchanted with the research committee's intention to work as a group to write an educational textbook aimed at furthering internationalism. "I can't rise to that task," he complained. "I'm naturally a solitary worker. Team work for me is like using a razor to carve marble." Then, clearly for the first time, he introduces his current project. "For some time I've thought of writing an Outline of History as a sort of experiment in teaching arrangement. I believe the History of Man can be [written] as easily as the History of England" and that a world "educated in universal history" would be "a different & better world altogether. I think after I have rested I shall go on with that."[23] He does not solicit Murray's help.

A clear indication that Gilbert Murray became involved with *The Outline of History* only well into 1919 is provided in a letter Wells wrote to him on June 15, 1919, after much of *The Outline* had been drafted, from his flat in St. James's Court. "Don't forget," he began, "I've got my eye upon you to help out my history. It's a rash tale of stuff I warn you & I screw up to this exaction, but I simply must get help. It's the Outline of History from the incandescent globe stage to this year of grace 1919." He goes on to mention that he has got J.F. Horrabin of the *Daily News* "doing endless maps" and "good outline drawings of extinct beasts," while Sir Ray Lankester is providing help with the early chapters. Sir Harry Johnston, it appears from the letter, has yet to make his contribution, since Wells expresses his hope that "I think I can count on" him "for the Ethnology." Wells now proposes to send Murray what he has written – the chapters up to "about 1000 AD." Murray's task? "What I want you to do is to blue pencil howlers & to note serious disproportions in your own regions of special interest. That is what I mean by checking but what I mean by support is something different and I don't know whether you will care to do that for me."[24]

Wells makes it clear in the letter that the "support" he asks for is not that of an expert's research on the book; instead, it is the weight of Murray's scholarly reputation. "The book," he warns Murray, "will rouse anybody in the history textbook & history teaching line to blind fury. It is a serious raid into various departments of special knowledge . . . It is a necessary counter to nationalism & imperialism. There will be a sustained attempt to [represent?] me as an ignorant interloper & dispose of me in that way." That is why Wells needs the weight of academic authority. "Well, what I want is to be able to name some indisputable names on my title page," Wells concludes, expressing his hope that Murray will be willing to lend his name in just such a way. Not until late July 1919 does Murray receive the first stack of typescript Wells has promised.[25]

Like the involvement of the other experts, Ernest Barker's contribution to *The Outline of History* was neither early nor sustained. Compared with them, he was a young pup of forty-four in 1918, a scholar whose star was still on the rise. At the time a Fellow and tutor at New College, Oxford, Barker was a political theorist and historian who had established his reputation with the publication of *Political Thought of Plato and Aristotle* in 1906. His support of the cooperative movement and of the Workers' Educational Association and the National Council of Social Service furthered his reputation as a man of politically progressive views, and this obviously appealed to Wells. Barker and Murray corresponded occasionally in late 1918 and early 1919, but the letters made no mention of Wells or his project.[26]

Barker's contribution to *The Outline*, like Murray's, did not begin until the summer of 1919, when he received the typescript to vet. Barker took his responsibilities seriously, and perhaps because he was younger, more healthy, and less preoccupied with other matters than the other collaborators, he was able to provide Wells with detailed notes on the text. They included suggestions from Oxford colleagues in fields such as Chinese and Indian history, as well as references to the main books on various subjects. This was helpful, but only to a point. It was the kind of aid required at the commencement of research, but he offered it only after Wells had already drafted much of his book. Barker later expressed his amazement at what Wells had been able to achieve. "The sweep of the panorama," he said, "makes me almost breathless: it is what I imagine an aeroplane flight is like in the material world."[27]

The achievement was enough to take almost anyone's breath away. Biographers of Wells uniformly fall back on the "team approach" to the research and writing of *The Outline of History* when they attempt to explain it, especially when they must account for its production at a time when Wells was seeing *Joan and Peter* through to publication, continuing to campaign on behalf of the

League of Free Nations idea, writing *The Undying Fire* (1919), and carrying on life at Easton Glebe as well as his on-again, off-again affair with Rebecca West.

Even those who, like Barker, knew how quickly Wells wrote and how prolific an author he was remained astonished at his achievement. For most such people, the presence of the names "Mr. Ernest Barker, Sir H.H. Johnston, Sir E. Ray Lankester and Professor Gilbert Murray" on the title page of *The Outline of History*, just below the notation that the book had been "written with the advice and editorial help" of these distinguished men, was sufficient to explain the accomplishment – particularly the speed at which it had been executed. If this was not enough, Wells thanked nearly fifty of his friends by name. These people had helped him with many details; at times, they had disabused him of interpretive errors. But, like the title-page collaborators, they did not advise him on the overall conception or structure of the work. Instead the long list of their names added to the aura of expertise that the title page had established, one that helped explain the mystery surrounding the writing of *The Outline*.[28]

Arnold Bennett, the author's closest literary friend, was himself a sufficiently adroit writer that more than once he had drafted entire novels in the span of weeks, but even he was incredulous. He had spent a good deal of time in 1918 with Wells at the Reform Club and knew exactly how busy he was. "The more I read of H.G.'s *Outline* the more staggered I am by it," he was to write to Jane Wells early in 1920. "How the fellow did the book in the time fair passes me . . . I cannot get over it. It's a life's work."[29]

When the book appeared, Wells minimized his own capacities as author. "His disqualifications are manifest," he wrote in the introduction, using the third-person singular as if to distance himself from the process. Wells pointed, instead, to his hard-working wife and collaborators: "Such work needs to be done by as many people as possible, he was free to make his contribution, and he was greatly attracted by the task. He has read sedulously and made the utmost use of all the help he could obtain. There is not a chapter that has not been examined by some more competent person than himself and very carefully revised."

By all accounts, Jane Wells, once more a silent voice at a crucial point in her husband's career, was his saving grace in the creation of *The Outline of History*. "Without her labour in typing and re-typing the drafts of the various chapters as they have been revised and amended, in checking references, finding suitable quotations, hunting up illustrations, and keeping in order the whole mass of material for this history, and without her constant help and watchful criticism, its completion would have been impossible."[30] There they were at Easton Glebe, state his biographers Norman and Jeanne Mackenzie – H.G. and Jane, "often working long hours at a stretch, pillaging references and blending them up into a smooth mixture."[31]

Three of the most experienced and prolific professional historians in the world, James Harvey Robinson, Charles A. Beard, and James Henry Breasted, had required several years to research and write their collaborative history of Western civilization. Wells and his ever-faithful wife ventured into their first and only exercise in the writing of history with few research notes and little intensive help from others, and somehow managed to accomplish the task in a span of time so short that it beggars the imagination. In mid-November 1918, nothing on the project had advanced as far as the typescript stage. By February 5, 1919, Jane had produced 50,000 to 60,000 words in typed form. Twenty days later, her husband had reached the 125,000-word mark – halfway through the projected book. He had written between 75,000 and 80,000 words in under three weeks, researching along the way. In mid-August, Jane sent the first five polished chapters off to Newnes for serialization; *The Outline* began to appear on November 22, 1919. At the end of the year, the whole manuscript was complete.[32] The achievement was nothing short of miraculous.

George Brett was a very busy man in a highly competitive industry. New, aggressive, and very accomplished book publishers had entered the New York publishing scene since his early days in the business – Knopf, Doubleday, Random House, and others. To succeed, it was essential to stay focused on important matters, not be distracted by extraneous issues. Yet there on his desk lay a letter of complaint of the sort he did not need. In it, a Miss Laura B. Durand informed him that under John Saul's direction she had written for Macmillan of Canada a work on astronomy intended for children. After she submitted her manuscript to the editor, he had refused to publish it. The woman was distraught. What, Brett wrote to Wise in May 1919, were the circumstances of the case?[33]

Wise replied within three days, as if to snip the Durand issue in the bud. Miss Durand, he told Brett, had for many years been an occasional writer of "society items" for the *Globe* newspaper in Toronto. "She is an intolerable nuisance and reminds me a good deal of our late friend, Mrs. Hogan, whom you will remember as a frightful pest in the days when I was with you." Then he placed the blame for Miss Durand's complaint on his recently departed editor. "Unfortunately, Saul had a bad habit of compromising himself with many authors who came. His instructions from us were specific that under no circumstances was he to even encourage an author until the matter has been submitted to me. Of course, when he was out on a trip he had a certain latitude in getting options on MSS, until they could be submitted, but for anyone in town there was no excuse whatever for his departure from the set rule."

Whatever problems the Toronto branch had with errant manuscripts or irate authors, Wise suggested, they lay with Saul, not himself. He had warned Saul not "to compromise himself" in such situations. When Miss Durand had spoken to Wise about a manuscript of hers on apple trees, for the rights of which she had been offered $800 from another publisher, he had advised her "to hire a taxi and rush over before they changed their mind, and keep the taxi to take her to the bank to have the cheque marked." He had never seen her again, he said. "But I suppose Saul must have deceived her by his abominable inability to say 'no.'" If Brett wished, however, Wise would get in touch with the troublesome Miss Durand. If her astronomy book was any good, perhaps he might be able to interest a couple of the western provinces in it for school library purposes.[34]

With such assurances, Wise no doubt thought the matter had ended. But it would resurface a decade later, and with more sinister implications.

One of the reasons why Frank Wise responded so quickly to George Brett's inquiry about Miss Durand was that it reminded him of an awkward and potentially embarrassing situation in which he and Saul had found themselves a few years back. Early in the century, when still with Morang, Saul had commissioned the superintendent of the Ottawa school board, J.H. Putman, to write a history text for him. The book had been published in 1904 as *Britain and the Empire: A History for Public Schools.* Years later, Macmillan had compiled its own history text for schools, and Putman discovered that it contained substantial portions of his book. He had consulted his lawyers and then threatened to bring legal action against Macmillan. The case had never reached the courts, however, in part because the Crown, not Putman, held copyright. But Putman had insisted on an interview with officials at Macmillan, and he brought along his lawyer. Saul admitted that he had "used Dr. Putman's material." An arrangement was then made to purchase Putman's silence by acquiring the rights to his book for $1,500.[35] With that, a potential lawsuit over plagiarism had ended. No paper trail on the matter was left in the Macmillan files.

The following month, Brett had much more to worry about over Frank Wise. Early in June 1919, an anonymous letter crossed his desk, and it was of sufficient gravity that he immediately sent a copy to Sir Frederick Macmillan in the London office. Written in point form, it was marked "Private and Confidential," and for good reason. It read, in full:

Facts which the Macmillans should know –

1. Both Mr. Wise and Mr. Purver's time while [*sic*], I presume, Macmillans pay for, is being devoted almost entirely to "The Times History of the War."
2. A large part of the staff is being employed on this.
3. The name of Macmillan is being used to solicit orders for this, otherwise they would not get the business.
4. They have some crooks as representatives, whom Macmillans would not wish associated with them.

5. Mr. Purver is not the kind of man who should be second president. He is not straight, nor could he be if he tried.

6. The Macmillan Co. is devoting its time and energies to everything but Macmillan business. This latter takes second place.

7. It would be in the interest of the directors to find out how much Mr. Wise and Mr. Purver have made out of the Times history, in addition to their salaries, during the past six months.

8. Good honest people will not stay with the Canadian Macmillans, and when they leave Mr. Wise sits and blackguards and writes lies about them.

9. I just give them a year longer, and their competitors will have all the business out of Macmillans hands – they are very busy now, while Macmillans are employed on *The Times*.

10. Their education department is going to the dogs. They have a problem running it.

If you don't believe the words of a well-wisher, find out for yourself. This is true, I assure you. I have made careful investigations.[36]

Brett did not know quite what to make of these astounding charges. He ventured the guess that the letter had come from John Saul, for he knew the opinions of Frank Wise on the circumstances of the editor's sudden departure from the firm. Saul "has, I am told, since he left the Company endeavored in every possible way to interfere with its business and detract those in authority in the Canadian office."

Nevertheless, the accusations remained extremely serious. Brett and Sir Frederick had continued to be concerned about the lax accounting methods of the Canadian branch. Now had come the even more troubling suggestion that by being involved in the *Times* history project, as Sir Frederick told Brett, Macmillan's employees "had become shareholders in another book-selling concern." To the head of the parent company, this was intolerable. "Our own idea is to say to him frankly that either he must confine himself entirely to the work of the company or he must resign his position and be replaced by somebody else."[37]

Brett had already been in contact with Wise over the absence of monthly financial reports. When he had attended the annual meeting of the Canadian company a month or so before, he had discovered that the accounts ending on March 31 had not yet been closed, that the annual statement and auditor's report had not been ready, and that in spite of an increase in sales revenue to $280,000, the deficit on educational contract business had continued to increase. No doubt, he had expressed his concerns directly to Wise at the time. Perhaps he also sensed that hidden motives lay behind the dismissal of the company's original secretary in 1917.

Wise admitted to Brett in July that possibly he had left the matter of profits accruing to Sales Unlimited vague. Such profits arose only through the new distribution and sales agency created in Winnipeg, MacVicar-Newby, to handle Sales Unlimited's business in the west. His own company was therefore left without direct profit, "which, of course, is eminently proper under the circumstances." A week later he wrote Brett again. "Next year will mark my twenty-fifth year with the Macmillans, and I shall never forget my entry and the ever kindly manner in which you recognized my attempts to further the interests of the concern."[38]

The Canadian publisher's uncharacteristically obsequious words did little to lessen Brett's worries. The situation was even more complex than he had thought. Not only was the existence of the Canadian manager's private company a fact, but another sales agency had apparently become involved. And it was by no means clear where the profits went or what the activities of these companies really were. He conferred with Sir Frederick in London and was instructed to take personal control of the Canadian operation. This was the last thing Brett needed, and he suggested in return that he much preferred that initiatives concerning the Canadian business come from the London directors. He informed Wise of these views.[39]

Wise now recognized that his position in the company was threatened. He wrote to Brett blaming Saul for conducting "a most determined assault" on him in the west. "It has also come to me from New York, Winnipeg, and Montreal, that Saul has stated several times that he was after me, personally, as well as Macmillans. I should not be at all surprised to learn that his propaganda has been carried not only to yourself, as was evident last time I saw you, but also to England."[40]

For the most part, the smooth talk worked. Brett wrote to Sir Frederick Macmillan that Wise had received "a severe lesson" and that it would now be "quite safe" to leave him in charge of the Canadian office. He had instructed Wise to divest himself of shares in Sales Unlimited, and he recommended that no final decision should therefore be made about any change in the Canadian management. Then he added that if such a decision became imperative, he had someone on hand who could "properly and efficiently undertake this work."[41] Late in 1919, Wise wrote to Brett stating that he had resigned from any connection with Sales Unlimited.[42] For the next six months the situation appeared to stabilize.

In the spring of 1920, a full year after she had retrieved her copy of "The Web" from the offices of Macmillan of Canada, Florence found herself with sufficient resolve to begin revisions to the manuscript. For this purpose she used one of the two carbon copies, not the original she had left with Saul. A few months later, having made significant progress, she had occasion to look at that original. She retrieved it from her room, unwrapped it, and was astonished. As it lay in front of her, she found it "soiled, thumbed, worn and torn, with over a dozen pages turned down at the corners, and many others creased as if having been bent back in use."[43] Yet at the time she had submitted it, the manuscript had been fresh from the typewriter, its pages in pristine condition. For a manuscript seen by only two or three people, it had been left in a badly worked-over condition. She could certainly not show this copy to any other publisher.

She assembled the pages used for her revision into a neat pile and put it on the living room table. The paper in the stack had not been treated with any particular care, and it showed. The original copy of "The Web" was next to it. Then she asked her mother and sisters to look at them and tell her which seemed to have been more soiled. "They did not know which stack of paper was which, but they all independently agreed that the returned manuscript from Macmillans definitely looked the most used."[44] The whole business seemed very peculiar, but Florence soon returned to her revisions, and the women thought no more about the little mystery. Not until she picked up her copy of *Saturday Night* on a cold December night later that year, and read Hector Charlesworth's review of *The Outline of History*.

That same spring, George Brett discovered that a recent advertisement in the *Canadian Medical Quarterly* had given the address of Sales Unlimited as 70 Bond Street. How could Wise have severed his connection with the sales company when it continued to operate out of Macmillan's Toronto office? Wise tried to explain that the company was merely a tenant in the Macmillan building, but the excuse was a weak one. Brett remained alarmed. And what about this journal, advertised as a Macmillan of Canada publication? Since when did the Canadian branch have its own medical division? What else did it do? What were its employees up to? He travelled immediately to Toronto to investigate the matter.

It did not take him long to discover the seriousness of the disorder in the Toronto office. Its staff seemed ill at ease. At one point Wise's personal secretary even asked to have some words with him in private. But Brett did not want to be distracted, and besides he was too pressed for time. So he told her to put whatever she had to tell him in writing.

Not long after his return to the New York office, a lengthy letter arrived from Toronto. It was from Miss May Mercer, secretary to Mr. Wise, dated May 19, 1920, and marked "Without prejudice and confidential."

> I shall endeavor, in as concise a way as possible, to place before you a few facts in regard to the Toronto office.
>
> In the first place I think the worst feature of the situation is that Mr. Wise is not dependable. He misrepresents things horribly, and I myself have found that he is not to be trusted. Not

only is this the general opinion of the heads of departments of the Company, but I find it is that of the trade, the Governments, and practically everyone with whom he comes into contact. When I tell you that even the janitor in the building has confided to me that he would not trust Mr. Wise, to use his own words, "as far as the corner," you will perhaps have some idea of what is responsible for the disorder that exists in the Toronto office . . .

When I tell you that never in all my experience have I seen or heard of any firm being run in the wholly disastrous manner the Toronto house is pursuing, you will perhaps better understand how it is that the annual returns are so thoroughly disappointing. Caprice, whim, self-gratification and self-glorification would seem to be the guiding motives rather than ultimate benefit to the Company or what is in accord with the name of Macmillan; in fact, more often than not Macmillan is entirely lost sight of.

I have always felt that the business could be run in a much more economical manner, and have so expressed myself on many occasions to Mr. Wise. While he has listened very attentively to the suggestions I have put forward and coincided in many of them, I have found it simply to be a "waste of breath" on my part since he does not want any ideas that might prove of benefit to the Company but would prefer rather to take advice from those who are really working for their own ends. One "extravagance" is the Medical Department, which has really never paid for itself but is, I consider, a sinking fund for the money derived from the paying end of the business. I have held that this could be run, in the case of the Toronto house, under the General Sales Department, and thus do away with a medical staff who are simply "eating their heads off." . . . Then, as of course you know, Mr. Purver has had charge of both the medical and bookkeeping departments all along, which possibility accounts for the very good showing for this department in the annual returns. This Medical Department has also been the campus for Mr. Wise's "favorites" and at the present time shelters Dr. Routley, whose car is at Mr. Wise's disposal when

required, and his medical service within call of the Wise household. The latest adjunct is a Mr. Britton – a thoroughly worthless fellow – who has been getting the advertising for the
Medical Monthly but was formerly, I understand, in the shirt-
making business in London. Only a few months ago Mr. Wise
had no use whatsoever for this man on the staff of Macmillans.
There is also a Mr. Thomas connected with the Medical
Department, who is making a good thing out of Macmillans.

Perhaps from what I have said you will understand how the
morale of the place has been thoroughly destroyed. There is no
incentive for a conscientious worker who has the good of
Macmillans at heart, but every encouragement for the unscrupulous individual, who is ever granted a hearing by Mr. Wise . . .

I do not know whether the Directors are aware of the fact or
not, but Mr. Wise is not confining his efforts solely to the
Macmillan business in Macmillan hours. Further particulars of
this I can give you when I have the opportunity. You can understand, therefore, how it is that Mr. Wise has completely lost hold
on things Macmillan – he does not even know the Macmillan
books always . . .

I also wish to put on record the fact that I was not given the
report which went to the Directors in regard to the Times History
of the War. This was dictated to Mr. Purver's stenographer, partly
by Mr. Purver. I know the true facts of the case were not put
before you and that Mr. Wise purposefully avoided dictating this
report to me, the reasons for which I think are obvious.[45]

The letter confirmed Brett's worst suspicions. Wise seemed to
have put the whole Macmillan operation in Toronto to use as his
personal fiefdom. Sloppy accounting, slush funds, private busi-
nesses, personal factotums and lackeys, a chauffeur, and a private
medical attendant – what else might be going on? So these were the
reasons why the medical journal had lost $7,000 over the past two
years! Furious, he instructed Wise bluntly to dispose of the journal.
"Moreover," he added, "the account bears some evidence of having
been unduly favored in the matter of expenditures and, perhaps,

also favored in the matter of receipts, at any rate the account is, as I gather, made up wholly or in part by those who are interested in having you still carry on the publication of the Journal." The next day, he sent a copy of Mercer's letter to Sir Frederick in London, concluding it by telling Sir Frederick that similar concerns had been expressed by Hugh Eayrs, a young Englishman who had recently replaced Purver as secretary of the Toronto branch.[46]

Brett was now very near the end of his patience with Wise and informed him that both he and the London directors were "very much dissatisfied with the progress of the Toronto house." He noted that rumours now circulated that Wise was about to tender his resignation, but said nothing more about them. For his part, Wise blamed the high costs of the Toronto firm on John Saul.[47]

Matters did not improve. In October, Brett reported to Sir Frederick that Wise had still to dispose of the *Canadian Medical Journal*. The same month, Sir Frederick learned that the Kiplings, with whom Frank Wise had such bad relations, had decided to end their relationship with Macmillan and move to Doubleday. Wise offered to negotiate with the author and his wife, but Sir Frederick told him in exasperation not to do so under any circumstances. Hugh Eayrs reported on a visit to New York that Wise did not appear at his office until eleven and was seldom there after four. And – the final straw – the MacVicar-Newby agency now threatened to sue Macmillan over Wise's irregular dealings with it.[48]

In December, Brett informed Sir Frederick Macmillan that Eayrs was about to visit the London firm and that its directors should look him over. "I believe that Mr. Eayrs is a young man of considerable enterprise, great energy, and possessing a fairly good taste in literature and matters pertaining to books."[49]

Wise knew that his career at Macmillan was over. In a letter of January 27, 1921, he informed George Brett that his resignation as president of Macmillan of Canada could be expected in the mail at any time, and that he was tired and worn out. Eayrs wasted no time in consolidating his position as Wise's interim replacement. At the end of the month, he instructed the company's solicitors to provide in writing the instructions he had received to take control of the internal affairs of the company and asked them to provide "any information required from, or banking attended to by Mr. Wise."[50] A meeting of Macmillan's Canadian board of directors early in February formally accepted the resignation of its founding president.

9   *Devils in Details*

> "It's an unpleasant business. More like some detective's job . . . I will say one thing though: as historians we've got to tell the truth about the past as far as we know it, but that's quite a different thing from searching into the truth of people's lives here and now. All this prying and poking about into what other people prefer to keep hidden seems to me a very presumptuous and dangerous fashion."
>
> Angus Wilson, *Anglo-Saxon Attitudes* (1956)

ONE EVENING DURING THE WINTER of 1920–21, Florence finished reading the second thick volume of H.G. Wells's *Outline of History*. She had already been struck by the fact that Hector Charlesworth's review of the book might just as well have been about "The Web." Now she understood why. Both works had been highly critical of militaristic thinking and of the age-old desire to gain the property of others; both authors held out hope for an eventual unity of mankind – Wells through some kind of socialist world order, Florence through the spirit of altruism. Each surveyed the entire history of the world, from earliest origins through the full span of human habitation. She was so annoyed that a few days later, books in hand, she took the streetcar to Eaton's and demanded her money back.

Before long, however, she reckoned that she had made a mistake. Her emotions had gotten the better of her, and she had acted in haste. The two works had so much in common in presentation of fact and in theme that, apart from its acknowledgments of helpers and authorities, Wells's preface could quite easily have served as her own. But one matter especially alarmed her: both works had at times made the same mistakes. The revision to which she had subjected the carbon copy of "The Web" over the past year had made her aware of a number of factual errors and omissions of important events in the original she had submitted to Macmillan. Yet the same errors and omissions also marred *The Outline of History*.[1] How could this be?

A thorough comparison of the two works was clearly in order, so she returned to the department store and bought *The Outline of History* again. First, she began her analysis of the two works by studying their structures; then she turned to comparing them word by word and line by line, for content, for omissions, and for verbal similarities. She knew that to the casual observer "The Web" and *The Outline* would appear very different. *The Outline* was more than twice as long, and Wells went into much more detail than she had. As a professional writer, he had the capacity to make prose leap off the page. His book was dramatically written, opinionated, and imaginative. By comparison, her own prose seemed amateurish and florid. "The Web" contained a lot of material about woman in history, but she was scarcely mentioned in *The Outline*. The 1,276 pages of text in its two volumes, written by a champion of feminism, resulted in only eight index references under "women."

As she grew intimately familiar with the two texts over the months that followed, Florence did not find any lengthy passages from her work incorporated into *The Outline*; instead, she found a general similarity in plan. "And here it was," she wrote later. "These two histories were virtually the same in plan and treatment and in these respects they differed from all other written histories of the world. THE OUTLINE OF HISTORY contained the very vital portions of 'THE WEB', the portions which comprised its real value, and which in THE OUTLINE OF HISTORY produced a result similar to that produced in 'THE WEB.'"[2]

Her comparison consisted of two columns, with passages from "The Web" on the left and those from *The Outline* on the right. By the time she had finished, she had a typed, single-spaced document on legal-size paper that ran to seventy-nine pages. She also made a list of subjects inadequately treated or omitted in both works. These included: "1) the making of the earth; 2) any adequate account of the early civilizations of Egypt and Western Asia; 3) the great range of oriental civilization which had entered Rome; 4) Rome's contribution to modern civilization; 5) the social and agricultural organization of medieval Europe with its manors or villas and its lords and tenants; 6) the territorial organization of medieval Europe and the development of centralized authority; 7) any account of the United States of America from War of Independence 1776 to Monroe doctrine 1823. From 1823 to opening of Japan 1854. From civil war to end of century." There were, she added, "many other cogent examples."[3] As a Protestant of Lutheran background, Florence had naturally placed considerable emphasis on Martin Luther; but while she mentioned Calvinism several times, Calvin, the great Genevan predestinarian, appeared in "The Web" only once. In *The Outline of History*, a work hostile to the Christian religion, Luther received prominent attention; Calvin did not appear at all.

Unlike almost all other works of general history, "The Web" and *The Outline* began not with Mesopotamian, Egyptian, or Greek civilization but with the solar system. Florence began with the sun. "There floated in the immensity of space a speck, comparatively, but, in reality, a prodigious nebulae [*sic*] which in the course of time became concentrated into the focus of heat and light known as – the Sun." Wells began with the earth, "a mere speck in the greater vastness of space." Her sun "at times threw off masses of cosmic matter," which became the planets; his was "a spinning mass of matter" from which fragments detached themselves, forming the planets. Wells's sun had "not yet concentrated into a compact centre of heat and light."

This was very significant. It was one thing for words of similar meaning, such as "The Web"'s "atmosphere" and "revolve" and *The Outline*'s "gaseous fluid" and "circle," to appear in the opening pages of the works. But the near duplication of a distinctive phrase about the formation of the sun was quite another matter. An outside observer might conclude that the two authors had simply come up with similar phrasing independently. But Florence knew better, because she remembered where she had gotten her words.

She had extracted the phrase "concentrated into the focus of heat and light" directly from Victor Duruy's *General History of the World*. In retrospect, she realized that she should have placed them within quotation marks, but the fact was that she had not. Here in front of her were Duruy's words on Wells's page, yet nowhere did he indicate that he had consulted Duruy's book.[4]

Florence began to see a sustained pattern of common use in the two works, less in the use of common phrases (Wells was after all a wordsmith with an extraordinary vocabulary) than in the sequence in which he presented his facts. Pages of "The Web" that had been folded down at the corner when she retrieved it from Macmillan had contained passages about the Phoenicians. She drew up the sequence of factual treatment in her columns:

THE WEB	THE OUTLINE OF HISTORY
1. Phoenician Fleets	(a) Phoenician shipping.
2. found their way to Indies	(b) was making its way to the East Indies
3. Their caravan	(c) the caravans.
4. Traversed the land of Asia	(c) toiled . . . across Africa and Arabia and through Arabia and through Turkestan (Arabia and Africa)
5. gathering up the best Productions	(a) with their remote trade.
6. Ivory from Ophir	(c) ivory from Africa (Ophir)
7. the most beautiful	the most beautiful
8. of pearls . . . precious	(c) there was hardly a variety [of] precious stone that had not been found and . . .
9. silks from China	(c) silk . . . from China.
10. glassware and purple	(c) pottery and porcelain.
11. the skill, especially of women, was responsible for rare productions.	(c) Men had learned to weave fine linen and delicate fabrics of coloured wool they could bleach and dye.

By revisiting her sources, Florence found it possible to reconstruct exactly which words had been her own, and which had been those of Duruy or of her other main source on the Phoenicians, *Chambers' Encyclopedia*. Original wording she marked with an "a" in parentheses; the words of Duruy became (b); those of *Chambers'* were designated as (c). In this way, she found that she could establish "the same unusual features, the same order of details, the same original language, and the same original mistakes as in 'The Web.'"[5]

Florence found such mistakes to be revealing. She had relied on the mythical rather than the historical explanation of the origins of the Persian Wars. So did Wells, and the relevant page of "The Web" had again been folded down. In an attempt to use modern terms, she had spoken of the Roman general Sulla as "aristocratic." But she had been mistaken in this. Contemporary authorities seldom, if ever, used the anachronistic term. Quite properly, they said he was "patrician." But to Wells as to Florence, he was "aristocratic." "The Web" had stated that Charlemagne became emperor of the Holy Roman Empire in 800 AD, when Leo III placed on his head the crown of the Caesars. This, she now recognized, was the kind of error an undergraduate might make. Work on her revision had taught her that the Holy Roman Empire had not been founded formally until 962 by Otto I ("the Great"). Charlemagne's coronation had made him emperor of the revived Roman Empire. An arcane distinction, perhaps, until Florence examined Wells's cited source: James Bryce. But Bryce had given the proper date, 962. Why, then, did Wells use 800? Where had he gotten his information?[6]

Then there was the matter of Columbus's first voyage. Both "The Web" and *The Outline* claimed, falsely, that he believed he had found India. Florence had since learned that not even Columbus had believed this. Yet the mistakes remained common to both works.[7]

With such mistakes in both her own work and that of Wells, common use of language that otherwise might have been considered mere coincidence became pregnant with meaning. Early on, when writing about the subjection of women, she had written, "Tribal wars were engaged in for the sole purpose of seizing women . . . The captured women were adopted into the tribe." *The Outline* read that "the captive woman and children were assimilated into the tribe." Her "Roman society" had been "a festering mass of . . ."; his "was festering with . . ." In "The Web," Leonardo da Vinci had been surrounded by "a brilliant galaxy of stars"; in *The Outline*, he was associated with a "galaxy of names." When she discussed the era of Columbus, she said at one point, "On a beautiful morning . . . the little expedition set sail"; for Wells, "The little expedition . . . stood out . . . in beautiful weather." She had spoken of "the unquenchable spark of divine love"; he had written of the "unquenchable personality of Jesus." In dealing with the Stuart period in England, Florence had quoted seven passages from Green's *Short History of the English People*, four of them lengthy ones. *The Outline of History* contained the same four passages, word for word. All seven passages from Green used in "The Web" found their way into *The Outline*, and in precisely the same sequence.[8]

It took Florence most of the year 1921 to make her comparison of the two works, to compile a list of the books cited as sources by Wells, and then to examine them in the downtown library. "I prepared a list of hundreds of such verbal similarities," she wrote, "phrases, clauses, and parts of sentences; whole sentences and paragraphs slightly changed or colourfully altered but containing the same details and original features of THE WEB, and mistakes. All of these were applied to the same time and subjects and ran in the same sequence order of arrangement. About one hundred were identical in wording . . . Not one similarity in the above list was traceable to any one of the two hundred and fifty, or more, sources and authorities cited by Mr. Wells in THE OUTLINE OF HISTORY. The significance of this comparison lay, not only in the actual language employed, but also in the piling up of many similarities. The cumulative effect became overwhelming."[9]

She now saw a heavy reliance of *The Outline* on "The Web" from its very first pages. One conclusion, and only one, was possible, from the fact that Wells had used the words she had copied from Duruy while nowhere indicating that he had consulted the French historian's book: that, with "The Web" or with notes from it in front of him, H.G. Wells had simply copied down Duruy's words from "The Web" and they had become his own.

To Florence, *The Outline* seemed to draw upon her own work in a myriad of ways. Yet there was one major difference: the treatment of women. So prominent in "The Web," they were virtually absent in *The Outline*. Even in this case, however, a comparison of the two works proved revealing. Her portrayal of woman as "a constructive force in civilization" became, in *The Outline*, omission or disparagement. It was as if, with "The Web" or passages from it on the subject of women in front of him, Wells had written his own few accounts of women as a direct rebuttal to her claims. Thus, when Florence had stated that woman domesticated fire and "constructed ingenious stoves to cook the food, and as vessels were needed for cooking, she moulded the earth into shapes and dried and burnt them so pottery was produced," Wells had said: "They do not seem to have cooked their food . . . they had no cooking implements . . . they had no pottery." In her view, women "kept and tamed the animals brought back from the forest by the hunters, the goat for its milk, the cat to kill the mice in the granaries"; Wells had written, "It is improbable that they had yet learned the use of animals' milk as food . . . they had little to do with any sort of domestic sheep or cattle . . . There were no cats . . . no mice or rats had yet adapted themselves to human dwelling." "The Web" said, "Men built habitations . . . to take the place of the tree shelters and the tents and huts which woman had built, and their great activity in agriculture drove women more and more to indoor labour to which confinement some scientists attribute the diminution of her size and physical strength . . . Lastly she manufactured her own dyes by extracting the juices from vegetables and plants." *The Outline* said, "They had no buildings. It is not even certain that they had tents or huts . . . they had no cultivation of grain or vegetables of any sort . . . The women were probably squaws, smaller than the men."[10]

There were devils in such details and in their sequence of presentation. The results of her comparison now became as much a subject of conversation in the Farnham Avenue home as "The Web" itself had been during the war years. All the Deeks women were incensed at what Wells had apparently done. Late in 1921 the family matriarch, Melinda, spoke to her son George about

Florence's predicament. He then asked Florence what she thought. Mabel later reconstructed the conversation: "She told him that she was convinced her manuscript had been used in the writing of *The Outline of History*." Florence reminded him that in 1916, having made good progress on her book, she had taken out interim copyright, which registered her intention to publish the work in the near future. A short time later, George, who in Mabel's view "had great regard for her judgment," arranged to have his lawyer explore the legal implications.[11]

In the view of George Deeks's lawyer, the interim copyright might still exist, since "The Web" had not been published and the act governing copyright in Canada did not contain any provision for the length of time in which "an action to recover damages for infringement" might be brought.[12] But there was a caveat: the Ontario statute of limitations would be applicable in the absence of any provision to the contrary in Dominion legislation. This meant that if Florence Deeks wished to bring any action in the matter, it had to be initiated within six years of the unauthorized publication of the work in question – in this case, *The Outline of History*.[13] The Newnes company had begun publishing the work as a serial in 1919. Florence could not launch a lawsuit later than the fall of 1925.

With the publication of *The Outline of History* in 1919 and 1920, H.G. Wells became more wealthy than he could ever have imagined. Never a good manager of his finances once royalties came in, he spent freely and his expenses were substantial; but he had always been a shrewd negotiator of contracts with publishers. "Earning a living by writing," he wrote to a friend in 1919, "is a frightful gamble. It depends neither upon knowledge nor literary quality but upon secondary considerations of timeliness, mental fashion & so forth almost beyond control." By deciding to reduce his output of fiction in order to work on his *Outline*, he had taken an immense gamble, and he was determined to make it pay. Not one to trust publishers, he harried them constantly about contracts, marketing, and especially advances on royalties. "I always ask for as big a cheque as possible," he later wrote, "because from my point of view it will guarantee that the publisher will go all out for the book in question. It is his role, not mine, to take risks on the book and lose if the book fails."[14]

Considered as a product for sale rather than a body of text, *The Outline of History* was not one book, but three, for Wells saw it from the first as having at least three different markets requiring as many publishing agreements. By arranging with Sir Frank Newnes to have it sold in twenty or twenty-four cheaply produced parts, he could reach those who could not afford the full price of a cloth-bound edition or who wished to read only about certain periods of history. Then there were the British and American markets. To secure the former, he had contacted both Sir Frederick Macmillan and Newman Flower of Cassell & Company. Macmillan had turned him down, but Flower proved enthusiastic. "I am very keen to have the handling of this book," he wrote, "because I believe, with our many ramifications, we could make a big thing of it." In spite of his misgivings about the vagueness of Wells's plans for the book, George Brett, too, had been optimistic about its possibilities in America.[15]

However, when Brett sent Wells a draft contract a month later, as a negotiating tactic he stressed the heavy editorial and produc-tion costs and minimized the potential market. From his perspec-tive, the proposal for royalties was generous. The publisher offered a royalty of twenty per cent for world rights of the regular edition, with a £1,500 advance against those royalties. He also offered a royalty of ten per cent for any cheaper school edition, instead of the usual rate of six. Wells was not satisfied, nor would he concede world rights to Brett since he already had English publishers lined up. He noted that these English publishers, not Brett's firm, would be assuming most of the production expense, such as the produc-tion of maps and plates. Wells agreed substantially to the financial terms Brett laid down, and Brett retained publication rights for all of North America.[16]

Sir Frank Newnes, too, thought himself to be generous in what he offered. He was willing to pay £600 for the serialization rights and £1,000 in advance of a ten per cent royalty based on the published price of each part. Again Wells objected. His name, he said, "must account for something" in determining the number of sales. "I'll agree to £1,000 for the first 25,000 of each part and then [a] royalty of 10 per cent. on the sales of each part [above] 25,000 with a guarantee of another £1,000. That is, if after the whole thing is published the royalties after 25,000 do not amount to £1,000, you will make up the deficit." This was the agreement to which both parties eventually agreed.[17]

Wells exacted an even better agreement on royalties from Cassell & Company, publisher of the British edition. His advance was to be £2,000 against a return of twenty-five per cent on the sales price of twenty shillings. For each volume sold in the "Colonies and Dependencies" (Canada excluded), he was to receive one shilling and eightpence.[18]

From the moment of its first publication, The Outline of History was immensely profitable. It struck a responsive chord in English-speaking countries around the world, for in the wake of the catastrophe of world war people sought to understand what had made civilized nations go so wrong. Wells offered an answer infused with hope for the future. Within a few years, sales in the United States and England alone exceeded two million copies. From 1920 to 1927, Macmillan in New York shipped over 11,000 copies to Canada. The book continued to sell year after year.[19]

Wells no longer needed to worry over finances: he was set for life. But in other ways, he was a desperate man. In the fall of 1920, during a trip to Russia, he had renewed his acquaintance with Maxim Gorky's alluring secretary, the twenty-seven-year-old Moura Budberg, whom he had met during his first trip to Russia in January 1914. To Wells, this woman – who had divorced her first husband, whose second had been murdered by Bolsheviks, and who had then married the Baron Budberg – remained "gallant, unbroken, and adorable." At his entreaty, one night she came to his room in Gorky's spacious flat and into his embraces. Another thread had been woven into his tangled love life, and it required a sorting out. He loved Jane "steadily and surely," he said; his commitment to Rebecca only neared love; but his new paramour, Moura, a creature of pure impulse, "had magnificence."[20] The sorting out, however, came much later. Upon his return from Russia, he was in a distraught mental and emotional state.

At the time, Rebecca West was in the final stages of recovery from a nasty infection resulting from a fall into a cistern in Cornwall in the spring. H.G. had neglected her badly during the preparations for his trip to Russia, and she was scarcely mollified by his suggestion that she confer with another of his female acquaintances, the visiting American reformer of sexual mores Margaret Sanger, about the best methods of birth control. He wanted Rebecca to continue their relationship, he later said, because it suited his needs. She acceded, so they continued seeing each other, spending half-days and evenings together either at the flat he had taken in Whitehall Court just after the war or at hers in Kensington. But to Rebecca, this was not enough. He seemed less committed to her than ever, and she insisted that they either marry or separate.[21]

There is more than a hint at her anger and frustration in a brief passage, otherwise out of place, in her 1941 masterpiece of political and social commentary on Yugoslavia, *Black Lamb and Grey Falcon*. In it, she speaks of "a kind of lowness that is sometimes exhibited in the sexual affairs of very vulgar and shameless people: a man leaves his wife and induces a girl to become his mistress, then is reconciled to his wife and to please her exposes the girl to some public humiliation."[22]

H.G. and Rebecca quarrelled constantly after his return from Russia. The trip had thoroughly unsettled him. Jane faced the prospect of a hysterectomy, and he would not abandon her; nor would he let fade the enticing image of Moura. During one of the arguments he let slip to Rebecca that he had been unfaithful with Moura, estranging her further. As always, his writing proved therapeutic, and he worked on his next novel, *The Secret Places of the Heart*. The book was published in 1922. In the view of a serious student of the relationship between Wells and West, Wells intended it "to be an admonition to Rebecca." It carried a refrain as tired as it was familiar: an ambitious genius struggling against the forces of capital and labour is hampered by a mistress whom he sees as "a rival" to his duty. He is the steadfast one, she the source of inconstancy, and in the end he dies a broken man. Martin Leeds, the mistress to whom Wells for some reason gave the name of a man, is left at the side of his coffin, crying, "Oh! Speak to me, my darling! Speak to me, I tell you! Speak to me!"[23]

The author sought to breach the gulf between himself and Rebecca in late 1920 by writing her a series of letters, steeped in contrition, in which he professed his undying love. At the same time, however, he had discovered in himself a deep "affinity" with Margaret Sanger. Rebecca would have to wait her turn.

Wells and Sanger had met that summer in London through a mutual acquaintance, the sexual reformer Havelock Ellis. To Margaret, the prophet was already a figure of heroic stature. When she had run into legal trouble in 1915 over the notorious Comstock Law, an act of the American Congress passed forty-two years earlier aimed at suppressing obscenity in the mails (Anthony Comstock, author of the act, had once gone so far as to describe George Bernard Shaw as an "Irish smut dealer"), Wells had signed his name to a letter to President Woodrow Wilson, protesting the indictment. On her 1916 lecture tour, Margaret recalled, "his name had been on everybody's lips."[24]

Meeting Wells in the summer of 1920 was "the event" of the American social reformer's visit to London. She knew of his reputation as an advocate of sexual freedom; in that respect, as in others, the two were of one mind. Attracted by the openness of his personality, she was delighted when she discovered that "his twinkling eyes were like those of a mischievous boy."[25]

Wells was certainly interested. At forty-one, Margaret Sanger remained a very attractive woman, a second coming of Ann Veronica not only in her freedom of spirit but even in the uncanny resemblance she bore to the physical description he had provided of his heroine. And since her reputation brought with it an obvious openness to sexual adventure, he wrote to her proposing a rendezvous in New York in December.[26]

It was not yet to be. In early winter H.G. came down with pneumonia, and Jane was still recovering from her hysterectomy, so he cancelled the American trip. His own inner life perfectly mirrored that of the protagonist of *Secret Places of the Heart*, Sir Richmond Hardy: unsatisfied by success, restless, confused, dreaming of love but never finding it. "Often I cared nothing for the woman I made love to," Sir Richmond admits. "I cared for the thing she seemed to be hiding from me."[27]

H.G.'s life was now one of drift on uncontrollable tides of desire. A trip to Malfi with Rebecca in January 1921; back to Easton Glebe in March; with Rebecca in her London flat during the summer; two months in the United States late in the year on the trip postponed from the previous year, including time in New York alone with Margaret in an apartment she rented at his request."[28]

After their liaison, Wells left America for Spain and Rebecca, although he continued to correspond with the woman he addressed affectionately as "Dear little Mrs. Margaret." He and Rebecca quarrelled, and in Algeciras early in 1922, emotionally fragile, he forced her into the role of the "the ill-treated mistress" of an older man, demeaning Rebecca so often in public places that a concerned hotel proprietor offered her the fare home.[29] Fortunately, Wells left for England and Easton Glebe, to which he had invited Margaret.

To those who knew him only by his reputation as a novelist and as the author of *The Outline of History*, he continued to impress. Cornelia Otis Skinner, later to become a successful writer and humorist, was a young American innocent, abroad with her family and a friend, and eager for the Twenties to roar. When she and her family paid a visit to Wells at Easton Glebe one Saturday (thanks to an earlier introduction of her father to the famous Englishman), he impressed her with his cheerfulness and his "teeming vitality," the strange mixture of his guests, and the peculiar games he insisted they play.[30] When it started to rain, Wells pronounced that they all must rush out to the barn-like structure behind the house. "This was obviously Mr. Wells' *Rumpus Room*," Cornelia said to herself. Soon they found themselves outfitted in ill-fitting tennis shoes, divided into teams (Americans versus Europeans), and madly running around engaged in a Wellsian combination of volleyball and tennis – subject to arbitrary rules of the creator's making as the game progressed. One player, described to Cornelia by the host as "the greatest educationalist in all England," took a serve from her in the face; others, young men fresh from Cambridge, answered to nicknames like Bungy and Poodles. An American woman named

Sanger, a crusader for the cause of birth control, remained on the margins of play. "Mrs. Sanger wasn't so bad, and I don't believe she was so good either," Cornelia Skinner remembered, "but at least she was moderately inconspicuous. The remainder of us were awful."[31]

Those who knew Wells rather better than this had come to hold a less benign view of his life in the early 1920s. Sidney and Beatrice Webb visited him in the summer of 1923, and Beatrice found that he seemed to have "coarsened." As she noted in her journal: "He is far too conscious of literary success, measured in great prices for books and articles – he has become a sort of 'little god' demanding payment in flattery as well as in gold . . . Moreover, he has another and even more damaging consciousness – he feels himself to be a chartered libertine. Everyone knows he is a polygamist and everyone puts up with it. He is aware of this acquiescence in his sins – an acquiescence accompanied with contempt. And this contemptuous acquiescence on the part of friends and acquaintances results in Wells having a contempt for all of us, because we disapprove, and yet we associate with him."[32]

Some, however, remained fiercely loyal to H.G. and to all he represented. One such person was Wells's long-time friend Richard Gregory – now Sir Richard, for he had been knighted for his service to the cause of British science. It was a much-deserved honour. He had become one of the most eminent popularizers of science of his generation, a worthy successor to the mantle of Huxley. But it was his dear friend Wells with whom he identified. In part, this was because he shared with Wells a rise to eminence from very humble beginnings.

Born in Bristol in 1864, Richard Gregory was the son of a cobbler, John Gregory, the Methodist "shoemaker poet" of the city, a man heavily involved in the local socialist movement. The son, too, became a champion of the cause of the working man.[33] Unlike Wells, he had flourished at the Normal School of Science, securing first-class honours in astronomy and physics in 1889. Gregory's subsequent career as a writer and lecturer was meteoric. By 1893, Sir Norman Lockyer had made him assistant editor of *Nature*, and so began his long association with Macmillan, which owned the journal.[34]

172 THE SPINSTER AND THE PROPHET

By the time he received his knighthood in 1919, Richard Gregory had long made his mark and was in heavy demand as a public speaker. In addition to his many articles, he had published several popular books, such as *The Vault of Heaven* in 1893, followed by *The Planet Earth* in 1894. Macmillan had appointed him its scientific editor, specializing in educational matters, in 1905 (a position he was to hold until 1939). Virtually the editor of *Nature* under Sir Norman's nominal direction since 1907, he had been instrumental in enhancing the journal's reputation as a "clearing-house for new ideas" in science. He assumed the editorship in the same year as his knighthood. Little wonder that in October 1918, when his friend Wells had sought information about astronomical temperatures and other matters in the distant past for his work on *The Outline*, it was to Sir Richard Gregory he turned, and the scientist had quickly provided the required information. Such was Sir Richard's sense of affinity and regard for Wells that the only photograph he kept to the end of his life of a person not related to him was of the young H.G. Wells.[35]

B y the spring of 1922, her comparison now completed, Florence Deeks was more convinced than ever that H.G. Wells had seen "The Web" and had made use of it in writing *The Outline of History*. To her, the correspondences between the two works made its infringement of her proprietary rights and copyright nothing less than "appalling." Her detailed analysis of the texts was shown to George's lawyer, W. Norman Tilley, K.C., of Tilley, Johnston, Thomson & Parmenter. After examining the materials, Tilley informed George Deeks that in his view Florence had a prima facie case and that action should be taken immediately. George, however, was more cautious, and suggested to his sister that she should "work up" the case first.[36]

Florence had no idea by what means "The Web" had reached Wells, only that somehow it had, and she sensed that John Saul must have some idea of what went on. It was time to pay Mr. Saul a visit. Accompanied by Mabel, who thought it best to be with her sister on important occasions such as this, she found Saul in his office at Gage. Nearly four years had passed since they had met, but he remembered "The Web" and the situation surrounding its submission. Later, she reconstructed their conversation.

I said: "Mr. Saul, I should like to speak about a manuscript I gave you when you were with the Macmillan Company."

He exclaimed: "What! That history of yours? Have you never got that back yet?"

I replied: "Yes, I got it back but it has been used by Mr. H.G. Wells for writing 'The Outline of History.'

Mr. Saul (surprised, silent for a moment): "Well, things like that do happen sometimes through unscrupulous writers. Why, the Dent people put out a new encyclopedia. It was no sooner published than the Encyclopedia Britannica came down on the Dents and accused them of taking material from the Encyclopedia Britannica. The passage in question was examined, Mr. Dent said, 'Well, gentlemen, I see that your work has been used. I knew nothing of the matter. But my hands are up – You will have to make your demand and I shall meet it!' It cost the Dent people 16,000 pounds. The money was paid over and the two books went on, just as if nothing had ever happened."

I remarked upon Mr. Wells' use of my entire work, and Mr. Saul then informed us that: "Just the other night there was a man came up to my house and he accused the Macmillans of using a manuscript that he had submitted to them. He said there were paragraphs taken out of his manuscript with just the words turned around. He showed me some and they were a good deal alike too.

"Has Mr. Wells got whole sentences like yours – three would be enough to prove that he had taken it."

"He has not whole sentences identical," I replied, "but he has many passages with the wording slightly changed – or the words changed round."

"That is the same thing," Mr. Saul assented. "If I could see your material I could tell in twenty minutes if he had copied it. I would not ask you to bring it to the office; I would go to your house to see it at any time that would suit you – morning, afternoon or evening. If he has used your manuscript to write THE OUTLINE it would be a piece of plagiarism to go down in the history of literature for 200 years to come," and "if this comes out the Macmillans might just as well close their doors."[37]

Saul's sympathetic attitude encouraged Florence. A day or two later, she telephoned him at his home. His wife, Lillian, answered. Her husband, she said, had told her "all about the matter," and she thought Miss Deeks would feel more comfortable if she understood this. She added that, in future, perhaps it would be better to discuss this business at their home rather than at her husband's office.

Florence was pleased to oblige and expressed her happiness that Mrs. Saul "understood things."

The conversation between the spinster and the wife continued amiably. "She said Mr. Saul was terribly agitated over it," Florence recalled. He had gone upstairs to his study after supper on the evening of their conversation, and when Lillian Saul joined him he was pacing up and down the room. "Well, I can't tell you what he said on the telephone," said Mrs. Saul, "but I never heard him use stronger language."

Saul's sudden agitation alarmed Florence sufficiently that she did not let Saul see her comparison list. But she and Mabel decided to keep the case "constantly and in detail before his mind" through further visits and telephone calls, so that he would not forget his involvement in it. She recognized that it would be some time before her legal action could be launched, particularly because she wanted to have some literary experts compare "The Web" and *The Outline* and report their conclusions to her. Meanwhile, she decided to concentrate her energies on finishing the revisions to her work, and in such a way as to render it publishable. She was no longer content simply to make alterations to "The Web." Her new work would be a different one altogether.

She decided to call it "The Highway of History." Not without regret, she had already eliminated most of the more speculative references to women, but to her mind she had made up for this by basing it on more up-to-date scholarship. To make certain that her new history possessed scholarly respectability, she made her way to University College in the University of Toronto. Its Department of History was located there, and it was within its impressive, ivy-covered stone walls that she encountered Professor W.P.M. Kennedy.

In a department populated mainly with graduates of Oxford, W.P.M. Kennedy was something of an anomaly. Appointed by George Wrong in 1916 to teach constitutional history, he had graduated from Trinity College, Dublin, and among his fellow historians he was the only one to hold the doctoral research degree. He was also one of the department's few Roman Catholics. By the time of his encounter with Florence Deeks in June 1923, he had risen to the position of assistant professor at a perfectly respectable salary of $2,750 per year.[38]

Kennedy was not a congenial colleague. He was mercurial, cantankerous, and arrogant, and by the early 1920s George Wrong was by no means certain he had made a wise choice in appointing him to his department. So irritating and eccentric were Kennedy's ways that at one point Wrong solicited the advice of the university's distinguished psychologist George Sidney Brett about him. "He said that his peculiarity would probably intensify as he grew older," Wrong later reported to the university's president, Sir Robert Falconer, "and considered him as distinctly abnormal." Everything had convinced Wrong of Kennedy's "lack of sane mentality." Kennedy claimed he was an official adviser to the Irish state, bragged that "all the Canadian provinces" consulted him, and did not pay the bills for the books he bought on credit.[39]

When Florence met with Professor Kennedy and asked him whether he would help her render "The Highway of History" into publishable shape – for a fee, of course – he leaped at the opportunity. He expressed "great interest in the book" and told her that not only would he help her revise each chapter but he would also write a preface, help find a publisher, and see the book through to publication by reading galley proofs. At first, Florence was impressed by the Irishman's enthusiasm and encouragement, and she did not object when he charged a sizable fee for each chapter he examined. "He enjoyed secrecy with regard to his private help," she later wrote to her lawyer. "He especially did not want Prof. Wrong, the head of his department, or Sir Robert Falconer to know."[40]

Initially the work with Kennedy went well, but, as he worked on each chapter, he revised his rates steeply upward. Eventually Florence became alarmed at the costs and asked him to establish a firm and fixed charge for his services – "from which," she later wrote, "he constantly deviated." But what was she to do? She needed the kind of expert scholarly and editorial advice Kennedy could provide. Since George "made no serious objection" to the costs and her book seemed to be progressing well, she continued to take advantage of the professor's help.[41] George dutifully paid the bills.

Gradually she came to suspect Kennedy's good faith, with respect not only to his fees but also to his services. He began to make changes in the manuscript that she thought weakened rather than improved it. Then he suggested the addition of ten or more chapters. This left her shaken, for her brother had already disbursed a considerable sum of money. Cautiously, she withdrew from accepting any more of his help. There were others at the University of Toronto on whose expertise she could draw, and she did. By the time she had finished revising "The Highway of History," she had secured "the valuable services" of some of the most able members of the university's academic staff. Among them were numbered George Wrong himself, his son Murray (then at Oxford), the economic historian C.R. Fay, and the diplomatic and political historian Ralph Flenley.[42]

One day during a conversation with George Wrong, Florence "almost accidentally" mentioned Kennedy's earlier involvement. Wrong became indignant about his colleague and proceeded to tell her, as she later recalled, "a few things about him which, he said, I might tell my brother & our lawyers but no one else." Just what these matters were, she did not say; but she was beginning to catch a whiff of conspiracy. This was reinforced by a later conversation with John Saul, who told her "that Prof. Kennedy & Prof. Stewart Wallace, the university librarian, were completely 'tied up' with the Macmillan Company. It was said – generally – that Prof. Kennedy,

Prof. Wallace & Mr. Eayrs (President of the Macmillan Co. of Canada) were on especially good terms of friendship."[43]

Catherine Wells was no doubt touched. The morning post had brought with it a charming letter from Sir Harry Johnston, who had turned sixty-five only a few months before. As usual, Sir Harry complained about his frail health, this time his recent bout with influenza, which had kept him cooped up in his flat in St. James's Court far too long. The main concern expressed in his letter, however, was for Jane. "You seem, from all account, to have had a trying and exhausting two years, involving operations and strain on your constitution; and if I had more control over you I should have prescribed and insisted on carrying out a two years' rest cure, to date from Jany. 1st, 1923; during which you were only to be approached by a select band of visitors, all of them rich, talented, beautiful and generous."[44]

She must have appreciated the thought. The past several years had been exhausting ones. She could scarcely bring herself to think about the hundreds of hours she had spent between late 1918 and 1920, helping with *The Outline*. The search for books on a host of subjects; the flagging and transcription of passage after passage from various weighty historical works, for her husband's use; the typing of H.G.'s scrawling manuscript, understandable only to her and to a few others, into clean copy; the endless correspondence with H.G.'s friends, with the illustrator, Horrabin, and with the publishers. It had all but broken her.

No sooner had the bulk of her work on *The Outline* been done, it seemed, than she had faced her operation and the months of recovery from it, often alone, for H.G. seemed less capable than ever of staying in one place for any length of time. On the occasions when he returned to Easton Glebe he surrounded himself with as many people, and as much activity, as necessary to feed whatever unfathomable hunger gnawed at him. Through it all, she had driven herself to remain the supremely competent and unflappable Jane everyone knew and expected her to be. She had been with this man for thirty years, but still she could scarcely guess what drove him from book to book, from place to place, and from woman to woman. She did know that his was a complicated, driven, unsatisfied soul.

None of her husband's relationships with other women was now, or for some time past had been, a mere *passade*. The word, she knew, had been a convenient fiction of the early years of their marriage, intended initially to bolster her sense of security, if not her dignity. Margaret Sanger she knew from 1920, when the American woman had visited them at Easton Glebe, and she was aware that H.G. had continued the relationship during his trip to America late in 1921. Sanger's appearance in *The Secret Places of the Heart* came as no surprise.

Sir Richmond Hardy, distraught and under psychiatric care because his life is without meaning, finds renewal in a young woman, Miss Grammont, an attractive and soft-spoken American woman who is an advocate of birth control and world population planning. Sir Richmond and Miss Grammont become minds in harmony, and they go on to talk about the history of the world, the ruins left by the Great War, and the coming crisis of civilization.[45] It remained to be seen how abiding this harmony might be. Would it burn itself out, like the affair with Amber Reeves, or would it prove durable, like H.G.'s affair with Rebecca West, now a decade old?

Everything about her husband's life seemed somehow to have become unhinged, without a centre, almost out of control. Oh, he was as productive as ever. The lectures from the American tour, following the international success of *The Outline* and its crusade for a world-state, had been published by Cassell in 1921 as *The Salvaging of Civilization*. He had set forward his views on the Versailles settlement in *Washington and the Hope of Peace* the next year, and had found the time to condense parts of *The Outline* into *A Short History of the World* and to see *The Secret Places of the Heart* through the press. But *Secret Places*, she knew, was scarcely H.G. at his best: there was too little self-knowledge in it, and too much self-pity. Even the novel he was about to publish, *Men Like Gods*, showed signs of its author's emotional disarray. Nominally a return to the themes of his famous novels of the 1890s, with a protagonist who is transported to Utopia, the book was less scientific romance than it was escapist fantasy.

He had not been able to escape from his latest adventure: Frau Gatternigg. The sorry business with her seemed to symbolize just how much Wells's private life had grown beyond his command and how tragic the consequences could be.

The affair had begun when a young Austrian journalist, Hedwig Verena Gatternigg, began to correspond with Wells during the winter of 1922–23, just when his relationship with Rebecca was nearing the breaking point. Answering her request for a meeting to discuss problems of the educated classes in Austria, he invited her to his flat in Whitehall Court. There, Jane served tea. Wells saw in front of him a petite and attractive woman in her late twenties, with dark hair and big brown eyes with long curling lashes. As he later wrote: "I hate to snub an exile in distress, and she was an extremely appetizing young woman."[46]

Hedwig Gatternigg proved to be more than open to the prophet's advances. She arranged to stay in a house in Felsted near Easton Glebe, and when Wells arrived there to meet her hosts, he found them gone and his favourite exile "minding it in a tea-gown and little else. 'This must end,' said I, 'this must end' – allowing myself to be dragged upstairs." The invitation to tea became a weekend of passionate lovemaking. To Wells, such infidelity was no betrayal of Jane. The thought never entered his mind. It was Rebecca he had betrayed, and even then he excused his behaviour by convincing himself that she had flirted with the American novelist Sinclair Lewis.

Before long, Wells concluded that the fling was well out of hand, and he determined to end it. He instructed his maid that should Hedwig call at Whitehall Court, she was not to be given access to the flat. Instead, in order to cool her ardour, he suggested that she meet with Rebecca West.

For her part, Rebecca had come to the conclusion that her own relationship with Wells must end. At the outset of a trip to America in the spring of 1923, a sanctimonious Boston clubwoman had even tried to have her held up at Ellis Island on charges of immorality. Her earlier insistence that he either leave Jane and marry her or end their affair had become an ultimatum, and it now reached its all-too-predictable conclusion. He would remain with Jane. Rebecca was bitterly disappointed, but she sensed his confusion, and its attendant drift. His routine had come to consist of "a feverish week-end at Easton, from Monday to Tuesday in the London flat, two days with me, two days at London again, back to Easton. He was then," she recalled, "very chesty and in poor condition, and often in a pitiful state of overwork and exhaustion. Of course it was death to his writing." Much later, recounting the last year of their relationship to Wells's biographers the Mackenzies, she said: "He went round and round like a rat in a maze."[47]

By the late spring and early summer of 1923, it had become well past time to end their shared agony. If Wells insisted on staying with Jane, Rebecca demanded as settlement a guaranteed income of £3,000 per annum. Eventually, she settled for £500 per annum until she married or was "otherwise with a man."[48]

Hedwig Gatternigg presented herself at Rebecca West's London flat on a June morning in 1923, accompanied by a letter of introduction from H.G. The Austrian woman was clearly distraught, her manner so strange that West's maid took it upon herself to go to the street to see if a policeman was on duty at the end of the block. "I was puzzled," West later recalled, "to know why H.G. had sent me this peculiar person."[49] On June 20, a day that reached 91 degrees, Hedwig showed up unannounced at Wells's Whitehall Court flat, wearing not much more than a raincoat, shoes and stockings. "You must love me," Wells recalled her saying, "or I will kill myself. I have poison. I have a razor." Wells's account of the scene portrays him in heroic action, seizing the razor from the distraught woman, putting her in a chair, "bleeding profusely," and rushing off for cold water to staunch the flow.

"Let me die," he recalled her saying. "I love him, I love him."[50]

Soon the hall porter appeared, and then two policemen. She was taken away to Charing Cross Hospital, "still asserting her incurable passion for me." Wells's first thoughts were that his shirt and cuffs had become bloodstained, that he would need to replace his carpet, and that he had missed his dinner party. The next day, the *Star* broke the story. It was like something out of an H.G. Wells novel:

a hysterical woman, presumably a stranger, gains access to the flat of a famous author, attempts to cut her throat, and is saved from herself only by his quick thinking.[51]

For Rebecca, beset by reporters about the Austrian woman because of an allusion to her in the *Star* account, the episode confirmed the wisdom of her decision to break with Wells. She was disturbed by the unseemly events in his flat, and although she agreed to stand by him and his story about the business with Hedwig, she was also profoundly annoyed at the needless way he had involved her, and at his attitude towards her. "Not once did he say 'I am sorry I have got you into this,'" she recalled. "He simply used me for his protection, and had no other thought about me . . . I was desperately anxious from that moment to get quit of all connection with both H.G. and Jane."[52]

The sentiments are understandable, but a question remains. Given the circumstances, why mention Jane at the end of this particular passage? Unless, that is, Rebecca knew that Jane had been present when Hedwig arrived. Nowhere in Wells's account, or in the newspaper stories that relied on it, does she make an appearance. Yet in *H.G. Wells and Rebecca West*, by the distinguished Wells scholar Gordon Ray, another view is offered. Of the suicide attempt, Ray, who had full cooperation from Rebecca West when writing his book, states: "That evening Frau Gatternigg attempted to kill herself in Wells's flat. Wells was absent at the time, and it was Jane who discovered her at 4 Whitehall Court. Jane called the police, who saw to it that Frau Gatternigg was taken to a hospital."[53]

That is all. We are left with two incompatible versions of the same events: the dramatic rescue told by the famous novelist, and the cleaning up of a messy situation by a protective, faithful, and all-enduring wife. Given the peculiarities of the *longue durée* of the marriage of this husband and this wife, one is inclined to accept Ray's account, very likely provided by West, as the accurate one. Always there, always half visible in the background, stood the faithful Jane, waiting for the moment when her husband needed her. As she knew he would.

In 1925, with a lot of effort and expensive advice, "The Highway of History" was ready for publishers to see. Any number of University of Toronto professors of history had helped Florence with it, and for it they had been handsomely paid. Early in April, she received a letter from George Wrong. He noted that his son Murray, the historian, had finished reading the final chapters and had made comments on them and on the book as a whole. Wrong enclosed the twelve-page report. "What I have read," Murray Wrong wrote, "seems to me to flow easily and to read quite well . . . The parts that I have read seem to me readable, interesting, and generally quite convincing. My impression is that little difficulty would be found in getting a publisher, and that the book, with a few maps & some well chosen illustrations, would be quite useful."[54]

Armed with such a lofty academic assurance, Florence and Mabel travelled to New York City that summer with freshly typed copies of "The Highway of History" in their baggage. They spent several weeks there, making the rounds of the most prominent publishing firms, lugging copies of the bulky manuscript and asking to see the people in charge. It was daunting to be in the heartland of North American publishing, but Florence was convinced that at last she had written a publishable book, offspring of "The Web" but much improved on it. So after each interview she and Mabel left a copy with the firm. Then, after a bit of a holiday, they took the train back to Toronto. "The Highway of History," by Florence A. Deeks, sat on editors' desks at Doubleday, Page and Company, Charles Scribner's Sons, Ginn and Company, Houghton-Mifflin, and Little, Brown and Company. Safely home on Farnham Avenue, the two sisters waited each day for the postman to arrive.

The letters followed a few weeks later. Rejections, all of them. Charles Scribner replied personally, writing that while "The Highway of History" was "a very readable and comprehensive outline of the world's history," his firm could not undertake its publication "with quite the degree of confidence" it liked. Houghton-Mifflin responded with the good news that "we are impressed with the thoroughness and care with which you have done the work, and we can readily see a probability that if published the work will get a welcome from some students and other readers who need just such a guide"; the bad news was that, from the firm's point of view, "it does not seem clearly a book for us to take up." Ginn and Company admitted that it was "tempted" because "your work . . . is so good," but the publisher found it "not at all feasible" to publish the book because several successful general histories already existed in the marketplace.[55]

The most prominent of these books, of course, was *The Outline of History*. How frustrating and infuriating it must have been for Florence, then, when Beecher Stowe of Doubleday wrote that he had decided to reject "The Highway of History" because "it so nearly duplicates the Wells outline," or when an editor at Little, Brown, the last of the publishers to respond, informed her: "Your book would be subject to comparison with Wells' 'Outline of History.' For that reason I think you will have difficulty in securing a publisher at the present time."[56]

IO   *Accusations*

> "It's a question of intellectual honesty . . . Oh, a
> small one maybe. But you say yourself you don't
> know where it may lead, what accretions of untruth –
> if it *is* untruth – may gather round it. This is a matter
> of historical truth, of course you must speak up."
>
> Angus Wilson, *Anglo-Saxon Attitudes* (1956)

W HEN HE SETTLED IN at Frank Wise's old desk
on the morning of Wednesday, September 14, 1925, Hugh Eayrs
had no reason to think the day would be different from any other.
Macmillan of Canada was doing very well in spite of the turnover
of staff in the early post-war years. Few of the current employees
knew of the turmoil caused by the president who had resigned so
suddenly in 1921.

But Eayrs, with his sandy hair swept back and to the side and
his rather wistful, basset hound countenance, remembered. He had
wasted no time in establishing himself in Wise's office once George
Brett and Sir Frederick Macmillan had offered him the presidency.
Within days, he had written to Hodder Williams, of Hodder and
Stoughton, asking to have an announcement of his appointment
placed in *The Bookman*, the book trade magazine Williams con-
trolled. Eayrs noted that he was the proud son of Dr. George Eayrs,
LL.D., F.R.H.S., of Leeds, that he had emigrated to Canada from
England in 1912 (at the age of eighteen), and that he had entered

the publishing industry immediately after his arrival in Toronto. He had collaborated with Thomas B. Costain in a novel, *The Amateur Diplomat*, published by Hodder and Stoughton in 1916, and had written a brief biography of Sir Isaac Brock for Macmillan of Canada's "Canadian Men of Action Series" late in the war. Eayrs concluded his autobiographical sketch with the request that in particular he did not want the announcement to emphasize his youth or mention his age.[1]

Not yet twenty-six at the time he became president of Macmillan of Canada, Eayrs was understandably sensitive about his relative lack of experience. Nevertheless, he had assumed firm control of the firm. He knew that Brett and Macmillan held high opinions of him, but he was also aware that they thought themselves able to control the actions of a young and untested president in a way they had failed to do with Wise. If so, they had underestimated him. In his first months as president, he had managed to convince his own sales manager as well as George Brett, against their better judgment, that Macmillan of Canada should publish W.H. Blake's translation into English of Louis Hémon's lyrical novel, *Maria Chapdelaine*, a work of mythic proportions about the spirit of a rustic and devout Quebec people. Beautifully illustrated with woodcuts by the Toronto graphic artist Thoreau Macdonald, it instantly became an international success.[2] Thereafter, the New York and London offices of Macmillan had given Eayrs considerable latitude in deciding what the Canadian firm might publish.

Hugh Eayrs was a young man who possessed great force of personality and an infectious sense of humour. He had a clear sense of direction, but he was impulsive and took offence easily, whether with business associates or reviewers of Macmillan of Canada titles. One junior employee was immediately impressed on joining the firm by "the drive and charm" of the man. But John Morgan Gray soon witnessed another side to his boss. At times he would bang the desk with his fist to make a point. "Hugh Eayrs had a low boiling point," Gray recalled, "and was not famous for reasonable argument. He fired and hired on impulse, or would cut off a bookseller's discount for criticism of our service or prices." A worried

Winnipeg bookseller inquired in 1924 whether it was true that Eayrs might still "harbour some ill feelings" against his company over certain business dealings. Eayrs explained that he was going through "a bit of a nervous breakdown" and was about to "get right away from business for a month or six weeks."[3]

Eayrs played as hard as he worked. "I have several stories to tell you which I shall treasure until I next meet you," he wrote to a friend in England in 1924, "in view of the fact that my temporary secretary is a very tender young thing who might resign if I dictated these stories to her."[4] On at least one occasion, his adventures got him into trouble. "I wish to do in writing what I did to-day personally," he wrote to an acquaintance during his first year as president, "offer you a sincere apology for my part in the unfortunate incident which took place to-day at the 60 Club. I do this first, because I want to, and second because the Commission of the Club asks me to do so." Then he left the name of his attorney, with whom the offended man's own counsel should communicate.[5]

On this September day, Eayrs accepted a telephone call. On the other end of the line was a reporter from the Toronto *Star*. What could Eayrs tell him about a writ just taken out at Osgoode Hall against one of Macmillan's authors, H.G. Wells, over his *Outline of History*? Who was this woman, Florence A. Deeks, whose lawyers had secured it? What did Eayrs think about the $500,000 in damages the woman sought for the illegal use of her unpublished manuscript in the writing of *The Outline*?

What indeed? Eayrs was stunned and managed only to mutter that he had no comment to make. All he knew about these extraordinary claims was what the reporter had told him. What *was* this all about? Where to begin? Perhaps when the writ was served he would learn more. Meanwhile, all he could do was wait.

The next day, the Toronto *Star* and the Toronto *Telegram* made the charges public. The *Star*'s account was brief but prominent. "Toronto Writer Asks Wells for Big Sum," ran its front-page headline, just below one that announced formal German approval of the Rhineland Pact at Locarno. The *Telegram*'s headline, like its article, was longer:

AUTHORESS HERE SUES H.G. WELLS FOR $500,000
Claims Outline of History Contains Part of Unpublished
Work by Miss Florence A. Deeks

In the absence of any contact from the woman's lawyers, all
Eayrs had to go on was the newspaper accounts. They were not particularly helpful. She was seeking an injunction restraining Wells's
publishers from selling, advertising, or distributing *The Outline of
History* without the plaintiff's consent, because it contained "a
reproduction in whole or in part . . . of the unpublished literary
composition or work known as 'The Web.' "[6]

"The Web"? Eayrs had never heard of it. The Deeks woman had
also asked for "a mandatory injunction directing the defendants,"
Wells and the publishers of *The Outline*, "to deliver to the plaintiff for destruction all books, manuscripts and other documents
containing such reproduction; for an account of all sales by the
defendants; and for an account of all profits." Finally, she sought
the half-million dollars in damages for "the illegal use, appropriation and reproduction of the plaintiff's said unpublished literary
composition or work and for infringement of her proprietary
rights therein."

One can imagine Hugh Eayrs, later that day, stepping up to
14 Elm Street, the old St. George's Hall, after a brisk walk from the
Macmillan offices. This was where the Arts and Letters Club had
established its quarters in 1920, and the club was where he often
relaxed over more than one drink after a hard day's work. Many of
the city's most prominent artists, writers, academics, and patrons of
the arts belonged to it. The journalist Hector Charlesworth held
court there. Vincent Massey, heir to the Massey farm machinery
fortune, frequently brought guests of international stature, like G.K.
Chesterton, to its premises. Artists of the Group of Seven, such as
J.E.H. MacDonald, could be found at the table they regarded as their
own, arguing amongst themselves. The composer Healey Willan
presided this year as the club's president.[7] It was a place where minds
could meet and, when it suited their fancy, men could be boys.

Much of the club gossip that day was no doubt about the
charges levelled by Florence Deeks and the $500,000 she sought

from H.G. Wells and his fellow defendants. This was not the kind of attention Hugh Eayrs sought. But as he fortified himself with his usual dose of liquid courage, he appears to have learned a little from his friends about Miss Deeks. Later that day he penned a short letter to George Brett in New York, informing him of the situation and enclosing clippings from the *Telegram* and *Star*. As publisher of the North American edition of *The Outline of History*, Macmillan in New York had been named as a defendant. "None of us have heard of this person, Miss Deeks, and I am trying to find out what I can of her but the prevalent impression amongst writers here is that she is lightminded." Meanwhile, he said, he would consult Macmillan's Toronto lawyers.[8]

Hot in pursuit of sensation, the next day the *Star* gave the story a headline: "Miss Deeks' Suit Over Wells Book Causes a Big Stir." The story's lead paragraph reflected the mood at the Arts and Letters Club the day before: the charges had "set literary Toronto agog." Friends of Miss Deeks had told the *Star* that she meant business, that this was no "freak action," and that she had the full support of her brother, who had "a large construction business." The woman's lawyer had refused to say anything about the case other than that "if it was by a coincidence that the material in Wells' 'Outline of History' was so similar to the material prepared by Miss Deeks for her manuscript 'The Web,' then it was a most remarkable coincidence."[9]

Contacted by the newspaper, Macmillan in London denied any knowledge of the matter and noted that it had not even published *The Outline of History*. One Toronto publisher wondered why Miss Deeks had waited five years to bring her action and pointed to the use Mr. Wells had made of famous collaborators such as Sir Ray Lankester and Sir Harry Johnston. Another defended the facts of history as matters of common possession easily used by different authors for their own purposes. Nevertheless, sources close to Miss Deeks had indicated that Macmillan of Canada had possessed "The Web" for a considerable length of time, during which, she claimed, it had somehow reached Mr. Wells. "Striking similarities" existed between the two works, it was said.

Eayrs received a letter from the firm of Tilley, Johnston, Thomson & Parmenter the same day. He was now more than a little worried. The woman's charges might be outrageous, but she had retained the services of the city's best lawyers, for W. Norman Tilley was renowned in the province as the Law Society's leading litigator.[10] Of all the members of the Law Society of Upper Canada, Tilley was probably the last one who would allow himself to become involved in a frivolous action. And the letter from his firm pulled no punches. "You of course are fully conversant with the use that was made of our client's manuscript while the same was in your hands and it is, therefore, unnecessary for us to go into further details at the present time for the purpose of substantiating the facts and circumstances relied on in support of the claim now made." The letter then suggested that if Macmillan of Canada was willing to entertain a settlement, negotiations should proceed.[11]

Eayrs was dumbfounded. Wells had written and published his book half a decade ago, when Eayrs was still secretary of the company, during the days of Saul and Wise.

Saul and Wise. What went through the mind of Wise's successor when he first made the connection between the events in question and the final years of the disgraced president? He must have dwelt, if only for a fleeting moment, on the unsavoury circumstances surrounding the dismissal of Frank Wise from the firm. Like George Brett and Sir Frederick Macmillan, he knew that Wise had engaged in more than a few dubious activities before his days as a publisher had ended. What fugitive thoughts began to gnaw at Eayrs's presumption of his firm's innocence in the matter of these outlandish claims? Did he recall the signed statement he had obtained four years earlier from Miss E. Millership, a secretary during Wise's final days? In it, she had stated that Wise had telephoned her, asking her to find copies of certain letters he had written and to mail them to him. Fortunately, she had had the good sense to speak to Eayrs about the request, and he had written to the ex-president refusing to allow him access to any of the company records. Wise "then asked me," Miss Millership had written in her statement, "if we had found certain papers which were supposed to be unfindable in the files. I said no."[12] At the time, Eayrs had suspected that the papers in question were about Sales Unlimited. But were they? Wise's inquiry could have been about any number of highly irregular schemes.

If he wanted to get to the bottom of this scandal in the making, Eayrs had a lot of legwork to do, and quickly. First he met with John Saul; then he spoke to Professor George Sidney Brett at the University of Toronto. Rumour had it that the Deeks woman had consulted the noted historian of psychology a few years earlier about her work. By the time Eayrs sat down to report his findings to George Brett in New York and Sir Frederick in London, he was alarmed at what he had learned. The suit, he wrote to Brett, was "beginning to appear much more serious than I had supposed." Both Professor Brett and John Saul had told him essentially the same story. Miss Deeks had indeed consulted them, and apparently others, after New York published *The Outline of History*, complaining that Macmillan in Toronto had held her unpublished manuscript for a very long time, and that after it was returned to her it was "thumb-marked and pencil-marked." She had then claimed that some of her material "had been copied word for word" and had found its way into *The Outline*.[13]

This was not the worst of it. Saul had told Eayrs that after consulting with Frank Wise about the manuscript, he had not only told Miss Deeks that her manuscript was good but also had proposed to her, "with Wise's approval," that he (Saul) "forward" it to Macmillan in New York for possible publication. More alarming still, both Professor Brett and John Saul had assured Eayrs that there existed "a resemblance between the material in Miss Deeks's manuscript and Mr. Wells's OUTLINE OF HISTORY so extraordinarily marked as to be a matter for amazement."

The Toronto scholar who shared the New York publisher's name had said "that coincidences of this kind were not likely . . . on the whole to be regarded as anything but coincidence." But Eayrs was scarcely put at ease when the professor added that there was a possibility, nevertheless, "that the court would look at it differently." Eayrs concluded his letter to Brett in New York by insisting that no one currently at the Toronto house had had any intimation of Miss Deeks's activities or had even heard of her. But he added that its lawyer Robert L. Johnston, a Macmillan of Canada director and partner in McLaughlin, Johnston, Moorhead & Macaulay, insisted on a meeting very soon between himself, Eayrs, and the president of the American branch.

Eayrs quickly followed his letter to Brett with one to Sir Frederick Macmillan, assuring him, too, that no one in the Toronto office had ever heard of Miss Deeks. "Upon the appearance of the first notification in the press," he wrote, "I thought the woman light-minded but I have now gone deeper in to the matter and find it is likely to assume a more serious complexion." After complaining that her lawyers had seen fit to release details of her charges through the press, he suggested that Sir Frederick trace whether her manuscript had ever been sent to Macmillan in London. Her lawyer had insisted categorically that the manuscript had been sent to the London branch of Macmillan through "Mr. Brett's house." In addition, Eayrs felt obliged to mention one complicating factor: he had been told "on good authority" that Frank Wise had been "in touch with this Miss Deeks for some time past and is in close touch with her now."[14] He concluded by saying that he and the company lawyer, Mr. Johnston, were watching the matter "most carefully."

While Eayrs publicly assumed the stance that the claim that Wells had used "The Web" was unfounded and laughable, in fact, with each day that passed he grew more worried. John Saul lived in the affluent Rosedale district of Toronto, in a pleasant home with warm, multicoloured brown brick, its two gables facing the street. At 30 St. Andrews Gardens, he was separated by only three houses from Eayrs's own home, larger but more austere than Saul's and in plain red brick, at number 55. Every time the two neighbours chatted, Saul seemed to tell a different story. Later in the month Eayrs told Robert Johnston, in worried confidence, that Saul now thought "The Web" had indeed been "forwarded to England."[15]

In a flurry of letters whose bravado scoffed at the idea, the three branches of Macmillan now began an extensive quest amongst themselves to determine just which of them had possessed "The Web," and when. Eayrs spoke of "this ridiculous case" to Sir Frederick Macmillan, but insisted politely, using the words of his lawyer, that it was of utmost importance "to find out if the manuscript by this Miss Deeks was ever sent to your house and when returned," and whether the British publisher possessed "any correspondence with our house either with Mr. Wise or Mr. Saul confirming it."[16]

Macmillan's Brett initially thought that "The Web" might indeed have been sent to his firm. "We have not yet been able to find out what happened to this MS after it was received by us," he wrote. But before mailing the letter, Brett had second thoughts about the words he had chosen; so he pencilled out the word "after" and replaced it with "if."[17] The next day he sent a delicately worded letter to Wells, outlining Miss Deeks's suit, proclaiming that it was "so ridiculous that no reasonable person would give a moment's attention to it," but urging him to give it "every possible attention." A week later, now convinced that the case was serious indeed, in a letter written in the stiff syntax of legal formality, he asked Wells directly whether he possessed proof that the outline of his book was his own, and whether, either directly or indirectly, he had ever heard of "Miss Florence Deeks or of her manuscript, or seen it, either prior to or subsequent to your decision to undertake the book, 'The Outline of History.'"[18]

Wells did little to illuminate matters. The Toronto *Star* interviewed him in London. "I can say nothing about it, because I knew nothing about it," he said. By the time the Toronto *Telegram* reached his flat in Whitehall Court, its correspondent found only his secretary there. Wells, he was told, had left for "the country," but he had left the message that "it was only a newspaper story." When the reporter asked why someone would launch a frivolous action if the consequence would be to incur the costs of the suit, the secretary replied that Mr. Wells was of the view that "the lady must have taken proceedings on account of an unpublished work of her own. In that case she herself must have given that work to Mr. Wells if he used it for the 'Outline of History,' and he says he knows nothing about it."[19]

It was a curious thing to say. On one hand, the author of *The Outline of History* appeared to offer a categorical denial of any knowledge of the Toronto woman's work; on the other, he declared that if he had used her work, she must have given it to him of her own accord. Each statement by itself made sense, but taken together they seemed to swing on a hinge of negation.

Florence thought it best to defer to Mr. Tilley as to when the writs should be served on the defendants. Meanwhile, she had much to do before her action could be brought to court. Furious that "The Highway of History" had been rejected by the New York publishers because it so much resembled *The Outline of History*, she had vented her frustration at George. Now she needed another kind of support, that of expert witnesses to testify on her behalf.

But who? For his defence, Wells would no doubt call upon some or all of the authorities listed on his title page. She needed scholars of a similar calibre. Professor Brett at the university had encouraged her to think that the action might succeed, but it was evident that he would rather not be involved in a legal action. Who among historians in Canada possessed the most impeccable authority? What was the name of their professional body? Armed with such questions, she soon found the address of the Canadian Historical Association. Thus began her contact with Lawrence J. Burpee in Ottawa, its founding president.

Like many other members of the historical association he had helped to bring into existence, Lawrence Burpee was not a professional historian attached to a university department. Instead, he was a former federal civil servant who, having worked for three successive ministers of justice in the 1890s, had resigned in 1905 to become librarian of Ottawa's public library, leaving this post seven years later to accept appointment as the first Canadian secretary of the International Joint Commission. It was a position in which he would remain until his death in 1946, at the age of seventy-three.

His first loves, however, were history, literature, and geography. A man of seemingly limitless energy, he had published several books on the adventure of exploration as it related to Canada, including *The Search for the Western Sea* in 1908, *Scouts of Empire* in 1912, *Pathfinders of the Great Plains* in 1914, and *Sandford Fleming, Empire Builder* the year after. At the time he received Florence's request to examine "The Web" and *The Outline*, his activity and output had scarcely slackened: he had just assumed the presidency of the Canadian Authors' Association and was preparing the first historical atlas of Canada for publication. In 1925, many of his most distinguished historical contributions were still to come.[20]

Burpee was intrigued by the tale told by the Toronto woman. She had sent him a copy of her comparison and had explained the circumstances by which her manuscript seemed to have been removed from the Macmillan vault during the very months in which H.G. Wells had apparently begun to write *The Outline*. His curiosity got the better of him. He agreed to examine the two works and soon began the laborious task of his own comparison.

He sent his report to Florence on January 11, 1926. "What I have been asked to do," he said, "is to make a careful examination of 'The Web' and of the 'Outline of History,' and to say whether or not a comparison of the two books reveals, in my opinion, any evidence of the plan, scope, spirit or language of one having been appropriated and incorporated in the other. If the facts are as stated, the appropriation obviously could be only from 'The Web.'"[21]

Burpee declared that, having just seen both works for the first time, he had brought to his assessment "no preconceived ideas as to the character, scope or language of either." He had compared "The Web" and *The Outline*, and then proceeded to examine critically Miss Deeks's typewritten analyses of their frameworks and substance. At the outset, he said, he had doubted that coincidence alone could constitute "evidence of deliberate plagiarism." But only "up to a point." By the time he had finished his own assessment, he had compiled his own lengthy list of parallel passages and had reached his own conclusions. Florence lingered over Burpee's concluding paragraphs:

> The impression left upon my mind by this detailed study of all the material, is that to a considerable extent the plan, scope, spirit and language of "The Web" have been incorporated in "The Outline." I have already said that coincidences, as such, are not necessarily evidence of plagiarism; occasional similarities may be coincidences and nothing more. But here the thing

to my mind, gets beyond the reasonable bounds of such an explanation. One finds the same general plan – a distinctly original treatment of an unusually broad and intricate subject; striking similarities in the framework; similarities in treatment; and also perhaps equally significant dissimilarities, as the stressing of woman's place in the history of the world in "The Web" and its avoidance in "The Outline"; and coincidences of language until it becomes impossible to regard them any longer as merely coincidences. Equally significant is the appearance, at least to some extent, of the same underlying thought in both works, the striking idea of the history of the world considered as a web or fabric into which is woven the story of man and his deeds, good and evil. One might take each item in these lines of comparison separately, or even each line of comparison, and perhaps remain unconvinced, but the cumulative effect of the whole is overwhelming.

Without attempting an analysis, I think it must be patent to anyone who reads and compares the "Web" and the "Outline" that they are not only curiously alike in plan and structure, but equally unlike any previous attempt at a world history . . .

In regard to similarities in the actual language employed by the authors of "The Web" and "The Outline" – that is, the presentation of similar ideas in the same sequence, and clothing them in substantially the same form of words, – the instances are far too numerous to even begin to present them here. In this respect perhaps more than in any other, – the significance of the comparison lies not so much in the individual example, which in itself may be often insignificant as evidence, as in the piling up of innumerable such instances. And as I have already said, it is the cumulative effect of very many similarities, in this as in other directions, that compels one to the conclusion that some of those who were engaged in preparing material, at some stage, for 'The Outline,' must have had access to the manuscript called 'The Web.' "[22]

This was support beyond Florence's wildest expectations. One of Canada's most distinguished men of letters now agreed with her. Burpee had even appended his own five-page list of similar words, phrases, ideas, and mistakes. She felt vindicated, almost triumphant.

One expert on her side, however, was not enough. So, wearing her new-found confidence like a bright spring coat, she went to the university to talk to some of her academic acquaintances. Later she walked east across Queen's Park Crescent to St. Michael's College to speak with Sir Bertram Windle.

If degrees and honours after a name imply academic respectability, Bertram Coghill Alan Windle, K.S.G., M.D., LL.D., Ph.D., D.Sc., F.R.S., F.S.A., was its very hallmark. After a distinguished academic career in England and Ireland, Sir Bertram had retired in 1919 at the age of sixty-one from the presidency of University College, Cork, to Toronto to remove himself from the turmoil of Irish politics and to be near members of his family. When authorities at the University of Toronto discovered his presence, they leaped at the chance to secure his affiliation with the institution.[23]

Son of an English vicar, Windle had been educated at Trinity College, Dublin, where he studied medicine. After graduation, he took up practice as a surgeon and pathologist in Birmingham and became a member of the original staff of the University of Birmingham. But interests in medicine and education alone were insufficient to quench the relentless curiosity of this Victorian polymath, for his intellectual interests ranged from natural history and anthropology to the histories of science and religion. Indeed, it was for his work in these subjects, not his authoritative *Manual of Surface Anatomy*, that the British reading public had come to know him. Among his popular books on archaeology, science, and religion were *The Prehistoric Age* (1904), *A Century of Scientific Thought* (1915), and *Science and Morals* (1919).

For eight years after his retirement to Toronto, Sir Bertram (he had been knighted in 1912) gave an annual series of public lectures at the University of Toronto, regularly attracting such large audiences to the theatre of the Physics Building that Convocation Hall often had to be used to accommodate the overflow. His book *The Romans in Britain* had appeared in 1923, incorporating some of his lecture material. It reached a second, then a third printing within a year. A resident of Toronto for only seven years by the time

Florence went to speak with him, he was nevertheless one of the city's best-known scholars.[24]

Windle chose to associate himself with St. Michael's College in Toronto because, influenced by the Oxford Movement when studying in Dublin, he had converted to Roman Catholicism in 1883. Founded by the Basilian order in 1852, St. Michael's was the only Roman Catholic institution affiliated with the University of Toronto. For his services to the faith, Windle had been appointed Knight of St. Gregory the Great in 1909 and had received honorary degrees from Rome (Ph.D.) and from Marquette University (D.Sc.). His book *Miracles and Other Matters* had appeared in 1924, and when he listened to Florence's story and considered her request that he examine and compare "The Web" and *The Outline of History*, he was busy at work on a "who's who" of the Oxford Movement and *The Catholic Church and Its Reactions with Science*, due to appear in 1927.

Quite independent of the merits of the case of Miss Deeks, Sir Bertram Windle was scarcely predisposed to be enamoured of the anti-clerical H.G. Wells, whose well-known view of the Roman Catholic church was that it was a colossal failure as an institution and a nefarious and stultifying influence in cultural and intellectual life, especially in Ireland.[25]

Now sixty-eight, Sir Bertram was eager to live a life free of controversy, and he told Florence this. Nevertheless, the genial man listened to her fears and agreed to examine her work and *The Outline*. It took him several months, but in the spring or summer of 1926 he sent her lawyers a lengthy report. His duty, as he recorded it, was not to make a case against the author of *The Outline of History* but simply to express his "honest opinion on the matter." His method was to examine the "skeleton" or "framework" of each work, to read them section by section and side by side, making "copious notes" as he went along, and to scrutinize the "Analysis so carefully prepared" by Miss Deeks. He added, however, that by the time he had completed his own evaluation, he had found that the notes he made in his travels through the two books corresponded "to a large extent" with her comparison.[26]

Sir Bertram's report read like a paraphrase and elaboration of Burpee's. Similarities between the two books, it began, could only be accounted for in one of three ways: (1) that both authors worked from the same model; (2) that the framework was an inevitable one and could not therefore be avoided; or (3) that "one author copied from the other." The first possibility he discounted on the grounds that no earlier model existed for such unique accounts of the history of civilizations, and neither Deeks nor Wells had indicated that they had found or used one. As to the second, Sir Bertram noted that even he could think of other ways in which the authors might have constructed their works – so nothing was "inevitable" about their themes or structures. That left the third explanation, and it was the one he thought most likely: that one author had copied from the other – "and in this case," he wrote, "it is perfectly obvious that the copying could only have been of the 'Web' by the 'Outline.'"[27]

He did not find "any absolutely crushing and final piece of evidence" but concluded that there was nevertheless "a good literary *prima facie* case" for plagiarism. The general frameworks were identical, and great similarities existed in the choice of theme, incident, and detail. His report discounted some of the details in Florence's comparison as likely coincidences in wording; too much reliance on them in court, he advised, would weaken her case. Yet having stated these reservations, he added that there remained "a number of passages the similarity of which is quite startling."[28]

Sir Bertram provided several examples of parallel passages. One from the Deeks manuscript, for example, said:

> But notwithstanding all the vicissitudes of the Greeks they still preserved their national unity by means of the institutions of the past – their language, religion, games, Amphyctionic councils and oracles. At the Amphyctionic councils the deputies of a dozen peoples met together and discussed common interests; and in order to consult the chief oracle, which was at Delphi, people flocked from all parts of the Greek world. The importance of their games may be judged from the fact that their first existing historical record is connected with the Olympic games. In B.C. 778 the name Coroebus was inscribed on the public register of the

Elians as having won the prize of the Stadium, and it became customary to take this date as the starting point of history.

The corresponding passage from *The Outline* read:

> Yet there was always a certain tradition of unity between all the Greeks, based on a common language and script, on the common possession of heroic epics, and on the continuous intercourse that the maritime position of the states made possible. And, in addition, there were certain religious bonds of a unifying kind. Certain shrines, the shrines of the god Apollo in the isle of Delos and at Delphi, for example, were sustained not by single states, but by leagues of states or Amphictionies . . . A still more important link of Hellenic union was the Olympian games that were held every four years at Olympia.

Considered as strings of words, the two passages appeared quite different. Yet as with many other such passages in "The Web" and *The Outline*, the obvious stylistic differences masked the underlying structural identity, for evidence of plagiarism rested here, as Sir Bertram pointed out, less in identical wording or facts in common than in the strong parallel in the sequence of presented detail.

THE WEB	THE OUTLINE
national unity	certain tradition of unity
language	common language and script
religion	continuous intercourse
Amphyctionic councils	certain religious bonds
common interests	of a unifying kind
Delphi	Delphi
Olympic games	Olympic games[29]

Such sequences would not at once be evident to the casual reader of both works, for he would be struck by the considerable differences in expression; but they stood out to those, like Sir Bertram, who became serious students of the two texts.

What most struck Sir Bertram, however, was the place of women in both works. In "The Web," he observed, women were central; in *The Outline* they were almost completely absent. This was a mystery where meaning, as with Sherlock Holmes and the hound that did not bark, arose at times from silence, and he placed great emphasis on it:

> The curious thing is that the female side of world history is so completely ignored as to cause one to wonder why even such a historian as Mr. Wells should have written two large volumes on the world's history and eliminated from them almost every important woman whom history has known . . . In fact the exclusion of women from the book is so marked a feature that one is obliged to wonder why it exists. This at least may be said that, if one were anxious to cover up one's tracks after copying from a book, the natural method which would suggest itself to the mind would be to make a very great difference in some way or another between the two books. Miss Deeks of set purpose, and perhaps at times even a little out of season, insists on women all through her book. Mr. Wells also, it would seem, of set purpose, ignores them all through his. I wonder why? . . .
>
> I confess as I went through the "Outline" it did occur to me time after time that there was some reason – unexpressed – for the studious omission of almost any mention of women. They may not have been so important in the history of the world as Miss Deeks would have us believe, but yet there were quite a lot of them who counted for so much in the tale of the human race . . . Time after time I have found myself asking "What is your reason for completely ignoring women? Is it because you want to make a difference between your book and another?" . . . This is clear to me: – if I had cribbed from another book and wanted to cover up my tracks I would select one or two points and in those points I would make my book differ just as widely as possible from the other . . . I stress this point because it is quite obvious even to the legal layman that the defence would run on the lines to some extent of "Look at The Differences."[30]

In his report, Sir Bertram concluded that he was not in a position to venture an opinion as to whether such a literary comparison would carry weight in a court of law. Miss Deeks had a case, but a difficult one to sustain in spite of the evidence at hand. "The whole thing," he concluded, "depends on how the evidence on the two sides would strike a body of common-sense men coupled with the amount of probability which could be shown for the access to the MS which is claimed to have taken place."[31]

Florence received Sir Bertram Windle's report with more than a little satisfaction. His conclusions were almost identical to those of Burpee, and both reports exactly paralleled her own analysis. She hoped that, like Burpee, Sir Bertram would agree to appear in court on her behalf. Later in the year, she sent him an enlarged version of her analysis to consider. Towards the end of November, a second report arrived from him, to which were appended several more pages of notes and passages from the two books. "I consider the analysis a marvel of labour," he said, "knowing intimately, as I do, both Outline and Web." Sir Bertram was now more convinced than ever that Wells had committed an egregious act of plagiarism. "I confess it is difficult to avoid coming to the conclusion that the writer of the second book had had access to the MS of the first," he wrote. "I hesitate to use the word 'impossible' for my scientific training has at least made me cautious in choice of words, but it would greatly surprise me if the contrary could be proved."[32]

Even after he had submitted his second report, Sir Bertram continued to study the two works and the additional materials Florence occasionally sent him. In April 1927 he expressed his willingness to serve as an expert witness on her behalf. There were "few things on earth" that he "more detested than going into Court as a witness," he said. But he was willing to do anything he could "to obtain justice."

> I have all along thought that one at least of the most important lines of argument is this: – Wells notoriously made no early study of history. Science was his line and his early tales show that. Then his time was filled by writing social novels. That takes time. Suddenly he comes out with an elaborate if inaccurate

outline of history. Now this I am prepared to swear to anywhere
– no man who had not made a prolonged study of the subject
could by any kind of possibility have drafted the scheme of the
book. It is utterly impossible to conceive anything of the kind
and I could bring powerful examples to show it. Then he got
that scheme somewhere. From a book? Let him produce it – I
don't know of one . . . From a friend? Let him produce the friend.
From your book? It certainly could have been found there.[33]

After making her rounds of New York publishers with "The
Highway of History," Florence had sought expert American advice
from members of the New York literary community. An acquaintance she described only as "a gentleman of high attainments in the
world of literature and business" provided her with a letter of
introduction to H.G. Leach, editor of the *Forum*, a magazine
founded in 1886 for the discussion of controversial public issues.
With it tucked securely in her handbag, Florence and Mabel made
their second trip to New York in as many years.

In the *Forum* office, her sister at her side, Florence explained the
situation and prevailed upon Leach for the name of a prominent
expert to look over "The Web" and *The Outline*.[34] He did as he
was asked, referring her to one of his friends, Henry S. Canby, a
Yale University professor and the editor of the recently founded
Saturday Review of Literature, and to C.K. Ogden, a prominent
British writer, linguist, and member of the editorial board of the
Forum. In this way, knowledge of her accusations began to perco-
late beyond the precincts of Manhattan publishing houses and into
the larger world of New York intellectuals.

Florence knew only that these men were distinguished literary
and linguistic experts, and she sat with Mabel in their hotel room,
waiting for the telephone to ring and the mail to be delivered to the
front desk, little knowing their networks of intellectual association
or those whom they admired. In doing so, she was unaware that one
thread in the web of interest common to Canby and Ogden alike
was H.G. Wells.

Canby had a working relationship with Wells going back to the
war. A champion of the League of Free Nations idea, Canby had

been invited to England by the British Ministry of Information early in 1918 to help promote "mutual understanding among the associated nations." He had been one of those present that summer at the Reform Club dinner party at which Wells had charmed the guests with his ideas on a League of Free Nations and on history in general. When the *Saturday Review of Literature* was about to be launched in 1924, with Canby as its founding editor, Wells wrote to congratulate him.[35] For his part, Ogden, founder in 1912 of an intellectual weekly, the *Cambridge Magazine*, had solicited contributions from Wells. H.G. was quite interested in Ogden's idea of developing a form of English as a universal language.

Canby and Ogden responded to Miss Deeks's request for help. Ogden admitted to being a personal friend of Wells's illustrator and "many of his authorities and advisers."[36] Each was understandably guarded in offering advice. Canby warned her that a "conclusive argument" for plagiarism by Wells would require "evidence supplied from a thorough study of both books by a historian thoroughly versed in world literature" in order to examine them in the context of earlier work. "I do not believe that a charge of plagiarism can rest upon the verbal resemblances alone . . . I find, in short, the verbal resemblance[s] striking but not in themselves convincing."[37] But then, he admitted, his duties at the *Saturday Review* prevented him from devoting enough time and attention to detail required of the task.

Ogden spent several evenings comparing Florence's marked passages from "The Web" and *The Outline*, and concluded that no reputable historian would provide an opinion without at least a month of study. He suggested to her that she should settle the matter out of court. Perhaps an indication that the New York friends of Wells were worried, Ogden also told her that he and Canby had conferred. The two had agreed to sign a letter (along with Leach) advising Wells to look carefully into the matter "in view of the fact that he may have had many collaborators and assistants, any one of whom might have failed to state the source of material supplied."[38]

There was another indication that Ogden and Canby viewed the accusations of Miss Deeks as extremely serious ones. The British theorist of literary criticism I.A. Richards happened to be in New

York visiting Ogden and other friends. He and Ogden had collaborated three years earlier in a pioneering and influential study of the resolution of philosophical problems through linguistic analysis, *The Meaning of Meaning*, and the two scholars continued to pool their ideas. Like Wells, Richards was very interested in Ogden's development of the idea of Basic English, his international language consisting of only 850 common English words. Ogden decided to seek Richards's views on the Deeks accusations.

Richards's visit seemed perfectly timed for Ogden's purposes, as well as for those of Miss Deeks. So, nominally on her behalf, Ogden asked his friend to compare "The Web" and *The Outline* in conjunction with her comparison. Richards was no historian, but the Cambridge scholar could make a fair claim to being the world's leading expert on literary criticism. His *Principles of Literary Criticism* had appeared in 1924 to great acclaim, and by mid-1926 work was well advanced on its companion volume, *Practical Criticism*, which would be published three years later.

Richards extended his New York stay by ten days in order to study the two texts in question. Towards the end of May, Ogden's letter arrived at the hotel in which the women from Toronto were staying. He had now seen a rough draft of Richards's report and hoped to be able to forward a copy to her before she left New York. "It . . . expresses the conclusion that there is a *prima facie* case for an indebtedness both in general structure and in detail from which, whatever its explanation, a formidable legal action could be developed."[39]

The assessment by the Cambridge critic, when at last it arrived, was called "A Report Upon Certain Resemblances Between The Outline of History and The Web." It began with the bald statement, "The prima facie resemblances between THE WEB and THE OUTLINE are plentiful." Richards's initial research strategy had been to look for "possible common sources" that might explain any resemblances between "the more interesting correspondences." He did not discover any. What he did identify was a number of curiously similar passages. Like Sir Bertram Windle, Richards drew attention to the one on the unity of the Greeks and the rise of the Olympic Games. Such correspondences, he said, were frequent.[40]

As another example, Richards reproduced passages from treatments of Pericles. "The details chosen to give this picture of Pericles human interest" in *The Outline*, he said, "are those which are to be found in the WEB." Richards added that the special prominence afforded to Pericles in *The Outline* did not arise out of a consensus of scholarly opinion.[41] Instead, it mimicked the idiosyncratic treatment of Pericles in "The Web."

Other "curious similarities," he said, "were also frequent in the chapters on Roman history," and he proceeded to provide an example. "Such a resemblance is of course by itself without significance. But the repetition of such parallelisms becomes suggestive, and many passages could be cited which have quite as much the air of being paraphrases worked up in later revisions."[42]

Richards was profoundly interested professionally in the use and meaning of words. He paid particular attention, therefore, to "similarities of diction where the word or phrase concerned is hardly an obvious choice." Once again, no individual example was impressive in itself; "but cumulatively," he added, "their effect is considerable, occurring as they do in works whose intellectual temper and style are so different. They give the impression that an earlier draft which may have been more like the WEB has been revised and expanded into the published form of the OUTLINE."[43]

As Florence read Richards's report, she revisited many of the acts of literary commission or omission common to both works that had already been identified in her comparison or pointed out in the reports of Sir Bertram Windle and Lawrence Burpee. The misattribution of the founding of the Holy Roman Empire to Charlemagne instead of Otto the Great; the neglect of monasticism and feudalism; the absence of any discussion of chivalry or the guild system; the remarkable similarities in accounts of Columbus and the navigators. Richards also noted a curious footnote in *The Outline* that said: "This is not the same Simon de Montfort as the leader of the crusade against the Albigenses, but his son." Curious because, as Richards pointed out, "The Outline had not mentioned this Simon de Montfort in its account of the Albigensian Crusade. The Web mentioned him twice."[44]

Florence paid careful attention to the Cambridge scholar's conclusions.

> The parallels offered by the remainder of the work are, with some exceptions, of a kind which would require consideration of a statistical rather than of a literary order. Granted the possibility of the assumption that the Web had been used in the writing of the Outline, there are a very large number of correspondences – in the selection of details, in their arrangement, in the emphasis laid upon them – which would enormously strengthen this possibility. But these correspondences would not, I think, in themselves necessarily impose this assumption upon us. Yet the force of so many parallel passages cannot be neglected . . .
>
> I have noticed many other such instances of a possible influence from the Web. They have, of course, by themselves, not the slightest evidential value. But they are suggestive once the assumption of a connection between the two works is admitted.
>
> To sum up, I do not regard the internal evidence that can be gathered from a comparison of the two books and an examination of their sources as in any way conclusive, and would regard a legal action which proceeded on that basis alone as unlikely to succeed. On the other hand, I have no doubt that a case could be prepared which would create a powerful impression that an indebtedness had been by some means incurred. A skilful defence, however, would, I believe, probably succeed in breaking down that impression in the minds of a jury.
>
> My own opinion as to whether the Web has or has not been used in the composition of the *Outline* would depend upon the other evidence. It seems to me possible, though improbable, that the very numerous correspondences may have arisen through the use of common or allied sources . . . But if this were the whole truth of the matter, I should have to admit that the long arm of coincidence had been remarkably active in the affair. If

on the other hand it were shown that the manuscript of the Web had been in London during 1918, then the fact that the similarities which I have noticed are quite as close and quite as numerous as I should expect to find had the manuscript been extensively used, is plainly relevant. Failing strong external evidence of this use, however, I am of the opinion that the internal evidence is insufficient to prevail in a court of law, though sufficient to arouse a strong suspicion.[45]

The carefully prepared report of I.A. Richards troubled the New York friends of Wells as much as it delighted Florence and Mabel. The apparent reliance of *The Outline* on "The Web" was striking. In the absence of any proof that "The Web" had crossed the Atlantic and reached Wells, however, the evidence was also inconclusive. But if it had? Then the parallels and correspondences became very damning indeed and Wells would be in serious trouble. Aware of this, Ogden and Canby hurriedly conferred at New York's Harvard Club in June with Richards and Leach. There they laboured over the delicate wording needed in a letter they were about to sent to Wells over their several signatures. It read, in part:

We understand that you have already been informed of this action, and have considered it sufficient to deny any personal knowledge of "The Web"; and that the same attitude has been taken by Macmillan's representatives in New York & London. We feel, however, that you should not be allowed to let the legal proceeding attain the serious dimensions now contemplated, without giving the matter full consideration from every angle. If, for instance, you had been misinformed as to whether the MS of "The Web" (or a copy of it) ever left the Toronto office, or if it were possible that some assistant or collaborator failed to acknowledge to you the source of material supplied, a very undeniable situation might arise. We consider the correspondence to be such that in the hands of lawyers an impression could be created which, however little justification it might have, would be much regretted by many of your admirers.

In an apologetic cover letter to Wells, this time written from the Yale Club, Ogden hinted that perhaps the best solution was to have Macmillan publish a revised version of Deeks's book: "An advance royalties payment," he added, "would allow for compromise."[46] If words were gestures, these constituted a friendly nudge and a knowing wink.

Wells misunderstood the intention of the letter, thinking that his friends had decided to "back up Miss Deeks," and he sent Ogden an angry reply. In September, Ogden tried to assure Wells that he and his friends had written the letter in order to draw his attention "to the fact that a *serious* Lawsuit seemed likely to develop."[47] Ogden had warned his friend of this as best and as forcibly as he could.

Florence, meanwhile, pressed on in pursuit of further support from experts. Following advice from Ogden, she contacted Harry Elmer Barnes, the politically progressive and prolific advocate of the American "New History," in Northampton, Massachusetts. Responding to receipt of her comparison of the two texts, he replied, "There certainly seems to be an astonishing similarity." Then he asked for more information about how Wells could have come to use her manuscript. She complied, and the result was a conference between Barnes and Ogden over lunch about the matter and six weeks later a further letter from Barnes. "My fairly thorough examination of your material leads me to this general conclusion, namely, that you have the basis for a perfectly just contention that Mr. Wells or his clerical secretary have seen and made use of your MS. in the preparation of the *Outline of History*."[48]

Barnes had placed himself in an awkward position by being so forthright, for along with his friends James Harvey Robinson and Charles Beard, he was a historian heavily critical of "traditional" political and constitutional history and its Brahmin practitioners in New England and old. In this struggle, the iconoclastic Wells was a helpful ally and Barnes could not afford to alienate him. So Barnes took on the role of academic broker, suggesting that he contact an acquaintance at Andover College – "a moderate critic" of Wells – to examine the two works in greater detail. Later, after explaining his reasons, he wished her the best of luck, suggested a fee of $200 for the Andover historian, and thanked her for the $50 cheque for his own services.[49]

He would come to regret that his involvement with Miss Deeks was purchased at so cheap a price.

11   *Investigations*

"I'm afraid . . . that he's always tried to make history a substitute for life. And, of course, it won't work."

Angus Wilson, *Anglo-Saxon Attitudes* (1956)

Florence and her lawyers had announced their intention to sue H.G. Wells and his publishers in the autumn of 1925, but they did not serve the writs on any of the defendants at that time. As a result, throughout 1926 and most of 1927 public interest in the case waned, helped in part by the stance taken by Wells himself that the case was fraudulent and frivolous and if ignored would go away. There was, however, a good deal of activity behind the scenes.

It is fair to say that without George S. Deeks, his sister's case against Wells would never have arisen, for he was the one who paid the bills. By the 1920s, he was at the peak of his career in engineering, construction, and real estate. An intensely private man, he had quietly supported his sister and her cause since she had first grown suspicious about the origins of Wells's book. He had sent her to his own law firm and had continued to meet requests for money from her.

Yet even he had limits. By 1927, Tilley, Johnston, Thomson & Parmenter had been retained on the case for six years. Reimbursements had also been issued to a number of historical experts.

George's cheque stubs bore the names of G.S. Brett, W.P.M. Kennedy, G.M. Wrong, C.R. Fay, R. Flenley, I.A. Richards, H.S. Canby, H.E. Barnes, L.J. Burpee, B. Windle, and others.

Two years into the legal action, Norman Tilley had still not served the writs on the defendants, possibly because he had not yet uncovered proof of the means by which "The Web" had been secured by Wells. He expected that the case would be won or lost on such evidence. Florence had suspicions based on a chain of circumstances, but he needed proof.

Whether it was George Deeks or Tilley who took the initiative, George stopped his financial support for his sister's lawsuit shortly after returning from a Florida vacation in February or March of 1927. As a consequence, early in May, Tilley, Johnston, Thomson & Parmenter announced its withdrawal from the case. "After full consideration of the facts and circumstances," R.H. Parmenter wrote to George Deeks, "including The Analysis of the two works prepared by Miss Deeks, I am still of the opinion that without conclusive proof that Miss Deeks' manuscript was actually in the hands of Mr. Wells no judge would find in her favour even though the action was undefended by Mr. Wells . . . If notwithstanding what I have said you still desire to proceed with the action I am afraid we shall have to ask you to let us retire from the case."[1]

Parmenter went on to remind George Deeks and his sister how time-consuming and costly any continuation of the case would be. First, there was the difficulty and the expense of examining the defendants and their records in Toronto, New York, and England. This task, in itself, was enormous and expensive. But adequate preparation would also require knowledge of the most arcane of historical details. The Deeks lawyers would need to have at their command nothing less than "a comprehensive study of the whole scope of both works, including the reading and consideration of all available authorities on the historical and other subjects dealt with therein." Life, Parmenter and Tilley may well have concluded, was far too short for them to undertake an informal but advanced course in the history of the world since creation.

Florence was disappointed but undeterred. To her mind the New York publishers had confirmed that, had Wells not produced

The Outline, her "Web" would probably have been published, for there was a definite market for such a book. Now she was on her own, so she immediately contacted Gideon Grant, of the prominent Bay Street firm of Johnston, Grant, Dods & Macdonald. She admitted that her backing for the case was now uncertain, but Grant was sufficiently struck by the woman's obvious sincerity that he agreed to take over the action.

George Deeks had no sooner withdrawn from the case than one of those unlikely Dickensian coincidences took place that supposedly do not happen in "real life." As his sister later put it, almost as if to preserve the mystery, "Just then a friend came to our assistance." Nothing is known of this "friend," except for Florence's use of the pronoun "he." Was the person a member of Bloor Street United Church, her congregation? Is it possible that "he" was not a man at all, but a rich matron of the affluent upper-middle-class district in which the Deeks families lived? Or did Florence's mother or her sisters manage to find the means of further support for her cause?

Was this mysterious benefactor, in fact, an individual at all? Until she became consumed with writing her book and pressing her lawsuit, Florence had been involved in a wide range of activities. If she had been of a mind to mount a private fundraising campaign in support of her cause, she certainly would have had the capacity to do so, for she could draw upon many contacts and – just as important – had access to their addresses. Was such an appeal made, and if so, to whom? The matter remains a mystery.

Somehow, Florence did find the means to press on. Judging by her legal and other correspondence, if she received funding from a single benefactor, it must have come to her episodically and in small amounts, for that is how she paid her bills.[2]

W ells had not really recovered from the sense of drift and ennui noted by others earlier in the decade. In the aftermath of the near-scandal over Hedwig Gatternigg, he had attempted to convince Rebecca West to remain with him. The overture did not work, for she rebuffed his enjoinders. Even so, still "haunted" by her, he said, he continued to write love letters into the second half of 1924. Meanwhile, he spent time with Jane in Paris that spring. Occasionally Rebecca consented to a visit, and Margaret Sanger perked him up somewhat during her tour of England.[3]

It was not enough. Still restless, the dogs of depression nipping at his heels, he announced his intention to take a world tour in late summer. Its first stage was Geneva, not least because it promised a rendezvous with Odette Keun, a woman the fifty-eight-year-old author had not yet met. Born in Constantinople, daughter of a Dutch diplomat and an Italian mother, she had for the past year written him fawning letters that spiralled towards intimacy. In one, she dramatically pleaded with him to "take" her before she died.[4] Given the circumstances of Wells's personal life, he was not of a frame of mind to spurn the attentions of a woman – any woman. And this one, at thirty-six, was ripe.

On Odette's instructions, staff of her Geneva hotel sent Wells up to her room. "She flung herself upon me with protests of adoration," he recalled. "She wanted to give her whole life to me. She wanted nothing but to be of service to me. 'If you feel like *that*,' said I." Odette had turned off the lamp before he entered the bedroom and they coupled without having seen each other at all. "I did not know whether he was a giant or a gnome," she recalled, "but it did not matter."[5]

In the cold light of the days and months that followed, Wells came to see his relationship with Odette as a refuge from his discontent. Jane continued to keep an impeccable house at Easton Glebe, but she had grown distant, had her own circle of friends, and had managed to carve out for herself an existence almost independent of him. He found that he could no longer work there. Rebecca had rejected him, and Margaret was seldom available, so he took shelter with Odette in a rented farmhouse named Lou Bastidon in Provence, near Grasse. "I wanted someone to keep house for me," he said of Odette, "and I wanted a mistress to tranquillize me and companion me. She would be there. She would never come to Paris or London with me or invade my English life."[6]

At first, bathing in the afterglow of having captured such a famous man, Odette Keun behaved in ways that met Wells's approval. But before long, much to his chagrin, "she began to assert herself." Having forgotten her part of the bargain he thought they had made, she took apparent delight in displays of outrageous sexual exhibitionism and words intended to shock those around her. She argued with him. She nagged. "She was," he recalled, "from certain points of view, a thoroughly nasty and detestable person; vain, noisy and weakly outrageous." But, in her "warped" way, Odette was affectionate and she made him laugh. In some respects she met his needs. When he could no longer abide her, he escaped to England; when he was merely bored with her, he could invite Margaret Sanger to visit Grasse. And he did.[7]

During the months after Florence Deeks launched her "literary piracy" suit against him in the fall of 1925, Wells buried himself in his work. His major novel was *The World of William Clissold*, and it occupied much of his time in 1924 and 1925. Published the next year, the two-volume epic, dedicated to Odette Keun ("Self-forgetful friend and helper"), proved to be the lengthiest novel he was to write. In part, it was a revisitation of themes that had informed *The Research Magnificent*, the thinly disguised story of his relationship with Rebecca West, published in 1915; now, he brought the story of his affairs with Rebecca and other women up to date.

The plot was a familiar one: William Clissold, educated at the Royal College of Science, is a successful businessman bent on fame and fortune. After a failed early marriage to Clara, followed by "quite a lot of promiscuous love-making," he finds several years of contentment with a mistress named Sirrie, followed by another called Helen. The former dies, and he eventually quarrels with the latter and they separate. So he flees, first to Geneva to see the League of Nations at work and then to the south of France with Clementina, a woman he has picked up in Paris. At last, in the coddling warmth of Provence, he finds the detachment and peace of mind necessary to engage in the world of thought, and to "define at last the Open Conspiracy that arises in the human will to meet and wrestle with the moulding forces of the universe, that Open Conspiracy to which in the end I believe I shall succeed in correlating all my conscious being."[8]

Define he does, not only the Open Conspiracy (a benign alliance of bankers and industrialists who will rule the world by bypassing legislative democracy) but much else. For the final 250 pages, using Clementina and his brother Richard as foils, William Clissold directly or indirectly informs the world of his considered views on social change, leadership, force and violence, race, education, universities, politics, sex, women, love, and much, much else. Only the death of William and Clementina in an automobile accident staunches the relentless flow of words – and even then not quite. For in the final pages of the 797-page novel, Wells affords Richard an elegy to brother William, allowing their creator the luxury of penning an obituary of himself that was as generous as it was premature.

Wells intended *The World of William Clissold* to be a summing-up of his mature philosophy and the main contours of his life. It was also a settling of personal accounts in ways suitable to his needs. The novel was so patently autobiographical that Wells took the extraordinary measure of writing a seven-page preface denying any truthful resemblance between his life and loves and those of his protagonist. Yet there they were: Isabel as Clara, Catherine as Sirrie, Rebecca as Helen, and Odette as Clementina. And in each case, in this therapeutic recasting of his real life, the major failings were of their making, not his. The portraits Wells drew of the women in his life remained true to their originals in certain traits of character and in some of his attitudes towards them.[9] But he departed from reality in order to explain the end of his relationships, and his inventions were clearly intended to shift the burden of responsibility from him to them.[10]

Oblivious to Wells, but abundantly clear to his readers, his critics, and his biographers, was the fundamental lack of self-awareness Wells exhibited as Clissold. He thought he was demonstrating that he understood his women; but what he created instead was a sustained and painfully obvious essay in self-dramatization. Unconsciously but clearly, he confirmed for others, in the words of the biographers Norman and Jeanne Mackenzie, the "profound truth about his attitude towards the women he desired sexually:

that the search for passion in successive infidelities led him to devalue, and then discard, the women he possessed."[11]

At last, in mid-September 1927, Florence's new legal representatives served writs on both North American branches of Macmillan. "We thought this wretched thing was done with, but I am not worrying," Hugh Eayrs wrote to Sir Frederick Macmillan, informing him that he could expect a visit from Miss Deeks's English lawyers. "The whole thing is a bluff," he assured George Brett in New York. But Brett was not convinced. It was, he replied, "possibly a very serious matter, indeed, and if . . . you are thinking that the present move is a bluff I advise you to remove such an idea at once from your mind . . . Personally I think we shall have to take considerable pains in this matter to make sure that we shall not be beaten in the case." Chastened by this rebuke, Eayrs replied that he had meant only that the Deeks woman was probably after an out-of-court settlement – but this implied that, if true, the "bluff" could be a costly one to the defendants. He might have added, but did not, that it would be perceived as an admission of Wells's guilt. Bluff or not, one thing was now clear: it was essential for the defendants to mount a defence.[12]

Establishing a coherent case for the defence was logistically difficult, since at that point it involved legal firms located in two continents and three countries. Individually, those charged were the Canadian branch of Macmillan and its English parent company, whom the plaintiff accused, respectively, of secretly sending and receiving "The Web"; George Newnes Limited, London publishers of *The Outline* in its initial serialized form; Cassell & Company, publishers of the English edition; and the Macmillan Company, Inc., of New York, publishers of the North American edition. Then there was the peripatetic Wells himself, whose correspondents found him by 1927 variously in London at his flat or at the Reform Club, at Easton Glebe, or wintering on the Continent. That is, when he was not staying in his recently established apartment in Paris.

Beyond the vicissitudes of transatlantic and cross-Channel mail boats, there was the problem of determining just what Wells's defence would be. Finding their client was difficult enough, but pinning his thoughts down on the subject seemed near impossible. His legal advisers found it difficult to obtain any information from him, except that the whole matter was preposterous.

When the suit was first launched in 1925, Wells had sent a "Memorandum of the Case of The Web" to George Brett in New York.

> Either the claim is a genuine but silly claim or it is a blackmail-ing claim based on a faked MS.
>
> In the former case the resemblances of the MS. to the Outline will be due to a common obvious idea and to the use of common sources – which should be easy to establish.
>
> In the latter the MS. has been extensively altered since it was in the hands of Macmillan & Co. This should be proveable by the testimony of the reader or readers of Macmillan & Co. to whom it was submitted in 1918. Our case will be that the Web has been rewritten to substantiate this claim since the appear-ance of the Outline.
>
> In either case Messrs. Macmillan must substantiate that the MS. never left the hands of their representatives in the period during which their responsibility lasted and could not have been seen by Mr. Wells.
>
> Mr. Wells denies having seen such an MS. or being in the least obliged to any report of it. He broached the idea of an Outline of History at a lunch of representative American visi-tors before the end of the War. A history of the origin of the Outline can no doubt be made up from Mr. Wells' letter files, but it would be a tiresome business and he does not propose to do that until he has the statement of the claimant's case and knows what points need refuting.[13]

Wells's memorandum was an outline of possible defence strat-egy, but it was a peculiar declaration of moral outrage for an inno-cent party. Rather than do the obvious – offer his lawyers the original draft of *The Outline* to examine, along with any notes he might have made – he threw the responsibility for demonstrating his innocence instead onto his publishers. It was up to *them* to ensure that no evidence existed that "The Web" had left the possession of Macmillan. Since the officers of the three branches of the company were by no means confident that this was so, they were left with two conclusions: first, that the case, far from being frivolous, was a serious one; second, that if *The Outline* did indeed resemble "The Web," the possibility that the Deeks manuscript had been altered after publication of *The Outline* required investigation. Wells, clearly, had little intention of helping his lawyers clarify the circumstances surrounding his writing of *The Outline*.

The possibility that "The Web" had been revised to resemble *The Outline* was certainly on Sir Frederick Macmillan's mind when he rejected George Brett's assertion that the suit was "possibly of serious consequence." Alteration of "The Web" would explain everything. Wells's solicitor, W. Sanders Fiske of Gedge, Fiske & Gedge, was of similar mind, for he advised Wells that, based on Deeks's vague statement of claim, the whole affair amounted to "an attempt at blackmail."[14]

Because Wells had for the most part been silent on the Deeks affair, except for suggesting that blackmail might be involved, Hugh Eayrs and his lawyers in Toronto decided to initiate their own lines of inquiry. Perhaps Deeks had indeed copied from Wells. Eayrs knew that she had been working on at least one version of her history after *The Outline* had been published.

This trail of assumption inevitably led to the earlier involvement of W.P.M. Kennedy in the preparation of "The Highway of History." Could it be that, as Wells suggested, the entire exercise was some kind of elaborate smokescreen, a way of incorporating elements of *The Outline of History* into a second Deeks manuscript and then somehow slipping them into an altered version of "The Web" as if to suggest they were Florence Deeks's original thoughts?

That this was a very real possibility emerged when Eayrs learned late in 1927 from the sociologist Robert M. MacIver, who had just left the University of Toronto for Columbia University, that Florence had consulted him no fewer than three times about "The Web" and *The Outline*, and that he had advised her to drop the case. Rumour had it that her lawyers had recently declined to continue and that she was going to stop her action. To establish whether this was true, Brett determined to speak with MacIver in New York.[15]

Following his interview with Eayrs, MacIver filed a "Confidential Memorandum" with Macmillan New York. It detailed a discussion he had had with George Wrong in 1925 about W.P.M. Kennedy's involvement in the Deeks affair. The precise details of Kennedy's role remained sketchy, but what had annoyed MacIver most about the involvement of his colleague was that while Kennedy had originally demanded $100 per chapter, it was rumoured that he had eventually managed to extract as much as $15,000 from the woman for the work he had done, in part at his rented summer cottage. Miss Deeks had complained of these "heavy expenditures" for Kennedy's work in her conversation with MacIver. Professor Wrong had been worried after learning these details, since far more money had been involved than any Toronto faculty member, even its president, earned in a year. Should the facts become known, the university community would be outraged at Kennedy's apparent greed.

Not stated in MacIver's memorandum, but clearly implied, was the notion that Kennedy would only have charged such an exorbitant amount if he had been involved in something of great risk to himself and his career. Had the mercurial Irishman become a party to plagiarism? If so, it was important to find out exactly when Kennedy had taken the Deeks manuscript to his cottage. This might determine which manuscript he was working on – "The Highway of History" or "The Web." Or perhaps both at the same time? As Brett put it, rather laboriously, to Eayrs: "Whereas formerly it seemed a perfectly honest and innocent suit it now apparently becomes a plot to rob this and the other companies attacked in this suit not only of their money but of their good name, Miss Deeks evidently relying upon the fact that two manuscripts prepared on the same subject by herself, assisted by Mr. Kennedy, and Mr. Wells on the other hand, must necessarily, the subject being the history of mankind, closely resemble each other in many important particulars as they deal with the same facts throughout."[16]

The publishers thought they had found a serious fault line in the armour of sincerity worn by Miss Deeks. If it could be proven that she and Kennedy had conspired to alter the text of "The Web" after publication of *The Outline*, and in a way that made her manuscript resemble Wells's book, her case would collapse. Perhaps Deeks had copied from Wells! Eayrs and Brett agreed that if discreet inquiries "were made in the proper quarters by a man of the right calibre" they might learn more about Kennedy's involvement. The question was, Just who should this person be? The obvious choice to put pressure on Kennedy was Sir Robert Falconer, the Presbyterian minister, professor of theology, and president of the University of Toronto since 1907. But Wrong had compromised Falconer on this matter a few years earlier, when, in confidence, he had expressed his worries about the large sums Kennedy was charging for his off-campus services. To involve Falconer now, it was thought, would involve the betrayal of that earlier confidence.

Eayrs therefore sought the advice of the librarian of the University of Toronto, W. Stewart Wallace, and asked him whether it was wise to consult the president, "the idea being that Sir Robert might inform Kennedy of his knowledge of the transaction and considering it somewhat unsavoury from the standpoint of the University bring pressure to bear on Miss Deeks through Kennedy."[17] Perhaps, subjected to such pressure, Kennedy would admit the true nature of his involvement.

The whole business was singularly confusing, with not one Deeks manuscript now to worry about, but two. It was, as Eayrs wrote to his lawyer, "of utmost importance that we differentiate between the original manuscript Miss Deeks submitted to this Company, and the latter manuscript which has been revised by Professor Kennedy. How are we to know which manuscript is put in by this woman for examination, that is to say, how can we be sure that the *original* manuscript is the one put in?" The only way, it seemed to Eayrs, was to make the culprits somehow reveal their duplicity.[18]

Brett was receptive to the idea but warned Eayrs that "it would be a great misfortune indeed if Miss Deeks and her lawyers were to ascertain the amount and the kind of information we have already obtained . . . and which I am hoping you will be able greatly to enlarge in detail."[19] By this time, an agent employed by the defence had interviewed the owner of the cottage Kennedy had rented at Kincardine in the mid-Twenties, and knew the rough dates and exact amount of rent he had paid. Two hundred and fifty dollars for the summer season. Probably in 1924.[20]

Hugh Eayrs eventually decided that he would let the decision about Falconer's involvement rest with Macmillan's lawyer W.W. McLaughlin, who had taken over the file from his colleague Johnston.[21] But the documentary record does not reveal what happened next. The letters of Falconer, Wrong, and Kennedy in the University of Toronto Archives are silent on the matter, as are the publishers' records, but this is not surprising since such a delicate combination of academic diplomacy and espionage was the kind of business usually conducted in senior common rooms or private clubs.

What can be said is that Falconer would not have been surprised had he received a polite note from Wrong or someone else in the university asking him to do something about Kennedy's behaviour, for the Irish scholar had been the problem child of the history department for many years. Not much time had passed, in fact, since Wrong had complained to his president of Kennedy's lack of sanity.[22]

Whatever was done, if anything, the stratagem did not work. The defendants gleaned nothing further about the relationship between "The Web" and "The Highway of History" before the trial took place. By then it did not matter, for all the while "The Web" remained in its original and unrevised state on Farnham Avenue. But by writing "The Highway," Florence Deeks had inadvertently thrown an awfully large red herring onto the path of the defence.

T he year 1927 was H.G. Wells's *annus horribilis*. He felt assaulted by a world that did not understand him. *Clissold* had been a critical failure, doubly damned. The preface in which he insisted that the novel was not autobiographical had been dismissed as disingenuous, while the tenderness with which he had intended to enfold the story of his loves had endeared him to no one. Few were enthusiastic about his idea of the Open Conspiracy that alone, he believed, could usher in a new world order of peace, prosperity, and progress. D.H. Lawrence described the book as a "mouse's nest," while Bernard Shaw condemned it as not a novel at all, but a blend of history and sociology. "Clissoldism" had become in public parlance a term of ridicule, a word for the pretentious meddling of any busybody who sets out to reshape the world according to a blueprint of his own making. The novel had even inspired a parody, in H.A.M. Thomson's *The World of Billiam Wissold*.[23]

While his friend Shaw told him that, in publishing *Clissold*, it was as if Wells had returned to writing *The Outline of History*,[24] his masterpiece had itself come under severe attack. The previous year, Hilaire Belloc, the brilliant but cantankerous champion of a revitalized but nostalgic Roman Catholicism, had subjected *The Outline* to venomous scorn. Few could command the English language like Belloc, and he put his talent to extraordinary use in a series of articles denouncing Wells's history for its treatment of the Catholic religion and much else. The book was "provincial," Belloc wrote. "A schoolboy ought to know better than to write this." "So much for the book," he concluded. "It will have a prodigious vogue in its own world and an early grave."[25]

As painful to Wells as the harsh and personal criticism itself was Fleet Street's lack of interest in publishing his rebuttals to Belloc. He was vexed by the refusal of the Catholic weekly the *Universe* to print his response to Belloc's articles, even when he offered it free of charge. That the English daily press did not find his views to be newsworthy was even more troubling. It was an implicit assault on the public persona he had constructed for himself.

Against the advice of friends and acquaintances, whether Arnold Bennett or G.K. Chesterton, Wells entered the verbal fray after Belloc published his articles in book form as *A Companion to Mr. Wells's Outline of History*. Almost lost in the din of controversy that surrounded the acrimonious exchange of insults between Belloc and Wells was Chesterton's response to *The Outline*, published at the end of September 1925. Much more restrained and dignified in tone than Belloc's polemic, *The Everlasting Man* was Chesterton's own *Outline of History*, a Roman Catholic indictment of "the rationalist treatment of history" on which secular historical scholarship and scientific speculation were based. It was to become Chesterton's neglected classic.[26]

Belloc relished a good war of words; Wells, congenitally defensive, was not temperamentally suited to wage one. Nevertheless, his tract *Mr. Belloc Objects to "The Outline of History"* appeared in 1926. The exchange of argument and insult did little to enhance Wells's reputation. Belloc stood on the foundation laid by Aquinas; Wells on that of Darwin and Huxley. But even on such familiar ground, H.G. ran into trouble. When he challenged Belloc to uncover any contradiction in *The Outline*, Belloc delighted in noting that at one point Wells had stated that paleolithic man "did not know of the bow." Yet there before him, "in Mr. Wells's own book, were reproductions of cave paintings, with the bow and arrow appearing all over them."[27]

Wells gradually retreated, although Belloc continued his relentless attack, with mounting sarcasm, on the inadequate scientific foundations of *The Outline* and its author's lack of acquaintance with up-to-date scholarship. The vituperative dispute immediately became the stuff of literary legend. One story had it that the two enemies encountered each other at the Reform Club shortly after Belloc had declared victory to be his. "Still looking for Neanderthal Man, H.G.?" asked Belloc. "No – Woman," the prophet is said to have replied. [28]

When the secretary of the Cassell publishing company wrote to H.G. Wells on September 23, 1927, to inform him that his firm had just been served with a writ "in the case of Miss F.A. Deeks v. Wells, Macmillan, Newnes and Cassell," the author was not disposed to pay it much attention. The war with Belloc and the reception of *Clissold* remained on his mind. Neither the substantial and highly favourable review of the novel secured by Sir Richard Gregory for *Nature*, nor the way the editor had rallied his journal in support of Wells in the dispute with Belloc over history, had improved H.G.'s mood.[29] Wells was preoccupied for a more painful reason than these. Jane was dying, and her husband had all but predicted it.

In the final pages of the account of William Clissold's relationship with Sirrie Evans, Sirrie finally succumbs to tuberculosis. Devoted William is with her to the very end. "A tired, flimsy, pitiful frame she had become, something that one just took care of and treated very gently," the novelist had written. "Her motionless eyelashes touched my cheek, and she passed away so softly that until, with a start, I noted her coldness, I did not suspect that she was dead."[30]

The account, ever so tender, was sadly prophetic in more ways than this, for the novelist had inadvertently given two different years of Sirrie's death, 1905 and 1908.[31] It was as if the true date remained to be filled in, and to the extent that Sirrie was Jane – both were devoted gardeners, voracious readers of novels, and passionate travellers – the year might just as well have been 1927. For in April 1927, shortly after the wedding of their son George to Marjorie Craig, Catherine consulted a surgeon about severe abdominal pains. Wells had already returned to his recently constructed villa – Lou Pidou – in Provence, to be with Odette.

While H.G. was there, Catherine underwent exploratory surgery. The result was the worst possible: a diagnosis of advanced and inoperable cancer. She had at most only months to live. Wells received the news from his son Frank. Writing from his French retreat, he was now all love and tenderness. Genuinely concerned, yet forced to play the role of Clissold in real life, he wrote to Jane: "My dear, I love you much more than I have loved anyone else in the world & I am coming back to you to take care of you & to do all I can to make you happy." Only now did the terms of endearment of the early years return to him: "My dear, my dear, my dearest heart is yours. Your loving Bins."[32] The precious words came far too late.

He returned to Easton Glebe to play his part in the final real-life chapter, the doting husband constantly at his wife's side – except for the trip he made each month to spend two days at Lou Pidou. Friends such as Charlotte Shaw and Arnold Bennett wrote letters, offering him the support they thought he needed and his ailing wife the attention they had not always previously been mindful to furnish. Wells was without question deeply distraught, but there was an element in him that relished the pathos. He would not attend the World Population Conference in Geneva, he wrote to Margaret Sanger, because "my little wife has to die of cancer & I want to spend what time remains of her life with her."[33]

Catherine Wells died early in the evening of October 6, 1927, her husband at her side. She was cremated at Golders Green,

London's crematorium, a few days later. A memorial service followed, attended by many friends. Lent a book of stock funeral addresses, Wells had altered the eulogy, bit by bit, constantly finding "some new way of fitting it more closely to this special occasion," until it became "almost entirely a personal testimony."[34] "The best and sweetest of her," the eulogist told the sombre gathering, in words penned by the grieving husband, "is known only to one or two of us: subtle and secret, it can never be told. Faithful, gentle, wise, and self-forgetful, she upheld another who mourns her here to-day: to him she gave her heart and her youth and the best of her brave life . . . She was a noble wife, a happy mother, and the maker of a free and kindly and hospitable home . . . She could forgive ingratitude and bore no resentment for a slight . . . She was a fountain of pity and mercy, except to herself."[35]

The Shaws were present when these words were read next to the coffin, with the furnace of the crematorium in plain sight. Charlotte Shaw was appalled at what she witnessed, and said so in a letter to T.E. Lawrence.

It was dreadful – dreadful – *dreadful*! I haven't been so upset . . . for a long time . . . The organ began a terrible dirge. We all stood up – and stood for what seemed hours and hours . . . while that organ played on our nerves and sense and knocked them to pieces. H.G. began to cry like a child – tried to hide it at first and then let go. After centuries of torment the organist stopped . . . and we all sat down and pseudo-Balfour [the classicist T.E. Page] began to read a paper, written, as he told us, by Wells. It was terrible beyond anything words can describe; a soul in torment – self torture. He drowned us in a sea of misery and as we were gasping began a panegyric of Jane which made her appear as a delicate, flower-like, gentle being, surrounding itself with beauty, and philanthropy and love. Now Jane was one of the strongest characters I ever met. She managed H.G. and her good curious sons and her circle generally according to her own very definite and very original theories – with almost unbroken success – *from the point of view of her theories*. Then there came a place where the address said "she never resented a

slight; she never gave voice to a harsh judgment." At that point
the audience, all more or less acquainted with many details of
H.G.'s private life, thrilled, like corn under a wet north wind –
and H.G. – H.G. positively howled. You are no doubt aware that
he was not a conventionally perfect husband . . . O it was
hideous – terrible and frightful. I am an old woman and there is
one thing I seem, at least, to have learned. The way of trans-
gressors is hard.

As the biographers of Wells who quote this passage add, with an
acid of understatement infusing otherwise innocent words: "A few
days later H.G. left for Paris, and by November he had again established himself at Lou Pidou."[36]

Words uttered at a funeral had by no means met Wells's need to
address the meaning of his wife. Safe again in his sunny French
villa, he set about writing a memoir of his life with her. It was published by Chatto and Windus in 1928, as a forty-four-page "introduction by her husband H.G. Wells" to a collection of Catherine's
little-known short stories and poetry. He chose to call it *The Book
of Catherine Wells*. After thirty years or more as Jane, she had at
last regained her rightful name. Wells had already written the
deathbed scene, in *Clissold*, but, undeterred, he found fresh words
to convey the real-life setting: "She spoke no more, she became a
breathing body from which all token of recognition had departed,
and an hour or so later, with her unresponsive hand in mine, she
ceased to breathe."[37]

Biographers and critics have often commented on the husband's
portrait of his dead wife, but they have said little about the wife
herself. Seldom have they dwelt on the ways in which her stories
and poems may have reflected her thoughts and feelings. If words
are any measure of their interest, those who have read and commented on the book seldom penetrated beyond page 44. The identity of Mrs. H.G. Wells became of fixed construction the moment
her husband penned his introductory declamations about Jane,
"the tangible Catherine," the woman who "made decisions freely,
while Catherine herself stayed in the background aloof."[38]
Catherine Wells has remained, for subsequent observers, this mute

voice and this fixed image. The collection of her writing bore her name, but nowhere on its title page was she designated as its author. Instead, she became the long-suffering and compliant wife of literary legend, still silent and in the background.

B y the autumn of 1927 everything about the case seemed to lead to unceasing frustration, delay, and expense. As they waited for Florence Deeks to provide them with a copy of her list of parallel passages, the Macmillan lawyers decided to see whether they could gain access to the reports Windle and Burpee had prepared for her. Hugh Eayrs and George Brett had learned that J.F. McCormick, editor of the New York-based Catholic journal the *Commonweal*, had once discussed the Deeks case with Sir Bertram Windle. The two Roman Catholic scholars shared a deep disdain for Wells and all he represented, so the publishers convinced McCormick to write a seemingly innocuous "fishing letter" to his fellow Catholic. Brett's assistant, Curtis Hitchcock, reported to Eayrs that if he got a promising response he would convince McCormick to "run up to Toronto" to see Sir Bertram – and with any luck return with a copy of his report.[39]

McCormick's letter to Sir Bertram was penned on the day Catherine Wells died. In it, he reminded his colleague of their discussion of the Deeks manuscript over lunch a year or so back, and noted in passing that he had recently learned from Macmillan that it was involved in a lawsuit involving H.G. Wells. For the rest, McCormick feigned forgetfulness. "When I learned this, I mentioned the fact that you had said something to me about this manuscript, but it so happens that I had almost entirely forgotten the incident. The details, of course, had left my mind completely, but whether you said there was a 'deadly parallel' or just the opposite I cannot remember. They, of course, are very anxious to find out what your reaction was . . . If you do not mind, I wish you would let me have for my own personal information a summary of what you told me that day regarding the manuscript."[40]

Sir Bertram marked his reply "private and confidential," for he was wary. He reminded McCormick that the discussions between

Miss Deeks, himself, and her lawyers were "of a private nature." That said, he was willing to tell McCormick what happened provided the details not be used other than in conversation with the gentlemen McCormick mentioned. He noted that he had undertaken the task of comparing the Deeks manuscript and the Wells book with great reluctance. "But I was pressed and offered a fee which I could not afford to refuse and did so. It was the weariest job of my life for though I did not have to correct or even point out mistakes I was sick to death of Wells and his grossly over rated book before I had done with it." Sir Bertram had made his report, but had heard nothing; that was the only reason he had been willing to discuss the matter with McCormick. Then, when the case revived, he had expressed his willingness to testify in court if his view was deemed "worth expressing." He had not used the phrase "deadly parallel" in his report, he said, so he could not have used it in their conversation. When he had last heard from Miss Deeks's lawyer – "some months ago" – the case was apparently not going to proceed.[41]

Sir Bertram Windle's cautious letter provided the defence with nothing of value to its case, and it was obvious that its author was not going to do so. "Evidently we should have a good deal of trouble in persuading Windle to let us see the report," Brett's assistant told Eayrs, "and Mr. Brett feels on the whole that it would be wiser not to make any more efforts in this direction for the present." Eayrs agreed, but meanwhile he had found out a little about the report. "It is reiterated to me by Saul and Watson (the former being at one time the Editor of this Company, and the latter being the Manager here for Thomas Nelson's and Sons) that Windle's report is overwhelmingly favourable to this woman's claim, although both these gentlemen take pains to add that it goes into little or no detail. Sir Bertram's anti-Wells bias is, of course, well known."[42]

Sidney Watson, to whom Saul had confided about the report, frequently played golf with the editor from Gage. This was not to be the only important secret Saul and he would share concerning the Deeks affair.

The defence did not pursue Sir Bertram further, much to his relief, for the aging scholar had heard more than enough about

Deeks and Wells. His involvement, he had told McCormick, had given him "far more trouble than it was worth." He had hoped not to testify, and he would be granted his wish. In 1929, at the age of seventy-one, he died. The case of *Deeks v. Wells* threatened to become the Canadian equivalent of *Jarndyce v. Jarndyce*, the lawsuit in Dickens's *Bleak House* that went on so long that its expenses consumed the inheritance at stake in the first place. Miss Deeks's action against H.G. Wells had a long way to go yet before it could reach the courts, and she now needed to find another expert to take Sir Bertram's place.

Eayrs, meanwhile, had discovered that one of Deeks's experts had been his "old friend" Lawrence J. Burpee, and he reported to Brett his amazement. How, he wondered, could someone as eminent as Burpee arrive at "an opinion favourable to her views"? Burpee's explanation, said Eayrs, was that "Miss Deeks wrote to him and assured him that the manuscript had been passed to Mr. Wells, and taking her assurance at face value he then compared her parallel passages and constructive similarities. He said that he did think there were here and there marked similarities between THE WEB and THE OUTLINE OF HISTORY." Eayrs risked straining his friendship by writing to Burpee in Ottawa, asking him for loan of his report and his correspondence with Deeks. Burpee agreed to do so, but only because, as Eayrs told his lawyer, "I have stormed him until he did." As with the intelligence McCormick had gleaned from Sir Bertram, the material was to remain strictly confidential.[43]

Eayrs had been able to understand Sir Bertram's willingness to take the side of Deeks. He knew that almost everything Wells represented, as novelist and historian, and in his personal life, was repugnant to faithful Roman Catholics. And Eayrs well remembered the acrimonious dispute a few years earlier between Wells and Belloc. Sir Bertram, it might be claimed, had used his assessment of "The Web" as a means of declaring his devotion to Roman Catholicism.

Burpee's involvement, however, worried him, for he had no religious or ideological axe to grind. He also held a substantial reputation as one of Canada's foremost and most popular historians and men of letters. He had published with Musson, Newnes, Ryerson, Lane, and Morang. The latter had been absorbed by

Macmillan in 1912, so, in a way, Burpee was a Macmillan author. Clearly, anything he might say on behalf of her case would carry the weight of great authority. Surely he would not risk damaging his reputation by appearing in court on behalf of a case he thought was lacking in substance?

Eayrs sent the Burpee report and correspondence to W.W. McLaughlin and to Brett in New York. Brett read it, and concluded that Burpee had found resemblances between the two works only because he had been preconditioned to find them when led to understand that the Deeks manuscript had been sent to Wells. Once again, the defendants agreed that the fate of the case would hang on the whereabouts of "The Web."[44] And that meant pinning down John Saul's story.

12   *Delays and Discoveries*

> "I think all you historians are frauds really . . . No more fiction for me now, historical or otherwise, just dreary old fact."
>
> "You are lucky . . . to be able to distinguish between them."
>
> Angus Wilson, *Anglo-Saxon Attitudes* (1956)

FROM THE OUTSET OF THE CASE, John C. Saul's precise role in it was a mystery. No one perpetuated the intrigue surrounding it more than Saul himself. About the only matter all the litigants agreed upon was that when Florence Deeks had stepped into the Toronto offices of Macmillan of Canada in late July 1918, Saul was the editor to whom she spoke and to whom she submitted her manuscript – and by the time she retrieved it in early April 1919, Saul was gone. As the editor responsible for the manuscript, Saul, more than anyone else, should have had direct knowledge of the whereabouts of "The Web" during the crucial months when it had been in Macmillan's possession.

But did he? Hugh Eayrs and his co-defendants could not have been reassured by Saul's mercurial memory. In October 1925, just after Florence Deeks announced her intention to sue Wells, Eayrs had asked him what he had done with "The Web." Saul had told him he had sent it to New York; then he said he thought it had been "forwarded to England." In October 1927, Eayrs had what he called "a long chat" with Saul, and took along correspondence from the office files. Eayrs reported his gleanings to Brett in New York. Saul had changed his mind again. "He is now quite sure in his own mind that the Deeks manuscript was never sent to England, or to you, and indeed, so far as he knew, it did not leave this office."[1]

Saul could scarcely have forgotten the part he had played. Over the years since his departure from Macmillan, Florence and Mabel had visited him, by his own count, no fewer than twenty-five times. It was too much to say that he and his wife had become friends with the Deeks sisters, but by the spring of 1927 their attitude appeared supportive enough that Florence gave him part of her comparison to look over. "A few days later," Florence recalled, "my sister and I were talking to him and I said 'What do you think of the similarities?' He replied 'I think you have your case all right.'" For Florence, this was tantamount to "a positive admission that he had sent the Ms. to England and, further, that he considered the similarities sufficient to win the case."[2]

Twice in 1927, Deeks's lawyer, Gideon Grant, had approached Saul about the same question, and his response had been that he "could not remember either one way or the other." Once his erratic memory was jogged by the conversations he had had with the woman in his own study, however, Saul sent Eayrs a mixed message. On the one hand, he said that the office correspondence assured him the case would fail because "proof that the manuscript was sent from this House is lacking." But on the other, he mentioned "that there is one paragraph precisely the same in The Web and The Outline, excepting that the introductory sentence in the one case is the closing sentence in the other; but for that the paragraph, which is a long one, is precisely the same."[3] This did not bolster Eayrs's confidence.

Saul gave Eayrs this ambiguous reassurance on October 12, 1927, but he continued to tell different tales to different people. In the spring of 1928, George Brett informed Wells, "[Saul] tells us that he may possibly have suggested . . . that he might send the manuscript to New York but that he is perfectly sure it never was done."[4] By the autumn, Saul was just as certain he had said and done something else. He suddenly recalled telling Florence Deeks in 1918 that he would probably take the manuscript on his next sales trip to the

Canadian west. He was now certain he had carried it with him the whole time, from the second week of August to nearly the end of October 1918. "He is positive of this," wrote Eayrs to Brett. "He may also have had it when he was in Quebec in November, but of this he is not sure; however, of the months of August, September and October he is sure. This, of course, limits the time of the manuscript's actual lying in the vault of this office, and also, limits the time of availability of sending the manuscript out of the office."[5] Several weeks later, however, Saul had still not committed his latest story to paper, and only after Eayrs badgered him to submit a memorandum about his dealings with Florence Deeks did he send one, late in 1928, to Eayrs's lawyer, W.W. McLaughlin.[6]

John Saul was not the only person who had come to regret his earlier recollections concerning "The Web." By the spring of 1928, Harry Elmer Barnes in New York also had a good deal to worry about. To begin with, for the past year he had been heavily criticized for his scathing ad hominem attack on the University of Chicago historian Bernadotte Schmidt over Schmidt's views on the Great War. In making his accusations, Barnes had clearly transgressed the tacit code of civility that still held sway within the academic guild. As the brilliant Cornell historian Carl Becker put it, such "an exhibition of extremely bad manners" was simply unacceptable. Even Barnes's very good friend and mentor, the historian Preserved Smith, chastised him for being "discourteous" and indulging in "personalities."[7]

Barnes had very nearly done irreparable damage to his reputation, and needed to avoid further controversy – at least for the time being. But just then he received a letter from H.G. Wells, his ally in the progressive cause. The English author asked him to find out about "the manoeuvres of Miss Deeks." Barnes could scarcely have forgotten his own involvement with Miss Deeks, particularly the strong words he had used. Not only had he mentioned the "astonishing similarity" between "The Web" and *The Outline*, but even worse, in a later letter he had told her she had a "perfectly just contention" that either Wells or his secretary, or both, had "seen and made use" of "The Web." In the late winter and spring of 1928, Barnes lived in fear that the Deeks case would reach trial, that his correspondence would surface, and that he would therefore bring down upon himself the considerable wrath of Wells and his friends.

The result was a frantic exchange of letters. Early in 1927 Barnes had suggested to Florence that she might contact Hugh Keenleyside of the University of British Columbia ("a very reliable historian") as a possible expert witness against Wells. A year later, Barnes wrote to Keenleyside to ask what was happening. "I have just received from H.G. Wells a letter expressing some curiosity about the manoeuvres of Miss Deeks. Can you tell me what she is up to? Did she start suit? If she is quoting me I could start a counter suit as she promised me that nothing I said to her would be used in the case, but would be highly confidential." Keenleyside, to whom Florence Deeks had apparently not written, forwarded Barnes's request to Eayrs in Toronto. Meanwhile, Barnes contacted Florence, insisting that his earlier correspondence and views remain strictly confidential; then he replied to Wells about the state of the Deeks case, saying he did not know what stage it had reached but, understandably, maintaining silence about his own involvement.[8]

The entirely typical transatlantic merry-go-round of the mails increased in speed. Wells wrote to his solicitor, Fiske, then to Curtis Hitchcock of Macmillan in New York; Hitchcock wrote to both Eayrs and his lawyer, W.W. McLaughlin; McLaughlin wrote to Eayrs; Eayrs replied in letters to Hitchcock and to his boss, George Brett.

The carousel continued, but with little gained. The two North American branches of Macmillan agreed that it might be wise for someone to speak to Barnes. "We are inclined to think," wrote Hitchcock to Eayrs, "that it may be worth while having a talk with him to get his point of view and whatever facts he may care to give us about his relations with Miss Deeks." Eayrs replied: "You are very wise in seeing Barnes. It may be that there is some point you can get as to Miss Deeks, which has not turned up yet. Barnes is a very approachable fellow: he is a great friend of Alfred Knopf's. I met him once at a luncheon if I remember correctly." Three months later, Hitchcock reported to Eayrs that he had at last spoken to Barnes, but that he had nothing significant to add to their case. Florence Deeks's original letter to Barnes had apparently contained "a rather full explanation of this case from her point of view," but Barnes had managed to misplace it.[9]

Lawyers for both sides faced imminent examinations for discovery, the presentation of witness statements for possible use at trial, and hurriedly made what preparations they could. By January 1928, representatives of Wells and the publishers had been given a mimeographed copy of Miss Deeks's list of passages from "The Web" and *The Outline*, which acquired the title "Comparison" for purposes of the lawsuit, and had begun to study it; but since Wells had not yet filed a defence, their clients – Eayrs of Macmillan in Toronto among them – complained among themselves that the author's silence meant that little progress could be made.[10] After discovering from Wells's Toronto representatives – the well-known Ontario firm of McCarthy & McCarthy – that Wells had still not established his defence, W.W. McLaughlin informed his client Eayrs in exasperation on February 28 that "his principals in London have difficulty in persuading Mr. Wells to treat the matter with the seriousness it deserves." Even McCarthy & McCarthy did not wish to proceed until they had "better information from Mr. Wells."[11]

Eayrs conveyed McLaughlin's concern to Sir Frederick the next day. A few weeks earlier, while in London, the Canadian publisher had met with Sir Frederick and Sir Richard Gregory, who had recounted his close friendship with Wells since their schooldays together. Privately, Eayrs urged Sir Frederick to see whether he could get Sir Richard to convince his friend "that he ought to take this matter seriously, and do what his lawyers think necessary to get it cleared up." Not, he added, that there was "anything serious in this woman's plan" – just that "she is herself taking it seriously, and it has got to be disposed of."[12] Under pressure from both sides, Wells's own solicitor, W. Sanders Fiske, urged him to cooperate. "I should very much like to see you . . . as adequate preparations must be made for your Defence," such as the possible selection of an expert witness. Besides, all parties were complaining about the "heavy costs and expenses which have been and which may be incurred."[13]

More than two years after Florence Deeks announced her intention to sue H.G. Wells, his legal advisers had still not determined the circumstances surrounding the writing of *The Outline of History*. Incredibly, they possessed no confidential statement, no copies of correspondence with historical advisers for the book, no copies of Wells's plans for the organization of it, nor a sample of its manuscript pages. In mid-March 1928, after a telephone conversation between them, Fiske sent Wells a bundle of papers prepared by their legal team on the other side of the Atlantic. He also advised Wells to make an affidavit "showing what documents relating to the matter are in your possession," as well as any relevant correspondence concerning arrangements for publication of *The Outline*. "If you have the original MS. in your possession still," he added, "that ought probably to be disclosed."[14]

No doubt Wells found the requests for details about his writing of *The Outline of History* bothersome, but he could no longer delay helping his solicitors and co-defendants establish a defence. After all, their liability rested largely on the nature of his own earlier actions. But instead of providing Brett with a statement about how he came to write *The Outline*, Wells asked questions the answers to which would flesh out the line of defence he had suggested in 1925. What evidence was there that "The Web" had left Toronto? Could Miss Deeks's assertion that he had "made extensive thefts from it," or that he had possessed it, be disproved? "I deny having heard of or seen her MS. How far can we dispose of the necessary preliminary story?" Was it not possible, he wrote, that the 1918 version of "The Web" had been "written, doctored, changed or expanded" subsequently to resemble *The Outline* since its publication in 1920? If so, could this be proven?[15] Instead of providing a straightforward declaration of his innocence and a means of establishing it, he chose to point the finger of accusation at the woman who had come to plague him.

The case for the defence thus existed in a state of confusion. Wells's London solicitors had written to Eayrs, asking him whether and when Macmillan in Toronto had sent "The Web" to Macmillan in London. In a state of complete uncertainty about the whereabouts of the Deeks manuscript, they found themselves continuing to inquire "whether the MS. of 'The Web' was either in our possession or in the possession of Macmillans of London at the same time as the MS. of 'The Outline of History.' " Was there "any possibility," they asked, "of any part of 'The Web' having been seen" by Wells "or referred to by Macmillan of Canada when writing to him?"[16]

That Wells's solicitors felt obliged to ask whether their own client had seen "The Web" is understandable. What was strange was why the author asked whether his New York publisher or his solicitors had proof he had not made "extensive thefts" from "The Web," when the only person who could definitively answer the question was Wells himself. If he was telling the truth and could demonstrate that the idea for *The Outline* was his alone, and if he had the notes and manuscript to prove it, did the whereabouts of "The Web" really matter? His advisers remained puzzled at the evasiveness of their client.

As late as mid-April 1928, the Toronto lawyers for the defence were still "quite convinced" among themselves that Wells did not "regard the action very seriously." This worried them, since Miss Deeks, they knew, was "quite in earnest in her claim" and somehow still possessed the financial means to "carry it through to a finish." Lawyers for the defence expressed their confidence that she would not be able to prove that her manuscript had ever left Toronto or that Wells had used it, although given the questions Wells was asking they may have wondered how honest his denials were. They were clearly troubled about Deeks's claim that "the great body of 'The Outline of History' [was] very similar in construction, thought and language to her own manuscript." Much would therefore depend on how much information Wells provided about the sources he had used. "The evidence we will require," the Macmillan lawyer in Toronto wrote to Macmillan in New York, "will be whatever evidence Mr. Wells is able to give us that will prove that the language or idea was not obtained from Miss Deeks's manuscript." Any neglect in preparation of the evidence on Wells's part, he added, would be "a great mistake."[17]

The defendants also had great difficulty obtaining an affidavit from Wells, an essential element in the construction of their case. Only after Eayrs wrote to Sir Frederick Macmillan, asking him to get Newman Flower of Cassell to pressure Wells to file an affidavit, did the author take any action. Finally, it seemed, Wells had come to accept the necessity for cooperation. "It is a tiresome business," he wrote to Brett in mid-March of 1928, "but I suppose it is better to be bothered now than run the risk of being skinned." Florence's lawyers received his affidavit, along with one from Sir Frank Newnes, towards the end of May, and by June 19 they had received statements from all of the defendants.[18] It was not until August, however, that Wells allowed the original draft manuscript of *The Outline of History* to leave England for examination by the plaintiff in Toronto, and then only after she obtained a court order that compelled him to do so.[19]

All the delay on a case that seemed to be getting nowhere merely added to Wells's legal expenses, and his London solicitor was more than a little annoyed at the inability of the author's Canadian law firm, McCarthy & McCarthy, to move the case along. "Little progress is being made on the other side with the action," Fiske wrote to Wells. "I think it very unlikely it will be heard before the autumn."

Within the month, Fiske had had enough, and his exasperation was transparent. "I find it almost impossible to work with Messrs. McCarthy & McCarthy," he fumed from London in late July. "The one idea firmly fixed in their brains is to extort money on account of costs from us, and nearly every letter of theirs refers to this question of remittances for costs." The firms representing Cassell and Newnes, he added, shared the same opinion. "They were highly recommended in the first instance, but they give us no real assistance, and although I have months ago asked them – as they say they think seriously of the case in some of its aspects – to point out anything in the 'Comparison' in which they can suggest a breach of copyright, they have always failed to do this, and they write in such general terms, and so indefinitely that one does not know where one is . . . I do not like swapping horses, etc., but I do think that McCarthy & McCarthy are not good to us." Fiske suggested that they be replaced by another reputable Toronto law firm – Elliott, Hume, McKague & Anger. Wells agreed. By the end of September the primary defendant, like the plaintiff, had changed lawyers.[20]

Real progress at last. Florence and her representatives had sought for some time to examine the original manuscript of *The Outline of History* as well as the notes on which it was based. Eventually, and with some fanfare generated by the $100,000 insurance value its author placed on it, the precious manuscript arrived in Toronto.[21] It was August 1928.

Notebooks in hand, Florence and Mabel made their way to Osgoode Hall, the chambers of the Law Society of Upper Canada, where the original version of *The Outline* had been placed under protection of the courts. This was Florence Deeks's first tangible contact with her literary enemy, and she remembered the experience well.

They arrived, and were delivered to Osgood [*sic*] Hall. There in a comfortable little room my sister and I were established to examine them – practically under the eye of various clerks and officials. The notes formed a large parcel, and when Mr. Smiley [*sic*; Percy Smily, one of Florence's lawyers] opened them he warned me to be careful not to overlook anything that might be of importance. I assured him that I would exercise the utmost care, and when he departed I set to work.

Those notes were a great mixture. To me they seemed to be adroitly selected. Some were hand-written, but the majority were typed. In general the wording was the same as the published text of "The Outline" but at times I would come across a passage, colourably altered, or a key word, phrase, clause, or part of a sentence or a mistake which was identical in wording with "The Web," and which was changed in the published text of "The Outline." This, to me, seemed positive proof that Mr. Wells had copied "The Web." I made careful note of those passages and later I attached copies of them, as a third column, to the list of similarities between "The Web," and "The Outline" as "Mr. Wells' original notes." . . . Days were consumed in the examination of those notes.[22]

The more Florence examined Wells's manuscript, the more verbal resemblances she found. Other clues added to the suspicion and mistrust the two sisters now shared.

Many years after the case was over, Mabel felt compelled to put her own view of the case on paper. Exactly why she did so is not certain, but judging by the general appearance and tone of the neatly typed twenty-six-page account she left behind, she wrote it after Florence's death as a kind of final reckoning of the affair that had forever changed their lives. The document is unsigned, undated, and without a title. "These few 'links in a chain,'" it begins, "is an authentic story as it is first hand knowledge, and a true legal story." At one point in this testament, Mabel recalls a significant discovery:

> My sister and I went to Osgoode Hall every morning and spent the day until she had finished with the reading. Towards the end of that manuscript she found a small slip or piece of paper on which was written a note by Professor Ernest Barker, of Oxford University, and a noted authority on history, correcting a mistake which Mr. Wells had copied from the original manuscript of "The Web" (then in possession of the MacMillan Company of London) and which apparently Mr. Wells had evidently been in too great a hurry to correct. According to Coppinger [*sic*; Copinger] and other authorities on copyright law, one mistake is a positive proof of copying. But there were others.[23]

With Mabel's concurrence, Florence decided that the matter should be pursued further in the proceedings for discovery and at the trial itself. Meanwhile, she continued doggedly in her examination of *The Outline* and its notes while Mabel sat at her side. It was not much of a phalanx, just two women well into middle age. The classical architecture of Osgoode Hall and the rows of imposing portraits of important jurists within it had been known to intimidate the most self-confident of men.

A fine line exists between dedication and obsession. Florence Deeks was certainly coming to be possessed by her cause, and those associated with the defence side came to see her as an obsessed old woman. But Mabel saw things differently. She observed in her sister a single-minded commitment to seek justice in spite of the series of obstacles she faced, and she admired her sister's dedication and perseverance in the pursuit of it. For both sisters, however, everything had come to carry the freight of heightened meaning – signs and symbols of larger forces at work could be found everywhere. Florence and Mabel had become suspicious of lawyers, yet Florence was fully dependent on them. As they sorted through Wells's notes they found such men at times literally looking over their shoulders.

Florence and Mabel both wrote of one such encounter. Their recollections are intriguing. Florence:

> Occasionally some one would enquire as to our progress, and one day Mr. T. a lawyer enquired about the gentleman who had been sent out from England to settle this case. This was a surprise. Mr. T. then explained that he had heard from Professor L. that, at a recent dinner at Hart House (University of Toronto), this case had been mentioned in the conversation, and it was stated that a gentleman had been sent out from England to settle it. And Mr. T. added, "This gentleman did not speak to you about the settlement?" I told him that this was the first intimation I had received of any settlement having been made. "Well, well," he remarked, "and you the plaintiff and he did not speak to you about the settlement!"[24]

Mabel's memoir, written much later, takes the matter a little further:

> After my sister had finished with the reading of Mr. Wells' manuscript one of the officials from the office came in to ask how we were getting along (for he was very much interested in her task) and to ask if we had heard about the banquet at Hart House the night before. No! she replied. He then told us he understood that the MacMillan Company of London had sent a representative over to Toronto to settle the case.
>
> "That is very interesting" answered my sister, – But he added that he only went to see Mr. Tilley. "He did not come to the plaintiff?" "No" she replied, "he did not come to the plaintiff." "Strange," he replied, "he did not come to the plaintiff."
>
> This came from that large banquet of important professors from the University of Toronto, as well as from some other important universities, held at Hart House, University of Toronto,

where, as we had been told, it was discussed at some length (I understand practically the only subject discussed) and with a great deal of interest and that the MacMillan Company had sent a representative over to Toronto to settle the case, but that the representative only went to see Mr. Tilley (my sister's counsel) who soon after retired from the case. Why?

When Mr. Tilley was given the case he had taken it up eagerly and pronounced it to be "a good prima facie case and interesting too." Then why did he give up a "good case" so soon? "But straws show which way the wind blows."[25]

Mabel corroborates her sister's story, except on one vital matter. In her account, Mr. Tilley, rather than merely hearing of the visitor from England, had in fact met with him. Florence was suspicious because as far as she knew neither she nor her legal representatives had been contacted about what seems to have been an overture to an out-of-court settlement some months before the writs were served. Mabel was even more alarmed, since in her recollection Tilley's withdrawal from the case came very soon after the visitor had made contact with him. Neither sister directly says it, but it appears they believed Tilley had been bribed. The matter remains a mystery, but one thing is clear. To both sisters, all lawyers seemed alike, and none seemed truly to serve the cause of justice.

One of the original parties to the case, the London branch of Macmillan, was no longer a defendant, at least in a formal sense. The British firm argued that the plaintiff's claim did not provide any credible evidence that its offices had been a conduit through which "The Web" had been passed to Wells, and indeed, Florence's case was vague on this point. The London house, unlike its New York counterpart, had not published *The Outline of History*; therefore, except for its necessarily close working relationship with the American and Canadian branches, it had had no direct involvement in the matter. Nor would the British Macmillan have had reason to help any rival publisher produce the work.

This was its stance before the courts, and on November 21, 1927, the Supreme Court of Ontario had set aside the writ served against Macmillan of London. The dismissal revealed the greatest flaw in the case of the plaintiff: it seemed to lack an adequate theory – much less proof – of how "The Web" might have made its way to Wells and what motive Macmillan in London would have had to become involved in the transaction.

Hugh Eayrs had written to Sir Frederick Macmillan and George Brett of the good news. "This is encouraging," he reported, to which Brett's gruff response was: "As you are inclined to congratulate yourself on this action I should be glad if you would kindly explain to me how you think it affects the other suits." Eayrs, rather chastened, found himself admitting that the same officer of the court who had dismissed the writ against the London house of Macmillan had refused to do so for Wells. As if in atonement, he sent along a cheque for $500 as his current share of the legal expenses.[26] For his part, Sir Frederick Macmillan thought it prudent to maintain presence of counsel in order to protect his firm's interests, especially after Eayrs found it necessary to remind George Brett that Deeks had "never amended her claim in respect of how the manuscript of her book had got to . . . Wells either via your House or London's. She named the three Macmillan companies as co-defendants," Eayrs added, "but she made no statement in her claim that the manuscript had been sent to New York or to London, either one or the other."[27]

In 1928 the examinations for discovery at last began. The major part of Florence's testimony took place before the Master in Chambers at Osgoode Hall, beginning on October 15. She found the experience exhausting. One session alone took six half-days. She answered more than four thousand questions. A single copy of the transcript cost her $77.[28]

W.J. Elliott, K.C., representing Wells, had posed most of the questions.

> *What complaint have you got, Miss Deeks, against Mr. Wells in this action?*
> That portions of my book were used in the writing of The Outline of History.

> *Outline of History being a Work of Mr. Wells?*
> Yes.
> *And your complaint is then, as against Mr. Wells, that he used your manuscript, did he?*
> Yes . . .
> *Do you suggest that Mr. Wells deliberately took that material out of your book?*
> I never said that.
> *Well, what do you say as regards it?*
> I say that The Outline of History contains my book.
> *Do you know who did compile The Outline of History?*
> It is said that Mr. Wells did it.
> *And that is the reason you say that Mr. Wells took your material?*
> Yes.

Elliott drew out from the plaintiff the facts that two publishers, J.M. Dent and Sons and the Methodist Book and Publishing House, had already rejected "The Web" before she submitted it to Macmillan of Canada, and that at no point thereafter had she sought to contact Wells directly in order to confront him with her accusations.[29] Clearly, Elliott implied, even if Wells had had occasion to see her manuscript, like the publishers he would have judged it to be a thoroughly inadequate piece of work.

At play were several basic factors fundamental to cases involving literary theft. The trial would involve the intricate interplay of two distinct kinds of evidence. The first was of an intrinsic sort, the kind that would be furnished by evidence based on a detailed comparison of the two works. This comparison would, or would not, demonstrate that one had made illegal use of the other. The second was direct evidence of the facts of the case. This would include the provenance and whereabouts of the two manuscripts, the facts concerning their origins, the research that went into them, and the manner and timing of their writing. If Florence Deeks was to prove that her book had reached H.G. Wells by some means, it was through direct evidence that this would need to be established.

During his discovery examination of Florence, Elliott contested the facts on both evidentiary fronts. First, he pursued the basis of her belief that "The Web" had made its way to England, and when she had arrived at that conclusion.

I think you have told me that you submitted it to Macmillans
    in August, 1918?
The end of July or first of August 1918.
And you got it back from Macmillans on April 3rd, 1919?
About that time.

The precise date of the return of "The Web" to Florence Deeks was a crucial element of her case, and both sides knew this. Florence was adamant that she repossessed it only in April 1919. Yet plaintiff and defence alike were aware that the Macmillan of Canada manuscript logbook clearly indicated that "Feb.5/19" had been entered as the date of the return of the manuscript. If this were so, the amount of time "The Web" could have been at Wells's disposal was significantly circumscribed. In Deeks's view, this entry was simply "false" – and she had written this in the margin of her copy of the manuscript logbook.

And where do you say it was in the interval between those two
    dates?
I do not know.
As far as you know it was with Macmillan & Co. all the time?
I gave it to Macmillans.
And you have no reason to believe that it ever left their
    possession?
I have reason to believe it did.
You were told it did?
Yes.
When were you told?
In 1925.
Can you tell me the date in 1925?
In the fall.[30]

Elliott was leading towards an event, involving John Saul's loose words, that he knew was potentially damaging to his side. He probed carefully.

> *I see in the examination that you had with the other*
> *   Macmillans that you put the date about October 14th,*
> *   1925 . . . I presume that is correct, is it?*
> I should think it would be . . .
> *Is that the first time that you connect Mr. Wells in any way*
> *   with your manuscript?*
> No.
> *That is what I meant. This was the first time that you had any,*
> *   what I might call direct evidence that it ever went to his*
> *   possession?*
> I understood it was sent over in the beginning.
> *Well I am dealing with the time you were told in October; that*
> *   was the first time that you had any direct evidence that it*
> *   had been sent to him at all?*
> Yes, I think it is – I never said it was sent direct to Mr. Wells . . .
> *I appreciate what you say. You had no evidence that it went*
> *   to Mr. Wells, but your information was that it went to*
> *   Macmillan & Company in England?*
> Yes.

Florence was in a quandary, and she was becoming flustered. She knew very well who the informant was. It was Sidney Watson of Thomas Nelson publishers, John Saul's golf partner. In a memorandum she wrote later to her lawyer, she reported that Watson had confided to her (in the presence of Mabel) a remark Saul made while playing a round of golf. The former Macmillan editor had said he had sent "The Web" to England. Under advice of counsel, she could not identify Watson by name since she had not been able to secure his presence as a witness. Elliott persisted:

> *Could you just tell me the language that was used when you*
> *   were informed of that?*

The person who told me said that this person said "I sent it to
  England myself."
That is the language that was used?
Yes.
And that is the whole of it?
"You don't think it would be made use of by them over there,
  do you?" – "Of course it would."
Who said that?
The two people that were speaking.[31]

Elliott then tried an old lawyer's trick to catch witnesses off
guard. He turned briefly to unrelated matters, and then quickly
switched back to the mysterious witness and the important admission he had allegedly heard from Saul on a Mississauga golf course.

*This person that said they sent it to England themselves, was
  that person employed in Macmillan & Company, with
  which you had left your manuscript?*
Yes.
*. . . And . . . this employee of Macmillans told this third party
  that he had sent it himself?*
Yes.
Did he say when?
No.
*And of course you know, but I presume you do not want to
  tell me the name of the employee of Macmillan &
  Company?*
Yes.
You do object to telling me that name?

Smily intervened: "Yes, we object." Elliott persisted, suggesting
"that it would perhaps assist both of us" if Florence revealed the
name. But Smily repeated his position, and Elliott tried another tack.

*Where were these two people when this conversation took
  place between them? . . .*

I think on the golf course . . .
And one of the gentlemen who was playing golf repeated it to you?
Yes.
And whereabouts were you when the conversation was repeated?
In that gentleman's office.
And was that office the office of Macmillan & Company?
No.
Was it the gentleman that was in Macmillan & Company that repeated this to you?
No . . .
So then we have it this way: That the gentleman from Macmillans was playing golf with a second gentleman and they had a conversation on the golf links, and the second gentleman repeated the story to you?
Yes.
And that as you have told us, was in October, 1925?
Yes.[32]

Finally, Elliott turned to questioning Florence at length about the intrinsic evidence, the similarities and differences between "The Web" and *The Outline*. The evidence was intricate. Each contested fact of history seemed to require a familiarity with the nuances of historical interpretation, such as whether the Roman general Sulla was best described as an aristocrat or a patrician or when the Holy Roman Empire really began.

Meanwhile Hugh Eayrs continued to bring George Brett up to date. "Nothing, so far, of any importance whatever, has come out of the Deeks examination," he wrote on October 19. Two weeks later, he noted that the examination for discovery of Miss Deeks was still under way. To his eyes, the evidence she had given had not even established a prima facie case and her evidence showed up badly. But he added, "There is no doubt that the lady is very much in earnest in her claim," and there seemed no reason why she would not go forward with her action. A few weeks later, he reported along the same lines to Sir Frederick Macmillan. Her evidence, he said, "seemed to reveal nothing except the ridiculous quality of the case . . . I am sorry that you are to be bothered in this way, but it is apparently necessary to go on with this ridiculous affair until it comes to trial."[33]

It remained for the New York and London defendants to have their say, and their representatives moved immediately after the conclusion of the Deeks testimony in December to have their evidence given "on commission" so that the witnesses would not have to travel to Toronto. Florence's expenses, already onerous, now escalated exponentially. Percy Smily reported to her that $500 would be required to retain an English solicitor and another $100 to cover his own costs in travelling to New York or retaining counsel there.[34]

While Eayrs and McLaughlin made last-ditch efforts to obtain a memorandum from John Saul pinning down the story he would tell on the witness stand, and Wells made inquiries of his solicitor as to how costs might be recovered from Miss Deeks, Gideon Grant, Smily's senior, warned his client of further expenses she could expect. After discussing the matter with Smily, he reported that the case could not be handled in England for less than $2,000. A London solicitor needed to be employed, a great deal of typing done, comparisons of "The Web" and *The Outline* made, and commissioners and stenographers hired. At the trial itself, at least three expert witnesses would be required, at a cost running between $3,000 and $5,000. And then there would of course be his firm's own charges. "I think it is hopeless to consider going on with the case unless you can provide funds to the extent of at least Seven or Eight Thousand Dollars to take the case through the trial. I do not know any way of raising this money and unless you have some way of doing it it does not seem possible to get the action tried."[35]

Hugh Eayrs, fresh from the indignity of his own examination for discovery in February 1929, was annoyed and frustrated. Life was bearing down on him, and the Deeks business had become a supreme nuisance. "I am not feeling very fit just now," he groused to Sir Frederick Macmillan, "and am very very tired because of a good deal of heavy work this winter and more trips than usual, and the silliness of this whole Deeks suit irritates me. To waste good

250 THE SPINSTER AND THE PROPHET

time I could employ in other ways for the business, answering perfectly stupid questions on the part of an equally stupid cross-examiner is an annoyance . . . Periodically this woman holds things up because she has no more money, and cannot get any from her brother: then again she periodically persuades her brother to put up more money, and so the ridiculous thing goes on."[36]

If it had not occurred to George Deeks before, it would have become abundantly apparent to him now that the stakes involved in the case against Wells were not his sister's alone. The Deeks family name was at risk, and he could not let it appear that Florence had been abandoned by her kin. No doubt under significant pressure from several or all of the women in his life, he appears to have relented as the case approached trial. In Florence's words, once again he took "a kind interest in the case" and resumed responsibility for her legal expenses. If Gideon Grant's letter to Florence outlining her anticipated expenses in England had been an oblique attempt to extricate his firm from further involvement in the affair, it did not work. When the invoices arrived, they were paid.[37]

A good deal of preparation was necessary on behalf of the plaintiff before evidence from Wells and his co-defendants could be given in London, and this entailed yet more delay. The defence found this intolerable, but it did have certain advantages. Miss Deeks, they had learned, intended to travel personally to England to hear Wells's evidence. The defendants hoped that the combination of sobering advice by barristers from the City about the hopelessness of her ludicrous case, along with the severe legal and living expenses involved in an extended stay in London, would finally put an end to the farce.[38] Not so.

Florence and Mabel left Toronto on Victoria Day, 1929, and soon set sail for London. They found the three-thousand-mile voyage down the St. Lawrence and across the Atlantic inspiring and the distinguished passengers intriguing. The scenery and the people constantly reminded them of their mission. An ordinary citizen of the British Empire was to have her day in court – the experience of a lifetime! But at what price? "It all emphasized," Florence later recalled, "the fact of having to pay too dear for justice."[39]

They arrived in London on June 3, taking up residence at the Hotel Tudor, a pleasant but modest establishment on the northern border of Hyde Park, with a fine view of the Serpentine in the distance. After settling in, they visited the firm of Collyer-Bristow, which was to represent them. Florence's first act was to hand over a cheque for £500 – about $2,500 – to get the evidence on commission under way. Sir Duncan Kerley was to have been in charge of their case (for a retainer of £100), but the schedules of H.G. Wells and Sir Frederick Macmillan conflicted with his own, and he withdrew. At the suggestion of Smily in Toronto, Florence came to be represented in London by Norman Daynes; Sir Duncan's junior, a Mr. Corsellis, acted as second counsel.[40]

The hearings began on June 18, 1929, in a large and comfortable room in the Law Society's Hall in Lincoln's Inn, Chancery Lane. "A wave of timidity swept over me," Florence later wrote, "when our solicitor escorted us into the room fairly filled with witnesses and gentlemen of the legal world surrounding a great circular table in the centre of the room." Other players in the suit were already seated around the table. Daynes sat at its head, and Florence took a seat beside him. Mabel sat near Corsellis and the clerks. To their left was the chair reserved for witnesses. Next to it came the commissioner and the stenographer. On the right side of the table sat counsel for the defence, together with their solicitors and clerks. "To our unsophisticated minds," said Florence, "the *tout ensemble* appeared to be a formidable gathering. As for the great outside world it, apparently, knew nothing of the hearing which was privately conducted, nor was it in the least concerned. While the precincts of Lincoln's Inn were apparently serene and peaceful, London surged outside."[41]

And so, one by one, the defendants presented their witnesses. First came Sir Frank Newnes and Frederick Newstead, acting secretary of Cassell; then Sir Frederick Macmillan, Sir Richard Gregory, and Harold Geikie of Macmillan. They were followed a couple of weeks later by Gilbert Murray and Ernest Barker. Florence made mental notes. Sir Frederick was "imperious in appearance" and "impatient in manner." Sir Richard Gregory "was alert in movement, but his words seemed to be more studied," as did those of Geikie. Together, they gave Florence the impression that they had "been educated in the same business college."[42]

The appearance of H.G. Wells to testify was of course the highlight of Florence's experience in London. It was to be the first and only time they would meet face to face. She sized him up: "A man of moderate height and size, dark hair, sombre complexion, falsetto voice, and, what was said to be, a somewhat Cockney, or East London, accent; mild in manner, even when in confusion of mind." The prophet also took the measure of the woman who had come to so disrupt his life. "I saw her once in court," he recalled, "and I found her rather a sympathetic figure. She impressed me as quite honest but vain and foolish, with an imagination too inflamed with the idea of being a great litigant for her to realize what an unrighteous nuisance she was making of herself . . . , giving her profound and subtle instructions for the undoing of our dire conspiracy."[43]

After testimony had begun, Wells received a letter of commiseration from Gilbert Murray. "I am sorry that this absurd lady has taken it into her head to bring an action against you," he said. "I presume she is mad." Three weeks later, Murray had given evidence and had seen the infamous Miss Deeks "in the flesh." Her counsel, said Murray, "tried to make me say that you could not have written the book in the time unless you copied it from somewhere, and secondly that your scheme of history was so strikingly original that no two people could have thought of anything like it independently. I don't think he got any change out of me on either point, both being perfectly silly." The prophet replied three days later: "Warmest thanks for your kindness in giving evidence. The woman's just one of these things we must suffer in life."[44]

Nothing that Florence heard from the witnesses for the defence undermined her confidence in the strength of her case, and at the end of July she and Mabel embarked at Southampton for the return to Canada convinced that Wells and his supporters had made several telling admissions that could be subjected to close scrutiny at trial.[45]

The Atlantic passage was uneventful, "no fog, no storm, . . . nothing of special importance." But she found her imagination turning to the voyages of John Cabot in 1597 as the ship passed the coast of Newfoundland, to the explorer Jacques Cartier in 1542 as it made its way past the Gaspé into the mouth of the St. Lawrence, to the French intendants Jean Talon and François Bigot, and to the Battle of the Plains of Abraham, as it reached Quebec City. "A great and romantic history," she overheard a politician on deck say, as they viewed the approach to Quebec. "They say that book – *The Golden Dog* – was repeatedly plagiarised," he added. Another passenger agreed, and with the mention that people had made illegal use of William Kirby's novel of the British conquest of New France, Florence was abruptly brought back to her quest for justice and to a reality shorn of romance.[46]

While he waited for a date to be set for trial, William McLaughlin, representing Macmillan of Canada, pored over the evidence taken in England and uncovered an unsettling line of questioning in the cross-examination of Sir Frederick Macmillan. Deeks's lawyer had asked Sir Frederick if any Canadian authors had complained to him in the past about Mr. Wise, in particular a certain Miss Durand.[47] What, McLaughlin now asked Eayrs, was this claim by counsel for Deeks that the Durand woman had submitted a manuscript to Macmillan of Canada and that "a large portion" of the manuscript had been incorporated into another book subsequently published by the Canadian branch? Was it the case that, as had been stated in London, "this latter book was subsequently withdrawn"? McLaughlin insisted on particulars.[48]

Eayrs supplied them. The matter, he suggested, was another instance of a ridiculous woman making outrageous claims against a respectable author. Everyone back in the early Twenties, he assured McLaughlin, thought that Laura B. Durand, a Toronto writer and journalist, was a madwoman. "I think her particular type of lunacy was the sort of fanaticism which showed itself in the sort of fanaticism which characterizes the present plaintiff."

When McLaughlin read Eayrs's side of the story, his skeptical legal mind must have noted that there existed more of a parallel between Miss Durand and Miss Deeks than Eayrs let on. "I could never quite make out the burden of her plaint," Eayrs had written, "excepting that it was that her manuscript had been here for some time, and that it had been finally declined by Mr. Wise or by the house. Of course, John Saul was the editor in the case . . . unquestionably he would see the manuscript of Miss Durant [sic] when it was submitted to the house."[49]

Once again, accusing fingers seemed to point to John Cameron Saul. From McLaughlin's perspective, there was only one detail in Eayrs's reply to his query for which he could give thanks: that the lady in question had died a few years earlier.

At the beginning of October 1929, a tentative date in early November was at last set for the trial to begin. Defence lawyers conferred about the advisability of obtaining an expert witness to testify about the alleged similarities of wording in "The Web" and *The Outline*, since Wells had called upon none. McLaughlin and Elliott asked Eayrs for suggestions, and the result was the idea to approach Chester Martin, George Wrong's successor as professor and head of the University of Toronto history department. Martin would be an excellent choice, Eayrs wrote to George Brett and Sir Frederick Macmillan, in part because of his "very considerable" reputation, but also because he was "almost the only historian in Canada who does not publish with us."[50]

Eayrs's second reason was almost as strong as his first, for under his direction Macmillan of Canada was coming to position itself as one of the major Canadian trade publishers of the nation's historical scholarship. University of Toronto Press, thus far, was still a fledgling operation. Few other publishers were interested in the small Canadian university market for works of history. Only the Ryerson Press, under the strong leadership of its publisher, Lorne Pierce, equalled Macmillan in its interest in Canadiana. In fact, a friendly but very real rivalry had come to exist between Eayrs and Pierce.

The prospect of Chester Martin as an expert witness for the defence proved acceptable to all concerned. But it was thought prudent to provide him with an "understudy" in case Martin became unavailable. Again, Eayrs demonstrated his familiarity with the local academic community. "There is a young man here," he wrote to Brett, "F.H. Underhill, in the History Department of the University of Toronto, who is a very able research man." Eayrs's notion was to employ Underhill to assist Martin, by having him compare the Deeks manuscript with Victor Duruy's *General History of the World*, thereby making Martin's task in preparing to testify easier.[51] The understudy plan was wise indeed, because Martin, for unknown reasons, did not testify.

Was it a sign of confidence in the defence's case or of its general lack of preparedness that the defence sought to employ a historian as an expert witness only a few weeks before it believed the case would come to trial? Whichever it was, in securing Frank Underhill, Eayrs and his colleagues could scarcely have sensed that they had brought into their camp the most important element of their defence.

In the midst of last-minute efforts by Eayrs, McLaughlin, and Brett to obtain details from Wells about how quickly he had written not only *The Outline of History* but also some of his other books, came first a rumour, then definite word: Florence Deeks had again changed lawyers and the trial would again be delayed.[52] Gideon Grant had withdrawn from the case; the records provide no explanation. No one could now predict just when it would be brought to trial. Late January? February? An exchange between McLaughlin and a Toronto judge suggested the week of March 3, but when the case came before this judge on March 10, he granted the plaintiff's revised legal team, R.S. Robertson, K.C., and Percy Smily, their request for a postponement in order to make adequate preparation. "My own feeling," Eayrs wrote to Sir Frederick in exasperation, "is that this woman can secure no more money and that the delay on her attorney's part is simply to see whether or no [*sic*] she can."[53] W.J. Elliott, Wells's Canadian lawyer, wrote to his English counterpart to express his disappointment in the delay. "We learn," he added, "that two Professors at the University of Toronto have lately been retained by the Plaintiff and are now working on the manuscript. You may rest assured that we will persist in our efforts to have it disposed of. A woman obsessed is a dangerous woman."[54]

Whatever degree of commitment Florence Deeks possessed, at that moment she was a woman in mourning. On March 11, 1930, the very day that Elliott penned his letter to Gedge, Fiske & Gedge, her mother died at the age of ninety-four. A few days later, after George had returned as quickly as he could from northern Manitoba, where he was supervising the laying of tracks in 40-below weather for the line from Flin Flon to Churchill, the funeral cortege travelled to Mount Pleasant Cemetery. There Melinda Deeks was interred next to her late husband, gone now for thirty-three years. Despite the mother's great age, it was a terrible blow to the family. Their mother and grandmother had been the guiding force in the family, the vital link between the house on Farnham Avenue and the mansion on Admiral Road.

As the plaintiff and the defence neared trial, their fortunes could not have been more unlike. Shortly after St. Patrick's Day, H.G. Wells received a royalty cheque from George Brett for $10,000 on sales of 200,000 copies of *The Outline of History* in America. Brett and Sir Frederick Macmillan's brother, Maurice, were exchanging correspondence aimed at dividing the world for publishing purposes into British and American "spheres of influence." And Sir Richard Gregory received word from an anonymous member of Parliament that he had been recommended to Prime Minister Ramsay MacDonald for a peerage.[55]

Then, still in mourning over the loss of their mother, the women of Farnham Avenue received another devastating blow. On the first day of May, their brother George died of a heart seizure at his home on Admiral Road. He was seventy-one years old.

For the second time in as many months, a sombre procession made its way east towards Rosedale and Mount Pleasant Cemetery. The new gravesite was only a short distance from that of the parents. Despite George's prominence within the engineering and business communities, the funeral was a very private affair, for among George's effects had been found a letter stipulating that his burial should be a quiet one, with no flowers or "undue ceremony," and no publicity about his life or death. Out of respect for his achievements, the family permitted the silence to be broken and the

Toronto newspapers provided substantial obituaries of his life and accomplishments.[56]

Only the immediate family and a few very close friends were there to pay their respects at the freshly dug grave. Their minds dwelt on shared memories of their pasts with him; but members of the grieving family faced very different individual futures. George's sons were only then entering public life. Campbell, twenty-three, could look forward to a promising future with the investment firm he had joined after leaving university three years earlier – that is, if the stock market collapse did not pull the company under. Twenty-one-year-old Douglas was in his final year at Upper Canada College and was planning to enter the arts program at the University of Toronto in the fall. His younger brother, Edward, was ahead of him in this respect; at nineteen, he had almost completed his second year in applied science at the university.[57]

The aunts who did their best to comfort them at graveside must have seemed to these young men more than only a single span of life distant. Their father's older sister, Annie, would turn seventy-three in September. Less than two weeks earlier, their Aunt Florence would mark her sixty-sixth birthday. Of their close family, only Aunt Mabel, in her mid-fifties, a year younger than their mother, Helen, seemed even remotely linked to their own generation. The three sons of George S. Deeks had much more on their minds than the fate of their aunts. It would scarcely have occurred to them, as their father was laid to rest, that when their Aunt Florence went home to prepare for the trial the family had talked about for as long as they could remember, she would be doing so thrown entirely on her own resources and relying on the support of two aging sisters and a widowed sister-in-law still mourning, with her, their double loss.

13   *Enter King David, and So On*

Was it not after all a small point of historical truth
that mattered really very little to . . . specialists and
nothing, but absolutely nothing at all, to anyone else?

Angus Wilson, *Anglo-Saxon Attitudes* (1956)

For a building almost a century old, Osgoode Hall, standing firm in its practical brick and stately grey stone, continued to impress in 1930. Anchored by a central classical portico with six majestic Greek columns, it sat on the corner of Queen Street and University Avenue as if placed there to separate the din of the business district from the comparative tranquillity of the university and legislative precincts to the north at Queen's Park. For ninety-eight years it had been the seat of law and justice for the province. In it was housed the headquarters of the Law Society of Upper Canada, facilities for its benchers, and the courtrooms where the drama of the system of justice played itself out.[1] At times, visitors to the city mistook Osgoode Hall for the legislative buildings. Perhaps they were impressed by the entrance from University Avenue, or the expansive grounds, or the iron fence that surrounded the building. Clearly, they failed to notice its distinctive, century-old, iron cowgates, constructed so that people could leave but farm animals could not gain entry.

The original structure of 1832 had gained two additional wings and a labyrinth of corridors and offices. Coloured tile floors and an Ionic motif marked the interior. Florence had visited it two years earlier, when the manuscript of *The Outline of History* had been sent to Toronto to be examined. She and Mabel had taken some time to explore its public spaces, but many doors remained closed to women. She had not seen the lawyers' common room or the lecturers' offices. The Convocation Hall on the second floor was also for men only, preserved for the exclusive use of the benchers.

The Great Library, also on the second floor, had fortunately been open to all, and Florence and Mabel had spent some time in it. The vaulted room, its ceiling supported by a number of Greek columns, contained some 70,000 legal volumes from throughout the Empire, along with the 6,000 books of the Riddell Canadian Library. At one end of the spacious room was a memorial to those who had fallen in the Great War; at the other, a huge fireplace above which hung George Theodore Berthon's portrait of Sir John Beverley Robinson, first chief justice of the province. Roses, thistles, and shamrocks completed the thoroughly loyal decorative motif.[2]

By comparison with the Great Library, the courtroom in Osgoode Hall that Florence and Mabel entered on Friday, May 30, 1930, was unpretentious. The temperature inside was warm, almost uncomfortably so, and little fresh air seemed to circulate. Scarcely a seat was vacant. Florence did not know who most of these people were, but from where she sat she could recognize several leading members of the academic and publishing communities. Young men, perhaps law students, whispered among themselves near the back. Reporters also sat there, steno pads in laps. Near them, with a look of bemused detachment, a portly middle-aged man with a carefully trimmed silver beard waited patiently for the proceedings to begin. It was Hector Charlesworth, who so long ago had written the book review that had resulted in this day in court.

Counsel sat in their designated places before the bench, waiting for the judge to arrive. Collectively, they were among the finest lawyers the provincial bar had to offer. The Toronto firm of Elliott, Hume, McKague & Anger was one of the city's most prestigious.

W.J. Elliott, K.C., and E.V. McKague, representing Mr. Wells and the publishing firms of Newnes and Cassell, respectively, occupied one table. At another sat members of the equally reputable firm of McLaughlin, Johnston, Moorhead & Macaulay, acting on behalf of Wells's North American publishers.

At the table sat Robert Dunn Moorhead, K.C., representing the New York branch of the Macmillan company; next to him, Macmillan of Canada's lawyer, W.W. McLaughlin. With only ten years in practice, McLaughlin, son of a barrister, was the least experienced lawyer in court that day. But he was a member of Macmillan of Canada's board of directors as well as its official counsel, and his relationship with Hugh Eayrs had become very close. William McLaughlin may have lacked court experience, but he was thoroughly familiar with the goings-on at 70 Bond Street since the days of Frank Wise. Apart from Florence Deeks and Hugh Eayrs, no one in court knew more about the accusations against Wells, and the transatlantic reverberations they had caused, than he.[3]

Behind the table of the plaintiff sat P.E.F. Smily of Johnston, Grant, Dods & Macdonald, looking very much alone. Forty years old, the son of a registrar of deeds from Windsor, a veteran of fifteen years' practice, Percy Smily turned around every once in a while as though to have a few words with his client. But the seat next to Smily, reserved for the lead counsel for the plaintiff, was vacant.

All stood to attention as the clerk of the Supreme Court of Ontario announced the entrance of the judge, the Honourable William Edgar Raney. The seventy-one-year-old judge brought a very different background to the courtroom than did the representatives of the legal profession who stood before him. Called to the Ontario bar in 1891, within a decade Raney had opted for a career in politics and had served as attorney general in the "farmers' government" of E.C. Drury after the provincial election of 1919. After the defeat of the government in the next election, Raney remained in the legislature as a leader until an offer he could scarcely refuse came from the office of the prime minister in Ottawa. As a result, on September 16, 1927, William E. Raney had donned his robe for the first time as a judge in the Supreme Court of Ontario, High Court Division.[4]

The trial of *Deeks v. Wells et al.*, so long in the preparation and so often delayed, began at last. It was to be tried not by jury but by judge alone. Smily rose at once. His first words were to ask Mr. Justice Raney for a postponement until the following week. R.S. Robertson, K.C., lead counsel for Miss Deeks, had been delayed by a trial in Niagara and could not be present. Over the strong objections of the defence, Raney consented to begin testimony the following Monday and drew the proceedings to an abrupt close. For those not familiar with the slow if inexorable pace of justice, it was an instructive lesson: long anticipation followed by a distinct sense of anticlimax.

The trial started in earnest at eleven on Monday morning, June 2. Having rushed back from Niagara, Robert Spelman Robertson of Fasken, Robertson, Aitchison, Pickup & Calvin was now in his seat beside Percy Smily, at the front of a full courtroom. Born in the western Ontario town of Goderich in 1870, the tall, bald Robertson was a barrister of long and distinguished experience, called to the provincial bar in 1894 and appointed King's Counsel in 1921. The year 1930 saw his election as a bencher, and word in the legal community had it that an appointment to the bench lay in his future.

"Before we go on with the exhibits," he began, "I should like to say perhaps a little more than one generally does, because of the nature of the case, what we claim and how we expect to go about proving it." After explaining to Mr. Justice Raney why the English branch of Macmillan was no longer a party to the case, Robertson stated the basis on which it was brought. Raney intervened when he thought it necessary.

> The action as brought is frankly different from the ordinary infringement of copyright. The Plaintiff's work is an unpublished manuscript.
> *But copyrighted?*
> She copyrighted the name before the completion of the manuscript.

Now, what she says is this, that the manuscript having been deposited by her in a manner that will be stated to your Lordship with the Canadian Macmillan Company, that it remained in their hands, she gave it to them along about July or August of 1918. The completed manuscript . . . remained in their hands until the following spring, 1919.

That in the meantime, some two or three months after she left the manuscript with them we have the first . . . intimation of Wells beginning to develop an idea of writing a History of Mankind, and that his work was published first by Newnes in England in parts, that is in serial parts, that was beginning in the Fall of 1919. Afterwards Cassels [sic] published it in England as a book.

The Macmillan Company, the Incorporated company published it in the United States and in Canada, and the Macmillan Company of Canada, possibly, . . . are involved in the use of the manuscript.

What do you say about the Canadian Company representing –
The Canadian Company, the Macmillan Company of Canada possibly sold copies in Canada. I think we can establish that.
Copies of the Wells' book?
Anyway, they are involved in the whole story because it was to them that Miss Deeks entrusted her manuscript, and if wrong use was made of it, they are the ones who must be accountable, because it was to them she gave it. We say our manuscript having been entrusted to Macmillan for a particular purpose was used through them, and by the defendant Wells, and unfairly used by him in the preparation of his book. That, of course, is not exactly infringement of copyright. It is not the sort of action one brings under the Act, but it is a well known form of action. It is rather an equitable relief the Law gives to one that is the author of a book.
The manuscript was not copyrighted?
No, it is not under the Copyright Act we are suing, it is under another branch of Copyright Law, it is a well recognized right by an author of a manuscript to the property in it,

and if anybody improperly, and without the permission of
the author, takes that manuscript and uses it unfairly,
various expressions are used by the Court in describing
what is unfair use.

It would be a breach of faith by Macmillan.

In the first place, and a wrong thing to do on the part of Mr.
Wells if he did so use it. That is the character of the action
we bring.

Then as to the way we go about proving it. I say we will
show that this Deeks' manuscript was prepared before Mr.
Wells had written a line, and it was taken to Macmillan
and in their hands there in Toronto prior to Wells even
starting to write . . . Then, I do not know that we will be
able to get your Lordship a witness who will say that
Macmillans did send from Toronto to England this manuscript. We rather seek to make the connection between our
manuscript and Mr. Wells altogether in another direction,
that is, we say by expression of the work, he must have had
it before him. We say this, first of all, your Lordship will
appreciate, if a man is going to write a History of the
World, there are a great many ways in which he might set
about writing it. He might write it from various points of
view, there are innumerable instances in the history of
mankind that he might put in or leave out, depending somewhat upon their significance to the view point he was
adopting. Now, we will say, first of all, and hope to prove
this by evidence, that the plan of the two works is very
similar indeed, the resemblance in the general plan; the
things that are discussed, the things that are omitted, are
such that it is beyond credence that it could be a mere result
of coincidence. Then we go further than that, and we say
that there are many resemblances, verbal resemblances,
resemblances in expressions that are used, but I do not carry
it thus far. We do not say that Wells was drawing from the
events that he discusses necessarily the same lessons that
Miss Deeks would. Wells was a man who has ideas.

His philosophy was different.

Wells is a man who has well-known ideas along lines of
that kind, and his own ideas constantly appear beyond
peradventure.

Another thing that is quite striking is that Miss Deeks, I
think, puts forward women and the place of women in
history and her importance. Mr. Wells apparently has quite
contrary opinions about that sort of thing, and rather puts
man in the front at different times.
And puts man in the leading position.
And puts the woman in her place – your Lordship will bear in
mind, when we are making comparisons in that way in
detail, we are not contending at all that Wells did not do
any work of his own, that he sat down and slashingly
copied Miss Deeks' book, but we say further the use he did
make of it amounted to an unfair use. I think I am fair in
saying this, that if the resemblances are such as to lead your
Lordship to the conclusion that Wells must have had her
manuscript before him, I think there will be very little
difficulty in reaching the second conclusion that he did not
use it properly, because he has denied having it at all, and if
he did have it, and denies it, it would not be unreasonable
to reach the conclusion he denied it for a purpose.[5]

Robertson went on, briefly, to note that there existed curious
omissions and errors common to both works, and that he would
show that it would have been "humanly impossible" for any man to
have written *The Outline of History* within the limited span of time
he had "unless he did follow as is complained and from time to
time make use of some such work as the manuscript of Miss Deeks."
Accordingly, he proposed to call expert witnesses who would testify
as to the similarities and differences between the two works.

W.J. Elliott rose to put the case for the defence. He was brief and
to the point: "Perhaps your Lordship will permit me, just so that
your Lordship will understand what the defence is, as well as what
my friend says – we say that this Plaintiff's manuscript which is
unpublished, never left the City of Toronto, that it never crossed to
the Macmillan Company at London, that it was never seen by

Macmillan or by Mr. Wells, or by any of the people who assisted him in writing the 'Outlines [*sic*] of History.'"[6]

With the statements of the plaintiff and the defence now made, Robertson called his first witness, Florence Amelia Deeks. He helped her as gently as he could into the details of her testimony, and one of his first acts was to have "The Web" entered as Exhibit 1. Then he proceeded to elicit from her the origins of her manuscript.

> *Now, when did you set about the preparation of this*
> *manuscript?*
> I think it was in 1914, but it might have been in 1913.
> *Yes, and will you tell us briefly how you proceeded with the*
> *work, for example, speaking broadly, what is the nature of*
> *the work?*
> I first undertook to feature feminism in history.
> HIS LORDSHIP: *To feature feminism?*
> Yes, the woman and her work in history. In order to do that, I
> did not know how to work it, and I thought I would have
> to go back to Europe, then to Asia, then I said I will go to
> the beginning.
> MR. ROBERTSON: *Well?*
> So I went to the beginning and I gathered notes, with different
> notes from different things and different sections, many
> and many notes, and I wrote them and re-wrote them –
> *Wait a moment, for the purpose of doing that, or writing or*
> *drafting notes, what did you do – where did you go to get*
> *your data or information?*
> I gathered different books from the Library.[7]

Robertson soon entered as exhibits a list of her historical sources, and the 1916 registration with the registrar of the Department of Agriculture of interim copyright "for the Literary work entitled, 'The Web,'" its author identified only by the pen-name "Adul Weaver." Over the course of the afternoon, he drew out from Florence the basic circumstances of her quarrel with Wells: her submission of "The Web" to John Saul, together with her correspondence with him; her attempts to recover it; the harsh letter of rejection from

Montrose Liston, Saul's successor; her insistence that she had not regained possession of "The Web" until early April 1919.[8]

She continued with a description of her shock at reading Hector Charlesworth's review of *The Outline of History* in *Saturday Night* magazine in December 1920, the revisions she undertook in order to make another version of "The Web" publishable, and the "Comparison" she made (entered as Exhibit 6) of the plans and details of "The Web" and *The Outline*. Sorting out the different copies and revisions of "The Web," and explaining the peculiar three-column structure of her comparison, took no little time. A good deal might have been added about the intrinsic evidence, but Robertson knew from his client's testimony on discovery that she was not the best advocate of her own case. She was too nervous, her few words too guarded – as if she were the defendant. She had spent so long working on her comparison and poring over its details that she had a difficult time sorting them out. This aspect of the case would be better presented by her expert witnesses.

W.J. Elliott then began his cross-examination, on the direct evidence concerning "The Web" and its relation to *The Outline of History*. His object, in part, was to introduce the idea that Miss Deeks began to revise "The Web" so that it would resemble *The Outline*, and for nefarious purposes. But first, he decided to make fun of the singular way she had initially expressed her interest in Wells's book.

And then, having seen the review in "The Saturday Night,"
    you went to the T. Eaton Company and purchased the
    book, did you?
I think it was in December.
December, 1920?
Yes.
And what did you do with the book, did you read it?
I read it rapidly through.
Yes, and then where is it? That book?
I returned it.
You took it back to Eaton's?
Yes.

HIS LORDSHIP: *Sold it back to them?*

I returned it, and the money was refunded.

MR. ELLIOTT: *Your money was refunded, you were not apparently very much interested in it when you did not keep it, returned it and got back?*

I was very much interested, but it suited my convenience.

It suited your convenience, so . . . you, Miss Deeks, in 1920 saw this Review, and you were interested in it, and went to Eatons and got a copy of the book and went through it hurriedly and took it back and got your money back?

Yes.

And apparently then, it did not strike you as being very similar to your "Web"?

It did strike me as being very similar.[9]

Then Elliott turned to the serious business of her revisions, first of 1920 and then of 1923 and later, noting as he did so that she took no legal action until five years had elapsed and the revisions were complete. Elliott well knew, from what the defence had discovered of the involvement of W.P.M. Kennedy, that these "revisions" had nothing directly to do with "The Web" as a discreet work, but that they concerned a completely different work. But he had introduced doubt and confusion over whether "The Web" had remained unrevised after Florence had seen *The Outline*. The implication was clear: she had used Wells's book to improve her own.[10]

Elliott drew attention to John Saul's letter of January 31, 1919. His object was to demonstrate that "The Web" remained in the possession of Macmillan of Canada all during the time Wells researched and wrote his book.

Tell me this, when you got that letter with the manuscript apparently there, did you go down and ask for it?

No.

You did not believe it was there, you think that the man who wrote that letter was misleading you, and that it was not there?

The letter stated, "I am cleaning up everything before
   leaving," so I expected if he were cleaning up everything,
   he would return my manuscript, and when it was not
   returned, I just thought it was the business way of doing
   things. They had had the manuscript for over six months. If
   it had been there when he cleaned up everything I would
   naturally have expected he would have returned it . . .
And did you not go down to speak to him?
No.
*And you did not do anything further about it until the follow-
   ing March? On March, March the 25th, 1919?*
As far as I know, I wrote them a letter . . .

A letter of reply dated March 27, 1919, had been written by
Montrose Liston.

*He comes into the picture the first time – he does not say I
   have a letter, he starts off, "I have glanced through the
   pages of your manuscript, and wish to say quite frankly
   how it affects me, in reference to your idea"* –
HIS LORDSHIP: As though this had been a matter which had
   been inherited by him from the former Editor.
MR. ELLIOTT: *He apparently was going through the manuscripts there, came across this manuscript there, knew it
   was from Miss Deeks and wrote her about it.*
      *Now, are you sure that that letter refers to your manu-
   script "The Web"?*
It was the only manuscript they had of mine.
*Didn't they have a manuscript there of yours called "The
   Dawn"?*
No. He suggested in his letter that I write on "Love and War,"
   and I wrote a heavy pamphlet on "Love and War" and submitted it to them.[11]

As if matters were not confusing enough with Florence claiming
that "The Web" had remained in its pristine condition while the
defence suggested that in fact she had revised it not only once, but

twice, after reading *The Outline*, Raney now had two more Deeks manuscripts to sort out. "Love and War" had been just what she said it was: a pamphlet-length piece she had written after Liston had suggested that the general argument of "The Web" should be reduced to essay length. Elliott no doubt also knew this, but he chose to sow a little more confusion.

You called it "The Dawn"?
No.
Did you have a manuscript called "Dawn"?
"Dawn" is the subject of my first chapter.
You mean it had two names?
No, the opening of the first chapter.
HIS LORDSHIP: The opening of the book is "The Dawn."
MR. ELLIOTT: *Then, on March 27th, you got the letter from Mr. Liston, and you went down and got your manuscript?*
The week following.
I have it, I think you told us, on April 3rd, 1919?
About that time.
And who did you see when you went down?
Mr. Liston.
Meeting him for the first time?
Yes sir.
And he sent a young lady to the place where they kept manuscripts and got it out for you, and you took it away?
Yes.
And did you think to ask them anything about where the manuscript had been all this time?
I did not.
You had no doubt then it had left their office?
I thought it had been in England all the time.
How?
I expected they would send it to England when I –
Why did you expect that?
Because Mr. Saul said the English House would have to give their consent to the quotation from the Green's "History."

They would not have had to send it to England to do that?
I thought they would.

Elliott returned to "The Web" and its whereabouts during the crucial six months of late 1918 and early 1919.

Then, coming back to it, when did you say that it went to
England – can you give us any idea when it went to
England, according to your idea –
I do not know the date.
You do not know when it went, or when it came back?
I cannot give you the date.
Can you not say positively, one way or the other, whether you
know it went or not?
I know it went.
HIS LORDSHIP: *You do not know from any direct information,*
as I understand you?
Yes.
MR. ELLIOTT: *It is an inference you draw from the facts, is that*
right?
Yes.

Raney had heard enough, and adjourned the proceedings for one hour and lunch. Elliott had done his task well. He had peppered the plaintiff's testimony with a mixture of manuscripts and revisions, sown confusion as to the whereabouts and state of "The Web," and demonstrated that Florence Deeks had no direct evidence that her book had ever made its way to England.[12]

When court resumed at two o'clock, Elliott shifted to the matter of intrinsic evidence. His task now was to make a mockery of Florence's claim that a comparison of the two works demonstrated Wells's use of "The Web." His chosen weapon was ridicule.

He knew that she would attempt to demonstrate her claims by pointing out similarities, so he drew attention to the fact that, to Miss Deeks, Mr. Wells would be damned even when he had presented views the opposite of those in "The Web." The lawyer pointed to the fact that *The Outline of History* was far lengthier than "The Web," and that Wells had used far more authorities. Moreover, Elliott added, many of Wells's authorities were those to which she also had had access and used. Was it so surprising that the two works should, in some ways, resemble each other?[13]

Elliott decided it was time to show how preposterous the claim was that "The Web" and *The Outline* were alike in any fundamental way. He would have some fun and play his trump card.

> *Now, Miss Deeks, the theory of your book, the "Web," is the theme, dealing with women in history?*
> That is one feature.
> *That is the main theme running all through?*
> One of the main things.
> *And when you wrote the "Web," started out to write it, your idea was to place in prominence the position of women in the affairs of the World?*
> Yes.
> HIS LORDSHIP: *Did you ever abandon that theme? I think Mr. Saul suggested that you should abandon it, didn't he?*
> In my last revision I made it very much less prominent . . .
> MR. ELLIOTT: *. . . In chapter two, you deal there with the influence of women in the world?*
> Yes.
> *You discuss specially the love of the beautiful?*
> I think it comes in prominently.
> *And you discuss women as the architects and builders?*
> Yes . . .
> *Medical science, they instituted medical science?*
> Yes.
> *And the institution of poetry was also with the women?*
> Yes.
> *That they were responsible for the clothes worn by the race?*

"And still are," Robertson added. Even he was caught up in the spirit of Elliott's questioning.

And that they were supreme in Government in those days?
I did.[14]

Elliott knew exactly what he was doing, and why. The more he
drew Miss Deeks out about her views on the contributions of
women to history, the more preposterous they would seem to this
assembly of intelligent men – and, although he did not yet state it,
the more different her interpretation would appear to be from that
of Mr. Wells. So he continued to stretch the credulity of the learned
judge and the courtroom audience. In rapid succession, he drew out
from Miss Deeks the role she gave women in parenthood and in
Greek civic culture, and showed how at every point she contrasted
women's pacific virtues with men's aggressive instincts.

> HIS LORDSHIP: Mr. Elliott, what is the purpose of giving partic-
>   ularly all these features in this way, and getting the
>   witness's assent to all these now?
> MR. ELLIOTT: I just want to show through all these things that
>   the whole work is dealing with women . . . In doing this I
>   was going to ask her if there was any similar dealing with
>   these matters in Mr. Wells' book?[15]

With that, Elliott turned once again to the witness.

> *So, Miss Deeks, after going through these various chapters,
>   the theme all through your book at this time was women
>   and their position in the world?*
> Was one of the themes, the position of woman and specially
>   her position in democracy, and the position of man in
>   general, and the leaders in particular.
> *. . . And your object in writing this book was to bring before
>   your readers the best of women in ancient and modern
>   times?*
> History in general has never had woman's position incorpo-
>   rated in it as a whole, and I endeavoured to do it as a
>   whole, and her position seemed to fit in with democracy.
> *Yes?*

The great success of *The Outline of History* made H.G. Wells a rich man and might have left most authors satisfied; but the 1920s brought him only increased restiveness.

Easton Glebe was the converted rectory in Essex where H.G. and Catherine Wells lived from 1912 until her death in 1927. The site of many parties, and of several of Wells's amorous *passades*, it was seldom a happy home.

Catherine Wells found refuge in the persona of the supremely competent, always compliant "Jane" of legend. Her private writings told of deeper needs, unwelcomed and unmet by her husband.

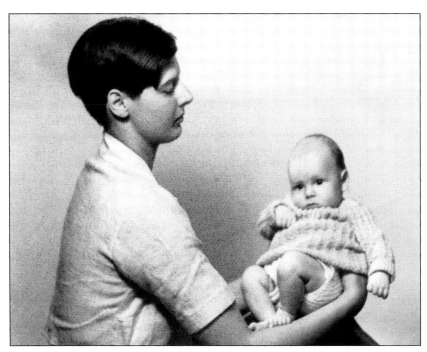

The affair between Wells and Rebecca West resulted in the birth of Anthony West on August 4, 1914, the day the Great War began. But this new bond was not strong enough to make H.G. leave Jane for Rebecca.

The abiding friendship between Sir Richard Gregory and H.G. Wells spanned more than six decades. After H.G.'s death, Gregory wrote: "I became his disciple as well as his friend, my attachment to him has always been stronger than to any friend in the world."

Hugh Eayrs spent his presidency of Macmillan of Canada from 1921 to 1940 at St. Martin's House, 70 Bond Street, Toronto, the headquarters that his predecessor Frank Wise had built. During these years, Eayrs transformed the company into an institution central to Canadian letters.

Sir Frederick Macmillan (left) and George P. Brett (right) presided with creative but firm hands over the London and New York branches of Macmillan from the 1890s until their deaths in 1936. When Miss Deeks launched her lawsuit in 1925, neither publisher was certain whether "The Web" had been sent to his office or not.

The centre of justice in Ontario since 1832, Osgoode Hall came to represent something else for Florence Deeks. "The Web" was a work about patriarchy and injustice for women through the ages. Her experience in this building ironically recapitulated the argument of her book.

The Supreme Court of Ontario (Appellate Division), 1934. Three of the four judges who heard *Deeks v. Wells* on appeal are present: Hon. Mr. Justice W.R. Riddell (second from left); Hon. Mr. Justice C.A. Masten (centre); and Hon. F.R. Latchford, Chief Justice in Appeal (far right). Mr. Justice J.F. Orde had died in 1932.

Author	Address	Title of MS
Dawson Erma	Goderich Ont.	"Niche do I condemn"
de Giffone A.	37 Somerset St. W. Ottawa	article on "Reinforced Concrete Slabs, Beams"
Deeks Miss F.R.	140 Farnham Ave San Francisco, Cal	"Come into the Garden Maud"
Douglas V.	944 Pacific Bldg	"Soulmates in Parkerland"
Dean H.H.	O.A.C. Guelph. Ont	"Dangling"
Dean H.H.	O.A.C. Guelph. Ont	Holly - Story of Farm Life
Dempster S.	206 Bloor St. East City	A Tragedy of Two Perns
Dagger F. Gordon	155½ Yonge St City	Songs of the Aftermath
Durand S.B.	11 Oriole Gardens, Toronto	Short Stories
Defries A.W.	Box 414. Nassau, Bahamas	Human Side of Pulp
Davies E.J.	Can. Bk. of Commerce Calgary. Alta.	Poems
Defries S.W.	Box 414. Nassau, Bahamas	In an Forgotten Country
Devlin B.J.	346 Daly Ave., Ottawa. Ont	Sonnets and Poems
Dunlop Miss E.W.	48 Chicora Ave.,	Story Million of Leading
Duffey Mrs Laura	4319 Pandora St., Vancouver. B.C.	The three Nations
Dale E.	33 Kintyre Ave City	"Jim" Blanks
Deeks Florence	140 Farnham Ave City.	"the Web"
Durand Laura B	11 Oriole Gardens City	Children's Book on Acting
Deeks F.J	140 Farnham Ave,	"The Dawn"
Defries Irma	London England	The Human Side of Pulp
June Mrs	Toronto	(Spiritual Studies)
de B. Huggins H.		

≠ G 2968

The Macmillan of Canada manuscript logbook was a crucial piece of evidence in *Deeks v. Wells*. The entry for "The Web" (fifth from the bottom) is followed two lines later by the entry for another Deeks manuscript: "The Dawn." But "The Dawn" was the title of the first chapter of "The Web." "False," Florence wrote next to the

Page of the Record Book of Manuscripts of the Macmillan Co. of Canada Limited

return dates on her copy of the exhibit. She believed that March 26, 1919, shown as the date "The Dawn" was received from her, was actually the day "The Web" had been returned to Bond Street from wherever it had been sent.

CLAIM AGAINST H. G. WELLS

Miss Florence Deeks (left), the Canadian authoress, snapped with her sister in London, where she will appear before the Privy Council in her appeal claiming £100,000 damages from Mr H. G. Wells for alleged infringement of copyright.

At the age of sixty-eight, Florence Deeks arrived in London to argue her appeal before the Judicial Committee of the Privy Council. On October 31, 1932, a Scottish newspaper photographer caught her (left) and Mabel in his lens. Moments later, as she made her case, came "the blow" from the Law Lords.

And democracy seemed to be opposed to militarism.

And just as you put it, that was to set these things out you wrote that book?

I set these things out when I wrote the book.

HIS LORDSHIP: In other words, she had a motive besides the motive of writing history.

MR. ELLIOTT: Yes. *Then, you do not suggest, Miss Deeks, that Mr. Wells' book deals with any such proposition?*

Mr. Wells' book omits women of course, altogether. He instances a few cases, a few names.

As you put woman forward, he does not seem to deal with her at all?

In another way he does deal, it is in an uncomplimentary way, whereas I have overstressed the point . . . Mr. Wells apparently overstresses it in the other way.

So you are at opposite ends of the pole as regards that?

Yes.[16]

W.J. Elliott had made his point. Far from conforming to Miss Deeks's thematic "plan," Wells had written his book from an entirely different point of view. How could he possibly be accused of plagiarism? This, too, diminished her credibility in the eyes of Raney and the other men in the courtroom.

He now turned to the matter of correspondences and parallels. If Raney found matters confusing thus far, he had heard nothing yet. Elliott's questions concerned the significance of Florence's "Comparison."

Miss Deeks, I see you took a great deal of pains in preparing this –

HIS LORDSHIP: She must have put in an enormous amount of work. The work in preparing the manuscript and then in comparing it with this book . . .

MR. ELLIOTT: *First, tell me this – do you claim that Mr. Wells copied your ideas?*

Oh, no – I am claiming that he copied my work as it stood in "The Web" –

> *Did you claim that he copied your language?*
> Very often.
> *And do you claim that the ideas that you displayed in your*
>   *book were copied by Mr. Wells in his book?*
> Sometimes the conclusions that I drew, he drew, and the result
>   I make, he makes.[17]

Elliott had made it appear that the witness contradicted herself. Having earlier indicated that "The Web" and *The Outline* were far apart in their consideration of women, she had now been made to suggest that he had sometimes copied her ideas.

In Florence's mind, no such confusion existed, but to sort the matter out would require much time and great attention to detail. Elliott took full advantage of the fact that no one except those who had seriously studied the two works could easily understand what she meant. He turned her attention to the treatment of Greek history in the two works.

> *Let us just look at it. Where does he take and copy your story?*
>   *. . . Let us deal with at page 21 – now you give us this case*
>   *as an outstanding one?*
> It is one of the outstanding ones.
> *Now, let us look at it – you say that VI (2) on the left hand*
>   *appear in your copy[;] in "Outline" it is XXII (304) on the*
>   *right?*
> That was it. I say that these two sections there –
> *You have to use what numbers of the section?*
> I say section VI (2) and VI (3) contains the statements of facts
>   which are contained in Wells XXII (304).[18]

Such details of identification were taxing in the extreme. Elliott, Deeks, and Raney had a copy of her list of comparisons in front of them as they attempted to identify corresponding passages in "The Web" and *The Outline*, but the sheer difficulty of locating them took attention away from the significance of the passages them-selves. Having expended mental energy enough in simply finding them, Raney may well have thought that the litany of historical detail hardly merited the effort.

As one of her examples of parallel passages, Florence drew attention to the discussions of Columbus.

> HIS LORDSHIP: I suppose this story has been told ten thousand times . . .
>
> MR. ELLIOTT: *You told us to come to page 46 – what do you see there?*
>
> We both speak of "beautiful weather" . . .
>
> *That is your part there starting, "Early on a beautiful Friday morning"?*
>
> The fact we both call the weather beautiful . . .
>
> *And what is the passage of Mr. Wells?*
>
> It says, "Early on a beautiful Friday morning," so and so, "the little expedition set sail." He says, "The little expedition went south to the Canaries and then set out across the unknown seas in beautiful weather with a helpful wind" – we both used the words, "Little Expedition," and the term "beautiful" . . .
>
> *In discussion of Columbus sailing, we agree that it was a small expedition, there were only three ships in it?*
>
> Yes, there were three ships.
>
> *You cannot complain because he says it was a little expedition?*
>
> I do complain of it.[19]

Florence was trying to explain that the key to proving that Wells had her work at hand rested in the pattern of the similar use of language, not in the individual instances; but each time she tried to point this out, Elliott deflected attention from language to the fact that each author was describing the same events. In what ways would they *not* use similar language to describe them? She and Robertson, as well as the experts they had consulted, knew that each instance of common language appeared insignificant in itself. The impact of the evidence was, instead, cumulative – in the gradual accretion of hundreds of such examples. She found it difficult to make her case when each instance was considered in isolation from the others.

Elliott asked her to provide another example. She decided to use the voyage of Vasco de Gama, and quoted from "The Web."

> "Also in 1498 the Portuguese under Vasco de Gama sailed around the African Continent and reached Calicut on the Malabar Coast." Wells says, "In 1497 Vasco de Gama sailed from Lisbon to Zanzibar and then with an arab pilot he struck across the Indian Ocean to Calicut in India" – but in his first note –
> HIS LORDSHIP: *What does he say?*
> In his first note, I have here, Vasco de Gama sailed around the African Continent," and his next note, he has "In 1498 Vasco de Gama sailed from Lisbon – "[20]

To Florence, this was a key passage. As she attempted to explain to the court, in "The Web" she had taken a sentence from Duruy stating that de Gama sailed from Lisbon and landed in India in 1498. But in her attempt to paraphrase, she had taken the date and placed it at the beginning of her own sentence – which then lent the erroneous impression that de Gama had set sail in 1498. In her view, Wells, who at no point acknowledged Duruy as one of his many sources, had initially made the same mistake in the date. He had managed to find and correct the error in the text of the published version of *The Outline*, but he had neglected to correct the dates provided in his footnotes.

Florence provided further examples of the way passages from her work dependent on Duruy had also mysteriously found their way into Wells's work. Elliott's rebuttal was simple: she got facts from Duruy; Duruy got them from some source of his own – and so did Mr. Wells. The plaintiff, he suggested, was not talking of correspondences at all, but of the historical record that was the common possession of any serious student of the past.

R.D. Moorhead, on behalf of Macmillan of New York, cross-examined Florence briefly after Elliott had finished. His main concern was to suggest that Macmillan of Canada had returned "The Web" to its author in early February 1919, and not in April as the plaintiff claimed. Later in the trial, when examining John Saul's secretary Mabel Hopkins, Moorhead would establish that this was the date given in the Macmillan of Canada logbook for the return of "The Web."[21] But, like Elliott before him, he also had to address the matter of Miss Deeks's mysterious manuscript "The Dawn." He drew attention to the fact that the Macmillan of Canada logbook of manuscripts had an entry for a manuscript called "The Dawn," dated as received on March 26, 1919, as then placed in the vault, and as having been returned on July 15, 1919. "The Dawn," he suggested, must have been a revision of the first version of "The Web."

Florence strenuously denied the assertion. She stated that the manuscript that had been returned to her on July 15, 1919, had been not "The Dawn" but the pamphlet Liston had asked her to write, "Love and War." But she had an answer about the mystery of "The Dawn."[22]

Towards the end of the trial, Robertson recalled Florence to the witness stand for a final time with one purpose in mind: to eliminate the confusion over "The Dawn" and its relation to "The Web," and to emphasize the importance of the entry concerning it in the Macmillan of Canada logbook of manuscripts. Under his questioning, Florence once again insisted that "The Web" had been returned to her not in early February, as the defence claimed, but in early April. He drew attention to the entry for "The Dawn" in the logbook for the date March 26, 1919. She insisted that she had submitted no manuscript at that time. Moreover, no such manuscript called "The Dawn" existed. Did she subsequently submit a manuscript to Macmillan? Yes, but it had been the pamphlet "Love and War," solicited by Montrose Liston in his letter rejecting "The Web." She had not delivered it to Macmillan until June. The pamphlet "Love and War," thrown into court by the defence, simply masked a significant point: that Liston's letter rejecting "The Web" was written the day after "The Dawn" had been received by Macmillan as an apparently new manuscript from Miss Deeks.[23]

To Florence Deeks and to R.S. Robertson, only one rational conclusion could be drawn concerning the receipt of a manuscript that did not exist. On March 26, "The Web" returned to Macmillan of Canada from England, where it had been for several months.

Florence was certain she knew what had happened. A clerk only recently employed by Macmillan, and therefore unaware of the existence of "The Web," had hastily examined it, thinking it to be a new submission. The author was identified only by a pseudonym. This would make entry of the submission into the Macmillan manuscript logbook difficult, so, uncertain what to do, the clerk had taken her problem to the new editor, Mr. Liston. He seemed to know a little about the manuscript, and after he had told her the author's name she left the manuscript with him. Then she returned to the outer office to make the entry in the logbook so that the manuscript would be recorded as having been duly received.

In doing so, however, the clerk had made two mental errors. First, she got Miss Deeks's initials wrong, writing them down as "F.F." Then, still relying on her memory, she put "The Dawn" rather than "The Web" down as the title of the work. The phrase "The Dawn" had been prominently displayed on the first page of the manuscript: it was the title of Chapter One of "The Web."

Montrose Liston had immediately sharpened his critical tools and put them to good use on the manuscript in front of him. Unlike the clerk, he knew that this was not a new submission, and he had not mistaken the chapter title for that of the book, so when he checked for the title "The Web" in the manuscript logbook, he found the author's Toronto address easily enough. The next day, he sent his harsh letter of rejection to Miss Florence A. Deeks.

That, at least, was how the author conceived that the situation had unfolded back in 1919.

Apart from a brief cross-examination by Moorhead, Florence's day in court had ended. Although Moorhead introduced the manuscript "Love and War" once again, Raney was clearly intrigued by the implications of Robertson's clarification of the mysterious existence and fate of "The Dawn." "It would almost seem," he said, "as if these entries in the book and this letter, were all designed to lend mystery to these transactions."[24]

Florence left the witness box and took a seat next to her lawyer. It was time for her first expert witness to be called. After the death of Sir Bertram Windle, she had needed to find someone to take his place. Fortunately, towards the end of 1929 she had found a scholar who proved willing to consider her request. Like Sir Bertram, he had been reluctant at first; but by the time he had completed his own comparison of "The Web" and *The Outline of History*, his initial hesitancy had evaporated. In fact, he seemed positively enthusiastic.

Professor William Andrew Irwin of the University of Toronto settled into the witness stand in the middle of Monday afternoon. Prompted by R.S. Robertson, he began to describe his credentials as an expert witness for the plaintiff. He had been a student of Oriental languages at the University of Toronto between 1908 and 1912, graduating with honours. After spending a year or two on the Canadian prairies, he had returned to Toronto for two years of graduate work towards a master's degree. Then he left the country to study further at the University of Chicago. At present, he held the rank of associate professor at University College in the University of Toronto, but he had just accepted a position as full professor at Chicago.[25]

What Irwin could have stated, but did not, was that he had been a University of Toronto gold medallist in 1912, that he had studied for the Methodist ministry at Victoria College (his time in the Canadian west had been his period of ministerial probation), and that he had been ordained in the Methodist Church of Canada in 1919. In the same year, he married the daughter of Professor J.F. McLaughlin, Victoria's head of the Old Testament department (and later dean of theology), and took up his new position at University College. Whenever possible, he had returned to Chicago to advance his research.[26]

Irwin was as unlike Florence Deeks as any witness could be. At the age of forty-six, he was in the prime of his career, immersed in the history of the Near East and a champion of the intellectual battle in the graduate seminar of the research university. He was fearless and opinionated, even brash. From the moment he took the witness stand, R.S. Robertson knew he would not need to draw Irwin out. The professor had firm views on the subject at hand and was eager to give them voice.

After he had confirmed that Irwin had examined "The Web" and *The Outline of History* over a period of five or six months, Robertson asked his first and most important question: "Now, are you able to say from a comparison of the work and assuming that Miss Deeks' manuscript was written as now stated in the evidence, and that Mr. Wells' work was begun not later than the latter part of 1918, are you able to tell his Lordship whether in your opinion the manuscript of Deeks was before or in the hands of the writer of the 'Outline of History'?"

Irwin did not hesitate: "I would say, your Lordship, the evidence is overwhelming that it was in the hands of the author of 'Outlines [*sic*] of History' before he wrote, and during the time he was writing."[27]

Robertson noted that Irwin had prepared a lengthy and elaborate report, from which the witness proposed to read during his testimony. The lawyer had already provided a copy to the defence; now he gave one to Mr. Justice Raney. This was unusual, but with the agreement of the defence, Raney accepted it. He reminded Elliott that the document might provide good grounds for cross-examination. Besides, he added, "we do not want to be all summer trying this case."[28]

Irwin began his testimony by emphasizing that he had "sought throughout to weigh the matter judicially," and not "to make out a case for or against anybody." Indeed, he said, he had undertaken to ignore Miss Deeks's charges. He had simply placed the two works side by side, compared them, and drawn his own independent conclusions. He had made an especially close study of those sections of the two works that dwelt on the history of the Near East, his area of expertise.[29]

It seemed "inherently improbable," Irwin read from his report, that an author so well known as H.G. Wells would possibly have occasion to rely on the unpublished manuscript of a writer as obscure as Miss Deeks. Wells had among his circle of friends many outstanding minds, and his collaborators constituted "a group of brilliant literary men." What concerned Irwin, however, was not Mr. Wells's reputation; "the question rather is whether Mr. Wells of the 'Outline of History' has shown himself there a master of literary craft and an expert in historical science so far removed from the level of Miss Deeks' works that his having borrowed therefrom is *a priori* absurd." The answer, he said, "must be an emphatic negative," for *The Outline* was "a very shoddy ill-digested piece of work devoid of literary excellence. I cannot recall a single passage that commends itself as the work of an artist."

W.J. Elliott was on his feet, objecting. This was not the measured testimony of an expert, but the barbed judgment of the academic. But Irwin continued: "As history it is commonplace in the extreme. The work has no merits that would preclude it being dependent upon an unknown writer. Indeed on the contrary, the striking deficiencies and inaccuracies of Mr. Wells' treatment, taken in connection with his imposing array of scholarly collaborators implies rather cogently that there is something deeply wrong."[30]

Elliott could stand no more. "My Lord, this could never go in as evidence in chief from any witness, and it is rather abusive, and I do not think it should go on the record, because there is nothing to substantiate it, and it is a thing that you would not expect from any man who professes to be a Professor of Toronto University." Irwin's statements, he said, were nothing less than libel and should not be permitted to become part of the record. R.D. Moorhead, for Macmillan New York, concurred. Elliott remained in shock at the scandalous breach of judicial decorum, but Raney permitted Irwin to continue. "Never mind," said the judge, "the critics are not very tender of one another."[31]

Thus encouraged, Irwin began to justify his harsh views. "With advisers such as those," he began, "why did he not produce a first class history of the World?" Instead, Wells had produced a slipshod work containing such a range of similarities with "The Web" as to constitute dependence on it. But an even greater clue to the reliance lay in their differences. Irwin elaborated. Both works were of similar scope, had similar plans, and neglected "to the point of omission" the whole phase of human cultural achievement. Both were "sadly out of balance," and in similar ways. Their treatment of the ancient

East was inadequate; they gave disproportionate space to Greece, Macedonia, and Rome, they overlooked "Achaemenia Persia," and they neglected the Seleucid and Ptolemaic empires, of India and Syria and of Egypt, respectively. Their treatment of Israel and Juda was unsatisfactory but in similar ways; they gave only casual reference to the Ottoman Turks and neglected Tamerlane.[32]

Irwin's comments thus far were broad and very general. But he had only just warmed up. Florence listened with satisfaction as he went on to discuss at length the first chapters of each book. Her own initial suspicions had begun with the way Wells had appeared to depend, like "The Web," on Victor Duruy's account of the origins of the universe and the solar system; yet he had not listed Duruy among his authorities. Irwin focused on the same point: "You will find step after step there tracing practically identically the same points, and points where the plans of both are wrong, sadly out of proportion with implications that simply they are contradictory of known facts of history upon that point, in a detail where both go wrong here, and the peculiar thing is, in the face of these works which Mr. Wells submits as his authorities, he has refused to follow the correct course of his authorities, has chosen rather to go wrong with Miss Deeks' plan."[33]

He went on, word by word and line by line, comparing the first few pages of "The Web" and *The Outline* with Duruy's account. Each incorporated the same words, the same phrases, the same facts, the same order of detail, the same errors. "The interrelation here cannot be explained as dependent upon a common mere suggestion; the dependence is documentary. Either, one is dependent upon the other, or both have used a common source and followed it closely." But Irwin had examined the sources Wells had cited. Their accounts were different from his. They had rejected, for example, the old Laplace theory of the origins of the solar system. But Wells had not: it was vital to his explanation, just as it had been in "The Web."[34]

All this was enough to make the head, not merely the world, spin. It was late in the day, and Raney adjourned the court until half past ten in the morning, in two days' time.

Reporters for the Toronto dailies scurried from the courtroom to their newsrooms and their deadlines. The day in court had been a long one, and they had found the testimony of Florence Deeks less than helpful in providing them with copy. She had been too reticent on the stand, too much on guard. She had seemed to view the whole proceeding with suspicion. But Irwin was another story. The professor was a man of words, and not equivocal ones. Irwin, so far, was the story. The next morning, the account in the Toronto *Star* contained nothing of the plaintiff's testimony, only her claim of $500,000 damages. But they quoted the professor.[35]

Later on Tuesday, Hugh Eayrs sent identical letters to Sir Frederick Macmillan and George P. Brett about Irwin and his testimony. The professor, he said, "has been rather a Bolshevik amongst the members of the Faculty and is thoroughly disapproved of by University authorities. He is a nasty greasy piece of work." He added that their own expert, Professor Underhill, had gone through Irwin's report and would find it easy "to riddle it."[36]

On Wednesday morning at the appointed time, Irwin resumed his testimony. It was clear that he had not yet done with the origins of life on earth, and he brought with him accounts by other authors in order to demonstrate how the matter could have been handled in ways very different from those chosen by Wells. How remarkable it was, then, that he had opted to open his book in a way identical to that of Miss Deeks! How could this be merely coincidental? Robertson was worried that the detail might threaten to overshadow the substance of the evidence. Irwin needed to be more concise, more closely focused. "How could this be of any significance as bearing upon the question raised as to the resumé of the Outline?" Robertson asked.

Irwin's bold reply was, "This illustrates how a man's mind will work when he is frankly copying. I want to make the point of the distance between this and Mr. Wells, as approximated between Mr. Wells and Miss Deeks." But Raney's mind was on the clock.

HIS LORDSHIP: *The difficulty is that if we pursue all the ramifications of discussion and exhaust all the things that appeal to you in detail, we shall consume an enormous amount of time, bearing in mind that we are dealing with eternity, almost . . .*

MR. ROBERTSON: We say that it is almost impossible that two people writing independently on the subject could have been so close on the whole of the history of mankind, and it is not found anywhere else.

MR. ELLIOTT: My friend should not give evidence.

HIS LORDSHIP: *I do not want to interfere, Mr. Robertson, with what is no doubt a carefully thought out plan of presentation; but the cross-examination is often much longer than the examination in chief.*

MR. ROBERTSON: We have taken great care, and since the witness was in the box we have seen if something should not be done to shorten it. The Professor is not going to make it any longer than is necessary to state his point.

HIS LORDSHIP: *There are practical limitations which, of course, are not binding upon Miss Deeks or Mr. Wells.*[37]

The language of justice in the Ontario of the day was one of decorum and restraint. It was clear to those in lawyers' gowns that the words of Mr. Justice Raney, uttered with just a hint at ironic understatement, had been a quiet warning: he wished the proceedings to be speeded up. This subtlety was lost on Professor Irwin. He took his lead, instead, from counsel. So he acknowledged the judge's wish for brevity and then proceeded more or less to carry on as he had done before. There can be little doubt that Raney made a mental note of the conduct of the witness.

A lot of history remained to be covered if the case of *Deeks v. Wells* were ever to end. Irwin sought above all the judge's attention; instead, he had taxed Raney's patience. To some in the court, Irwin seemed arrogant in the extreme. His academic training, he said, had provided him with "an unusually good training" for work of this sort, examining the internal evidence of documents. "I speak as one who has a right to speak." And speak he did, moving slowly towards his conclusions on the subject of Deeks, Wells, and Duruy. "The answer demands no intricate argument. The detail of verbal similarities, the identity in order of minor ideas, the sentences of similar structure show clearly that Wells' rewriting of Miss Deeks' story is not a re-telling of a remembered account read yesterday or even an hour ago. Making all allowance for possible unusual feats of memory the situation quite clearly was that the manuscript of Web was at hand as he wrote, if indeed it did not actually lie open before him. In any case his reading of this particular passage of it was so recent that his writing was to all intents and purposes a copying and expansion thereof."[38]

Irwin once again read from his prepared report. He had only reached the simian generations on earth, but once again he pointed to "the close identity of ideas, at certain points their identity of order and even in some cases identity of wording," for which he provided a tabulation of word sequences.

Web:	Millions of years.
Outline:	Millions of simian generations.
Web:	An animal with a relatively enormous brain case; a skilful hand.
Outline:	One particular creature . . . it was small brained by our present standards, but it had clever hands.
Web:	Dwelt in caves and trees and roamed the forest.
Outline:	It clambered about the trees and ran, probably ran well on its hind legs on the ground.
Web:	Feeding on nuts and fruits.
Outline:	It handled fruits and beat nuts upon the rocks.
Web:	Much the same as the man-like apes of Borneo today.
Outline:	It was half ape, half monkey.
Web:	Tendency to throw stones, flourish sticks, and in general defeat aggression.
Outline:	Caught up sticks and stones to smite its fellows.
Web:	Emerged from the animal into mankind.
Outline:	It was our ancestor.

"He was a nice animal to have as an ancestor," Elliott found himself saying, for the record.[39]

Some in the room, those with scholarly interests and backgrounds, would have been impressed by Irwin's close textual analysis, the detailed study he had made of "The Web" and *The Outline*, and the fact that he had examined in detail the secondary sources on which the two works had been built. He could state with authority quite precisely just when, and how, Wells had used his acknowledged sources – and, more important, when he had not. For the verbal sequence he had just outlined, he was able to demonstrate that "The Web" had used Christie's *Advance of Woman*, and a passage from the historian James Harvey Robinson's essay on the history of history; the latter had been found in *Source Book of Social Origins*. Robinson, in turn, had quoted from Sir Ray Lankester's *Kingdom of Man*. Irwin insisted that Wells had used none of them. "So we have conclusive evidence here again that Mr. Wells has taken a passage from Miss Deeks, only thinly disguising his plagiarism by a few slight alterations and . . . [it] is written so immediately from Miss Deeks' passage that he must have turned practically direct from her manuscript to his own writing."[40]

Irwin had one final point to make before turning his attention to the ancient Near East: the treatment of early women in the two works. He pointed to the way "The Web" eulogized "savage woman" and attributed to her great importance in the evolution of civilization and its first inventions, such as huts, agriculture, milling, medicine, baskets, fire, cooking, pottery, weaving, canning, and so forth. Wells mentioned such accomplishments, but not only denied woman a place in their discovery but did so in a tone of disparagement: "The information at this point that the women were small squaws and grossly fat is dragged in." The reference, said Irwin, was gratuitous and insulting. Why? Irwin had an explanation: "These ideas have no logical connection whatever so would seem to be suggested by some authority which Wells is following. And certainly Web provides just the required example . . . This would most readily explain his mood of contradiction here: he has found in Web information that he knows to be wrong so he denies it with emphasis; there was no pottery, no cultivation, no buildings, etc. His disparagement of women then becomes funny; he seems to say, Yes, your fine woman who was a paragon of virtues – she was nothing but a squaw and too fat at that!"[41]

To Irwin, Wells's treatment of the history of the Near East demonstrated even more conclusively that Wells must have had access to "The Web" and put it to use. For example, both works completely ignored one of the most important periods of Egyptian social and intellectual development, that of the Middle Kingdom. "If Mr. Wells were really following any of his imputed authorities, his oversight here would be unintelligible. I mean there that all his authorities deal with the Middle Kingdom, and they stress the social and intellectual attainments of the Middle Kingdom, and more so because it has the social values which Mr. Wells wants, and yet he ignores it." Why? Because he was relying on "The Web."[42]

Irwin pointed to the difficulties faced by scholars in the interpretation of hieroglyphics. Differences in vocalization had created a wide range of spellings of Egyptian names, and scholarship reflected this. Irwin had gone through the sources Wells claimed to have used, and found that "not one of Wells' authorities" used the names Wells had chosen. Only one work used precisely the same nomenclature: "The Web."

One particular Egyptian name, Irwin said, was in fact what had first twigged him to the dependence of *The Outline* on "The Web" and had made him suspicious. It was the name "Hatasu." In Florence's work, she was characterized as "Regent"; in Wells's, properly, as Queen. "The Web" knew little about her, *The Outline* rather more: that, for example, she was aunt and stepmother of Thothmes III and that sometimes on her monuments she was represented in male attire. But both works omitted much that was known to be important about her. Most significant of all, however, was the name. Irwin had worked in the field for more than twenty years and had never seen or heard of it until he started the current investigation. It appeared in none of Wells's authorities, or in any other recent works. "Only by special investigation did I discover it," Irwin concluded, "and that in old histories of 1890 and earlier. Since that time the accepted form of the name has been Hatshepsut."

For Irwin, this was usage in common of such an extraordinary nature "as in itself almost to prove interdependence." He added that in general such agreements were "so numerous and so peculiar as to provide again conclusive proof of inter-dependence; the question of authorities has already been assessed, so we can briefly summarize that we find proof that Outline was using Web."[43]

Again and again, as he slowly talked his way through the ancient civilizations of the Near East, Irwin found telling signs of H.G. Wells's reliance on the work of Florence Deeks. Why were their accounts so similar in detail while so different from all authorities other than Duruy? Of all things to say of the Phoenicians, why did both authors choose to mention their caravan voyages overland to the East? The Phoenicians were a seafaring people: they traded by sea, not by land. This was a fundamental detail of their history, known to all historians, but not to Miss Deeks, for she had spoken of Phoenician "caravans" plying their trade overland. And so had Mr. Wells.[44]

William Irwin had formed a mental picture that helped explain such identities of language, fact, and error, and he ventured it: "Suppose he had read the Web's passage just before starting this chapter, unless his memory is one of the most unusual power the similarities would be much less close than we actually find. The situation will however be satisfied by this theory. In his reading of Web this passage had attracted him; he had made a note of its character and location – the difficulty of locating passages in this manuscript, unprovided as it is with index or table of contents, implies strongly that his notes on relevant passages were written, not mental. Then coming to this section 8 he realizes that this summary of Phoenician commerce is just the thing he wants; he turns it up, refreshes his memory with a hasty glance, then pushing the manuscript aside writes this concluding section of his chapter.[45]

Irwin went on, in a similar manner, to work his way through the Wells and Deeks accounts of the history of Israel and of Greece. With respect to the Holy Land, the two works had of course relied heavily on the Biblical account, yet both also made "identical allusions" of a distinctive sort; both favoured, for example, an explanation of kingship at odds with contemporary scholarship. To illustrate his point, Irwin examined in sequence their treatment of Samuel, Saul, David, and Solomon.[46]

As to the Greeks, Irwin noted yet more instances of language in common, peculiarities of interpretation, and errors of fact. Both "The Web" and The Outline had suggested that Cyrus the Younger had been king of Persia. "We are driven to conclude that here again the two works agree in defiance of history." Florence had referred to Aspasia as the wife of Pericles; to Wells, she was "in effect his wife." Why this exact phrasing? Why, asked Irwin, had he not simply referred to her, like the authorities he claimed to have used, as a courtesan or as his mistress? The answer was simple: "The astonishing rendering is due to the influence of a source which Wells is following. And it is remarkable that this odd idea appears in Web also, save that there it is presented without apology."[47]

The evidence Irwin wished to introduce was not only that of expert opinion, but also of a physical nature. Florence had provided him with the version of "The Web" that had been returned by Macmillan of Canada in 1919, and he had examined key passages from it and *The Outline* to see whether the damning pages were those that had been dog-eared or otherwise showed signs of hard use. It was his view that there was indeed a correspondence between passages suspiciously alike and these pages. Irwin invoked the image of Wells at his desk: "The detailed similarities at these points show that the manuscript of Web was at hand as he wrote, and the dispersion of these key passages throughout a large part of this earlier section of the two works, as well as their linking up by a considerable number of minor similarities which I have not listed demonstrate that his reference to Web was no chance or sporadic thing but that the manuscript was one of his authorities, constantly available, lying close at hand at his work table and referred to repeatedly if not steadily throughout the progress of his writings. Sometimes it lay open before him and his writing was palpably a disguised copying of Miss Deeks' passage; at other times he made notes of her treatment and wrote more freely from these notes."[48]

If Raney was willing to allow such wild speculation, however well informed, into the record, Robertson was certainly not going to object.

Thus encouraged, Irwin plunged on, into a discussion of the similarity between the overall plans of the two works of world history. After the break for the lunch hour, Alexander and the Macedonian empires rose, Jerusalem fell, and so did Rome. By mid-afternoon, the Ottoman Turks and the Persians, India, China and

Japan, and all Central and Eastern Asia had made their appearance (although only because both "The Web" and *The Outline* had seen fit to neglect them). "We have found at point after point," Irwin concluded, "an amazing agreement as to selection of topics, as to order of presentation, and in the main as to proportionate emphasis. This agreement was frequently followed into peculiarities amounting even to errors, and this in the face very often of the combined authority of the best works in the field . . . Making all allowances for differences, it yet remains that the two works have one and the same plan; and that plan, we must conclude, Mr. Wells took from Miss Deeks."[49]

So the conclusion of the entire investigation, my answer to the problem which Miss Deeks set me last November, is this: –

1. Mr. Wells had read Miss Deeks' manuscript before commencing his work on what we now know as The Outline of History.

2. He analyzed her manuscript and made written notes of features which attracted him.

3. With but unimportant revision he adopted this analysis as a plan for his own writing. His use of the plan of Web was such as to justify the epithet "slavish."

4. Certain passages in The Web he took over in detail. He re-wrote them in such a fashion as might be hoped to obscure their dependence, but they remain a palpable copying.

5. He kept her manuscript readily available as he wrote, apparently at times it was actually open before him, and he made frequent reference to it.

6. He used The Web as his chief source and authority. He followed it very much more closely and continuously than he did any of the works to which he refers. Indeed, of some of these I can find no evidence of use whatever. His citation of them is no more than a bluff.[50]

Just how Wells had come to use "The Web" was a matter, Irwin confessed, he could not answer fully. But given that Wells had already stated in his discovery evidence that he "had never formulated definite plans for the book" prior to 1918, the professor was willing to try.

W.J. Elliott could abide this no more. The witness did not seem to understand the distinction between the evidence of an expert and the gossip of the senior common room. "Of course this is not evidence," he stated. "I am not objecting to this, because it is quite evident that this witness is carried away and wants to make a speech, I think; but it is quite evident that this is not evidence."[51] But Irwin went on, as if undisturbed at his University College lectern, his historian's imagination in full flight before the captive audience.

> It is quite clear that he regarded Miss Deeks' manuscript very highly; no man would make such extensive use of it otherwise. It must have roused him to a realization of the possibilities in publishing such a work at that time. But this is to be considered as well: having undertaken the project, he wrote under very high pressure . . . Moreover, the time which the evidence allows for the actual writing strongly corroborates this. Somewhere about October of 1918 he is fairly started; but the next July the work is complete save for some minor revision . . .
>
> In about nine months he produced a manuscript of about half a million words, surveying all the intricate and recondite subjects entailed in a history, not of mankind alone, but of the earth. It is simply stupendous. And if I understand aright his testimony, he denies that he dictated to stenographers; on the contrary he wrote it entirely himself in longhand . . .
>
> To do that in a bare nine or ten months is a task that might well stagger one. The mere writing was exacting. There could have been no time whatever for exhaustive reading, for collation of authorities and maturing of views and modes of expression. These things can be done only through years of quiet work, not in a few hectic months of feverish activity . . . For some reason he felt that speed was of importance. It may have been that he felt the market was peculiarly ripe for his purpose, and that he must hasten before the public mood changed . . . But there is no evidence against the view, and probabilities favor it strongly, that his reason was an anxiety to

forestall the publication of The Web. He must have known that he could retain the manuscript in his possession but for a limited time. [52]

From Florence's perspective, Professor Irwin had done no more than tell the truth. But there was a distinction to be made between the search for the truth and the system of justice. Irwin's initial criticisms of the literary value of Wells's work had been highly subjective and beyond the realm of his expertise. He was a historian, not a critic. That had set the tone of his subsequent testimony, just as, unintentionally, it had served the cause of the defence. It was not Irwin's task to settle the truth of the case as a whole, and in his highly speculative but unequivocal attempts to do so he had undermined the authority of his own testimony.

Irwin's opinions on subjects other than those in which he was an acknowledged expert may well have been interesting, but they violated the rules of evidence. In the eyes of the court, they neither tested nor furthered the evidence – they lacked probative value. His theories were just that – the academic musings of a professor who wanted to give a lecture. Every time he strayed from the detailed comparison of "The Web" and The Outline, he made his own motivations suspect. In fact, Irwin had made many extremely important points as an expert in his field, and he had proved that he possessed an unrivalled knowledge of the works of history in question. But as W.J. Elliott quickly recognized, each time the professor took it upon himself to solve the case, he deflected everyone's attention away from the evidence of real importance: the slow and damning accumulation of similarities and differences in use of language and in historical detail.

Under normal circumstances, counsel for Wells would have cross-examined the witness at length. Elliott, however, knew that this was not necessary. Crossing verbal swords with Irwin over the people and events of history, he knew, would place himself at a great disadvantage with so learned a witness. So he kept his cross-examination brief, and away from the validity of the internal evidence. Instead, he called into question Irwin's motivation in undertaking Miss Deeks's request, and pointed to the fact that she had earlier asked scholars as eminent as Harry Elmer Barnes and R.M. MacIver to do so, and they had wisely refused. He noted that Irwin had confined himself only to the early sections of the two books. He alluded to the fact that if it could be proven that "The Web" had been completed *after* publication of *The Outline of History*, his testimony would be worthless.

And what, Elliott asked, if "The Web" had remained in the possession of Macmillan of Canada to the end of January 1919, as John Saul's letter of the 31st of the month seemed to suggest? How could Wells possibly have had Deeks's manuscript in his possession long enough to have made use of it? Surely, Irwin did not suggest that the eminent men employed by H.G. Wells had done nothing to help the author out? Professor Gilbert Murray? Professor Ernest Barker? Sir Richard Gregory? How could Irwin possibly have stated that *The Outline* was shoddy and without literary excellence? Finally, Elliott asked, had Irwin really "read all the authorities Mr. Wells refers to?" Irwin answered with a question of his own: Had Elliott?[53]

Robertson's re-examination consisted of only a few questions. Had the request of Florence Deeks in any way compromised Irwin's independence of judgment? No. Was it not true that he had been asked to make his report because an earlier expert could no longer do so? Yes – Sir Bertram Windle, who was now deceased. And what of Wells's use of his learned collaborators? Their contribution seemed to have consisted only of comments the author lazily placed into his footnotes – comments that often contradicted the text itself. Finally:

MR. ROBERTSON: *In cases where you have used the argument that The Web and The Outline are in agreement, but they are both in disagreement with the known authorities, in that sort of instances did you read and search the other authorities upon the point?*

I searched them. Some of it was not necessary to read; I have known them well for years.

HIS LORDSHIP: He has been living with this subject for years.[54]

Court that day may well have seemed to span not the usual hours, but several millennia. Only the first expert witness for the plaintiff had testified. Two more were yet to come. As he sat waiting for the next historian to make his appearance, Hector Charlesworth mulled over the day's proceedings. "The witness naturally had a grand time when he got to Babylon and Egypt," he would later write. "That day in court was rather like an historical pageant. Enter the prophet Samuel, enter King Saul, enter King David, and so on."[55]

14   *Ripostes*

A trial may in theory be an objective pursuit of
truth, but in practice there are many subjective
factors which influence the course of events. Justice
may in theory be blind, but in practice she has altogether too human a perspective.

> Martin L. Friedland, *The Trials of Israel Lipski* (1984)

"There is some risk of one's being asked to become
a historian. Judges aren't historians."

> Judge Charles Gray, quoted by D.D. Guttenplan in
> "The Holocaust on Trial," *Atlantic Monthly* (February 2000)

ON WEDNESDAY AFTERNOON, June 4, R.S.
Robertson called his second expert witness, Lawrence Johnston
Burpee. The eminent Canadian historian and man of letters had
travelled from Ottawa a day or two earlier and was feeling under
the weather, but he knew that he was one of the main witnesses for
Florence Deeks.[1] He had spent many hours comparing "The Web"
and *The Outline of History*, and the hard work had gradually convinced him of the strength of the woman's case. What he heard from
the lips of Professor W.A. Irwin in court confirmed his judgment.

On the witness stand, Burpee quickly established his *bona fides*:
historian of northwestern America, Fellow of the Royal Society of
Canada, honorary secretary to the Royal Society of Canada and
member of its council, founding president of the Canadian Historical
Association, president of the Canadian Authors' Association, and, at
the present time, editor of the *Canadian Geographical Journal*.[2]

He testified that he had first examined Florence Deeks's manuscript in 1926, at her request, and that he had then compared it
with *The Outline of History* and submitted a report to her. Asked

by Robertson about the relationship between the two works, he stated: "I think The Outline of History shows . . . many evidences of its dependence upon the manuscript called The Web." To explain the relationship further, he added: "I would assume that either Mr. Wells himself or that someone acting on his behalf had had access to the manuscript . . . and made a very complete study of it."[3]

Perhaps Burpee had sensed Mr. Justice Raney's impatience over the length of William Irwin's testimony, for to save time he asked the court's permission to read from the opinion he had prepared in 1926. But he prefaced his remarks by saying that, because many of the grounds of similarity he was about to discuss had already been noted by Irwin, he wished the court to know that he had never before met Professor Irwin or seen his written opinion. He added that, until Miss Deeks had asked him to make his examination, he had never heard of her, and that initially he had approached his task "with the feeling, almost the conviction, that the charge was incredible."[4]

Burpee began to read from his report. The impression left on his mind had been that to a great extent "the plan, scope, spirit and language of The Web" had been incorporated into *The Outline*. Examples might be provided "almost indefinitely," he noted, but Professor Irwin's thorough analysis, with which he was in "substantial agreement," seemed to make this unnecessary. He did read into the record the many instances in *The Outline* where the metaphor of a web, or variants of it, occurred, citing them as characteristic examples (and by no means an exhaustive list) of parallel passages. Taken individually, they might appear "trifling," he said, but "in the mass" they became "convincing."[5]

Robertson asked Burpee whether there were any particular resemblances that reflected common errors in dates or in names. He cited the fact that, in their accounts of the dating of the creation of the Holy Roman Empire, both works used the crowning of Charlemagne by Pope Leo III in 800 AD. Most authorities, he pointed out, instead placed the date at 962, when Otto the Great was crowned by Pope John XII. "There would thus appear to be the same error in The Web and The Outline." He then read into the record thirty-three instances of parallel passages, similarities of ideas and language, and other instances of errors in common. "I once more point out that these few examples, taken almost at random, give no adequate idea of the extent of the similarities in these two books – it is the cumulative effect of many such examples that compels one to the conclusion that the 'Outline' leans heavily upon the 'Web.'"[6]

These were conclusions Burpee had drawn in 1926, after writing his initial report and a supplement to it; but as preparation for the trial he had re-examined the two books only a few months before. He had found "no grounds for changing the opinion then reached," but now asked for the privilege to add something to what he had written earlier. It concerned the kind of preparation required of a writer to produce a work of the sort represented by *The Outline of History*.

The witness freely conceded that H.G. Wells was without question an outstanding novelist. Nevertheless, until he had begun to write the book in question he had made no pretence of being a historian. Wells's examination for discovery, which Burpee had read, disclosed that he began writing in November 1918 and had substantially completed the book by July 1919. The idea for the work had occurred to Wells, by his own account, "a month or two earlier, but in October, 1918, he was still trying to persuade other people to undertake it; that he wrote the entire work himself, and that it runs to 250,000 words." (This projected length was Wells's early estimate, and it was to prove wildly inaccurate.)

Burpee wanted the court to know that in his view this was impossible. His own book *The Search for the Western Sea*, on a much smaller "corner of the domain of history," was somewhat under 200,000 words in length but had required eighteen months in the actual writing. Wells took upon himself the entire history of mankind and yet had done so in a little over eight months. "With the time at his disposal," said Burpee, "it would have been a heavy undertaking to have written a popular novel of the same length. When one remembers what he was actually doing, it sounds miraculous."[7]

He wanted the court to understand just what was required in the construction of a historical work of the magnitude of what Wells claimed he had done single-handed.

Think of it; we are asked to believe, that with no background as an historian; with no time to collect, study and digest his material . . . , Mr. Wells sat down to a work that no historian would dream of undertaking without years of most careful preparation . . .

May I go a little further. In practice the writer of a work on universal history must rely upon secondary authorities. It would be quite impracticable, and in many cases impossible, to go back to the original documents . . . But the secondary authorities, when we are dealing with world history, will embrace an almost incredible number of books and other printed material . . .

It is not necessary to assume that Mr. Wells would have to consult all the books that have been published in every branch of history, even if that were humanly possible; but it is necessary to assume that he would be on familiar terms with all the books that count in that very wide and complicated field. And no one who has carefully read the "Outline of History" can escape the conclusion that the author of that work either had gone himself very deeply into his subject, or that someone else had done it for him. All the evidence we have tends to deny the first alternative. The time within which his book was written precludes the possibility of Mr. Wells having made a deep or prolonged study of his subject at that time; and there is nothing to suggest that he might have done it before. For years past he had been very busily engaged in writing books of imagination rather than of fact, and he would have neither time nor occasion for studying the material relating to world history. We are thrown back upon the second alternative, that someone else must have done it for him.[8]

Burpee knew from the discovery evidence that Wells had involved "no collaborators" in the ordinary sense of helping an author to research and write his book, and he informed the court of this. The author had done this work himself; his "collaborators" had merely criticized what he had already written. Wells prepared the manuscript, and his wife did the typewriting.

W.J. Elliott rose to remind Burpee that Wells had given evidence in England that he "was writing along the lines of The Outline as early as 1893," but this did not deflect the witness from his line of thought. The fact was that, of any number of approaches that might have been taken to the subject of world history, Mr. Wells had chosen one that closely replicated the plan of "The Web." This was critically important, and Burpee chose to stress it in summing up his testimony:

> Faced with an immense volume of fact, traditions, opinions, the accumulation of thousands of years, one historian will decide to use certain of these and reject others, will arrange what he selects according to a certain plan, and will give a certain emphasis to one, and more or perhaps less to another. It is not reasonable to suppose – it is hardly even conceivable – that another historian, working quite independently, relying upon his own judgment, influenced only by his own point of view, will make the same selection, or anything very much like the same selection, from that tremendous body of information, arrange it in anything like the same way, and repeatedly put approximately the same emphasis upon given facts or incidents. Yet that is substantially what we find in comparing Mr. Wells' Outline of History with Miss Deeks' The Web.
>
> As one who has read with pleasure many of Mr. Wells' books of fiction, it is only with the greatest reluctance that I have been forced to the conclusion that his Outline reveals much unacknowledged indebtedness to The Web. One finds it in the plan, the framework of the book, and one finds it persistently in the details.[9]

Burpee had completed his testimony in chief and had now to face cross-examination. W.J. Elliott had not, however, read the witness's recent written memorandum and asked that cross-examination begin the next day. Raney agreed to the request, and in what remained of that afternoon's session, evidence obtained from the defence in England was read into the record.

R.D. Moorhead's cross-examination of Burpee on Thursday morning was brief. To the lawyer's suggestion that two works setting out to be world history would necessarily share the same "general plan," Burpee said he could think of no other works approaching the subject from the dawn of time. He did not profess, however, to be an expert in universal history. Moorhead pursued the point, and Burpee found himself admitting that since he was not an "Oriental scholar" he could not "corroborate Irwin's testimony in that area."[10]

The lawyer for Macmillan New York also had another fruitful line of questioning, that of dissimilarities between the two works. What kind of strange accusation of plagiarism was it, Moorhead suggested, that based itself as much on differences as on similarities? By "differences," Burpee responded, he had meant points where both "The Web" and *The Outline* differed from known authorities on points of fact, as when they made errors in common. And what, asked Moorhead, of Mr. Wells's use of the metaphor of a web? Was the witness not aware that the author had used it in his novel *Joan and Peter*, and in other works? Burpee admitted that he had not read the novel in question. Finally the defence lawyer asked about the matter of the "peculiar error" concerning Charlemagne, and the question of whether the Holy Roman Empire had begun in 800 or 964 (he meant 962). Was the witness aware that James Bryce, a noted authority, provided the date of 800 and the coronation of Charles as Charlemagne as its point of origin? Robertson objected on the ground that the counsel for the defence was himself posing as an expert witness, and Moorhead withdrew his question. The matter of which date was the correct one remained unresolved, but some damage had been done to this little corner of Burpee's testimony.[11]

The final witness for the plaintiff was Professor George Sidney Brett of the University of Toronto. In establishing his credentials, he noted that he had graduated from Oxford in history and philosophy; was the author of *The Government of Man* (1908), a study of political and ethical theories and history from Homer to John Stuart Mill; was the author of a three-volume comprehensive history of psychology from earliest times to 1911; and had written the entry on the history of psychology for the *Encyclopedia Britannica*. In a university where the political economist Harold Innis and the classicist and historian Charles Norris Cochrane had yet to make their mark, Brett could make strong claim to be the institution's leading scholar in the humanities or social sciences. In fact, he was perhaps the world's leading authority in his field.[12]

Asked by Robertson to explain his acquaintance with "The Web," Brett answered that he had examined it and compared it with *The Outline of History* in 1926 but had made no notes, for he had no intention of becoming involved in a court case. Nevertheless, he had found it "very difficult to avoid the conclusion that there was a relationship." It had taken him, he noted, "roughly twelve years" to write the three volumes of his history of psychology – a work that, however comprehensive, held but one "direct line" of thought. Accordingly, he had assumed that Mr. Wells, whose work was thematically much more complex, could not have written *The Outline* in the time he did without having had help.

> I think anybody undertaking a task like that, at the request of a publisher, would organize a gang of workers; that would be the proper thing for him to do; and I formed my own theory, which has no further value, that this manuscript had probably been, I would say accidentally included in material from which the final draft of the publication was made. That hypothesis would explain the whole thing; but I understand it has been categorically denied in the English examination.
>
> *What do you say then is your opinion now as to the relation between the two documents?*
>
> If that process was not gone through, then the single and sole author of The Outline must have been able at times to look at the other manuscript. . .
>
> HIS LORDSHIP: *That if there was not the employment of hack writers and access by one of the hack writers to the manuscript, and if the work was done by Wells, then what do you say?*

It seems impossible to avoid the conclusion that the manu-
script of The Web was available.
MR. ROBERTSON: *Was before Wells?*
Was before Wells.[13]

Brett noted that only four or five weeks before the trial he had
been asked to re-examine the Deeks and Wells material with the
purpose of serving as a witness for the plaintiff. He had agreed, and
subsequently had spent "considerable time" going over some "particularly selected passages." He remained, he told Robertson, of the
same opinion he had formed in 1926.

On what, Robertson asked, did the witness base his conclusions? Brett responded by drawing attention to the importance of a
good and comprehensive plan in undertaking a work that was
going to cover some 2,000 years of history. In this, he said, he could
speak from direct experience as a historian. The plan was crucial: it
was "the substructure" of the anticipated work. It determined
"what you are going to put in and what you are going to leave
out." Most plans for a work of universal history might appear the
same, but only superficially so. The question of whether one work
depends on another is not answered, Brett said, on the matter of
whether, for example, both works deal with Greece and Rome, or
begin with Columbus. The order of such commonalities is dictated
by chronology, and because of this there is no reason why two plans
should not appear "practically identical." Evidence on the relationship between two documents existed instead at a deeper level: it
"would turn on the question of peculiarities in his plan and of the
treatment of those peculiarities." In short, it would hinge on "what
the author did with the ideas."[14]

Brett went on to discuss briefly the similar – and peculiar – treatment of several historical figures by Deeks and Wells. The treatment
of Aspasia was out of all proportion to the importance afforded
her by other authorities. A passage discussing Socrates on virtue
and knowledge seemed "to have been transposed" from a passage
"which was used as a description of Plato's Philosophy in The
Web." The erroneous description of the Roman general Sulla as

"aristocratic" (when an authority such as Theodore Mommsen "went out of his way to point out that Sulla despised the aristocrats") was common to "The Web" and *The Outline*, but to no other known sources.[15]

Brett added another instance of a suspicious similarity of treatment: the one on Columbus and his "little expedition." It was, he said, "a very good test passage." On the basis of earlier depositions, he had examined the sources supposedly used by Deeks and Wells. Eighty per cent of Deeks's words had come from the *Encyclopedia Britannica*, although four or five sentences had also been taken from James Harvey Robinson's *History of Western Europe*. Wells, too, had relied on Robinson, and he had copied them "absolutely verbatim."

> HIS LORDSHIP: *In other words, your opinion is that the writer of that particular chapter on the Discovery of America had before him the Encyclopedia Britannica and Robinson and the Deeks manuscript?*
>
> Yes, they supply, I think, one hundred per cent of the material. . . . It is not a matter of authority but is a matter of copying.[16]

It was also a matter of copying, Brett added, when Wells misdated the origins of the Holy Roman Empire in defiance of his own stated authorities but in apparent common cause with "The Web." But adherence to Miss Deeks's plan could result in acts of omission as well as commission. When she had come to discuss the eighteenth century, she had neglected even to mention Adam Smith and *The Wealth of Nations*. So had Wells. This was a glaring omission, and to Brett was further evidence that the author of *The Outline of History* had been closely following "The Web."

Even Hector Charlesworth blanched at this minor revelation. It was, he later wrote, "a really singular coincidence."[17]

In his final few questions to Professor Brett, Robertson dwelt on the remarkable speed with which Wells had written his historical magnum opus.

> *Now as to the work or labor of a man single-handed prepar-*
> *ing a work of this kind in a period of, say, ten to twelve*
> *months, what do you say – writing it out?*

It is entirely incredible to me. I do not wish to judge other
people's powers. I think I could rank as a fast writer. Under
the circumstances under which I had to write the article
in the Encyclopedia, I wrote 27,000 words in a little over
a month. I was really making an epitome of my own work
and was my own authority. That is of course working
under the most favorable conditions that a man could
work under.

Robertson added that Wells had somehow managed an even
greater feat. Each volume of *The Outline* consisted of more than
250,000 words: that is, each month he had written in excess of
40,000 words. "Now, take a man whose work had not been
History before, and who sets about to write a History of Mankind,
with references to hundreds of authorities, the work being an original work, the plan being his own, and what would you say as, in
your opinion, to the possibility of a man doing all of that as his
own work?"

Brett's answer was blunt and to the point: "Starting out from
the blank to collect his material I would simply say I would regard
it as absolutely impossible. If I had to do it, I should do it by the
simple method of getting an existing work and working it over;
and I think I could defy anybody to discover that I had done it."[18]
With that, Robertson took his seat and waited for W.J. Elliott's
cross-examination.

Elliott began immediately. Did the learned professor know that
Mr. Wells "was not writing a history of the world to be used in col-
leges or to be used by professors," but by the general public?
Should such works not be viewed less critically than a work of academic history? Were Wells's collaborators not outstanding men in
which the witness would have confidence? What was wrong with
an author "saturating" himself in information gleaned from the
Encyclopedia Britannica and other sources?

Did you know that Mr. Wells as far back as 1893, was dealing with similar subjects to this?

Yes, I believe he was originally a school-master, and his reliance upon a book such as this, Robinson's History of Western Europe, would be understandable, from which he copied the statement about Columbus. I think he probably had a small library of school books around the house. Still that does not militate against the rather miraculous ability of striking the same phrase . . .

Do you agree with me in this statement that authors going to the same sources for information are likely to describe the same facts, possibly in the same language?

Up to a certain point; but I think the chances – the way in which I wish to express that is simply this, that in the cases which I have pointed out you have what I would call a miracle of coincidence. There are miracles and I do not wish to deny it; but it has just this disadvantage, that the odds are against it.[19]

Challenged to provide an instance of such "miracles of coincidence," Brett returned to the examples of Sulla the "aristocrat" and Socrates on virtue and knowledge. "He committed a double offence there?" Raney asked. "He copied from The Web, according to your view, and then he did a worse thing than that, he bungled it and put it in where it did not fit at all?"

"I think it is a case of survival," Brett replied, ambiguously. *Survival.* With the images of a frantic author scribbling away to meet his deadline, and of words carelessly taken from other sources remaining even after revision, the case for the plaintiff reached completion.

T hus far, a clear narrative thread had stitched the trial together. The plaintiff had sought to make her case through intrinsic evidence – that the written expression of *The Outline of History* led to the conclusion that Wells must have had "The Web" before him. Her expert witnesses had woven the theme of literary theft into the proceedings, and those sitting in judgment could now weigh their credibility and that of their evidence. But the trial was unusual in that few of the defendants were present in the court-room. Their physical absence made it much more difficult for people to assess how their evidence fit into the "story" of the case.

Most notably, H.G. Wells was nowhere to be seen. In 1929, he had sold Easton Glebe. Memories of life there with Jane, and the crankiness of the aged Lady Warwick, had proved too much to bear, so he had moved into a London flat in Chiltern Court. He spent less time now at Lou Pidou, with Odette Keun. For him, the bloom had gone off that particular rose.

Neither were the other non-Canadian defendants present to testify in person. Sir Frederick Macmillan and George Brett remained in London and New York, respectively, content to let Hugh Eayrs inform them of the course of the trial. The less impor-tant witnesses for the defence, whether Wells's collaborators or employees of the London and New York branches of Macmillan, were also absent. In fact, of the defendants, only Macmillan of Canada was a visible presence in the courtroom.

It was, of course, the right of the defendants not to present a defence at all if they did not believe it necessary. They did, but the manner in which they provided evidence had the effect of jumbling the trial's narrative structure. Whenever Mr. Justice Raney and the various lawyers found it convenient to do so – as, for example, when Elliott sought a delay in cross-examining Lawrence Burpee because he had not read Burpee's most recent assessment – they read the defendants' testimony on commission, given in London and New York, into the record.

Officially, H.G. Wells, Sir Frederick Macmillan, and other English defendants and witnesses testified at trial, but their voices were not their own but those of their lawyers. The judge and the courtroom observers could see none of these witnesses, could take no account of body language or tone of voice. They had only their words. The effect of this on those present can be measured by the accounts of journalists at the trial. They commented at length on the testimony of live witnesses but said virtually nothing about that of any of the others, even though theirs was of equal weight in the eyes of the law.

Reporters and others perhaps expected a story to develop, in a coherent fashion, informed by cause and effect and in a linear sequence. What they got instead, when they had to weigh most of the evidence of the defence, was a legal jigsaw puzzle, with pieces of the picture scattered seemingly at random over the length of the trial. To discern the overall pattern, particularly when evidence was read into the record by third parties, required real concentration.

One senses that when counsel for the defence began to read the evidence given on commission, attention flagged. The lawyers' flat voices, the haste with which they read the testimony, merely encouraged minds to wander.

From the perspective of Florence Deeks and those who supported her, however, the defendants' evidence required close scrutiny, for they knew from the discovery evidence that at times it was genuinely illuminating. Before and after his testimony, William Irwin sat in the courtroom as an observer. Many years later, his memory refreshed by the transcript of the trial, he wrote a lengthy account of Miss Deeks's encounter with the law and what he thought of the evidence, including his own.[20]

He understood that the case for the defence rested on two basic claims: that "The Web" never left Toronto, and that there existed insufficient similarity between the Deeks manuscript and *The Outline of History* to render Wells culpable. Professor Frank H. Underhill, due to testify late in the trial, would be responsible for addressing the second issue. But of the two claims, the first was in fact more important. If the defence could demonstrate that "The Web" had remained in the possession of Macmillan of Canada all along, any and all similarities between the two works must of necessity have been coincidental.

It did not surprise William Irwin when he heard a lawyer read the words of Sir Frederick Macmillan into the record, categorically stating that he had not heard of Miss Deeks until the action was launched and that at no point had he seen her manuscript. Sir Frederick said that his routine took him to the London office each day. No evidence existed that the company had ever received a manuscript called "The Web." Its manuscript logbook recorded all manuscripts sent to the company, but Miss Deeks's manuscript was not among those recorded in it.[21]

Irwin noted that only when under cross-examination did Sir Frederick learn of the correspondence between John Saul and Florence Deeks concerning her use of Green's *Short History of the English People*. In that case, the publisher conceded, Saul "ought to have submitted" her manuscript for his approval. "Certainly if they were going to publish a book which contained extracts from a book of which we owned the copyright here," he said, "we should expect to be consulted first."[22] In short, if company procedure as established by its senior branch had been followed, Saul at Macmillan of Canada was duty-bound to have sent the manuscript to England for approval.

Harold S. Geikie was a minor figure in the London office of Macmillan. But in one respect his position was an important one: he was the person responsible for entering into the company logbook the details concerning manuscripts it received. Although he had not been employed by the company at the time "The Web" had allegedly been sent to England, he was thoroughly familiar with office procedures and policy.

At a suitable moment in the trial in Toronto, W.J. Elliott read Geikie's evidence into the record, corroborating Sir Frederick's testimony that there was no entry for "The Web" in the manuscript logbook. But near the end of his cross-examination, there occurred this brief exchange:

> *Supposing anything was submitted to you to say whether you objected to something contained in it as infringing your copyright, would you enter it in that book?*
> No, certainly not.[23]

That was it. Three words, perhaps lost to those whose attention had waned. But what those words did, as Irwin immediately understood, was to put one significant piece of the puzzle next to another, elements in the difficult hidden narrative of the case's direct evidence, now coming together. Geikie's words meant that if John Saul had indeed followed company procedure and sent the Deeks manuscript to England because of its use of Green, the absence of an entry for it in the company's logbook would have been no more than standard practice.

Geikie's admission entirely undercut Sir Frederick Macmillan's contention that the absence of an entry for "The Web" in the company logbook "proved" that the Deeks manuscript had not reached his company. In fact, in combination with Sir Frederick's testimony, it demonstrated that no one in the London office could prove that "The Web" had not been received there.

What of manuscripts that the company did receive? How were they ordinarily handled if, for example, they were being considered for publication? Norman Daynes, representing Florence in England, had asked Sir Frederick about this, too.

> *Do you personally see any manuscript that is sent over? That would be too small a matter to bring to you; somebody at the office would see it?*
> Practically I see every manuscript that comes. We have at our Board meetings, which take place once a week, all the man-uscripts that have come and been reported upon and to be dealt with, put before us . . .
> *They are received by some particular official whose duty it is to deal with them before they are put before you?*
> No, not in the least. They are only received at present by Mr. Geikie and entered into a book.
> *Are they looked at, at the Board meetings?*
> Certainly; or may have been looked at previously by one of the members of the firm, one of the partners, or myself.
> *A Director might put it in his bag and take it home and read it overnight, and give his co-Directors his views upon it?*
> Yes; or he might send it to somebody else to read.
> *Some outside reader?*
> Yes, certainly.[24]

At this moment, Daynes had abruptly shifted his line of question-ing. But only apparently so, for an implicit chain of inference was now in play:

With regard to Sir Richard Gregory, what connection has he with Macmillans?

He is editor of "Nature."

That is one of your publications?

Yes, a newspaper.

Is he interested in the Company as a Director or shareholder?

No.

. . . I understand that you knew nothing of Mr. Saul, the editor?

I knew such a person existed.

You had never written to him, or seen him, or anything of that kind?

No . . .

I am sorry to have to ask you, but I think I must. You knew of Mr. Wise, at any rate, who was the President of the Canadian Company?

Certainly.

I think he was President of the Canadian Company in 1918 and 1919?

Yes.

And it would not be possible to say that he was a man of spotless honesty or integrity?

I do not know that.

I am sorry I have to put it, but I think I must: It would not be possible to say he was a man of spotless honesty or integrity?

We dismissed him, as a matter of fact.[25]

Daynes peppered Sir Frederick Macmillan with questions about his knowledge of other instances of alleged literary theft involving Macmillan of Canada. Had he received a letter of complaint from a Miss Durand, involving her work "Skyland Stars and Stories" and complaining of piracy? He had not. Did he know of an accusation regarding a "Life of Mr. Lloyd George"? Some medical manuscript? Or the case of Dr. Putman? Sir Frederick knew of none of them.[26]

Delivered as they were in the drone of lawyers' voices in a Toronto courtroom, the words of Sir Frederick would scarcely have betrayed the witness's state of mind. But when he left the stand in London, he may well have been a worried man.

The shift in Norman Daynes's line of questioning had been effective. First he had demonstrated that company policy required manuscripts needing copyright permissions to be sent to the London office, but that they would not be entered in the manuscript logbook. Second, he had established that manuscripts of any sort were often taken out of the office. Then he had linked this London-based information to the Toronto branch and to accusations of plagiarism when it had been under the direction of Frank Wise, a man of dubious character.

Perhaps the testimony of Macmillan of Canada employees would shed further light on what went on during the tenure of Frank Wise as president. Meanwhile, it was necessary for the lawyers to read a good deal more commissioned evidence into the record. For several hours on Wednesday afternoon, June 4, those in court listened as the testimony of H.G. Wells and three of his collaborators, Gilbert Murray, Ernest Barker, and Sir Richard Gregory, was read into the record.

As expected, Wells's testimony was lengthy, but no doubt it secured the attention of those in the Toronto courtroom. In William Irwin's judgment, its most revealing words were uttered near the outset. Confronted with a copy of his initial "Memorandum of the Case of The Web," which had huffed that the Deeks claims were either silly or an attempt at blackmail by means of a "faked manuscript," Wells admitted that he had thought at the time that "The Web" might indeed have been sent to the London office of Macmillan. This, he had said in his memorandum, "should be proveable by the testimony of the reader or readers of Macmillan & Co." Norman Daynes had probed further.

> *I am afraid you may have to have your attention drawn to a few passages. You go on: "In either case Messrs. Macmillan must substantiate that the manuscript never left the hands of their representatives." Is that the same thing as "readers"? Were you thinking of their readers when you say: "never left the hands of their representatives?"*

> Whoever the Plaintiff is accusing of handing over the manu-
> script to me, I suppose has to be interrogated to prove that
> nothing of the kind happened. I suppose she has to prove
> something somewhere in this case.
> *I was wondering why it was you were saying that Macmillans*
> *must substantiate that the manuscript never left the hands*
> *of their representatives. Supposing it had left their hands, it*
> *would not necessarily have implicated you?*
> No, but I suppose they can show – these are fine points – [27]

Momentarily, Wells had become flustered. Daynes had made his point. Instead of emphasizing the baseless nature of the claims, as an author entirely innocent of plagiarism would have done, he had acted in a manner that threw the responsibility for defending the accusation on Macmillan. Then, perhaps having recognized that he was in danger of implicating the publishing company, he had drawn back – "these are fine points." As Daynes had pointed out, the mere fact that "The Web" might have been in the possession of Macmillan in London in no way connected him to the Deeks manuscript. The answer was more explicable if Wells had been aware that his manuscript might contain passages that bore evidence of the connection.

A more sustained line of questioning drew attention to the vagueness of Wells's descriptions of his project in the fall of 1918, that as late as October 20 he was still only planning to write, and that at that time he anticipated that the book would be no longer than 200,000 words. Much of the assistance of his title-page collaborators had been provided by "word of mouth." Daynes asked whether his "helpers" had collected any materials for him; Wells replied, "No, my helpers were merely – the vulgar phrase is that they vetted the book."

Further questions about the involvement of Sir Ray Lankester, Gilbert Murray, and Ernest Barker drew forth the contrast between the infrequency of written contact between author and collaborators and the prominence with which their names came to be displayed on the title page of *The Outline of History*. Personally, Wells had made few notes, and even fewer abstracts from secondary sources. "I am afraid I have very little system in my work," he stated, "but if you want to know how the 'Outline' was written I should say that after these first few trials, the production of a manuscript, then most of it was typed at once by my wife, who was very much interested in the scheme."[28]

Daynes had demonstrated that although Wells's collaborators were learned men, they had not done his reading or writing for him and had provided no detailed research notes or memoranda from which he could draw. But what of the author's own reading? Wells drew attention to the many secondary sources mentioned in the footnotes, such as Winwood Reade's *Martyrdom of Man*, Breasted's *Ancient Times*, and Robinson's *Medieval and Modern Times*.

> *Were those the main works that you read?*
> All these books were consulted . . . I did not sit down and read
>   a number of works through and then begin writing.
> *When you talk about history text books, do you mean people
>   like Monson [sic; Mommsen], Prescott, Froude, Macaulay,
>   and so on?*
> You are asking for my intellectual autobiography.
> *I do not want to be curious?*
> I should have to spend a considerable amount of time before I
>   could really write a history of my historical knowledge.
> *You did not go to these books as special preparation for this
>   particular work?*
> No.[29]

If the collaborators had done little, if any, research for him, it was now evident that Wells himself had done little preparatory reading. It was as if either he had possessed the history of mankind as part of his general stock of knowledge, or it had simply popped into his head just when it was needed – and, it was alleged, exactly when "The Web" had disappeared from the vault of Macmillan of Canada.

Norman Daynes took Wells in detail through his "plan" for *The Outline*. It was one, the author said, that "must have occurred to thousands of people." Then Daynes drew the author's attention to the peculiarities of treatment common to *The Outline* and "The Web." The glossing over of Mesopotamian civilization; the absence of any consideration of the architectural achievements of Rome; the dismissal of Roman law in a single sentence (so remarkable that one of his collaborators rebuked him sharply in a few sentences that became a footnote in *The Outline*); the absence of adequate discussion of monasticism and the feudal land system. Why, Daynes asked Wells, did he, like Miss Deeks, say so much about medieval Florence but so little about Venice? This had been remarkable enough that Ernest Barker had taken issue.

> *Your view was that Venice was not of any very great*
>   *importance?*
> Did Miss Deeks have a difference with Mr. Barker?
> *No. In her work there is rather a similar view of proportion;*
>   *that is all?*
> I see. It makes me respect Miss Deeks' judgment.[30]

The humour was characteristic of Wells's defence of himself, his views, and his methods. His manner was that of amused detachment from the accusations that surrounded him, his projected image that of the hard-working author not quite certain what all the fuss was about. All the coincidences of commission and omission were no more than two writers' attempts to give expression to commonplaces of historical knowledge.

Why, he was asked, did he refer to Brutus as "the ringleader of the murderers" of Julius Caesar, when the more ordinarily accepted view was that Cassius had been the ringleader? What authority did he use? Wells mentioned the *Encyclopedia Britannica* and the author Joseph Wells, but then added:

> Has not Mr. William Shakespeare some share in this?
> *I think he mentions both Brutus and Cassius?*
> I think he does. Has Miss Deeks some special information?
> *I rather fancy Miss Deeks happens by some means or other to*
>   *take the same view as you did.*[31]

What was the point, Wells's attitude implied, of asking questions of such an eminent writer about why he chose phrases like "little expedition" or "festering with discomfort"? Did it really matter whether Sulla was a patrician or an aristocrat? H.G. Wells was a wordsmith, a genius, and a prophet. It would have been easy for the sympathetic observer to discount such apparently minor verbal correspondences between *The Outline* and "The Web." The problem was that they existed in abundance.

But would the suspension of critical judgment carry over into questions that carried more freight? At one moment Daynes queried Wells on Duruy:

> *Did you ever refer to a book of Duruy's, "History of the*
>   *World"?*
> I do not know; I do not remember.
> *It is one she relied upon; that is why I ask?*
> I do not know that. Is it mentioned in here?
> *I do not think it is mentioned in your authorities?*
> I do not remember it at all.[32]

How many of the important concessions, such as Wells's ignorance of the work of Duruy even though he had used the French historian's words, were lost on the judge and others in the courtroom when the trivial and the crucial were in quick juxtaposition, and found expression only in the flat tones of legal counsel?

Near the end of his cross-examination of Wells, Daynes returned to a matter raised early in the discovery phase: the speed with which *The Outline* was written. The "original" version of the book produced as evidence in court consisted of a typescript.

> *Is this the type that was done by your wife?*
> That was generally done by my wife.
> *Can you tell me whether it was done from your dictation?*
> No, from my manuscript.
> *It was not in one sense the first manuscript?*
> No, it was very often written in pencil, but I never dictated.
> *You do not think any of it in any way represented passages*
>   *that you had asked her to copy out for you to work upon,*
>   *or anything of that kind?*

> No, I think I seem to remember copying the passages of
>   Herodotus, but as far as I know he knew nothing of Miss
>   Deeks . . .
> *I think you told me in the examination for discovery, but I will*
>   *just make quite sure, you have not a manuscript from*
>   *which this was typed. This is the earliest thing you have?*
> That is all I could find.[33]

This, too, was an important concession. Asked to produce the original manuscript of *The Outline of History* as evidence, he had instead produced the first typed copy, accompanied by a few notes. More than any other document in the case, the original handwritten script would have provided important clues about any reliance on "The Web." No one involved in the case had apparently thought to ask where it might have gone.

Finally, Daynes wanted Wells to confirm the brevity of the period in which *The Outline* had been drafted. He drew Wells's attention to a letter of February 5, 1919, from the publisher Sir Frank Newnes to the author, looking forward "with keenest interest" to the 50,000 words that Wells had promised him soon.

> *It looks rather as if he was under the impression that you had*
>   *not then got 50,000 words ready; but I think you [indi-*
>   *cated earlier] that impression was probably wrong, and*
>   *that according to your recollection 50,000 or possibly*
>   *60,000 words had been done by that time?*
> Yes, but there was no fair copy in typewriting; that is probably
>   what I meant.
> *Do you think it is possible that you could have written 50,000*
>   *words or 60,000 words in three weeks?*
> No, I should not think so. I should think it existed before that
>   time.[34]

After Daynes had Wells confirm that on February 11 he estimated that the length of the completed *Outline* would be 250,000 words, he drew attention to the fact that, in a letter dated February 25 to

George P. Brett, Wells had said: "I have got, I suppose, nearly half way through it . . ."

> *That would be 125,000 words, would it not?*
> Yes; well, I have got, I suppose, nearly half way through.
> *. . . That would be about 125,000?*
> Yes, so I take it from that letter I must have had 125,000 in manuscript. . . .
> *Three weeks before you said you had 50,000 or 60,000. It looks as if you had done 75,000 in three weeks?*
> No, I had 50,000 to show; that is, I had it in fair typescript. There is no inconsistency there . . .[35]

Rather lost in the dispute over whether Wells had managed to write 75,000 words in a period of three weeks early in 1919 was the larger achievement. Earlier testimony had established that on October 20, 1918, he remained at the planning stage; nothing had been drafted. But by February 25, 1919, he had single-handedly researched and written 125,000 words of the first draft of *The Outline of History*.

A_mong the last of the phantom witnesses for the defence were Gilbert Murray, Ernest Barker, and Sir Richard Gregory, whose testimony was read into the record after that of Wells. It proved significant for what the "collaborators" did not know. Murray did not remember "at all" when the subject of *The Outline* first arose between them. He had not become acquainted with the author's "methods of work." He "could not possibly say" whether one year was the shortest period of time for more than 1,200 printed pages of a work of universal history to be written. The assistance he had given consisted chiefly of criticism.

Had Wells consulted Murray about his plan or his sources? "No."

Did the notes incorporated eventually into the annotations of *The Outline* constitute the whole of Murray's work?

"Yes."[36]

Ernest Barker's testimony was of a similar nature. His contribution to *The Outline*, he said, did not begin until midsummer 1919, when he began to receive typescript chapters. His work consisted of criticizing points of detail; he supplied no material.

During cross-examination, Daynes asked Barker whether he had ever received a letter from Mr. Wells "stating his point of view" on the accusations of Miss Deeks. In his own testimony, Wells had said that the first he had heard of her claims had been when he received a letter from her solicitors at the launch of the action in 1925. Barker's answer differed significantly: "I never received anything from Mr. Wells except one thing. I think I remember when I came back from Toronto, in 1924, writing to tell Mr. Wells that I had seen Miss Deeks, and to tell him as simply and as accurately as I could what the upshot of the conversation had been."

Barker's testimony corresponded with the memory of Florence Deeks, for when the Cambridge scholar had attended meetings of the British Association for the Advancement of Science in Toronto, she had taken advantage of the presence of one of Wells's collaborators and spoken with him about her intentions. Barker told Daynes that he had received a brief reply from Wells but had destroyed it and could not remember what it said.[37]

To Florence, Barker's lapse of memory was far too convenient. How likely was it that he would completely forget the response of a famous author and friend to an accusation of plagiarism, especially when the book in question had involved Barker himself? And why had he destroyed Wells's letter "at once" after receiving it? Barker's testimony placed Wells's knowledge of her charges more than a full year earlier than the date the author himself had given. To those sympathetic to Wells, the contradiction could be explained as a result of the failing memory of an aging man; to those like Florence, it was nothing less than perjury.[38]

Daynes asked Barker about Wells as a historian.

Although you had known Mr. Wells as a distinguished novelist, up to that time had you ranked him as a historian?

No . . .

Did he tell you at all, when you were discussing it at Oxford,
how long it had taken him to do?

No. It is very rapid.

That is what impressed all of us?

Yes. I do not think he had read very much, if you ask me . . .

Did he give you an idea of his method of work?

No. In the first proofs, the typewritten proofs, he occasionally
referred to the authorities he had used, and it made me
smile, because really they were authorities, from my point
of view, which were rather elementary. I used to write and
try to refer him to authorities that I regarded as more up to
date and more thorough. I thought he had written the first
draft on very imperfect reading.[39]

The next-to-final witness for Wells and the defence was Sir
Richard Gregory, who acknowledged that he was president of the
Royal Meteorological Society and editor of *Nature*, a scientific
weekly owned and published by Macmillan of London. He was
also the company's educational adviser. He insisted that he had
never heard of Florence Deeks until the legal action was launched.

Under cross-examination, he was asked when he first learned
about *The Outline of History*, and he accepted that "the first definite information" he received on the project had been shortly before
October 31, 1918, when he wrote Wells a letter giving information
about the earth and sun. When did he first see chapters of the book?
On August 8, 1919.

In concluding, Daynes revisited an earlier question.

When did you first hear of the Plaintiff in this action, or her
work "The Web"?

I think it must have been a year or so ago; it was either in conversation with Mr. Brett, or someone, that first I heard of
it. It came from the outside quite casually.

I suppose you had nothing to do with Mr. Saul, the Editor of
the Canadian Company?

No, I do not think I have ever met him. I have certainly had no
   correspondence with him.
Nor with Mr. Wise, the President?
No.
You probably know that Mr. Wise was not regarded as a very
   honest or satisfactory man, and had to be got rid of?
Even that I did not know.[40]

Sir Richard's testimony was in error in at least one respect. He
had corresponded with Frank Wise. The Macmillan of Canada president had written to him on December 20, 1917, to tell him about a
professor from Acadia University who admired one of his books.
Wise had also offered the distinguished scientist his personal "best
wishes for the Season."[41] Less than a year later, "The Web" would
allegedly be dispatched to England and the Macmillan offices.

Perhaps Sir Richard's memory failed him, but then perhaps not.
The scandal surrounding Wise's activities had been well known in
the London office of Macmillan, and it is difficult to believe that
someone with as wide a network of information as Sir Richard, and
holding as important a place at Macmillan as he did, could have
remained unaware of a major scandal within the company.

Reading the commissioned evidence for the defence occupied
much of Wednesday afternoon and continued well into the next
day. Fewer people chose to attend, and observers dropped in and
out of the courtroom. The proceedings had not made good newspaper copy, and reporters had to work at finding interesting new
angles. Reporting on H.G. Wells's evidence, the Toronto *Star* fixed
on the admission that he had "very little system" in his work, and
that his wife had typed most of *The Outline*. The idea for the book,
the newspaper reported, "had always been in his mind"; the apparent resemblances between it and Miss Deeks's book, said the
famous author, were due to "a common obvious idea."[42]

At last, word came that the court was about to
return to live testimony. The final witnesses for the defence,
employees of Macmillan of Canada and Professor Underhill of the

University of Toronto, had been seen in the corridors of Osgoode
Hall. Once more, on the Thursday afternoon, June 5, the courtroom
drew near to full capacity.

The clerk of the court called Hugh S. Eayrs to the witness stand.
R.D. Moorhead began the examination. For the most part, it was
perfunctory. What was his current position with Macmillan of
Canada? What position had he occupied in 1918 and 1919? Who
was president at that time? Eayrs told him about his own position
as secretary and sales manager and that of Frank Wise as president.
Asked about office custom in the handling of manuscripts, he stated
that the secretary of the president would pass them to the appropriate department. One like "The Web" would be sent to the editor
of the education division, John Saul.[43]

Moorhead asked Eayrs whether he knew anything personally
about the manuscript called "The Web." "Nothing whatever,"
Eayrs answered. The judge, too, asked him whether he had ever
heard of this manuscript.

"No, my Lord," said Eayrs.[44]

From the perspective of the plaintiff, Eayrs had never been a
"suspect," so in his brief cross-examination R.S. Robertson pointed
in a different direction, asking about his predecessor as president,
Frank Wise. "Where is he now?"

Eayrs had suspected and feared that this question would be put
to him. He now steeled himself and said he did not know. But
Robertson did, and he knew that Eayrs did too. So he pressed the
witness further:

Where was he when you last knew where he was?
He was, I think, in Kingston.

Kingston, at the juncture of the St. Lawrence River and Lake Ontario,
was a pleasant town dominated by three institutions: the Royal
Military College, Queen's University, and the Kingston Penitentiary, in a little sub-community.

Or a place called Portsmouth, near Kingston?
I believe so.

> *Was he sent to Portsmouth because of some irregularities at*
>   *Macmillans?*
> No.
> *Something else?*
> Yes.
> *He was discharged from Macmillans?*
> Yes.
> *At about what time?*
> February of 1921.
> *And there had been irregularities there on his part?*
> I understand so.
> *You were there?*
> Yes, I was there. I understand so.
> *Perhaps you know more about that?*
> No, I do not.[45]

Hugh Eayrs knew a great deal more than he let on, but he was not about to say so. This was dirty linen best laundered elsewhere.

Wise had not gone to the Kingston area for military training or to further his education. He was there at the pleasure of His Majesty, George V, as inmate number 1304 of the Kingston Penitentiary. In 1929, he had been sentenced in Toronto to two and one-half years in prison for uttering a forged document.

Just how Frank Wise had sustained himself and his family after his dismissal from Macmillan of Canada remains something of a mystery. For a while, he appears to have gone into fine bookbinding. Once, while in her lawyer's office around the time the writs were served, Florence Deeks accidentally discovered a business card that read "Mr. Frank Wise – fine liquors," or something to that effect. "Mr. Wise was said to be the aristocratic bootlegger of Toronto," she later wrote.[46]

Towards the end of the 1920s, however, Wise had found another means of gaining a livelihood. The case of *The King v. Wise*, tried before a jury in the Supreme Court of Ontario beginning in April 1929, had proved that he had conspired with several others, one an employee of the Italian Embassy in Ottawa, to secure visas and sell them to emigrants from Italy.[47] When Eayrs gave his testimony,

Wise was about to be released, presumably on the grounds of good behaviour.

Robertson did not press Eayrs further for details on Wise's misbehaviour while president of Macmillan or on his subsequent criminal activities. Everyone in the courtroom understood exactly what was implied when Eayrs had confirmed that Wise had been sent to "a place called Portsmouth, near Kingston."

However suspicious was the behaviour of people at Macmillan of Canada when the company possessed "The Web," Robertson knew that direct evidence of their culpability was immensely difficult to secure. This aspect of Florence's case had to be conducted by inference. He needed to convince the judge that the conduct of the Canadian defendants was such that sending her manuscript to England for nefarious purposes was not nearly as improbable or as ridiculous as, at first glance, it might seem. Forgery is kin to plagiarism, and Wise had been found guilty of the former. Was he not, then, at least capable of involvement in the latter? To link Wise to this possibility, Robertson asked Eayrs about office procedure concerning manuscripts such as "The Web."

> *When the manuscript came in, you suggest that this is the sort of manuscript which would probably go to Mr. Saul?*
>
> Yes.
>
> *Apparently there is not much difficulty about that here, because Miss Deeks says she took it to Mr. Saul, and he apparently got it. Then, if the common practice was followed with this manuscript, what would be done with it when it came in? Where would it be put at night?*
>
> It would be kept in the Company's vault.
>
> *And the Company's vault would be the common place and the proper place for it, unless someone was working upon it?*
>
> Yes.
>
> *That is where you would look for it?*
>
> Yes.
>
> *And did Mr. Wise have access to the vault?*
>
> Yes.
>
> *And Mr. Saul had too, of course, I presume?*

Yes.

And their Secretaries?

Yes.

I suppose in the daytime the vault was open?

Yes.

Was it open right off the main office?

It opens off a small sort of half corridor leading into the main office.

And there was no one person about there on guard?

No, it was generally in the care of the Secretary of the President.

That did not mean that either the Secretary or the President kept his eye on it to see who went in?

No.[48]

So much for the Macmillan "vault," an important word since it was the talisman by which the Canadian defendant assured the court that "The Web" had been kept in tight security and could not have left its office. Far from being a locked safe, as the term might suggest, the vault was in fact an open area of common shelving easily accessible to any employee who might pass by.

One of these employees was the company's former editor-in-chief. It was now John Saul's turn to be called to the witness stand.

Under direct examination by Moorhead, Saul acknowledged that Florence Deeks had delivered her manuscript of "The Web" to him, and that he had read it. He could not recall any details of his interview with her, but he had seen at once that her book "would not be one in which the Macmillan Company would be interested." Shortly afterwards, however, it occurred to him that a revised version might possibly be adopted by the schools of Manitoba. He could not be sure, but he thought he had taken the manuscript with him on a trip to Winnipeg.[49]

The judge asked him about the whereabouts of "The Web" at the time he left the employ of Macmillan of Canada.

To my knowledge the manuscript was in the vault of the Macmillan Company, as far as I know, sir.

Do you recall having seen it after you came from the west?
I do not, sir.
You do not recall definitely having had it with you in the West,
*   and so you cannot recall definitely whether after you*
*   returned from the West you had it put back in the vault?*
Yes, your Lordship.[50]

Moorhead drew Saul's attention to his letter of January 31 to Florence Deeks, which said, "I am leaving the manuscript here at your disposal." How, he asked the witness, had that come to be written? Saul replied that at the time, he felt certain that the manuscript was in the vault. "It would be naturally where I would expect it to be."

Robertson began his cross-examination. Had Saul read "The Web" a second time and, if so, had he taken it home? Yes, he always did that. If on a daily basis a manuscript was placed in the vault, or taken out of it, would an entry be made each time in the manuscript log? Not unless it was "sent out or mailed to somebody else." If Saul took a manuscript with him on a field trip, would such an entry be made? It was not the office practice.

Then am I putting it fairly when I put it in this way, that you
*   have no such definite recollection that you can swear to, of*
*   having seen the manuscript again at any time, except such*
*   recollection as you have in connection with reading it again*
*   at some time?*
That is correct, sir . . .
And from that time on you have no recollection of having seen
*   the manuscript?*
I have not.[51]

Robertson asked Saul whether it had occurred to him that the Deeks book might have been publishable and profitable if its author had been a well known figure. "If published as a general book, yes," Saul answered. And since Macmillan of Canada did not publish many books, would the Toronto office likely have tried to get New York or London to publish it? Saul answered in the affirmative.

Then Florence's lawyer turned to Saul's remarks to his golfing friend Sidney Watson, of the Nelson publishing firm.

> *Do you recall making a statement to him at one time that you had an impression that you might have sent the manuscript to England?*
>
> I will answer that question directly, if you will allow me to explain it afterwards. Yes. I made the statement to Mr. Watson in the course of a conversation, but whether I put it directly in that way I do not know. As a matter of fact, we were going around the Mississauga Golf Links, and the matter was in the air, and at that time I had not any distinct recollection of what had happened to the manuscript. What I have given you now I have pieced together since then by seeing the correspondence . . . We were canvassing the possibility of that manuscript having reached England. It was in the air, and everybody was talking about it, and the newspapers. I did not make any positive statement to Mr. Watson that I had sent that manuscript. I could not have said it because I did not know . . .
>
> *But you did go so far as to say that you had an impression of that kind?*
>
> Yes, I was thinking that I might have sent it, – I would say that.[52]

Saul's answers were crafted in a way to suggest that because his conversation with Watson took place half a dozen years after he had left Macmillan, the haziness of his recollections was understandable. Robertson knew better, for Florence and Mabel Deeks had kept in ongoing contact with Saul throughout the period. It would have been impossible for him to have forgotten the details of his involvement with "The Web."

> *Do you remember having a visit from Miss Deeks and her sister in the spring of 1922 . . . ?*
>
> No, not particularly.

*Do you recall having a visit from them two or three years after
you left Macmillans?*
Oh yes, many of them.
About this manuscript?
Yes, many.
*Did they suggest to you the possibility of the manuscript
having been used by someone?*
Yes.
And did you say to them that that was a possibility?
I do not think so . . .
*Had you known of another case in Macmillans of a manu-
script having been used? I am not suggesting any impropri-
ety on your part?*
No, never, that came within my direct knowledge.
*Did you tell these ladies, on the occasion which I have referred
to, that shortly before that a man had come to your house
and accused the Macmillans of using a manuscript which
he had submitted? The man, you said, showed some para-
graphs and you said they were a good deal alike?*
I have a dim recollection of something of that kind . . .
And you may have told Miss Deeks that?
Yes.
*And did you suggest that a comparison of the Outline with the
manuscript would be a good way to tell whether the manuscript had been used?*
I may have suggested that . . .[53]

To the question of whether he had ever told anyone that "The
Web" had been sent to England, he answered with vague questions
of his own. Pressed on the issue of whether he had earlier made a
statement to this effect, he said: "I cannot remember it at all." His
chosen words did not quite constitute a denial.[54]

John Saul's evasiveness on the witness stand must have been
evident to anyone in the courtroom that day. All things considered,
he had not been a credible witness. In William Irwin's view, he had
made a real contribution to the case, but scarcely to the defence.[55]

To the best of Saul's recollection, he had taken "The Web" out of the Macmillan offices, and out of the province, on at least one occasion, but somehow his memory failed him about its whereabouts after his return. And then there was his remarkable conversation with Sidney Watson while they played golf in Mississauga around the time the case was launched.

When the conversation on the golf links took place, Saul would surely have searched his memory to recall exactly what his role in the controversy had been. It was one thing not to remember just when he had last seen "The Web" in the Macmillan vault, but quite another to forget whether he had sent it to England. And if he remembered that he had not done so, or even if he merely doubted it, he would surely have disclaimed responsibility by denying it in his conversation with Watson. Instead, however, in an offhanded way between holes, and without giving much thought to the consequences of his words on a nice day for golf, it may well have been that he had simply told the truth to a friend.

To William Irwin, and to Florence Deeks, Saul's testimony about his words with Watson was "not less than astonishing." It fell just short of constituting "direct and positive evidence that he had in actuality sent Miss Deeks' manuscript to England."[56]

Like everyone else familiar with an office environment, R.S. Robertson knew that if you want to find out how things really work, you should ask the secretaries. Robertson had occasion to do just that, when, a little later, the assistants to Saul and Wise were called to testify. Under direct examination, Mrs. Mabel E. Hopkins, secretary to Saul, stated that she had been responsible for the entry "vault" next to that of "The Web" in the Macmillan of Canada manuscript logbook, but that the entry for its return in 1919 was written in a hand unknown to her. She had left the company in the first week of October 1918.

Robertson now wished to determine in greater detail what happened to manuscripts when they were left on one of the shelves that were designated as the Macmillan of Canada vault. Under his questions, Mrs. Hopkins stated that if Mr. Saul wished to examine such a manuscript, or take it with him while travelling, he would simply retrieve it. No entry would be made in the record when a manuscript was taken out or returned; it would be treated as if it were still in the vault. Mrs. Hopkins admitted that she did not attempt to account for the firm's manuscripts on a regular basis.[57]

As he questioned Mrs. Hopkins, Robertson drew the attention of the court to several examples in the Macmillan manuscript logbook where appropriate notations of receipt or return were missing, or where the word "vault" did not appear.

> *There is a good deal of guessing to that isn't there?*
> No, I do not think there is. You cannot expect me to remember everything . . .
> *And here is an entry, of Miss Dunlop, without even a date as to when it came in, – there is no date to show when it came in?*
> No.
> *And nothing to indicate what happened to it when it did come in?*
> It went into the vault. Probably that was taken for granted.
> *There was a good deal taken for granted about this whole record, was there not, – things that should have been in are not in the record, is that not so?*

Saul's former secretary had no answer, but the judge had a question. He pointed to the copy of "The Web" on the exhibit table. "Have you, Mrs. Hopkins, any recollection at all of this manuscript?"

"No, I have not, my Lord."

"You do not recall ever having seen it?"

"No, I do not recall it as a manuscript individually at all."[58]

As in the earlier testimony of Hugh Eayrs, once again the truth of the fabled Macmillan of Canada "vault" had been exposed. People could take manuscripts from these shelves whenever they pleased, and no record of the withdrawal was necessarily kept. And far from being able to vouch for its safekeeping, Mabel Hopkins could not remember ever having seen "The Web" at all.

For William Irwin, sitting in the courtroom, this was a moment of revelation. All the entries for "The Web" in the Macmillan manuscript logbook were in her hand, except for the date of its return.

She therefore must have handled it early on. But she had just testified, unambiguously, that she did not remember seeing it. Earlier,
she had confidently said that "The Web" had remained in the
vault; now, in fact, she could provide no direct evidence of this
claim. All to which she could truthfully testify was that it ought to
have been there.[59]

May Mercer, secretary to Frank Wise in 1918 and 1919, took
the witness stand immediately after Mrs. Hopkins stepped down.
Moorhead's questions sought to establish that, if Wise had ever sent
a manuscript to England or New York, she would have known
about it.

Mercer stated that she was the person who handled all manuscripts sent from Macmillan of Canada to Macmillan in England or
the United States, because "everything went through Mr. Wise."
Like Mrs. Hopkins, she remembered nothing about any manuscript
called "The Web."[60]

Cross-examined by Robertson about the working relationship
between Wise and Saul, Mercer noted that Mr. Saul would not have
sent manuscripts to the other offices of Macmillan in the absence of
Mr. Wise; on the other hand, if Saul was not in the office there was
no reason whatsoever why Wise could not do so. Wise naturally
had access to the vault.

But did Miss Mercer know about everything Mr. Wise did at
70 Bond Street?

> *There were important matters that Mr. Wise did that were*
> *concealed – don't you know that?*
> That were concealed?
> *Yes, that were concealed for some time, and afterwards*
> *created trouble, – did you know that?*
> No, I did not know that.[61]

Like Eayrs's statements earlier on the same issue, May Mercer's
denial of any knowledge of the details of Wise's misdeeds as president was perjured evidence. Eayrs had left a vast paper trail detail-
ing the misconduct in his correspondence with Sir Frederick

Macmillan and George P. Brett, and Miss Mercer had gone so far as to write a letter to Brett outlining her concerns. Both knew exactly what had gone on during Wise's final years, but their loyalty to the company outweighed their commitment to the cause of justice.

Frank Hawkins Underhill reminded some people of nothing so much as a bantam rooster. A short, wiry-framed, and balding man in his mid-thirties, he had an abundance of nervous energy and exuded a cocky self-confidence. Possessed of a way with words, he was already a widely acknowledged master of the bon mot and of witty repartee. He had spent more than a decade teaching history at the University of Saskatchewan, near the heart of Western Progressive political discontent, and in his journalistic writings for the left-leaning journal the *Canadian Forum*, he had demonstrated his discontent with the status quo, in his criticisms of Liberal politics and of British imperialism. He was iconoclastic by nature, and this, combined with his flair for the language, made him, despite his relative youth, a distinctive figure among the nation's historians – an H.L. Mencken of the left. As such, he was a natural ally of H.G. Wells and his progressive causes.[62]

Called to the witness box as the one and only expert witness for the defence, Underhill established his qualifications: an honours degree from the University of Toronto in classics, English and history, taken in 1911, followed by three years at Oxford in the course of *literae humaniores* and modern history. A native of Ontario, he had returned from Saskatchewan to his home province in 1927 to assume the position of full professor in Canadian history.[63]

Like William Irwin, his counterpart on the plaintiff's side, Frank Underhill needed little prompting from R.D. Moorhead. With Moorhead's question, "Well, what have you to say" about *The Outline* and "The Web," Underhill launched his testimony. "Well it struck me that in their general spirit and tone there was not very much similarity between them." The theme of feminism ran throughout "The Web," and there was nothing of this in *The Outline*. He had observed "that when you abstracted . . . the feminism there was not much left in The Web except a succession of narratives of facts, which would be fairly well known to any historian and would be found in most elementary history books."[64]

Underhill went on to say that he could not find any "striking originalities" in the plan of "The Web." The only ideas in it and not in other world histories were those points where "The Web" was original, but wrong. Besides, the proportions given to different people and events in the two works were vastly different. As to commonalities, "The authors of world histories are bound to deal generally with the same main events, and the same people; so that I cannot see the striking similarity on their framework and plan which has been seen by some other of the witnesses."[65]

Moorhead turned to the question of parallel passages. "What have you to say about that?" Underhill answered that he had not been struck by any when reading the two works through. He admitted he had not nearly had the time to work systematically through all the examples provided by Miss Deeks – "It would be almost a life's work" – but he did examine many of them. "My point is that the whole argument for The Web is that it is the cumulative force of these parallel passages that counts . . . And my argument would be that when you examine them, a great many of them just fade away to nothingness." Many sources existed to explain Wells's particular phrasings; it was not necessary "to have recourse to the hypothesis that Wells used The Web."[66]

Underhill went quickly through some of the examples cited in Florence Deeks's comparison. Why was it so suspicious that Wells should have begun his book with the earth's origins? After all, in *Joan and Peter*, his character Oswald had said that all history would be useless which did not begin with the geological record. It was perfectly understandable that Wells should have dealt with man's "ape-like ancestor," since he had been educated as a scientist in the heyday of Darwinism. "It seems to me," Underhill added, "that he had those ideas long before Mr. Irwin and I were born."[67]

The Deeks "Comparison" in hand, he skipped from example to example, speaking as he did so, punctuating his points with words of dismissal. Aspasia? A very good story told well by Plutarch, who

was all Wells needed. The aristocratic Sulla? Yes, "aristocratic" was
not the correct term to use; after all, it was a Greek word. But it was
used in at least two prominent North American textbooks to
describe the man. The reference to Brutus and Julius Caesar? Again,
Wells drew on Plutarch – and so, it seemed obvious to Underhill, had
Shakespeare. "The Holy Roman Empire" was a perfectly reasonable
popular term for Wells to have used in reference to Charlemagne.
What difference did it really make if in one passage Bryce said
"Empire" or "Roman Empire," instead of "Holy Roman Empire"?[68]

Again and again, Underhill circled above the examples that
Irwin had agonized at length over, circled and then pounced. Cite
the apparent correspondence, point to its triviality, dismiss it as a
coincidental attempt at the expression of a well-understood historical event. "Nearly all these things that I am skipping over, I may
say, seem to me to deal with facts that are pretty well known. They
are not abstruse facts. If there were in this comparison some particularly abstruse facts about history which could only have been
obtained by Mr. Wells as a result of long search, or by cribbing
them from Miss Deeks, there might be something in these Comparisons; but they all deal with fairly well known facts of World
history and therefore I am leaving many of them out."[69]

With this broad stroke, and others, Underhill appeared to rescue
the evidence of contested historical detail from the rarefied and
picayune world of academic expertise and to hand it back to the
common sense of ordinary people. Rather than meet the challenges
posed by the detailed testimony of Lawrence Burpee and Underhill's
two University of Toronto colleagues, he chose a simpler mode of
argument: to diminish their importance with clever words and curt
dismissal. Frank Underhill was not the kind of historian for patient,
detailed textual research. He was a man of the big picture, the glib
phrase. He had read *The Outline of History*, as he had also read
"The Web," but he knew that he had not given either work the same
depth of comparative analysis as that of the witnesses for the plaintiff.[70] He knew he did not need to, for he had learned that ridicule
would best research any day, whether in the magazine of opinion, in
the lecture hall, or in the courtroom.[71]

"This was a very large job that Mr. Wells undertook?" Robertson asked gently, as he began his cross-examination. Would it not require a good deal of preparation?

"Of course for a professional historian it would be quite impossible," Underhill acknowledged, "because he is too scrupulous about his authorities and he wants to verify all his references." Nor could a professional historian do this work in so short a time. "But Mr. Wells is an extraordinarily rapid worker, and I would express no opinion as to whether he could do it or not." So rapidly did Wells write his novels, Underhill opined, that "a good deal of his literary work is kind of slipshod."[72]

Robertson turned to the planning of a major work of history, and secured Underhill's agreement that the making of thematic outlines required a good deal of time and labour, and that a person would be greatly assisted if he had something to follow. Robertson asked whether Underhill had looked at "any other author dealing with the history of mankind or world history [who] is anywhere close to these books in detail." The professor replied, "I have been repeatedly quoting Breasted and Robinson."

This was the kind of generalization Robertson had now come to expect of Underhill – all assertion, little substance. He pursued his quarry:

> Yes, here and there. Have you compared them throughout, particularly compared them so far as the first book of The Web is concerned, or up to the time of the end of medieval history?
>
> Oh no, not throughout. I have not had time to do that.[73]

This confirmed Robertson's suspicion that Underhill's command of his material was less deep than he let on. He was just on the point of demonstrating that the witness could not identify the omissions in common noted by the experts for his client, when Raney brought the proceedings to an abrupt halt.

The court hours for the day had run their course. "I did not know that we were going to be up against these lengthy professors," remarked W.J. Elliott. "Rules which apply to ordinary witnesses do not apply to professors."[74] It was now 4:50 p.m., and the court adjourned until 10:30 a.m. Friday.

The final day of the trial began with Frank Underhill once again in the witness box. Robertson resumed his cross-examination. Had Underhill seen Miss Deeks's "Comparison" of the plans of the two works, entered as an exhibit, and had he studied it? Underhill answered that he had looked it over "at some time before the court sat this week." In answer to another question, he stated that he had indeed been in court to hear the evidence of Professor Irwin. Did the witness agree with Irwin that the general plans of *The Outline* and "The Web" were "closely alike"? Underhill answered that they were, but that they were also like any other outline of history he knew of.

Robertson was beginning to reach where he wanted to go.

> *That is the next thing I want to ask you. What other outline or book dealing with this subject, do you refer to as having a similar plan, a plan which is as near The Web as The Outline is?*
>
> Well, Robinson and Breasted, on the whole . . .
>
> *You have referred to Breasted. Breasted, of course, has nothing at all to say about the part that takes up the first few hundred pages of Wells's book?*
>
> No, I have already dealt with that.
>
> *You have nothing to say on that at all. I observe that in his case he puts the Babylonian civilization –*
>
> As I said yesterday, I do not know anything about Oriental History. I have not gone into it. I did not look into the Oriental part.[75]

Robertson had made his point; an expert witness had just admitted his lack of expertise.

> *I suggest to you that if you made a comparison of the plan, if it was worth anything, you would look to see whether they dealt with periods in the same order –*

> I did not have unlimited time at my disposal, but went over
>   them generally and went into detail in the periods with
>   which I was dealing.
> *Have you anything to say about the period of which Mr. Irwin*
>   *spoke. He can speak of it with more authority than you*
>   *can?*
> Yes.
> *And also he knows the subject better because you have not put*
>   *any time on it?*
> Yes, I guess that is right.[76]

The blithe self-confidence of the witness had all but disappeared
under the weight of questioning. Underhill became forgetful about
the amount of space "The Web" and *The Outline* had devoted to
the prehistoric era, claiming ignorance of geological periods. He
had earlier asserted the view, as Robertson pointed out, that all histories of mankind pretty much followed the same chronological
order, and now he reconfirmed it. But he had admitted that he had
not had time to examine closely any significant omissions from the
narrative of the two works. Robertson pursued him on the question
of Aspasia, pointing out that Wells's mention of her made little
sense, given the general neglect of women in *The Outline*. Further,
both Wells and Deeks made reference to her having an illegitimate
relationship to Pericles.

> *What do you say about that?*
> Wells said she was Pericles' de facto wife, – I have forgotten
>   the phrase . . .
> *What he says is that she was in effect his wife?*
> That is only part of what he says.
> *And he does not say that she was his mistress?*
> You are quibbling about a word. He makes it clear.
> *It is a matter of words. It is the words that we say are*
>   *significant.*[77]

Robertson shifted to another instance where words and their use
were critically important and perhaps revealing.

Then the other one, . . . the instance mentioning the "Old
   Man." I suggest to you that you did not quite do credit to
   the argument put forward by the witness on our side. The
   suggestion, I understand, was not at all that it was any-
   thing out of the way to mention the "Old Man" in the
   early life of man, but it goes on to say, and we suggest,
   rather absurdly, something against the "Old Woman," that
   she was nothing but a squaw and too fat at that. We
   suggest to you this, that it was the seeing of the phrase
   about the "Old Woman" in Miss Deeks' book, The Web,
   so stirred him up that he was moved to a contradiction?
No, I should say that suggestion is just absurd . . .
More than the phrase, the idea of disparaging woman, in
   saying she was subject to the man.
That is disparaging her anyway from Miss Deeks' point of
   view.[78]

A major difference existed between Robertson's expert witnesses' approach to "The Web" and *The Outline of History* and
that of Professor Underhill. The vital clues to the use of Deeks's
work by Wells did not lie in the "facts" or "events" they held in
common. It rested, instead, in the verbal formulations that surrounded their presentation. Irwin had recognized this; so had
Brett and Burpee, and, before them, Sir Bertram Windle and I.A.
Richards. But Frank Underhill would not countenance the notion.
The counsel for Miss Deeks pursued this important if difficult distinction. Each time he pointed Underhill towards a passage with
obvious verbal resemblances, the Toronto historian retorted that it
was events and interpretation, not words, that counted. Tempers
began to flare.

I put it to you that those three passages quite obviously are
   related, the passage from Web, the passage from Wells and
   the passage from Duruy are obviously related?
Again you are insisting upon asking me about significance.
   Obviously related, – maybe their language is, but I do not
   know whether that is significant. We are just wasting time.

> *Maybe we are and maybe we are not, for a moment longer. If*
> *you want to tell me that you are not here for the purpose*
> *of making comparisons of language or expressing any*
> *opinion upon them, we can shorten this very much.*
> I am here for the purpose of making comparisons on history
> about which I know something . . . I say it is useless to ask
> me whether there are significant similarities between these
> passages.
> *No, I ask you if it did not indicate inter-relation?*
> That is significance, isn't it?
> *Do they or do they not? If you say you cannot answer that*
> *question, I think that means a lot in this case.*
> There are verbal similarities, but whether that indicates inter-
> relation I do not know. That is about the twelfth time I
> have answered that.
> *I think, even if I do repeat the question several times, that I*
> *am doing it in fairness to you, because I do suggest to you*
> *that as an educated English-speaking man you ought to be*
> *able to answer the question. Do you say you cannot say*
> *anything more about it?*
> No, I cannot.[79]

For the observant, it was evident that Robertson had gotten
Underhill to reveal his unwillingness to engage in an exercise in
close, comparative textual analysis. From Underhill's perspective, it
was plainly silly to engage in protracted squabbles over the precise
moment when the Holy Roman Empire came into existence, or in
semantic entanglements over the meaning of those three words.

Robertson, too, was annoyed. "The witness, of course, my Lord,
is not getting this. What we are calling attention to is not the fact of
history but the phraseology that they use. Here are two people who
use a phrase that we say is not used by anybody else. If the witness
will confine his remarks to the question he is asked, instead of trying
to tell me what is important or what is not, we will get ahead."[80]

Towards the end of his lengthy cross-examination, Robertson
made one last attempt to get Underhill to address the verbal similarities between "The Web" and *The Outline*. The long day had

frayed the nerves of all, and the tension at the front of the court-room now affected everyone. Robertson noted that a few moments earlier, Underhill had referred to the mother of Alexander the Great, Olympias.

> *Let me again put this to you. I suggest to you, you have not got the point of our criticism, which is, that again with what The Web says, Mr. Wells has gone out of his way to say something about a woman?*
> As I said yesterday – I am merely repeating here everything said yesterday – if Mr. Wells went out of his way, Plutarch had done it too . . .
> *I suggest to you that you have not considered your answer. The reason I emphasize that is because of what has been said so frequently in this trial, that Mr. Wells would have nothing to do with woman in history, and here he is going out of his way to bring in a woman?*
> I never said Mr. Wells would not have anything to do with woman. My general impression of Mr. Wells is that he put women in their proper place.[81]

The court stenographer recorded the response of the audience. The word he used was "Laughter."

The case was effectively over. "The witnesses are all exhausted, my Lord," said Elliott, obviously relieved. His witness had been roughed up in the discussion of detail, but he had left a final impression that was bound to linger in the minds of the people who, even then, were beginning to make their way towards the exit. A wave of relief had spread throughout the courtroom following Frank Underhill's well-placed barb. Just as Mr. Wells had done with woman in general, in the near-final words of his testimony, Underhill had managed to put Miss Deeks in her proper place.

15   *Justice*

> "It's a far larger question of historical truth. This lie,
> if lie it is, has become the cornerstone on which a
> whole false edifice may be erected. And even if it
> wasn't so, even if it was just one single historical
> oddity, I see now that I've been wrong all these years
> in treating it lightly. If an historian has any function
> at all, it is to maintain honesty."
>
> Angus Wilson, *Anglo-Saxon Attitudes* (1956)

So QUIET WAS IT ON BAY STREET on the day after
the trial ended that William McLaughlin could hear the scratching
of pen over paper. He was alone in the office on a Saturday morning,
and his report to Hugh Eayrs provided a good opportunity to
reflect on the Deeks action. The trial, he wrote, had gone off largely
as expected, except for the strong testimony of Professor Irwin. "If
the action is dismissed," he concluded, "we think it highly proba-
ble that Miss Deeks will appeal, as she is just that type of obstinate
woman, that is, of course, unless she has run out of money."[1]

A week later, he reported to Eayrs again. Simple relief that the
trial had ended had now given way to a more sober evaluation of
the evidence brought before the court. No doubt, he had discussed
the case with his colleagues. "There is this to be said in favor of the
Plaintiff's case," he wrote. "There are sufficient similarities between
the two works to have enabled her to obtain the evidence of three
experts, whose honesty I believe to be beyond question, two of them
in particular going to a considerable length in giving it as their
opinion that it would be little short of a miracle that Wells could

have written 'The Outline of History' without having first read 'The Web.' In this connection we felt that we were very fortunate in having Professor Underhill's evidence. We feel that his evidence will be sufficient to satisfy the Judge that the other experts were mistaken. Mr. Justice Raney would have been in a rather difficult situation had we gone to trial without having expert evidence, as he would have found considerable difficulty in disregarding such definite evidence on behalf of the Plaintiff."

McLaughlin reminded Eayrs that Wells had specifically instructed Elliott not to engage an expert witness for the defence. As he had pointed out to Elliott during the trial, if Macmillan of Canada had not had Mr. Underhill "to fall back on," Wells's lawyer "would have felt himself at that time in a rather precarious position." Because of this, McLaughlin would do his best to have Elliott's clients assume a portion of the $750 that was deemed appropriate as Underhill's fee.[2]

For the remainder of the month, those involved in the case waited anxiously for Mr. Justice Raney to schedule final arguments, but he appeared to be in no rush. Towards the end of June, McLaughlin learned that the judge had indicated privately to Miss Deeks's lawyer Percy Smily that he did not see why he should hurry since it had taken his client "about eleven years to get this far." McLaughlin reported the conversation to Eayrs, care of the British Empire Club in London, noting that Raney had said he presumed that the defence was anxious "to have their names cleared." "It seemed to me," McLaughlin wrote with evident relief, "that he was not taking the plaintiff's case very seriously."[3]

At least three times that summer, by Mabel's recollection, Florence was summoned to Osgoode Hall to hear final arguments; each time, someone told her that the hearing had been postponed. Raney did not hear the lawyers' final arguments until Saturday, September 13, 1930. R.S. Robertson recapitulated the case for the plaintiff. It took him three hours, and during the presentation Raney constantly challenged him. Florence and Mabel had difficulty hearing Robertson at times, but what they did hear did not impress them. In Mabel's view, Robertson's argument "was not worthy of a public school scholar."[4] When Robertson had finished,

Raney announced that he did not think it necessary to hear argument for the defence and that he would hand down his judgment in a few weeks, after his return from circuit hearings.

Hugh Eayrs reported to Sir Frederick Macmillan that he had been impressed with Raney's command of the case and that "quite clearly . . . he did not think the charges made had any basis in fact." Eayrs did, however, take issue with one newspaper's account of the day's proceedings, and he wrote to Claude C. Jennings of the *Mail and Empire* to correct the matter. The newspaper had reported "that the officials of the Macmillan Company were not above reproach when the President went to the penitentiary and if he would do that he would surely steal a manuscript." Eayrs noted that the official in question should have been described as the former president, not the president. "I think we can fairly ask that you take your own way of amending the impression which might be left in people's minds." Fortunately, Eayrs had managed to convince the publishers of all the Toronto newspapers but the *Telegram* to suppress the news about Wise, his crime, and his whereabouts.[5]

Confident that victory was near, Eayrs and the other defendants began to consider how they could recover their costs once Raney announced the decision in their favour. Sources had informed him that Miss Deeks was "absolutely without money." The rich brother had died and he had left the bulk of his estate to his own family. Eayrs went on to say that the brother had left the Deeks sisters only the house on Farnham Avenue (worth "at the outside" $10,000), but nothing else. Robertson had received only twenty per cent of his fee on going into court, but "no more since," and, the source said, he was "exceedingly disgruntled." Irwin had been promised $2,000, but he too had not "seen a penny." Given her financial difficulties, Eayrs wrote to Brett, Florence Deeks would very likely not appeal.[6]

On September 27, 1930, in Toronto, Mr. Justice Raney read his reasons for judgment to a hushed courtroom. He entered the room, as Mabel recalled, "with his gown flying and looking *most* important and on his 'high horse.'"[7] Then he proceeded to dismiss the case outright. Florence and Mabel sat in shock and disbelief. Florence had been appalled at the antagonism the judge had shown to Robertson when he had argued her case a few weeks earlier, but she had never expected this! He now found the defendants not guilty and held her responsible for costs.

All her effort had come to naught. Of the entire judgment, she could agree only with the judge's estimate of the seriousness of her charges: that if they were well founded, Wells was guilty not only of plagiarism but also of "a peculiarly despicable form of literary piracy," and that Macmillan of Canada would therefore have been guilty of theft and conspiracy.

It was, in her view, an outrageous judgment. She knew that the direct evidence about the probability that "The Web" had made its way to England, and to Wells, had been circumstantial. But to her mind it had been extensive and, taken as a whole, powerful. Yet, later, when she came to read the written statement, she found that Raney had dismissed it in a single paragraph, saying only that there was "no evidence that the manuscript was sent to England, or that Mr. Wells or anyone else in England knew of its existence, or that the Macmillan Company of Toronto, or anyone else in Toronto, knew that Mr. Wells was writing, or had it in mind to write, a history of the world." No explanation; no weighing of the evidence. No mention of the mysterious mistakes in the Toronto manuscript log. No word about the evasive testimony of John Saul. Nothing at all.[8]

The judge had disposed of the intrinsic evidence in a similarly cavalier manner. He had not found any similarity between *The Outline of History* and "The Web" to be convincing, and he had gone out of his way to castigate the testimony of Professor Irwin. Raney accepted that "significant phrases" from Duruy had found their way into both works. He also accepted Irwin's contention that Wells had not used Duruy as a source. But his explanation was that a historian as eminent as Duruy had obviously been "a mine for later historical writers." For Raney, the fact that Wells was not a historian sufficiently explained his unfamiliarity with the French scholar. But, he added, "some of his associates were historians and were undoubtedly familiar with Duruy, and there appears to be plain evidence of the influence of Duruy in the opening chapter of The Outline of History."[9]

Had Raney actually listened to the evidence before him? Wells had testified that, in his recollection, he had not used Duruy. The testimony of Wells's associates had been, plainly and unambiguously, that they had done no research for him and that they had written none of his book. How, then, could Raney possibly attribute the presence of Duruy's words in *The Outline* to them? To Florence, Raney's explanation was incomprehensible.

Much of Raney's judgment consisted of lengthy extracts from Irwin's testimony, followed by immediate dismissal of his views. The common spelling of Hatshepsut's name as Hatasu, the judge said, was no doubt due to common use of a source written earlier than 1890; but this was almost the only instance of common usage or mistakes on which he had anything to say. He simply quoted Irwin's words, and then rendered his conclusion. "If I were to accept Professor Irwin's evidence and argument there would only remain for my consideration the legal questions involved in the piracy of a non-copyrighted manuscript. But the extracts I have quoted . . . are just solemn nonsense. His comparisons are without significance, and his argument and conclusions are alike puerile." The fact was, said the judge, that every writer of a work such as *The Outline of History* had necessarily to draw on facts used by previous authors.

Raney had little to say about the testimony of Brett and Burpee except that while they were "men of excellent standing in the Canadian world," and without doubt were qualified as "experts in their respective fields," they had chosen to provide evidence consistent with that of Irwin. That, in Raney's eyes, was enough to condemn the experts and the evidence alike.[10]

To Raney, it was scarcely necessary for the defence to have offered any evidence refuting "Professor Irwin's fantastic hypothesis" that Wells had had "The Web" at his side as he wrote *The Outline*. After all, Mr. Wells, an honourable man, had flatly denied this, and had stated that he had "never seen or heard of Miss Deeks' manuscript." Similarly, the evidence of the witnesses called by Macmillan, Raney said, had satisfied him "of the good faith of that company and that no improper use was made of Miss Deeks' manuscript."

And what of Miss Deeks herself? She had gradually come to believe "in the wickedness of the Macmillan company of Toronto

and of Mr. Wells." It was a belief that had grown in her from the
first moment she had seen *The Outline* in 1920, and it had gotten
worse – "as time passed it became an obsession." She was obviously
not "in a condition of mind to judge fairly of the very serious
charges she was bringing against a reputable publishing house and
an eminent and respectable author." This, said Raney, should have
been obvious to her legal advisers, but they had allowed her to libel
the defendants with impunity. "This action," he concluded, "ought
to have been discontinued after the examinations for discovery, and
certainly it ought not to have been brought to trial."[11]

Florence later recorded her surprise on reading Raney's reasons
for judgment. She had expected "an exhaustive presentation of
close-knit and critical reasoning," but what she got instead was a
document of thirteen and a half typewritten pages. Three of them
introduced and outlined the case, seven consisted of quotations from
Irwin's testimony, and another contained quotations and summary
of the testimony of the other two expert witnesses for the plaintiff.
Of the entire document, only a page and a half contained Raney's
"reasons," and – in Florence's words – "even here His Lordship
had given not reasons but vituperation."[12]

Florence Deeks begged to differ with Raney. "With complete
and respectful acknowledgment to the learned trial judge," she
wrote in her account of the case, "we can but apply to his judgment
of the case the words which he so inappropriately applied to the
scientific testimony on the documentary evidence," namely that it
was just "solemn nonsense," "without significance," and so forth.
"I have not the least desire or intention to injure anyone unneces-
sarily but I consider that respectability and responsibility are qualities which cannot be applied to the Macmillan Company and Mr.
Wells as brought out by the evidence in this case." Accordingly, she
decided that she had no alternative but to appeal Raney's decision.
What else could she do if justice was to be served?[13]

W̲ord spread quickly among the defendants that
they had won. Wells's London solicitor wrote to his client to tell
him the news. So did George Brett, who added that because of the

plaintiff's "failure of money supplies," he doubted very much whether anyone would ever be reimbursed for the heavy costs they had incurred. In another letter, Sanders Fiske told Wells that once the costs were awarded in Canada "we have to try & make the woman pay."[14]

For his part, Wells had inquiries of his own to make. He asked Fiske to find out who it was, "connected with some Authors Society," who had given evidence against him. On October 10, 1930, Fiske informed his client that the man was Lawrence J. Burpee, formerly secretary of what the lawyer believed to be called the "Canadian Society of Authors." He forwarded Wells a copy of the statement Burpee had read into the court record. A few days later, he sent him a copy of the *Mail and Empire* account of Raney's decision.[15]

Back in Toronto, Hugh Eayrs used the language of Raney's judgment to support his spin on the affair. Thanking a Kingston journalist for running a piece on the case, he added: "We were, of course, for five years, in point of reputation, the victim of a woman who, though perfectly sincere from beginning to end, was quite obviously obsessed." The same day, he learned that Florence had announced her intention to appeal. Recovery of costs would be delayed, and, as he informed George Brett in New York, McLaughlin was now in the process of trying to determine just what resources, if any, the woman possessed. Eayrs needed to know, because, as Fiske in England had informed Wells, he had begun to inquire of his Toronto colleagues whether it was possible to make Miss Deeks "give security for costs."[16]

The pressure of the case had eased, and Hugh Eayrs and W.W. McLaughlin ended the formalities they had adopted earlier in the salutations of their letters. "Dear Billy," Eayrs began a letter to McLaughlin dealing with reimbursement for legal expenses; "Dear Hugh," McLaughlin replied, suggesting that a sum of $2,000 would be sufficient as an initial payment. It was as though, the Deeks decision finally handed down, both men could at last drop their guard.

Formalities remained, however, when Eayrs and Brett corresponded, for Toronto and New York had begun to quarrel over the splitting of costs. Eayrs had suggested that the New York office carry half the expenses; Brett refused. As he reminded his younger colleague, "even though we are involved, having been sued jointly with you and others, the suit was really brought about because of happenings in the Canadian office." Eayrs could do little more than reiterate his hope that New York would split the costs equally after the appeal was heard, and to insist that the suit had come about through no fault of his company. "It was brought because a silly woman thought she had a case, and now, even after that most sweeping judgment, still seems to have the same idea in her mind."[17]

As the year 1930 yielded to 1931, the Toronto and New York branches of Macmillan continued to wrangle over the apportioning of costs. McLaughlin's firm alone had charged over $6,000, and Brett refused to pay half, so Eayrs sought support from Sir Frederick Macmillan. The appeal did not work. George Brett's son, George P. Brett, Jr., was now treasurer and general manager of the New York firm, and he had chosen to take a tough stance. In March 1931, he informed Eayrs that "we would not under any circumstances consider paying half of the lawyers fees." He did, however, offer Eayrs the olive branch of a cheque in the amount of one-third of the total expenses of the suit. Eayrs continued to press for half, much to Brett Jr.'s annoyance.[18]

Florence knew that the odds of winning an appeal were against her, but her faith in the inherent strength of the evidence remained unshaken. Her experts had told nothing less than the truth as she understood it. The trial judge had erred in fact and in logic, and he had ignored much of the evidence. She could not bring herself to believe that a second judge would do the same.

The odds were stacked against her in more ways than this. She was all but penniless. The deaths of her mother, and then George, had thrown all the members of the family into a state of uncertainty. In the mansion on Admiral Road, Helen, newly widowed, was now forced for the first time to handle the details of her family's financial affairs. George had left an estate of almost a million dollars, over half in stocks, a legacy that would need careful attention if its value was to be maintained in the failing international economy. Fortunately, the stocks were diverse and of the blue-chip variety: textiles in Monarch Knitting; mining in Kirkland Lake and International Nickel; utility companies in Montreal, Shawinigan, and Baltimore; Chrysler Motors; Dominion Construction; and others. The estate had also included $77,320 in bonds and $113,398 in cash and other real assets. George had owned the house at 140 Farnham Avenue outright, at a value of $9,750, and held $33,600 in equity in the mansion at 77 Admiral Road.[19]

A prudent man, George S. Deeks had provided well for his immediate family. His widow was to receive a sizable annuity from the residual estate until the eldest son turned twenty-four. At that age, he would receive $22,000, plus one-third of the income over the $12,000 per year granted to his mother; later, so would his two brothers. When each son turned thirty, he would receive an annuity of $5,000 plus an equal share in the residue of the estate.

The three sisters who lived on Farnham Avenue had not been neglected, but neither did they fare as well as their sister-in-law or their nephews. George had left them a life interest in the house they lived in, and an annuity of $1,800, which of course they were to share equally. If Florence was to continue in her quest for justice, she would need to do so on an annual income of $600 – $50 a month. She held no real property of her own. She had yet to meet the expenses for which Robertson and Smily demanded payment, and she needed to find resources to fight the appeal.

Somehow, she managed to appease Smily. One can only speculate how she did so. Even if Florence, Mabel, and Annie pooled their living allowances, they would not have been able to meet the legal costs. It is possible that one or several of the sisters appealed to their circles of acquaintance; evidence suggests that later they did.[20] At this point, however, with the court date for the appeal fast approaching, it is more likely that they sought help closer to home. Just how much enthusiasm Helen Deeks retained for Florence's cause after the deaths of her husband and her strong-willed mother-in-law is not known. It is reasonable to conclude that, perhaps after several requests from her three sisters-in-law on Farnham Avenue, she gave them what she thought she could afford – or perhaps what she believed to be appropriate.

R.S. Robertson had sat down with his client shortly after the decision and advised against an appeal. He claimed to believe that her charges were well founded, but, as Florence recalled his words, "he said the Judges of the Appellate Division would never take the trouble to go into all that evidence – they were too indolent, that's the word he used, I feel sure. And besides several of those judges were old . . . Mr. Robertson said the Appellate Division would just follow the trial Judge who had the advantage of seeing and hearing the witnesses."[21]

Robertson suggested that Miss Deeks seek some "brilliant young man" with more time on his hands if she wished to carry her case further, and he offered to brief the individual. This would have meant much more delay and expense, so Florence declined. Robertson helped his colleague Smily prepare the appeal, but soon afterwards he announced his personal withdrawal from the case. "Hope seemed to be doomed," Florence recalled of her reaction to the news.[22]

Few if any advocates in Toronto would now touch the case of the obsessed spinster. According to Mabel, "some loyal friends" began to urge her sister to argue it herself.[23] Florence's initial sense of hopelessness gradually gave way to the essential righteousness of her cause. "So strong was my faith in the ideal of justice permeating the British Judicial system and in the competence and fairness of the Canadian Courts that I was unwilling to forego the privilege of presenting the case before the Appellate Court, and I decided to undertake the task myself, well supported by friends."[24] She sat down to study the evidence presented at trial, and, with the help of Professor William Irwin and her "staunch friends," she prepared a lengthy written argument for use in the court of appeal.

When those still interested in *Deeks v. Wells* entered the Osgoode Hall courtroom on May 13, 1931, and saw the judges of the Appellate Division of the Ontario Supreme Court take their places, they were no doubt impressed. Four distinguished men swept into the chamber, their shin-length black robes in stark contrast with their upturned collars and brilliant white bibs. The judges, like the bibs, seemed cut from the same pattern.

The Honourable F.R. Latchford, K.C., Chief Justice in Appeal, led the way to the long, elevated bench at the front of the room. Of Irish parentage, the seventy-seven-year-old former attorney general of the province of Ontario, known as an able, industrious, and painstaking judge, took his seat at the centre of the judges' bench beneath the large gilt lion-and-unicorn coat of arms. Three colleagues followed him. John Fosberry Orde, a native of Nova Scotia, a long-time Conservative, and former president of the Royal Canadian Golf Association, was a comparatively youthful sixty-one, but having been appointed to the Appellate Division in 1923 he had as much experience in this court as did the chief justice. Cornelius Arthur Masten, seventy-seven, whose distinguishing mark was his black spats, was long familiar with Osgoode Hall, having learned his law there after attending Victoria College in Cobourg in the late 1870s.

The fourth justice was the eldest. Born in 1852, William Renwick Riddell, like Masten, had graduated from Victoria College. With his bushy moustache and long sideburns trimmed to a sharp point so that they nearly reached his mouth, he was not a man to go unnoticed. Of the four justices in the courtroom, the seventy-nine-year-old Riddell was easily the best known to the public, not least because among his other accomplishments he was a well-known Ontario publicist, man of letters, and legal historian. Notorious for the reluctance with which he parted with books he borrowed, he had donated his substantial collection of Canadiana to the library of the Law Society.[25]

In cases involving several litigants, judges were accustomed to seeing a battery of legal counsel before them. The presence of a sixty-seven-year-old woman acting as her own advocate made this one very different. Like the professions of medicine and engineering, the guild of lawyers called the Law Society of Upper Canada had proven to be formidably resistant to the presence of women within it. Women lawyers there were in Ontario, but as often as not they had been made to feel unwelcome as colleagues in the cause of justice. Only five years earlier, in the presence of parents, fellow graduates, and distinguished benchers, a judge had told one of the few young women about to be called to the bar at Osgoode Hall that while he greeted the male graduates, "it was constitutionally impossible for him to welcome the young women . . ." He went on, she remembered, to say that he regretted that the parents "had foolishly spent so much money to educate us for a profession in which there was no room for us."[26]

The legal position of women in Canadian society, while an improvement on that of the nineteenth century, remained a second-class one. In 1928, in a unanimous verdict, the Supreme Court of Canada had declared that women did not legally exist as "persons" and could not therefore hold public office as senators. Five women from Alberta appealed the decision the next year to the Judicial Committee of the Privy Council in London, which had overturned the Canadian verdict. Their Lordships declared it "a relic of days more barbarous than ours."[27]

When Florence Deeks stood before the four members of the Ontario court of appeal, she did so in the knowledge that only three months earlier Cairine Ray Wilson had made a mark for women in Canadian history by taking her place as the country's first woman senator. But apart from that, she was very much alone in front of the four judges. She knew from the harsh words of their colleague Mr. Justice Raney that she had been marked as a woman who, without husband or children, had simply found another outlet for her frustrations. In their eyes, she thought, she was just an old maid with nothing better to do with her life than to fix upon some slight of her own possessed imagining.

"I shall undertake," she began, "to show that the total of evidence, and the whole history of the case, is such as to vindicate fully my charge that the Macmillan Company put to an illegal use the MS. which I entrusted to their possession, that during the time the MS. was in the possession of the Macmillan Company Mr. Wells wrote 'The Outline of History' and that in this task he made use of my MS. I shall undertake to show that all this was done, not only in violation of my proprietary rights and copyright but also at the cost to me of severe sacrifice and injury."

With those words, she launched into a systematic review of the history of "The Web," of the implicit and direct evidence of its use in the creation of The Outline of History, and of the errors made by the trial judge. "I shall request your Lordships to observe that the Learned Trial Judge in his decision, failed to give proper weight, not only to the direct but also to the circumstantial evidence, in proof of my charges; and that his Lordship, notwithstanding his decision against me, yet, strange as it may appear, made admissions and even advanced arguments which amount to a virtual finding of fact in support of my charges and in accordance with the evidence and argument of my witnesses."[28]

For the better part of three days, Florence Deeks made her argument before the court, under three categories: the evidence in support of her charges, the evidence and position of the defence, and the judgment of Mr. Justice Raney. Mabel was proud of her older sister's cleverness and her "fine kindly dignity," and of how well she knew her case. She found the panel of judges decidedly less impressive, and when later she compared mental notes with Florence she found that they were of like mind. Orde seemed to nap in his chair each day after lunch; he seemed complacent, "almost handsome with his benign countenance and wealth of snowy white hair." Latchford made only a pretence at interest, and Masten really did appear quite deaf. Perhaps because of this, at times Mabel found on his face "a certain lassitude or bewilderment." All seemed to defer to Riddell. He sat erect, "with an attitude of firm self confidence – especially when his arms were folded securely across his expansive chest." He looked young for his age, and he was the one who did most of the talking.[29]

Gone was Florence's reticence during her testimony in the first trial, and she went over the case in detail, point by point, highlighting the contradictions and the outright evasions in the defendants' evidence.

What of Raney's uncritical acceptance of Wells's assurance that he had not heard of, seen, or used "The Web"? Wells, he had said, was an author of renown who must be taken at his word. Florence refused to accept the assertion. "Is Mr. Wells' mere word on an important matter affecting him vitally, to be accepted as of un-impeachable honesty?" She emphasized that "mere scandal-mongering" was "abhorrent" to her, but there were certain facts to consider. "Mr. Wells' reputation is far from spotless," she said, "and while I am well aware that popular repute is not legal evidence yet equally the bland assumption of the defence, and I fear too, of the Learned Trial Judge, that Mr. Wells is beyond criticism, is like-wise not evidence. That a man has written hosts of novels, some of them of very dubious quality, is not legal evidence nor even plausi-ble presumption, of his immaculate character. If the defence wish to attach any weight whatever to this point, they must first produce their evidence of Mr. Wells' high honour, and . . . we shall soon see whether or not it is true that where there is much smoke there must be at least a little fire."[30]

On she went, covering not only the evidence of the trial but also the reasons for judgment, peppering her argument with quotations from the 1927 edition of Copinger's *Law of Copyright*, the 12th edition (1923) of Pollock's *Law of Torts*, Oldfield's *Law of Copy-right* (1912), and cases such as *Duke of Queensbury v. Shabbeare* (1758) and *Albert v. Strange* (1849) that served as precedents in actions concerning rights to intellectual property.[31]

At times, she found herself distracted. At one point early in her presentation, in the midst of discussing the direct evidence, Riddell interrupted. "What about the mistakes – have you any mistakes between 'The Web' and 'The Outline'?"

"Yes, my Lord," Florence replied. "Would it be better to take up the internal evidence now and leave the further direct evidence until later?"

"Yes, let's have the mistakes now," he said, and with that Miss Deeks began hurriedly to shuffle her papers.

At other moments, the all-too-evident deafness of Masten made matters difficult. At times, Florence recalled, "he would hold his hand to his ear like a megaphone and say in a deep rich voice, 'a little louder please – I don't hear very well.'" The clerk of court advised her to aim her voice directly towards him. "I did my best," she later said, for "his Lordship was rather old as well as deaf; and to please him I even shortened my argument when he asked me to do so in order that we might finish this week as he wanted to leave town." As a result, she directed the attention of the judges to only a few of the many verbal similarities between "The Web" and *The Outline*.[32]

As time and circumstances permitted, Florence reviewed the intrinsic evidence her expert witnesses had provided so forcibly and in such detail, and she demonstrated how in so many ways the trial judge and the expert witness for the defence had chosen to discount it. To what extent had the lively testimony of Professor Underhill fundamentally addressed, much less countered, the issues at stake? Florence's flat answer was: Little, if at all. Underhill, she pointed out, "did not understand the nature of his task. It involved primarily and supremely the science of textual criticism, the examination of general and detailed features of documents to determine their interrelation." But what had Underhill done? He had dismissed this responsibility as mere "quibbling over words." She insisted that, once scrutinized, his evidence proved to be virtually "worthless."[33]

In the final hour or so on the third and final day of the appeal, Florence turned to the errors of Raney and the record of the defendants. Raney's conjecture that common use (and misuse) of Duruy had been due to reliance on the same sources, or that Wells's "helpers" had been responsible for them, she declared, was clearly at odds with the evidence. Raney had chosen to ignore and then to dismiss the testimony of the expert witnesses for the plaintiff because they did not fit his particular theories. Her experts had provided overwhelming evidence, yet "the Learned Trial Judge waves them aside with scorn, and himself undertakes to act as an opposing literary critic; and novice as he is in this field where only specialists may speak, he advances his own theories and upon them he bases practically his entire disposition of the case."[34]

She went on about Raney's judgment for some time, saying in conclusion: "There is in the entire judgment not a bit of sound reasoning or any major point, there is no approach to a comprehensive grasp of the evidence . . . It is apparent that his Lordship did not consider the nature of the evidence." Raney had simply concluded that because "the defendants were 'a respectable publishing house and an eminent and respectable author,'" her charges "and the weighty evidence in support of them must be waved out of court."[35]

"Surely, that is begging the question," said Florence, of Raney's assumption. What *were* the reputations of the main defendants? The president of Macmillan of Canada at the time "The Web" was in its possession was now in prison. Its current president had admitted under oath that during the tenure of his predecessor, a number of still unaccounted for "business irregularities" had existed. The senior editor had admitted under oath that "another Canadian author had complained to him of the plagiarism of his MS. while in the custody of the Macmillan Company of Toronto."[36]

To bolster this claim that accusations of plagiarism were by no means unknown to Macmillan of Canada, Florence drew the court's attention to a letter she had received from Dr. J.H. Putman, senior inspector of public schools in Ottawa and president of the Ontario Educational Association. Putman had written that by engaging in an act of plagiarism while employed by the Morang Company, John Saul had violated the copyright protection afforded to Putman's book *Britain and the Empire*. After Morang was taken over by Macmillan of Canada, Putman said, he had threatened legal action. The Ottawa author and educator now confirmed that Macmillan had settled the claim, "by a payment of a considerable sum of money."[37]

And what of the reputation of H.G. Wells? He had "repeatedly been embroiled in literary or social episodes that were far from creditable . . . It was said that he was 'frozen out' of the Fabian Club." Early in his career, Florence declared, "he was accused of pirating a book entitled 'A Plunge into Space,'" written by Robert Cromie, brother-in-law to a former English Ambassador to China. Induced to take action by his brother, a King's Counsel in London during the Great War, Mr. Cromie had launched his lawsuit. In a letter to Florence written shortly after she had initiated her Toronto litigation in 1925, the late author's niece, a Mrs. Eve, had drawn attention to the earlier charges involving Wells and her family. The case, she said, had been settled out of court.[38]

In what way, Florence concluded, was she a plaintiff who "was not in a condition of mind to judge fairly of the very serious charges she was bringing" against reputable, eminent, and respectable people? In what sense was her case an abuse of legal privilege? In which realm, she might have added – that of the plaintiff or of the defendants – did honesty and integrity lie?

The defence arguments had been brief, content on relying on the evidence and findings of the first trial. After the appeal, Hugh Eayrs

reported as usual to Sir Frederick Macmillan. "Miss Deeks conducted her case," he wrote, "explaining that she was too poor to
brief counsel further, and she had a much more sympathetic hearing
than she would have through counsel, these judges being kindly to
an old woman in such circumstances." A fortnight or so later, C.K.
Ogden wrote to his friend H.G. Wells: "I'm so glad the Deeks
woman is over. I *think* you should get costs. Someone in the family
had a lot of money for she offered me a handsome fee to refute . . .
I told her . . . she would do better to put £1,000 behind her own
book & get it out & die happy. But she & her sister were an obstinate couple, like ex-school matrons from Ashby de la Louche."[39]

Almost two months later, the Appellate Division announced its
verdict: it dismissed her appeal, with costs taxed against her.
Florence discovered this when she picked up the evening newspaper on the afternoon of August 26. Early the next day, she and
Mabel travelled to Osgoode Hall to verify the newspaper report
and to obtain the written judgments. When she read them she
found that the learned judges had accepted fully the earlier conclusions of Mr. Justice Raney. They rejected as inconsequential and
unconvincing the direct evidence of her case. "I am of opinion,"
wrote Latchford, "that her appeal must fail. To hold the contrary is
to accept as true her contention that the Macmillan Company of
Canada parted at some time with the possession of the manuscript
of 'The Web.' "

There had been circumstantial evidence strong enough to
suggest that this was at least a possibility. But could it even be coun-
tenanced, given the two sets of images that had sat in apposition
from the very beginning of the controversy? From the outset,
Florence Deeks had been the unknown woman, the frustrated spinster obsessed by a foolish cause, the amateur historian. And whom
had she accused? A famous author, a man of the world, the greatest social prophet of the modern age. How could not only he, but
also distinguished publishing houses, respectable publishers, and
hard-working editors, have been involved in the scandalous behaviour Florence accused them of? It was as if the judges simply could
not conceive the possibility.

Of the intrinsic evidence studied and presented by her experts, most of the judges had little to say. Masten wrote no opinion at all; he merely appended the word "agreed" to Latchford's three modest paragraphs. Their only comments on the direct evidence were those of repudiation. The two authors had merely drawn on well-known figures and events. "There can be no copyright in the facts of history or in their chronological sequence," Orde wrote. To Florence, it was obvious he had missed the entire point of the evidence presented by her experts.

Only Riddell, the lone historian among them, went further. He spent most of his lengthy opinion rebuking Professor Irwin and castigating his firm conclusions. "Perhaps the fact of the witness having graduated as recently as 1912," the judge wrote, "may account for some of this – it certainly does not err in over modesty or want of certainty in his conclusions." Then Riddell had fixed on a few isolated examples of correspondence – mainly those concerning Aspasia and Columbus – only to dismiss them with phrases such as "Can absurdity further go?" and "the utter worthlessness of this kind of evidence." They were, he said, "almost an insult to common sense." He dismissed outright the notion that any real commonalities existed, but he chose not to dwell on the matter. "So, too, without elaborating," he wrote, "it seems to me that there is nothing in any way conclusive as proof in any or all of the alleged common inclusions, common omissions, common errors, etc." As to the fact that Wells had written a great many words in very little time, the fact, said Riddell, was that "there are few, if any, Judges on our Bench who do not frequently reach and surpass that amount."[40]

"It is greatly to the credit of Miss Deeks," Latchford had written, "that her presentation in person of this appeal has been as full and effective as in the circumstances it could possibly have been argued by the most able counsel." Florence took no satisfaction in such words. She had done no more than her duty. Had the learned judges done theirs? She thought not. Their words reflected only "unpardonable inefficiency or bias," or both. In thus rendering such faulty judgment, she thought, they had deprived her "of all compensation for the enormous wrongs" thrust upon her "by rich and powerful defendants." She resolved that her search for justice would not end here.[41]

Florence reflected carefully before she took her next step. Two options remained open: appeal to the Supreme Court of Canada in Ottawa, or appeal to the Judicial Committee of the Privy Council in London. The Canadian court had proven hostile to women only three years earlier, when its unanimous verdict declared that women did not exist as "persons" within the meaning of the law. But the Privy Council had overturned the judgment. Besides, Florence knew that if she lost an appeal to the Supreme Court, she would be barred by law from any appeal to the imperial council.

A woman of inherently idealistic disposition, Florence possessed a limitless faith, if a naive one, in certain abstractions. The power of love was one. The sanctity of "British justice" was another. As the highest court in the British Empire, the Privy Council was above reproach – "obligated," she thought, "as it is by Act of Parliament to hear and to make a thorough investigation of every appeal brought before it, and invested as it is with unlimited power for discovering truth, and administering justice." To the Privy Council she decided to go.

Hugh Eayrs found out about the decision of the appellate court from the newspapers the morning after it was released. "I hope this really sees the last of the ridiculous affair," he reported to Sir Frederick Macmillan. A week later, he had less pleasant news to bear. He informed the senior George Brett that he had learned of Florence's intention to appeal the second judgment to the Privy Council in London. "What mystifies us is where she can possibly be getting her funds from. We can only surmise that her brother's widow and his family are supplying her . . . Surely idiocy could go no further than this new move. She is bound to be beaten again in London but the fact is the thing has become an obsession by now." Meanwhile, he added, McLaughlin had applied for a sheriff's order to collect the costs levelled against her.[42]

Informed of the likelihood that Florence would appeal to the Judicial Committee of the Privy Council, H.G. Wells responded with the words: "Can't we get security for costs for the appeal?"[43]

While Florence pored over the second judicial decision, the defence on both sides of the Atlantic began in earnest to pursue the best means of recovering the costs from her. Fiske wrote to H.G. Wells (through his daughter-in-law, Mrs. G.P. Wells, who acted as his secretary) that "we must try and make it as onerous as possible for her in the way of securing the payment of the costs." Eayrs informed McLaughlin that it would be a good idea, in calculating their expenses, to make them "as high as possible." A few days later, the lawyer replied that he was doing just that. "As you know," he wrote to his client, "we have checked up on the will of both Miss Deeks' brother and her mother. Any interest that has been left to Miss Deeks is so tied up that it would not be exigible. My own idea would be that if we were to lodge an execution in the hands of the sheriff and later have Miss Deeks examined as a judgment creditor we could probably force her into a position where she would be glad to make some offer of settlement."[44]

George P. Brett, Jr., fully agreed with this strategy. "I feel that the best way of keeping Miss Deeks from making an appeal to the Privy Council is by making it as hot for her as we can."[45]

At this point, Florence again changed lawyers, turning now to D.L. McCarthy, formerly of the firm that had originally represented Wells and his English publishers. On learning of his opponent's most recent moves, Hugh Eayrs could only shake his head. "We can get no trace of where she is getting her money from to continue at all," he wrote to Sir Frederick Macmillan. "She doesn't appear to have any funds which we can seize for costs, yet from somewhere she is able to find enough money to put up as necessary security for her next move."[46]

It was like a high-stakes poker game. The defendants moved in whatever ways they could in order to recover expenses incurred by the original action, only to have Florence reply with an often unexpected counterattack of her own. At the end of October 1931, she again appeared before Mr. Justice Latchford, this time to argue for permission to appeal the Appellate Division's decision to the Privy Council and to have the security deposit set at a total of $2,000. The defence argued in turn that this should be the amount for each of the defendants. Latchford sided with her. Somehow, most likely through continuing entreaties from the three sisters on Farnham Avenue to their sister-in-law on Admiral Road, Florence found the security.

Eayrs and McLaughlin fell back on the Toronto sheriff's department for redress. Eayrs reported to George Brett, Jr., that through McLaughlin he had instructed the sheriff "to seize any money and effects of Miss Deeks's on which he can lay his hands." He was not optimistic. "It appears that she does not even own the house she is living in and that the slight income she has from her brother's estate is safe-guarded in such a way that we cannot get our hands on it."[47]

A month later, Eayrs received a confidential letter from Graham Spry in Ottawa. Spry, at the time, was national secretary of the Association of Canadian Clubs. He knew a little about the Deeks suit, and thought Eayrs would want to know that "a collection is being made here among very wealthy people" on behalf of the woman's cause. A few of these people had come to Spry for more specific information, and he now asked Eayrs for details. The Macmillan president conferred with McLaughlin, and an exchange of letters with Spry followed. Eayrs provided him with copies of the judicial decisions. The claim of the Deeks woman, he said, was "simply wild from beginning to end." Supporting it would be a waste of people's money.[48] Spry's subsequent actions remain unknown.

By February 1932, with the appeal to the Privy Council now imminent, McLaughlin and Eayrs had given up hope of inflating their expenses in order to thwart the determined Miss Deeks. In fact, the Taxing Master had reduced the costs charged against her. Nor had the sheriff of Toronto met with success, for he had advised McLaughlin that he had been unable to determine whether she possessed "any goods or chattels" whatsoever. His return on the request had been "*Nulla Bona*." The simple facts were, as far as the sheriff could establish, that the woman lived in a house she did not own, and that her sole source of income was $50 monthly from the deceased brother's estate. She had admitted to receiving "gifts" from people, but had refused to indicate from whom they had come.[49]

Eayrs and McLaughlin weighed the merits of applying to have Florence Deeks declared bankrupt. McLaughlin recognized that such a case might be rejected; it would be all too apparent, he warned, that the defendants were doing so solely to prevent her from proceeding with an appeal. The sympathy of the courts would no doubt be with her. Eayrs rejected McLaughlin's advice and proceeded with the action, but a Toronto judge dismissed the Macmillan of Canada petition and levied costs against it. The next step, as McLaughlin wrote to Eayrs, would be to take "some steps to obtain a receivership for the annuity that she receives from her brother's estate."[50]

At the same time, lawyers for Wells informed him that Deeks had been seeking financial support from "some persons in England and Montreal." Did Mr. Wells, Sanders Fiske asked, have any idea who in England might "do such a thing"?[51] He did not receive a reply.

16   *Lancaster Gate*

"Great words and great phrases, like Justice and so
on, very often mean nothing and have serpents concealed in their folds."

> Ramsay MacDonald, cited by Florence Deeks as the
> final words of "The Case – A Literary Tragedy"

O N FEBRUARY 26, 1932, Florence and Mabel
Deeks left Canada for England. Passage through the deep swells of
the North Atlantic was rough, and the ship out of Halifax had to
veer several hundred miles southward in order to avoid the worst
of a winter storm. Ten days later they reached England, and their
spirits lifted. Later, Florence recalled her sense of the moment:
"Now, according to our well-established faith in British Justice all
was secure. It might take some months to carry through the Appeal
but at the end was justice – British justice. There was one misgiving
however, which at times loomed ominously. Namely, the fact that
the Defendants were English people and people of wealth and
power whereas we were Canadians and unknown to the world at
large. If only the Defendants were 'foreigners' also. But no, British
justice knew neither nationality nor power. That was our belief."[1]

As they had in the past, Florence and Mabel stayed at the Hotel
Tudor, off Lancaster Gate, in central London. First they needed to
engage a solicitor, for only through a solicitor could a litigant engage
counsel.[2] They found one, a Mr. Holden, and handed the court

documents over to him. A few days later, they received his reply. "There is no purpose in my wishing to pay you polite compliments," he wrote, "but I must say at once that I do not think that any member of the English Bar could have made a better, more closely reasoned, or more plausible argument than you did yourself in Canada . . . Any ordinary person must be most frightfully struck with the resemblance between your manuscript and the book published by Wells." Then he informed her that the costs of the action would be considerable. Junior counsel alone would require a fee of between £100 and £200, a sum that exceeded Florence's annual income.[3]

Florence decided that she and Mabel would do much of the solicitor's work themselves, and she would not engage counsel. Instead, she would again argue her own case. Knowing that her unfamiliarity with English legal ways put her at a distinct disadvantage, she sat in with Mabel on several cases then being tried before the Privy Council in its Council Chamber in Whitehall. Hearing these appeals, one of which involved Canada, gave Florence a renewed sense of confidence.[4]

They met with Privy Council officials to determine which documents should be in the official "Record of Proceedings" and the order in which they should be placed. At length the bulky document was ready, and it went off to the firm of Ayre and Spottiswood for printing and binding. In order to proceed, the company insisted that she deposit £300 in cash with the Privy Council.[5] When the "Record of Proceedings" came back, it ran to over 500 typeset pages. Six copies went over to the Privy Council and she waited for a date to be set for the hearing of her case, known as Appeal No. 18 of 1932. All the while, she worked on polishing her latest argument, incorporating into it her experience with the Ontario court of appeal. It was barely finished when she received news that the hearing was to be held on Monday, October 31, at 10:30 a.m.

The Council Chamber Florence Deeks and her sister entered on the final day of October was the one in which she and Mabel had listened to earlier cases. Grate fires blazed at either end, and along the two side walls large chairs had been arranged for spectators. Mabel took a seat at one and Florence walked nervously to the centre of the room. There, at a horseshoe-shaped table, sat the Law

Lords, in morning dress but with neither wigs nor robes. The lawyers stood in gowns and grey wigs in tight curls. Near them sat the clerks. Three members of the Judicial Committee of the Privy Council sat in judgment upon her, Lord Atkin of Aberdovey, Lord Tomlin of Ash, and Lord Thankerton.[6]

Florence stepped up to the lectern facing the judges and made some preliminary remarks, setting forward the points on which she based her claim and would argue for a reversal of judgment, and then proceeded to read the earlier decisions. Just as she began to inform their Lordships that the earlier judges had failed to take adequate account of the evidence placed before them, Lord Atkin interrupted: "Did no one ever tell you that this Board does not review a case of facts where there have been two concurrent findings in the courts below?" he asked.

Suddenly Florence felt faint and disoriented. All her dreams and aspirations seemed to have shattered with these few words. "This then," she later recalled, "was the return handed out for all the expenditure of time, travel, trouble and money it had cost to come to the Privy Council and for the fulfillment of every requirement laid down by its regulations. A sense of disappointment and defeat swept over me like an overwhelming wave. I dropped unconscious."[7]

It took several minutes before Florence revived from what she and Mabel came to call "the blow." Lord Atkin suggested that the hearing be postponed. But fearing that it might be cancelled altogether, she insisted on continuing. Perhaps shocked at what had happened, the Law Lords conferred briefly and then announced that in the present circumstance they would make an exception to the "concurrent findings" rule. Miss Deeks was to be allowed to argue her case at length.

Over the course of three days, Florence covered as many details of her experience with the earlier courts as she thought the Law Lords would permit. Point by point, she addressed the evidence against the Macmillan Company of Canada; the circumstances under which she believed H.G. Wells had reproduced her work; the irrelevance of "The Highway of History" to the case; the similar plans of "The Web" and *The Outline*; and of course the intrinsic evidence as set forward by her experts and dismissed by the justices.

At one stage, Lord Atkin asked: "Have you any idea how long it will take to present your argument?"

The question, as put, seemed ominous, and Florence felt intimidated. She tried to abridge her argument as she went along, but it struck her that the comment scarcely conformed to the ideal of British fair play.[8] After this, the Law Lords chose to make only a few interventions. She went on to discuss at length the verbal similarities she and her experts had discovered. She attempted to read Wells's evidence into the record – in her view it constituted "so much evasion, shiftiness, forgetfulness and contradictory evidence as to make his word worthless as legal evidence" – but their Lordships refused to allow it, on the grounds that "the evidence of Mr. Wells was quite clear and definite that he had never seen the manuscript." They also instructed her not to deal with the copyright aspect of the law. She could not understand this, since her case was based in part on the violation of the copyright she had taken out in 1916 to signify her intention to publish "The Web."

She accepted this direction with as much good grace as she could summon, and drew her argument to a conclusion, concerned that she do nothing to irritate or worry their Lordships. After all, the Law Lords represented the pinnacle of justice in the English-speaking world.[9]

The defendants had chosen Arthur Macmillan, of the publishing family, to represent them. He had lobbied long and hard to secure the case, and had succeeded. George Brett, Jr., had resisted the idea but Hugh Eayrs, eager to please the London firm, won the skirmish. Arthur Macmillan had thanked him for his efforts, saying, "I shall be very glad to help in the final squashing of Miss Deeks."[10]

Their Lordships had but one central question to ask of counsel for the defence, and Lord Atkin posed it. "How do you account for the falsity of the Macmillan Record Book? Take that entry of the 5th of February, 1919, how do you account for that entry?"

Arthur Macmillan had no ready answer to the question, except in his "imagination." Perhaps "The Web" had been returned on that date, and then Miss Deeks had taken it home and "worked it over"? Perhaps she then brought it back to Macmillan on March 26, 1919? Florence recalled the response of the Law Lords as being something akin to "What nonsense." What about the entry of July 15, 1919, the date shown for the return of one of her manuscripts? Again, Macmillan was hard pressed for an answer. Perhaps, he said, this was the date on which the "worked over" version of "The Web" had been returned. The Law Lords once again looked incredulous.[11]

On this third and final day of the hearing the defence rested its case and the court adjourned for lunch. During the recess, tea and sandwiches awaited the appellant and her sister in an anteroom, but neither Florence nor Mabel could stomach the thought of eating. They sat there alone, in silence.

After twenty-five minutes, the sisters were recalled to the Council Chamber. The judges had already taken their seats. They called in two stenographers. "All was still," Florence later recalled. She waited for discussion of the case to resume, but Lord Atkin now held in his hand a document and began to read it.

"Gradually the realization dawned upon me that it was the Judgement," Florence recalled. "What could it be? I listened spell-bound with my eyes fixed unwaveringly upon the reader. As he read, Lord Tomlin's right hand covered his face – as if in grief or pity. What did this really mean? A little later Lord Thankerton also covered his face with his hand and with a similar effect. Lord Atkin sat upright holding the paper before him and reading distinctly; his eyes were fixed upon the Appellant with an occasional glance at the Respondents."

Lords Atkin, Tomlin, and Thankerton had accepted the reasoning as well as the conclusions of the earlier courts. "As he read on, making statement after statement of error, ambiguity and contradiction I occasionally shook my head in silent protest, but when it came near the end there was one statement with which I indicated at least partial agreement, namely that 'It is very doubtful whether anything that this Board says, or that any court says will be likely to alter Miss Deeks's opinion of the merits of her case.' I nodded assent."[12]

That evening, sitting in their cramped room, the first impulse that came to them was to leave England "at once and forever." Yet justice had still not been done, and the sisters mulled over their options. Bright and early the next day they called upon Sir Charles Neish, registrar of the Privy Council. Sir Charles told them bluntly that any further appeal would be "useless," but Florence retorted that her objection to the Law Lords' judgment was not that it had been decided against her but that it went against the evidence. Eventually, the registrar informed her that she had the right to enter a petition for a rehearing, but that to do so would be an exercise in futility. Undeterred, she determined that she would submit the petition immediately, before the written decision of the Law Lords could be sent to Buckingham Palace.[13]

Since her sister was so preoccupied with other matters, Mabel took it upon herself to be the one to keep the family back home, especially Annie, regularly informed of their progress. She could not stifle her anger. "We are feeling terribly bitter at the so-called British Justice. I think Lord[s] Atkin and Thankerton showed a decided bias for the Macmillan Co. & in doing that they had to save Wells." As far as Mabel was concerned, the supposedly learned jurists had shown no interest in the case, only ignorance. Lord Thankerton, she told the family, "is nothing but a conceited pup. He appears to me to have a thoroughly swelled head."[14]

A month later, Mabel was still in a state of shock and disbelief. "This is certainly one of the worst blows I have ever had and dishonesty has been suggested from more than one quarter," she wrote home. She went on to lament the sheer stupidity of the Law Lords and their judgment and to say that she and Florence were "terribly worried over all the money." But this process could simply not be hurried, and had to be seen through to the end. She could report only one note of encouragement: someone had written to them to say that he believed that Wells "had stolen from one of his books," and that as a result it remained unpublished.[15]

The letter had come from Brighton, from a P.J. Harwood. At first, the sisters thought this was a woman, but they soon found that their correspondent was Percy John Harwood, a man of scientific training and the author of *Principles of Arithmetic*, published in 1925 by Methuen. "Did I tell you," he wrote, "that I suspect Wells may have used Part II (nearly all biology) of my Theory of the Solar

System (1928) for his 'Science of Life'? I sent him a copy of part I which his Secretary acknowledged. He may have used it like he probably used your 'The Web.'"[16]

This was a most interesting man.[17] Florence and Mabel decided that they would try to fit in an excursion to Brighton over Christmas.

The sisters took great care to keep their own counsel during the lengthy stay in London. They told no one in the hotel the purpose of their visit, but newspaper accounts of the Privy Council action mentioned their names.[18] Miss Mackenzie, the hotel manager, told them that she thought Wells would "hang himself"; they made no comment. A hotel guest, a colonel, offered the services of his lawyer; they declined.

The final act would be played without lawyers, and with due caution. "We must be careful," Mabel wrote to Annie, "for we do not want anyone to say we were mad because we did not win. So we are, & mighty mad too . . . This time she is going to tell them where to get off at, and not allow them to tell her, if that can be possible."[19]

Although H.G. Wells knew that Florence Deeks had appeared in London to present her case, he had no intention of meeting this source of such unrelenting annoyance. A fortnight before her appeal to the Privy Council was to take place, he wrote to his solicitor. "No doubt she will leave England as soon as possible after the appeal has been heard, but if very prompt steps are taken it might be possible either to obtain costs from her or to have her adjudged a bankrupt." Later, immediately after learning that she had lost once again, he urged Sanders Fiske to appeal "to our Canadian friends for the promptest and most vigorous action to recover costs." Sir Frederick Macmillan in London sent Hugh Eayrs a telegram consisting of three words: "Deeks Appeal Dismissed." Beneath them, Eayrs wrote four words of his own: "Three lusty British cheers."[20]

While Florence and Mabel tried to figure out the correct procedures for further appeal, an unsuspecting member of the executive of the Canadian Authors' Association, Howard Angus Kennedy, wrote an innocent letter to H.G. Wells. The association, he said, was about to hold its annual convention in "the mother country." Would Mr. Wells help assure that its members had the opportunity "of meeting their leading fellow-craftsmen, whose books they have so long enjoyed and admired"?

Wells scarcely saw the text of the letter, for his eyes had fixed upon the name "Lawrence J. Burpee" on the masthead. He answered immediately in words of outrage: "I doubt if your Association will be received with any excess of hospitality in this country so long as Mr. Lawrence J. Burpee adorns it," he began. "Naturally I shall object to the reception of Mr. Burpee's society in England. I am quite sure that Sir James Barrie, Sir Evelyn Wrench, Major Astor and Lord Burnham, when they realize the quality of their prospective guests, will think twice about your visit. They will share my views about this vexatious case and of the role Mr. Burpee and his fellow 'experts' played in egging on the Plaintiff in her campaign of defamation."[21]

Kennedy, clearly shaken and already in mid-passage aboard the *Duchess of York*, replied: "Your letter fell like a thunderbolt on my unhappy head." He had enquired of his association's first president, John Murray Gibbon, about Miss Deeks and her case, and assured Wells that while she had appealed to the Canadian Authors' Association "to take up her case," the association had refused the request. He insisted that the society was not the special preserve of Mr. Burpee and threw himself upon the famous author's "fundamental sense of justice." The appeal fell on deaf ears. Burpee was no ordinary member of the Canadian Authors' Association, Wells charged: he was one of its officers. "I cannot consider that my fellow authors in Canada have shown a proper sense of the gravity of the prosecution to which I have been subjected." A week later, Wells received word from his solicitor that he had instructed counsel in Toronto to attempt to force Florence Deeks into bankruptcy.[22]

Towards the end of December 1932, Toronto lawyers for Wells wrote in frustration to their English counterparts. Their application to Mr. Justice Latchford for payment of costs out of Florence's deposit had met with cablegrams from the appellant in London. She objected on two grounds: that she was petitioning to have the appeal reheard by another board, using a precedent involving Irish civil servants; and that the money belonged not to her, but to her sister. The whole business, W.J. Elliott said, was "a lot of nonsense but the peculiarity about it is that the Appellant's Solicitors here have great faith in the justice of the Appellant's case and that an injustice has been done. We can understand how the Appellant who is simply obsessed might have that view but we cannot understand how a sane Counsel can acquiesce to the same view."[23]

W.W. McLaughlin was a little more sanguine. "It is a pleasure to be able to advise you that this matter is now finally and absolutely disposed of," he informed Eayrs. Miss Deeks continued to claim that she would apply for a rehearing of the Privy Council decision, "but whether she realizes it or not, she has drawn her last bow." He assured the publisher that unless instructed otherwise he intended "to make it sufficiently uncomfortable" for Miss Deeks "that she will do what she can to have the matter disposed of finally." It was two days after Christmas 1932, and he concluded his letter with words of good cheer: "We know that it will be a pleasant prospect to all of us to start the New Year without our Deeks and Wells."[24]

No doubt, Eayrs shared the sentiment. Meanwhile, there still remained the problem of recovering costs. The strategy now was for McLaughlin to insist of Miss Deeks that she meet the $3,083.18 owed to the Canadian and New York branches of Macmillan as ordered by the courts, in the hope that at least $1,000 could be recovered. "I may say," Eayrs wrote to George Brett, Jr., "that in the meantime, of course, no suggestion of this compromise has been made in any way: on the other hand McLaughlin is scaring the life out of Miss Deeks with this writ of execution amounting to between three and four thousand dollars."[25]

Brett replied quickly, agreeing with the proposal to settle for a lesser amount. To Eayrs, there appeared scarcely any other choice. What little income Florence Deeks had, he told Brett, had been "very carefully left" to her sister. She was therefore "quite right legally when she says she has not one penny of any sort or kind."

By the end of January 1933, the two had begun to discuss the possibility of "attacking the principal" on the brother's estate.[26]

In London, after a wait of about six weeks, Florence had finally received a copy of the Law Lords' judgment. She and Mabel lost no time in beginning to study it in order to petition the Privy Council for another hearing. To Florence's mind, the decision was a perverse one. The judges had conceded that the "exact story" of what John Saul had done with the manuscript had not been "quite clearly recorded." They accepted as "incorrect" the February 1919 date in the Macmillan logbook for the return of "The Web." They even accepted Florence's insistence that she had received it in April 1919. They rejected the July 1919 date, acknowledging that it was for the return of the manuscript called "Love and War."[27]

The Law Lords also noted that the period in which "The Web" was in Macmillan of Canada's hands and allegedly disappeared was also the time when "Mr. Wells appears to have completed the manuscript of his book." But they accepted Saul's statement that to the best of his knowledge he had not parted with the manuscript. They also accepted, as if on faith, the declarations of Sir Frederick Macmillan and H.G. Wells that they had never encountered "The Web."

With respect to the direct evidence, the Law Lords expressed the view that strong intrinsic evidence could indeed constitute proof of copying, even if direct evidence pointed in the other direction. That intrinsic evidence, however, "must be of the most cogent force before it can be accepted as against the oath of respectable and responsible people whose evidence otherwise would be believed by the Court." They agreed that Miss Deeks had argued her case "with great candour and with great force," but concluded that she had not proven it.[28]

Appeal dismissed.

It was almost Christmas 1932, and Florence and Mabel were near the brink of nervous exhaustion. They decided it was time for their excursion to Brighton, and while there they would see if they could pay their visit to Mr. Harwood, the man who claimed also to have been a victim of H.G. Wells. The famous Royal Pavilion, the exotic but out-of-place symbol of the excess of George IV, left them decidedly unimpressed. But they found the sea air invigorating, and Florence knew the pair "needed a bracer."[29] Sometimes they just walked in silence down the Kings Road on the harbourfront, from West Pier to Palace Pier, admiring the Georgian terraces along the way.

If they managed to meet with Mr. Harwood, neither sister left a record of it. After two weeks they returned to London and their hotel at Lancaster Gate, rested and ready to steel themselves for the next step in their quest for justice. Over the next six months they would canvas every legal and constitutional option open to them, including what they should do if the Privy Council refused to grant another hearing. Mabel wrote home regularly, usually to Annie or her brother Charles – Charlie to her.

Collectively, this correspondence gives a fleeting glimpse of life and routine at the Hotel Tudor: their small room, always cold, overlooking Hyde Park; food that seemed to get worse as the days passed; a hotel employee said to have absconded with monies owed the tax man, leaving her employer £500 short; colds and chills and fevers that came and went, and that left each sister weakened and at times bedridden. During one particularly bad spell, Florence had a temperature of 103 degrees. She could not seem to shake her hoarse throat.

The sisters kept brandy on hand all the time now, and had taken to having a little each night before bed. Mabel took hers with sugar. Distraught days and unaccustomed nightcaps proved a powerful mix. Over the next few months, each sister had several nightmares. In one, Mabel was just about to have "some cake and fancy bread" when she was confronted by a man with a sharp knife, and she found it difficult to escape from him. In another, Florence saw "a big ocean wave coming & rolling right over the house & Mother was there." She awoke with the recollection that "it was going to be terrible & wash everyone away."[30]

Mabel did her best to keep spirits up and put the best face on things, and Florence managed, sometimes in bed, to write and rewrite the presentation intended for her new hearing before the Law Lords. The sisters decided that this time she would not hold back. "Flo. is going to play a good deal on the shock she received," Mabel wrote to "Charlie and all" in mid-February, "and also she is going to riddle their Judgment from *start* to *finish* . . . She is ready for a fight, & is not going to let them get away with one single point . . . If it had not been for the blow we would never have been so strong . . ."[31]

Money never ceased to be a problem. Their stay in London had gone on much longer than they had expected – almost a year now. To save pennies they heated their room as little as they could bear, and they ate sparingly. Mabel worried over her purchase of a pair of rubber overshoes; her little spats, she wrote home apologetically, were not adequate in the cold rain. Florence's old gaiters had also turned shabby, and had holes in them. She, too, had been forced to buy new ones.

In January, Mabel wrote to Annie: "We will have to have some more money for the rest of our passage & I do not know how you are going to get it." In the same month: "Hope you can get $100.00 from Helen." February: "The bank telephoned this morning to say 4 pound 17.6 had come to me and twelve pounds for Florence . . . Its marvellous how our money seems to hold out, & the way it has all been provided." But by early March, in a letter to Annie, the optimism had disappeared: "We really should have another $100.00." Two weeks later, hints of desperation: "Try & get 50.00 or 75.00 from Helen & perhaps you could spare $75.00 . . . Make Helen give you some more money for she can do it & never miss it."[32]

Florence had left her petition for a rehearing for leave to appeal to the Law Lords with the Office of the Privy Council. On February 28, the registrar, Sir Charles Neish, refused on the grounds that it was "frivolous." She appealed his refusal, and spent many anxious days waiting for word. "The more we see, & the more we study the judgement, the more strongly we feel there has been *some* influence back of it," Mabel told Annie in the third week of March. "Let us try & pull through to the right & justice, & above all keep well, for it will not be long now & we will be glad to be away from the horrible English cooking."[33]

After what seemed an almost intolerable delay, the Privy Council at last summoned Florence. She was to appear before the Law Lords on March 31, 1933. Five judges, including the three who had sat in judgment on her, heard her state the grounds of appeal. She resolved that her argument would not this time be cut short arbitrarily by interruptions or objections. Someone she had spoken to had told her that "it was the course of wisdom for a Counsel 'to stick to his guns,'" and she intended to.

"I came to the Privy Council with a supreme faith in England's administration of British Justice," she began her appeal, "and although –"

Lord Atkin interrupted, to say that he was sorry if her faith in British justice had been shaken.

"No, my Lord," Florence said, "that faith still remains strong, and although I feel that the Judgment is a miscarriage of Justice I believe this to be due to misunderstandings which have 'crept in,' and which could be explained away by a rehearing on a few specific points as set out in the petition."

Atkin again interrupted, saying that their Lordships had read the petition and had found nothing in it that constituted a reasonable cause for rehearing.

Nothing she said after that had any effect. No amendment she might make, they informed her, would change their mind. Their earlier decision was their final one. That decision had been a miscarriage of justice, she replied, and so would be the one they were about to render. Lord Atkin administered a mild rebuke for giving voice to words not permitted to be uttered in court, and with that he and his colleagues dismissed her petition for a second hearing.[34]

Almost immediately afterwards she mailed a personal letter, prepared earlier in case just this happened, to each of the Law Lords. The language of her attack on those who had sat in judgment of her was so strong that she now feared imprisonment for libel or contempt of court. "We re-read the letter and discussed it from various points and finally resolved to accept without resistance whatever verdict the Judges might see fit to pronounce. If I should be singled out for imprisonment my sister would remain where she was and both would remain dignified and firm in the faith of self-justification. With this decision once established we fell asleep, and the sun was high in the heavens when we awoke next morning."[35]

The letter of rebuke that arrived from Sir Charles Neish, informing her that her latest course of action had been highly inappropriate and that her letters had remained unopened, came as a great relief. But it did not succeed as a deterrent. Florence and her sister had come to dislike the man intensely, and she now replied brusquely that she had not knowingly committed an impropriety. Her sole aim, she told Sir Charles, had been "to obtain at least some measure of compensation for the injuries I have sustained. I feel that not only my own interests in particular but also the principles of justice demand of me an unfailing effort toward the effectual prosecution of the case I have entered."[36]

John A. Gedge, solicitor to H.G. Wells, informed his client of the latest rebuffs to the irrepressible Miss Deeks. In doing so, he advised Wells that there appeared no reason why the author should not now publish a letter to the *Times* he had drafted earlier but on the advice of counsel set aside. On Thursday, April 6, 1933, it appeared on page 5 under the title "Authors and the Law."

The letter outlined the troubles Miss Deeks had caused him, and quoted an extract from Mr. Justice Raney's verdict. Wells lamented the fact that the woman had been allowed to appeal to ever higher courts, even in the face of judicial defeat. The net result was that while at each level he had been awarded costs, the only charge levied against Miss Deeks by Canadian courts was the sum of $2,000; this, while he faced personal costs well in excess of £3,000. He concluded by saying that an "urgent need" existed to find "some more expeditious, more expert, and cheaper method" of handling such "highly technical" matters as plagiarism than through "normal pleadings in Court." As always, Wells seemed to suggest, he had the public interest at heart.

Word reached North America that Florence had found ways of appealing her case beyond that of the highest court in the British Empire. "Miss Deeks will not die, or perhaps it would be better to say, she doesn't know she is dead!" Hugh Eayrs exclaimed in a letter to George Brett, Jr. He wrote to W.W. McLaughlin the same day: "Dear Billy, . . . When you and I are in England in May, I suggest that we make a pilgrimage, hand in hand, and as a matter of fact travelling like a caterpillar tractor, that is upon our knees, and climb the steps to the famous room where Miss Deeks pleaded. There ought to be a faint atmosphere thereabout." Three weeks later, he wrote to Brett again, asking him to pay half of a Deeks-related bill of £5 16s. 8d. "The final kick from Miss Deeks," he promised.[37]

In a state of near-desperation, Florence and Mabel pored over the writings of Norman De Mattos Bentwich, a leading authority on international justice and equity and on the procedures of the Judicial Committee of the Privy Council. They discovered these passages: "When all else fails the King's personality stands in some substantial way between 'his people and wrong,'" and "every British Subject has a right to appeal to the mercy seat of the throne."

"This was encouraging," Florence later wrote. "The very name of 'mercy seat' had a soothing effect and it seemed to carry with it some nebulous assurance of Justice." So she decided to appeal to King George V. She drew up a graciously worded petition, and on what she recalled as "a glorious Spring morning," with "Nature becoming resplendent in verdure and bloom," she and her sister drove through Hyde Park and down Piccadilly, a fresh breeze bringing renewed hope. They did not mind missing the changing of the guard as they entered the Mall, because it had become a familiar sight. Finally they reached Buckingham Palace and its "great iron gateway."

"A tall soldierly figure" received them at the entrance, and she asked him to present the petition she carried to the private secretary of the King. Then, quietly, the sisters left the palace grounds.

They presented the petition on Friday, April 7. On Monday Florence received word that the private secretary of the King regretted to inform her that it was "not within his province to submit such communications to His Majesty. All petitions to the King must be sent through His Majesty's responsible Ministers."[38]

Miss Florence Deeks had run afoul of that institution most beloved of her fellow Canadians – responsible government. But she had not quite finished. She looked into just who the appropriate minister was, and discovered that he was the secretary of state for the Home Office, Sir John Gilmour. So she went about petitioning him, having studied the authorities and found technical flaws in the wording of the documentation that provided potential grounds for appeal. On May 1, she received a reply from Sir Charles. Her appeal to the King, he said, had been judged "frivolous."

Florence then resorted to a petition in the form of a personal letter directly to His Majesty, at the end of which she remained His Majesty's "Most Dutiful and Humble Servant."[39] On the second day of June she received her reply. The private secretary to the King again refused to submit the petition to the monarch on the grounds given in his letter of Monday, April 10. He suggested that she forward her letter to the Home Office, and she did so. After almost four weeks of anxious waiting, word arrived from Sir John Gilmour. He had personally laid her letter of petition before the King but had been "unable to advise His Majesty to issue any commands in the matter." "The entire system," Florence concluded, "seemed to be excellently arranged for accomplishing nothing."[40]

With little to lose, she mailed one final, short, and blunt letter to each member of the Judicial Committee of the Privy Council. She attached to it a concise outline of the case, the evidence, her treatment by the courts, and a copy of the Privy Council judgment. Sir Charles replied with stern words forbidding her from having any further communication with their Lordships. Her response to him described the Privy Council judgment as "a palpable misrepresentation of the Case." It left authors, she said, "at the mercy of publishers – unscrupulous though they may be." She had not won, but she took some satisfaction that hers had been the final word.[41]

Her cause was lost. She had exhausted all means of appeal. Deeply distraught, and eager to leave England forever, the two sisters prepared for the long and dreary passage home. They had been in England, at the centre of British justice, for almost a year and a half. Florence was nearing sixty-nine years of age, and she now felt dead tired, and very, very old.

17   *Voices*

She long'd her hidden passions to reveal,
And tell her pains, but had not words to tell:
She can't begin, but waits for the rebound,
To catch his voice, and to return the sound.

Ovid, *Metamorphosis*

A history of the world, yes. And in the process, my
own.

Penelope Lively, *Moon Tiger* (1987)

W HEN FLORENCE DEEKS RETURNED with her
sister Mabel to Toronto in the early summer of 1933, the consum-
ing passion of her life was spent. At first she had felt herself to be
the victim of a plagiarist, then a pawn in the games played by
lawyers. Ultimately, she came to believe herself to be a casualty of
the system of British justice. In the final, frantic months of her quest
for that justice, her activities, arising out of sincerity and conviction, had bordered on outright farce.

She experienced it as tragedy. In front of her lay the prospect
of an old age of thwarted ambitions and sullied dreams. She had
put almost all of her energy since the age of fifty into "The Web"
and her desire to see it published. For the rest of her life, it sat
untouched in her home, a court exhibit with its own silent past.

After they returned to Toronto, the sisters rested for a few
weeks. Florence's experience with the law, and the essential injustice done to her, became the subject of conversation at family gath-
erings. After all, her tangle with the courts had eventually involved
most of the older members of the Deeks family. It seems clear from

letters Mabel wrote home from England that her sister Annie and her brother Charles, as well as her sister-in-law Helen, had contributed to their loved ones' lengthy stay abroad. Family lore later had it that by the time the various appeals had run their course, the total cost to the family had reached $100,000. At the end of the twentieth century, the equivalent value of this sum would exceed $750,000.[1] Who knows what unkind words came to be uttered just beyond Florence's hearing, what brooding family resentments her past bore upon her future?

Despite her devastating setback, Florence continued to harbour ambitions to be the author of a published work of history. In fact, on the way home from England she and Mabel had disembarked in New Jersey so that Florence could see editors at Scribner's in Manhattan about the prospect of a new book. But before she wrote it, a different story needed to be told: the tangled tale of "The Web," its origins, and its fate in the hands of men responsible for administering English-speaking justice.

Florence spent the remainder of 1933 and part of 1934 writing of this experience. A wealth of court documents was at hand, and she prepared others, one called "Treatment Given by Privy Council," as aids. When finished, the typescript occupied two thick volumes. One consisted of an account of the case; the other, of the reports of her literary experts. The first of these alone was 246 single-spaced pages long. Clearly, she had aspirations to see it published in book form, for in the spring of 1934 she corresponded with the popular historian T.G. Marquis, and he offered advice about a possible structure and the essential "plot" of her story.[2] She may have taken her completed manuscript to local publishers, but if so, they did not accept it. Eventually, like "The Web" and her other papers, it simply collected dust.

In the mid-1930s, she made several attempts to write a work of comprehensive history, but whether called "The March of Civilization" or "Wings over the World," they resembled any number of textbooks on "Western civilization" available by then.[3] Among her surviving papers for the year 1935 are letters from several publishers and authors, including the historians James Harvey Robinson and Sir Percy Ashley as well as the classicist Ernest

Barker. Each granted permission to quote passages from his books.[4]

The new project went nowhere. Florence was now in her seventies, and the fire had gone. Mabel continued to believe that the effort would have been worthwhile. "I think she was too discouraged . . . that Macmillans had taken her manuscript and the rich market and the glory that belonged to her," she wrote many years later. "When I know how she worked and what she accomplished and how interested she was in her work and the result it would bring, I cannot help feeling as I do. I was her constant companion all through her legal work and she needed me – I do not know what might have happened had she been alone. We would not let her go out alone in the evening, not even to the post box half a block away."[5]

Mabel's sad but caring words hint at family worries about the health of Florence, and at the heavy toll her struggle had exacted on her, in mind as well as in body.

At this point, Florence Deeks all but disappears from view. Many of her papers contain information about her experience with publishers, lawyers, and the courts, but scarcely any of them tell us what we need to know. What occupied her for the remainder of her long life? What were her interests? Fragments of romantic novels, some co-authored with Mabel, have survived, and they record the continuing influence of the early years in Morrisburg, and the Loyalist myth that enveloped the town, on the sisters' imaginations. Perhaps the life of exile from a land of abundance and the story of survival in the face of hardship found resonance in these maiden aunts, confronting the privations of genteel poverty and the infirmities of old age. After Annie died in 1937, at the age of eighty, the two remaining sisters found a way to subsist on the strict economies exacted by their combined income of $1,200 per year.

In contrast, their three nephews reached maturity with no hint of want. Upon his marriage in 1930, George Campbell Deeks, the eldest son of George and Helen, gave his bride a diamond and ruby pendant and the couple took up residence in Toronto's affluent Forest Hill Village. For the rest of his life he served the firm of investment dealers he had joined after leaving university. Eventually he held several corporate directorships.[6] He was the one to whom Florence and Mabel turned whenever things needed fixing on

Farnham Avenue. And like his father before him, he did his best to help.

During the Second World War, Campbell served as a reserve officer of the Forty-Eighth Highlanders of Canada. Douglas twice won the rank of major while overseas during the war, once with the Fifth Wing battle school and a second time with the Forty-Eighth Highlanders in Italy, where he was wounded in action. Trained as an engineer, Edward founded Dominion Metalware Industries in 1940.

The brothers made successes of themselves and, like their parents, later contributed time and resources to charitable and philanthropic causes, such as the Victory Loan campaign, the United Appeal, and Boys' Village. Their mother, Helen, lived to 1945, when she died at the age of seventy-one. While her nephews forged their way in the public world, Florence remained, with Mabel, in the privacy of her own space behind the curtains at 140 Farnham Avenue, trapped in the skein of memories associated with "The Web."

Autobiography has traditionally been the preserve of men who, for reasons of their own, choose to write about their development as individuals. The sense they usually have had of themselves is that of individuation and autonomy: the Augustinian self at war with evil; the Rousseauian self at odds with society – the "essential self," the imperial self. Florence, like most other women, did not view herself in these terms. Female identity has traditionally been grounded, in the words of the feminist historian and critic Mary G. Mason, "through relation to the chosen other."[7] Yet it is one matter to feel this way, and quite another to express the sentiment. What was the "chosen other" of Florence Deeks?

Had she married and become a mother, Florence might have written of her life in terms of domesticity and family, of a life lived in relation to husband and children. The longing to love was always strong in her. But at a certain point in her life, for reasons of her own, she had chosen to remain unattached. In her own way, in the 1890s she had become a "new woman," not unlike Amy Catherine Robbins.

Florence found her sense of self in her hard labour as an amateur historian and her lengthy encounter with publishers, the legal

profession, and the law. Above all, she developed a clear identification with the women embodied collectively in "The Web." Florence's
"chosen other" resided there, in the way she had managed to place
woman at the forefront of history and to give her a voice.

By the time her struggle with the courts ended in 1933, the sense
of self-worth and confidence that had swelled within her during the
years of work on "The Web" was gone. On the advice of literary
men, she had earlier removed women from their central place in the
narrative of "The Highway of History." Now, when she attempted
to tell of the "literary tragedy" that had befallen her, she lacked a
means of articulating her personal voice, one that would keep her
at the centre of her own story.

She did write one document that began "I, Florence Amelia
Deeks," around 1930, but she intended it to help her lawyer and
serve her cause, not her self. Three paragraphs about her origins,
family, education, and interests gave way within a page to the story
of "The Web" and the men who had handled it. In its more sustained version, as "The Case: A Literary Tragedy," written after the
Privy Council decision, Florence presented herself only as a figure
subordinated to the central "character," her unpublished history of
the world. Family and friends appeared in it only at fleeting
moments, when in some way they served the cause.

Instead, several men took it upon themselves to tell the story of
Florence Deeks, and they had little good to say about her or her
quest for justice. Each in his own way provided the case for the
defence. In doing so, they proved incapable of conceiving, much
less comprehending, that there could be another perspective,
another version of the life and labours of the woman about whom
they wrote with such presumption.

Throughout the period when the Deeks case was before the
Privy Council, and during the months that followed, Wells spent
much of his time at his French villa putting the finishing touches on
the telling of his own story, published in 1934 as *Experiment in
Autobiography*. It set the interpretive framework for subsequent
published accounts of the litigious lady from the Dominions. When
the time came for the first mention of the woman who had plagued
him so, the wordsmith expressed himself carefully. Florence Deeks,

he said, was "a Canadian spinster who conceived the strange idea that she held the copyright to human history."

Wells was fully aware that the image of the frustrated and neurotic spinster remained a popular stereotype. Indeed, it had gained new currency in the age of Havelock Ellis and Sigmund Freud. Miss Deeks had reminded him, Wells said, of Miss Flite of Dickens's *Bleak House*, "in the way she fussed about with her lawyers, with much whispering and rustling of papers." But he could just as easily have drawn his allusion from the pages of *The Odd Women*, the "spinster novel" of his friend George Gissing, or, for that matter, from *Trial by Jury*, with Gilbert and Sullivan's harsh caricature of the "rich attorney's elderly, ugly daughter." And so, Wells suggested, with little hope and not much more to do with her life, Miss Deeks had found an outlet for her thwarted desires and had pursued them to the point of obsession and beyond. She was, he said, "quite honest but vain and foolish," a "faintly pathetic" figure.

The high moral ground remained his. "Life is too short and there is too much to do in it," he informed his readers, "for me to spend time and attention in hunting out whatever poor little assets Miss Deeks may have preserved from her own lawyers and expert advisers. She has to go on living somehow and her mischief is done. I hope she is comfortable and that she is still persuaded she is a sort of intellectual heroine."[8]

In fact, H.G. Wells had been decidedly less charitable than he let on concerning the disposition of Miss Deeks's remaining assets. He knew these were negligible, but as late as July 1933 he had instructed his legal representatives to secure them from her in any way possible, including forced bankruptcy. "It seems strange to Mr. Wells," his secretary wrote to his solicitor John A. Gedge, "that he can be pestered by this sort of thing while he cannot extract a penny from Miss Deeks. Mr. Wells asks if you are quite satisfied that everything has been done which can be done in the matter of costs."[9]

Canadian observers fleshed out Wells's brief but memorable sketch of the Canadian spinster. In his own way, Hector Charlesworth merely expanded on the interpretation initially placed on the Deeks story by Wells. In 1937 the veteran journalist and critic was in the

384 THE SPINSTER AND THE PROPHET

midst of preparing a third volume in his "candid chronicles" of people he had known and events he had witnessed during his long career as journalist. During the 1920s, Hugh Eayrs had published the first highly successful volumes, and he looked forward to the third, to be called *I'm Telling You*, not least because it contained two lengthy chapters harshly critical of the plaintiff in the case of *Deeks v. Wells*.

To help Charlesworth prepare his account, Hugh Eayrs and W.W. McLaughlin had provided Charlesworth with access to trial records and other documents. The journalist used them to such good effect that they feared Florence Deeks might sue. Eayrs made certain that McLaughlin read Charlesworth's text in order to delete libellous passages. They decided to keep in the passage about the woman's purchase, return, and repurchase of *The Outline of History* from Eaton's. It was amusing. McLaughlin had pleaded that Charlesworth be made to tone down his severe judgment on the extravagance of William Irwin's testimony, but he did so only because Irwin was married to his cousin. Eayrs insisted that Charlesworth's words remain intact. "After all consider my dear boy what this whole thing cost us," Eayrs wrote in one of his "Dear Billy" letters, "and really and truly Raney's view was that of most reasonably intelligent people." In contrast, the publisher and the lawyer agreed to soften Charlesworth's account elsewhere in his collection of the premier of Ontario, Mitchell Hepburn, in light of the company's "intimate relations with the Provincial Government."[10]

Charlesworth's December 1920 review of *The Outline of History* in *Saturday Night* magazine had provided the first substantial Canadian assessment of the book. With the publication of *I'm Telling You*, and its chapters entitled "The Amazing Case of Deeks vs. Wells" and "Wells Vindicated At His Own Expense," he furnished the basic account to which any subsequent chronicler of the affair had to turn. But Charlesworth's point of view was strictly that of the case for Wells.

The corporate correspondence he was allowed to examine had been carefully selected. Eayrs and McLaughlin kept from Charlesworth any company records that might have hinted at the troubles during the years of Frank Wise – such as the statement

Eayrs had secured from Miss Millership about Wise's attempts to obtain the letters that were supposed to be "unfindable" in the company's files. And of course they also kept from him any other troublesome internal correspondence. It would not do, for example, to let Charlesworth see the correspondence in which Eayrs himself had reported that John Saul had said that, with Wise's approval, he might indeed have sent "The Web" to New York – or even to England. Full access to the company correspondence would have informed Charlesworth that even George Brett had thought "The Web" might have been sent to New York.

Charlesworth's chapters on *Deeks v. Wells* served the purposes of author and publisher alike, and served them well. For Charlesworth, they provided a comic interlude in an otherwise fairly serious book of reminiscence. For Eayrs and his firm, they more or less ensured that no one in future would take the spinster's claims seriously.

Frank Wise did not exist in Charlesworth's story. The whereabouts of "The Web" during the months following John Saul's resignation Charlesworth dismissed as "a minor mystery." "The Web" had "clearly" been returned to Miss Deeks as early as February 1919. To think otherwise, Charlesworth proclaimed, was simply to go against the evidence. The "eminent experts" mentioned by Wells in his introduction to *The Outline of History* had provided "detailed assistance," while the professorial experts Florence had retained, William Irwin in particular, had deluded themselves into supporting a fraudulent cause. She had been able to retain the distinguished lawyer R.S. Robertson, K.C., only because "she happened to have a brother of considerable means who was a great admirer of her literary abilities and a firm believer in the rectitude of her claim."[11]

By such means, and with such skewed evidence and vested interest, something that appeared to be an authoritative version of the case took shape. It continued to build. In 1945, an amateur historian of progressive political sympathies wrote to H.G. Wells. Aware of Charlesworth's portrayal of the Deeks trial, Edwin C. Guillet had decided to write his own account for his "Famous Canadian Trials" series. He had obtained the evidence and judgments from

Osgoode Hall, and sent Wells the finished product of his research. He noted proudly that a journalist from the *Globe and Mail* had written a series of columns using information he had provided. Guillet had concluded that Florence Deeks's charges were "ridiculous," and the journalist, J.V. McAree, followed suit. The famous author, McAree said, had been the victim of "one of the most outrageous lawsuits ever instituted in Canada."[12]

Guillet wrote several fawning letters to Wells with what he claimed to be "more or less secret information" on the background of the case: stories of the rich brother; of the $15,000 W.P.M. Kennedy was said to have received for his services as editor; of William Irwin as a "fundamentalist religious crank" eager to attack the progressive Wells. This much H.G. would have appreciated; but when Guillet asked for a photograph, Wells's secretary wrote on the top of the letter: "It irritated Mr. W. so much to be asked for autographed portraits of himself like 'some damned movie star' that I am not putting it before him just now." Seven months later, after writing several other equally ingratiating letters, Guillet received his photograph.[13]

Perhaps inspired by Toronto newspaper accounts of *Deeks v. Wells*, in the 1940s the American writer Channing Pollock chose to include the case with others he deemed to be frivolous or vexatious, or both, in an article published in the *American Mercury*. He called his piece "The Plagiarism Racket."[14] In this way, Florence Deeks came to be associated with all manner of cranks, frauds, and hucksters.

Such a view of the Deeks case continued to the end of the twentieth century, unchallenged. In 1999 a book called *Toronto: A Literary Guide* was published to critical acclaim. Its author was Greg Gatenby, artistic director of the International Festival of Authors. Organized according to neighbourhood and street, it contains an entry for 140 Farnham Avenue.[15]

Gatenby tells the story of a hapless lady who one summer day in 1918 set out from her home to deliver an "over-the-transom submission" to Macmillan of Canada and ended up suing H.G. Wells for plagiarism. "The case," Gatenby assures his readers, "was absurd and that it lasted as long as it did is surely as astounding as the initial credibility given to any of Deeks's claims . . . The case was finally put down like a sick dog, but not before it had cost all parties a great deal – and more than just cash." A few lines later, Gatenby invokes the words of Hector Charlesworth, written in 1937, as final judgment on the matter. In the whole Deeks affair, Charlesworth tells a new generation of readers, "few gave consideration to the feelings and reputations of honourable men, who over a period of some years, had to face the accusation that they had been guilty of disgraceful conduct."

It is difficult to blame Gatenby for taking Charlesworth's conclusions at face value, for he merely repeated what history has stated to be truth. That is usually what amateur historians do. Donald Jones had told the same story in his 1992 book, *Fifty Tales of Toronto*. His was popular history, so it lacked the authority of the footnote; but the presence and authority of Hector Charlesworth lurked between the lines in that book, too.[16]

Half a century after Florence Deeks's death, it has become possible to suggest a resolution to the mystery of "The Web." She lost her case against H.G. Wells because the sizable body of intrinsic evidence suggesting a direct correspondence between the Deeks manuscript and *The Outline of History* came to be discounted. The direct evidence, the kind needed to prove that "The Web" had reached Wells, was judged insufficient to outweigh it. This was the verdict of the courts, but must it be the judgment of history?

Cases proceeding within the jurisdiction of civil rather than criminal law require a burden of proof based on a "balance of probabilities," rather than on "proof beyond a reasonable doubt." Historical records now available provide a far more comprehensive body of evidence than that heard in the courts. What, in the end, does it suggest?

If "The Web" was indeed sent to England – why, when, and to whom? How could it have reached Wells? The evidence leaves us with a series of hints that, when linked, point towards a concealed narrative. Propelled less by malicious conspiracy than by a mixture of helpful intent and self-preservation, it requires no particularly complicated scheme or complex network of villains. Instead, it involves a publisher and an editor currying favour, and a man helping his oldest and closest friend, just as he had done for many years . . .

John Saul has possessed "The Web" since the end of July 1918. At first he does not know what to do with it. He places it for the time being in the office vault. Its author, a Miss Deeks, has asked him to determine whether the lengthy extracts she has used from John Richard Green's *A Short History of the English People* go beyond "fair use." She does not wish to be accused of plagiarism. Copyright to Green's work is held by Macmillan & Company, Limited, of London. But for all its substantial length and interesting material, her manuscript is not publishable in its present state. It lacks any apparatus of scholarship, is written in a romantic prose far too old-fashioned for readers who have gone through four years of war, and is so strident in its advocacy of the cause of woman and in its denigration of man that the likelihood of its acceptability as a school textbook is not great. So why trouble the London office? Saul goes on his fall sales trip to the western provinces, and "The Web" sits on the shelf. It is still there when he returns in mid-September.

The transatlantic publishing world, however, while intensely competitive, is also collegial. Co-publication arrangements require the sharing of confidences, even gossip – especially about the goings-on of authors who might make them money. Few authors generate publishers more income than does H.G. Wells, and Wells has a new project. Rumour has it that he is working on a popular history of the world, for use in schools, and that he might offer it to Brett in New York. It is now October 1918.

But Macmillan's Toronto office already contains a history of the world more than 500 pages in length. What should an editor do under such circumstances? Should Wells not at least be made aware that another author is attempting to publish a book on the same subject? John Saul has some ideas, but he decides to speak with his employer, Frank Wise.

Neither publisher nor editor entirely trusts the other – Wise because there are affairs in the office he would rather keep to himself, Saul because he knows what is going on. He knows about the private company, Sales Unlimited, Wise has set up in the Macmillan building so that it could use Macmillan's resources; knows about the hijinks in the Macmillan medical division, populated by shady characters like the one whose sole duty is to act as Wise's personal chauffeur and factotum; knows about the dubious legality on which his British "cash for settlers" colonization scheme rests.

Nevertheless, they have maintained a good working relationship over their half-dozen years together. This particular October day is a chilly one, and Wise has kept a coal fire blazing in the brick fireplace in his office. The two men are seated comfortably in front of it, Wise in his favourite wicker chair, next to the coal scuttle. Saul has raised his problem of what to do about the Deeks manuscript. They are talking about Wells and "The Web," mulling things over, when Wise has one of his better ideas, if once again a shady one. He knows he is in trouble with both Brett in New York and Sir Frederick in London over declining profits, and also over Mrs. Kipling's threatened withdrawal of her husband's books from the Macmillan list because of his boorish behaviour towards them. He fears that his superiors may one day discover his very private sales company or the dubious practices of the employees of his medical division. He senses that his future with the firm is less than secure, and he is fifty years old. What can he do to regain favour?

Wise and Saul are well aware that H.G. Wells has been a Macmillan author, but they know that the author had fallen out with Sir Frederick over poor promotion of one of his novels a number of years back. Might Wells be secured once again to the Macmillan stable if, through some friends in the firm, he is offered use of "The Web" in the writing of his own history? The Deeks manuscript is not publishable, not yet anyway, but it certainly contains a lot of good material. Would Wells, a wealthy author, see fit to provide some kind of reward for such a service? Wise is acutely conscious that he owes Macmillan hundreds of dollars that he has misspent or otherwise allocated for his personal use.[17] He can certainly do with an unanticipated infusion of cash. So, for that matter, can Saul, whose passion for collecting rare books has kept him short of money.

And so, as Wise adds more coal to the fire, an idea takes shape. Saul, no innocent in these matters, will send "The Web" to England in such a way that it reaches Wells. For obvious reasons, it cannot be forwarded through regular channels – through Macmillan's editorial division, for example. That might involve entry of the author's name and title in the firm's manuscript logbook – as in Toronto. The basic problem is who should be selected as the conduit to Wells. Each possibility involves some risk. Directly to Wells? Too dangerous, too much like the direct receipt of stolen goods. An approach to him would need to be more subtle than this. Through George Brett in New York? Why start the chain of transaction on the wrong side of the Atlantic? Besides, is Brett well enough acquainted with Wells? Through Sir Frederick? Out of the question. The Victorian sense of propriety of old Sir Frederick was in part what had alienated Macmillan from Wells and his amoral novels like *Ann Veronica* in the first place. He would be furious if sent "The Web" with the direct suggestion that Wells use it for the purpose of his own work of history.

No, what is needed is a transaction that can masquerade as merely part of the normal business of publishing, or at least can be explained as such by people like Sir Frederick, and even Wells, if things go wrong. They need to be in a position to distance themselves, if necessary – to be able to provide a plausible explanation of the presence of the Deeks manuscript in England should its whereabouts become known.

Who, then, to approach? Wise and Saul mull things over, *sotto voce*, searching for an answer. Wise's office door is slightly ajar; but then only May Mercer, the president's long-suffering but loyal secretary, is within hearing distance. And Wise knows she has heard and typed confidences of much more dubious legality than this.

"The Web" is with them. It rests on Frank Wise's lap. He glances at the beginning of its first chapter, "The Dawn" – the strangest opening he has ever seen in a history book: the creation of the sun and the planets; the solar system; the cooling of the earth;

its envelopment with "a gaseous fluid saturated with carbonic acid and nitrogen." Pages on the slow evolution of the earth and its earliest prehistoric inhabitants. This is less the stuff of historians than of advocates of popular science.

Suddenly Wise knows where "The Web" should be sent: to Richard Gregory, with whom he has corresponded within the year. He has remembered that Gregory, one of the greatest and most popular scientific journalists of the day, is assistant editor of the prestigious scientific journal *Nature*, published by Macmillan and with its offices in Macmillan's own building in St. Martin's Street. He is also, conveniently, Macmillan's education adviser, and is often consulted by Macmillan when non-fiction manuscripts touch upon his interests and expertise. It would be perfectly in order to send this manuscript to him – not exceptional at all. And Gregory is Wells's oldest and most enduring friend, a pal since their schooldays together.

"The Web," they decide, will be sent directly to Gregory, nominally to ask him to look over its early sections for scientific accuracy, but with the informal suggestion that Wells might find the manuscript of some benefit in his work on the new book. Perhaps a covering letter, easily disposable, is in order; one suggesting that, if Wells deems the manuscript to be of help, he might wish to reward those responsible for sending it to him. There is no reason why Gregory should think anything is particularly out of the ordinary or worrisome about this, particularly when he can help out a dear friend.

Transatlantic passage, even in wartime, seldom took longer than a week, and the efficiency of the British postal service was legendary, with several deliveries daily. A parcel originating in Toronto would be in its recipients' hands in London easily within ten days.[18] Near the end of October, Richard Gregory receives the package, along with its covering letter. Well acquainted with his friend's domestic routine, he knows the division of labour in the Wells household. He does not send "The Web" to the author at his London flat. Nor does he trouble the great man as he holds forth at his table in the Reform Club. Instead, he forwards the labour of an author identified only as "Adul Weaver" to Easton Glebe.

392 THE SPINSTER AND THE PROPHET

Gregory has already received a request from Wells for information about the temperature of space and the diameter of the sun. A short while later, he provides the information in a letter sent to Wells's London flat. He encloses a copy of his edition of Huxley's *Physiography*, in the hope that H.G., as his friend puts it so unwittingly but so tellingly, will find it "of use in connection with the book you have in hand."[19]

The book in hand is not the one that will become *The Outline of History*. Like others, Gregory knows that Wells has not yet begun to write the book. He has referred, instead, to "The Web." It does not occur to him that there should be any reason why he should not acknowledge that the manuscript from Canada is in his friend's possession.

Like that of Florence, the story of Jane Wells became one told by men. As she took refuge in the persona of Jane, the compliant wife of a great man with powerful needs, Catherine Wells gradually lost the capacity to express publicly her inner longings. After her death, her image would be fixed immediately in the public mind by the words her husband chose for his introduction to *The Book of Catherine Wells*. In this respect, H.G. Wells would act as arbiter of the meaning of the life of Catherine Wells in a way paralleled a decade later by Hector Charlesworth with respect to Florence Deeks. The voice of the Canadian woman, quieted in the 1930s, lay embedded in the text of "The Web." Similarly, that of Catherine Wells rested in the book whose title carried her name. Her voice is a powerful one, yet her husband only hinted at its concerns. He observes the tone of "wistful melancholy" characteristic of her writings. "Desire is there," he notes, "but it is not active aggressive desire. Frustration haunts this desire."[20]

This much is so. But the husband's words do not convey truth. It rests, instead, in what the man neglects to say. The writings of Catherine Wells overflow with passionate desires, swells of loneliness, deep resentment against unfulfilled longings and the strictures of self-imposed silence, and a self-destructive need to please at any cost. To understand Catherine, her own voice must be heard.

Catherine's short stories make abundantly clear just how complete her transformation to Jane had been. Several of their titles speak of her desperation: "Fear," "Cyanide," "The Draught of Oblivion." The main subject of these stories is the release found in suicide by desperately lonely women, neglected and at times betrayed. In the final scene of "The Draught of Oblivion," a woman recognizes that she is destined to remain unhappy because her unfaithful husband "has ever the look of one who seeks."[21] Dorothy Richardson, Rosamund Bland, Amber Reeves, Elizabeth von Arnim, Rebecca West, Margaret Sanger, Moura Budberg, others: each took her toll on Mrs. Wells. Catherine yearned for her own draught of oblivion even as Jane went about her duties.

On and on the lonely and mournful lament of Catherine Wells continues in these stories and poems. It is clear that the rise of Jane within her did little to curb her unmet desires and longings. "In a Walled Garden" comes very close to a stark depiction of the secrets of Easton Glebe. Of all the pieces in *The Book of Catherine Wells*, this short story is the one that is most patently autobiographical. The story of this home uses the image of drawn curtains, intended to protect those behind the windows from the outside world. The hand that draws the curtain is that of Rosalind Bray, whose maiden name the narrator also provides, as if to suggest an existing identity that must not be forgotten. Her "suburban middle-class background" is akin to that of Amy Catherine Robbins. She has married Edgar Bray, who bears a strong resemblance to H.G. Wells, a man who "drifted into her world by the purest of accident, and profited by its limits." For this man, Rosalind has surrendered her Christian name, which had been Ellen, so that he could "fasten upon her a name that should better satisfy his ear."

Blessed by material success, the couple eventually finds a charming house with a "large and very beautiful garden." It is Easton Glebe by another name. But Rosalind becomes aimless and discontented. Bray comes to bore her. She begins to think that there must be other, more fulfilling ways of life than this.

Then, after an innocent encounter with a handsome young photographer, Rosalind falls truly in love. Everything is changed. Her walled garden is now a prison, her marriage an "absurd blunder."

On this tragic note the story ends.[22] Like Rosalind, Catherine is trapped within the garden walls – and by the Jane of her own creation. The deep longing for freedom, fulfillment, and above all for passion and love permeates *The Book of Catherine Wells*. But so does the need to be dutiful, to serve, to enable.

The few poems in *The Book of Catherine Wells* speak to the atmosphere of loss behind the curtains kept so carefully drawn closed. In "The Kneeling Image" a wife has somehow sinned and her husband has told her that she is dead to him. She retreats to a life of penance; meanwhile, the hypocritical husband builds a public memorial to a saintly wife. Through the years she weeps each night. And from "Two Love Songs":

> Let us clasp hands again, and play
> We're not apart.
> . . . .
> We sit in a quiet room;
> You are very far away;
> And very strange it is that I
> Who so easily could call you
> When I would,
> Can do so no more.
> You are very far away,
> Though so near;
> I sit alone in our silence,
> My dear![23]

These were the longings, the silences, and the unmet needs so wilfully diminished as "wistful melancholy" by a widower in mourning. There was, Wells noted, "a lover, never seen, never verified, elusively at the heart of this desire."[24] It seems not to have occurred to him that he was the person whose attention and love his wife Catherine so desperately sought. It is clear that Wells could not see that the short stories and poems he had chosen for inclusion in *The Book of Catherine Wells* were a powerful indictment of all that he represented as lover and husband.

There is a work that helps explain the peculiar chemistry that existed between this man and this woman. Written two millennia ago, Ovid's *Metamorphosis*, the great epic poem about time and history, chaos and decay, and the re-establishment of order, contains within it the story of Narcissus and Echo. Narcissus we know as the figure from Greek mythology, a young man of great beauty who, loved by all those around him, cannot love them in return. Instead, he reacts with scorn and remains heedless of their heartbreak. Only when he sees his own reflection in a clear pool does he truly love, and from that moment he is trapped.

It is not difficult to see Narcissus in H.G. Wells. Narcissism is above all a disorder of bonding. Everything about Wells speaks to this: the problematic relationship with his parents during his formative years; the incessant preoccupation with himself, to the extent that the image he saw of himself became the central character in most of his novels; the need for a "geographical cure," moving from one place to another to evade problems. Above all, we see it in his relations with women, which combined attraction and repulsion, love and loathing.[25]

Like Narcissus, Wells found it possible to connect with people only when he saw aspects of himself reflected in them. And when he found Catherine, and discovered in her a woman willing to transform herself in ways that met his needs, he reacted with deep emotion – the emotion of disgust, and with it withdrawal. He helped create "Jane." He stayed with her and he said he loved her. But he valued her only because she met his own needs, whatever the cost to the Catherine he wed. There was no genuinely healthy bond in this marriage.

This was a man and an author for whom everyone and everybody existed for the purpose of self-appropriation. He found women useful when they reflected elements of himself, but when they found their own voices he discarded them. And so it was, too, with the words of others.

Appropriation of "The Web" was special only because it reached the courts. In his book *H.G. Wells and His Critics*, Ingvald Racknem provides a comprehensive discussion of Wells's many literary plagiarisms. This meticulous scholar demonstrates exhaustively the many ways in which Wells borrowed, directly and indirectly, the words, phrases, and general outlines of a wide range of writers as diverse as Kipling, Sterne, Swift, de Maupassant, Poe, Flammarion, and Gourmont. Racknem finds the evidence so plentiful that he concludes: "Actually, every one of his publications suggests works by various hands; but Wells's inordinate versatility confused the critics, and it was difficult to ascertain to what extent he was influenced by others, and equally difficult to appreciate his writings."[26]

If he could lift material and ideas from published short stories and novels with such impunity, it is doubtful that Wells would have given a second thought to using the unpublished manuscript of an anonymous author. As writer, husband, and lover, H.G. Wells was a vast sponge that absorbed any work or any person that served his purpose.

It is the lesser-known figure of Echo, however, that we must dwell upon if we wish to understand the second wife of H.G. Wells and the appropriation of "The Web." Ovid's tale has a specifically contemporary resonance, for it provides a literally classic example of what those in the health profession have come to call "co-dependency." Short of separation, this was Catherine's only means of survival in this relationship.

Echo has been forbidden by Hera, wife of Zeus, from initiating conversation. Instead, she is condemned to repeat the words of others. When she falls in love with Narcissus, she is powerless to express her feelings towards him. She can only follow him about in the hope that he will notice her. One day, however, an opportunity arises when Narcissus calls out to his companions, "Is anyone here?" Thrilled, but hidden to him, Echo answers, "Here, here!" He responds: "Come!" and she echoes his word, only to find herself turned away from his outstretched arms. "I will die before I give you power over me," he declares in disgust. "I will give you power over *me*," she responds.[27]

In this way, we come to sense the existence of a second concealed narrative, one involving the Wellses and "The Web." In this case, however, the act is less one of conspiracy than it is of collusion, for it involves nothing more than a writer desperate to find a way of gaining an adequate command over the entire course of history and a wife willing to help her husband in any way she can . . .

Amy Catherine, the vivacious science student of the 1890s, has long since disappeared with the intensity of the marriage; but "Jane" is determined to keep her home intact at any cost. Jane manages the household. It is she, plain Jane, not H.G., who receives the mail and marshals the correspondence and determines which parcels and letters her husband will examine on a given day. It is she of whom a friend of Wells will later write: "What a bulwark of strength she was to him. I have seen her typing and correcting proofs by the hour, all this in addition to running the house so successfully."[28]

All sorts of unsolicited packages, from aspiring authors, friends and strangers alike, arrive at Easton Glebe for Wells's attention. But Wells sees only some of them: Jane is his gatekeeper.[29] Towards the end of October or in early November there arrives a manuscript called "The Web." This one gains her attention, however, for it has come from Richard Gregory at *Nature* and is accompanied by a most pleasant and helpful note from him. Jane Wells is not quite certain how useful this manuscript will be in her husband's work, but it certainly looks relevant; besides, it has always been her practice to ensure that H.G. receives anything sent along by his friend.[30]

In fact, from her perspective, anything that will help in the daunting task of assembling the new book is bound to be a godsend, for if this new history sells as widely as her husband thinks, it offers up the prospect of financial stability at last. Jane, above all others, knows that her husband is the poorest guardian of his own financial interests. Although the success of *Mr. Britling Sees It Through* in 1916 paid him handsome royalties, he nevertheless has, as one biography will later note, very "heavy outgoings – a house in London and another in the country, a growing family, the . . . relationship with Rebecca West, a taste for entertaining at home, dining out in good restaurants, and staying in expensive hotels."[31] Besides, he continues to drift further away from her.

The arrival of "The Web" has been providential. The more Jane examines it, the more interested she gets. It is an outline perfect for *The Outline*. H.G. really must see this. Perhaps her peripatetic husband can finally settle down and make some progress.

Wells is in his study at Easton Glebe, jotting down ideas for the plan of his outline of history. His work is not going well. The modern period is not a problem, for he possesses a good general knowledge of history since the start of the industrial era, and he has firm views on its consequences. The ancient history, however, is difficult. What sources should he use, and in what sequence? Time is pressing. He has decided to devote a year to the project, and several months have already passed with little progress. Encyclopedia volumes and other reference works lie open in front of him, but still there is the problem of finding the pattern, the point of departure. Where to begin? Once this is determined, he is confident that the writing will go well. His muse has never failed him before.

Jane enters the room, carrying a large sheaf of papers, by the looks of it a manuscript. She places the bulky work on his desk, telling him that he should have a look at it: Richard thinks it may be of some real use. And much to H.G.'s surprise, he finds himself staring at a general history of the world – some five hundred pages of it.

He spends the better part of the day getting an overall sense of this work, by "Adul Weaver," taking some notes on sources the author has used. It is by no means the kind of book he has in mind, not of the grand scale he conceives. But it is more than useful. He even finds the author's argument amusing, with its single-minded determination to place women in the forefront of history. He has his own thoughts on that subject.

H.G. Wells does not give much thought to the use to which he now puts this manuscript, "The Web," whose author remains unknown to him. He has always used whatever resources his mind has dredged up – the gist of stories and novels he had long since read, and of plots he could remember. Why should the experience of writing history be different? Many authors before him, he knows, have put past compositions and previously expressed words to good personal use: Laurence Sterne, Samuel Taylor Coleridge, Charles Reade, any number of editors of dictionaries and encyclopedias.[32] What he does is no more, and no less, than simply liberate from the printed page ideas and facts common to humanity and put them forward, in his own inimitable manner, for a new age. Is this not what a prophet must do?

What harm can come from using this neatly typed manuscript history as a general guide, if whole passages are not copied? Do the facts of history not belong to everyone? Judicious use of this "Web" is the means of fleshing out his idea for an outline history of the world. At last, without his having to waste valuable time by reading the sources himself, he can put Jane to good use, typing out notes drawn from "The Web" and searching his library for other sources. Before long, he has a lengthy list of names and topics for her to track down. He also has flagged a number of key pages, so that she might take the manuscript away to her typewriter.

Jane seems especially pleased about this. She has been awfully distracted lately. Now she can be assured that she remains invaluable to him, and he has given her a real sense of direction for the research. Whatever would he do without her? Thus far it has been all hit-and-miss, a frustration for each of them. Now, Jane seems positively keen to forge ahead . . .

In Toronto, it is mid-January 1919 and Wise and Saul are worried. Two months have passed, and no word from Richard Gregory. Nor has "The Web" been returned, and if they are any judge of Miss Deeks, she is bound to be asking about her manuscript soon. They have known her like before. The dilemma raises shades from their past, for this is not the first time they have been linked to the dubious handling of an author's work. Nor will it be the last.

Both men well remember the business with Putman, the Ottawa public school superintendent, while Saul was still with Morang. Saul had thought himself quite clever, allowing one Morang book to feed another, so to speak – until Putman found out. By then, Macmillan had purchased Morang and taken over its list, and he and Wise had managed to evade court action only after a thoroughly awkward meeting with Putman and his lawyer. They had bought Putman's silence, but only by arranging to purchase his rights. The little escapade had cost them $1,500.[33] They were lucky that time. And Saul is now wondering whether his luck might soon run out.

Saul has other reasons for concern. Wise does not yet know about the business of the other spinster, Miss Durand. She has been pestering Saul for some time about doing a book for Macmillan, and he has strung her along with vague promises in the hope she would leave him alone. But damned if she has not shown up with a manuscript at just about the same time as Deeks has with "The Web." The Durand is a children's book on astronomy, called "Skyland Stars and Stories." It is not very good, but like the Deeks it contains some interesting stuff that – used properly and by the right author – might just amount to something.

John Saul prides himself on his network of connections to publishers and authors alike, and he knows exactly who might be interested in some of Miss Durand's material. But Miss Durand returned to his office only the other day, and became indignant – all huff and puff – when he told her that Macmillan is not in a position to publish the book she now claims it "commissioned."

Saul has another surprise in store for Frank Wise.[34] He is about to leave Macmillan for good. The competition at Gage has offered him a position with more responsibility and support staff and a better salary. Besides, there have come to be too many skeletons in the Macmillan closet for Saul's liking, and several, he knows, are linked to him. First the business with Putman; then the attempt to put the Durand manuscript to good use. Saul knows, too, about Wise's other office intrigues, and fears that if they are discovered the scandal will draw him in. Finally, there is the business with "The Web." If he leaves at the end of the month, as Gage wants him to do, he will not be around to face Florence Deeks's accusations the next time she visits. What can he say if she shows up at the office and insists on immediate possession of her manuscript? She has already written a letter of inquiry this month, and is bound to turn up asking for her precious "Web" any day now. This alone is incentive enough to want to move on, and to place as much distance between himself and Bond Street as possible.

A few weeks later, Saul sits at his desk at Macmillan, putting his affairs in order. He is to leave for Gage the next day, and as one of his final acts as a Macmillan employee, he is writing a letter of some delicacy. The Deeks manuscript has still not returned from England. It has been overseas for almost three months now; had he thought it would take so long to be sent back, he might never have agreed to Wise's scheme. In fact, he decides, once he begins work with Gage he will quietly put the word out, among those who count, about some of the Macmillan president's unsavoury ways. If the Deeks woman creates a fuss, it is best that people cast the first glances of accusation in Wise's direction.

So, carefully, Saul writes his letter to Miss Deeks, worded in a way to allay any worry she may have and to suggest that although he is about to leave Macmillan of Canada her manuscript remains in safe hands on Bond Street.

Almost two months later, near the end of March, Frank Wise receives a package from England. He is relieved to find that it is "The Web," rather the worse for wear, but intact. After looking at it briefly, he gives it to one of the clerks to place in the vault. Later, when he encounters John Saul's successor in the hallway, Wise tells him that one of Saul's manuscripts needs attention. It is called "The Web." Wise suggests that Liston retrieve it, glance it over, and write its author the letter of rejection that Saul should have drafted before he left. Macmillan's president is still furious about the departure of his editor, made with so little notice. He feels betrayed.

Then Frank Wise returns to his office. He has just remembered that there is some correspondence related to the Deeks business that he would rather not have others see. He will put it in the spot in his office where he has secreted other highly sensitive papers.

What Frank Wise does not appreciate is that he is not the only person in the office with secrets to keep. May Mercer, his faithful secretary, has kept a mental checklist of all the improprieties she has observed taking place under her employer's direction. Already she is wondering whether she should report them to Mr. Brett in New York. And if she does, should she write a formal letter or an anonymous note? She is worried and confused, not certain of her course of action. Meanwhile, she will bide her time, and weigh the competing claims of loyalty and conscience . . .

A middle-aged man, a historian, sits on a lawn chair in Mount Pleasant Cemetery in Toronto's Rosedale district. It is the 19th day of June, 1999, the fortieth anniversary of the day Florence Deeks was buried here. On June 17, 1959, in her ninety-fifth year, she died peacefully in the home she had lived in for half a century. Her moment of release came in the very year the river she so loved was made to flood the land where she was born, in order to form the expanded shipping lanes of the new St. Lawrence Seaway.

The funeral was held at 140 Farnham Avenue. Later, the family gathered at the cemetery – nephews Campbell, Edward, and Douglas, their families, and a few remaining friends. And of course Mabel, the one person among them who had truly known this woman and her story.

It does not take long for the historian to find the Deeks family gravesite, for it is in a prominent section of the cemetery, and a substantial monument and plinth mark the parents' resting place. Carved oak leaves trim the corners of the large stone. If a person did not search for it, however, one would never find the burial place of Florence Deeks. To do so, it is necessary to kneel down behind the grave of her parents, and look for three half-buried stone markers set in the nearby turf. Hers is the one on the right; the others belong to her sisters.

The historian has scraped away at the crabgrass that threatens to hide the inscription. Time, he knows, has already erased enough. She has been dispossessed of a past in more ways than this. Finally, beneath the crabgrass, some words on stone: "In Loving Memory Of," followed by her name. No year of birth, not the merest hint at history or accomplishment. It is as if this woman lacked a life of her own and was to be remembered only because she eventually died.

This summer afternoon in 1999 is a fine one. The temperature hovers in the high twenties and the sky is a pale blue. A light breeze rustles the leaves of early summer. Sitting in his chair a few yards from the graves of the three spinster sisters, the visitor is thinking about history and silence and voice.

History and silence and voice. Is this what lies at the heart of the story of Florence Deeks? So much of it rests in voices that can easily evade the telling. And what *is* the story? The obvious one about a failed lawsuit over plagiarism? Stolen words? Is it a tale of a woman's struggle to make something of herself? Of her insistence that she have her own voice and make her own statement to the world? Is it about her right to do so, or about the incapacity of those who sat in judgment upon her to weigh evidence that went well beyond their competence or their understanding? Is it fundamentally about justice and injustice?

Or is the heart of the story something else altogether, something deeper? Florence Deeks might well have thought it was really about relations of women and men through the ages, about cooperation and confrontation, complicity and evasion and incomprehension, a narrative that somehow came to be recapitulated in the spinster's own struggles against patriarchy, whether the benign one within her family or its harsher variant in the publishing and legal professions.

Perhaps it is a story of who gets to write history and proclaim its truths in the public sphere, or about private truths hidden within walls and behind curtains. It may be a story of the depths of loneliness and longing, and of the need to connect.

It is all of this and more. For the historian in the graveyard, the narrative once involved only Florence Deeks, her ill-fated book, and her accusations. But as it has gradually unfolded in his mind over the years, her story has become inexorably linked not only to the famous author whom she glimpsed but once but also to the woman who was his wife.

Florence Deeks and Catherine Wells went to their respective graves each unaware of the life of the other. They lived in vastly different worlds, this impoverished spinster and this wealthy wife. But they held, as if in communion, silences unfathomable to those around them – longings and desires and unfulfilled aspirations common to women through the ages but somehow unique to them alone.

Each woman longed for a voice, desired to be heard. Only in unpublished writings did Catherine's own voice exist, and after her death, when her words were published, few if any people heard what she had to tell them. Florence found her voice in writing "The Web," but it too remained an untold story after the book failed to be published.

Graveyards are the final levellers of humanity, in spite of the different sizes of their monuments to the dead. Not far from the plot where Florence Deeks is buried, John Saul and Hector Charlesworth also rest, and the historian takes some time to seek out their resting places.

By the 1930s, John Saul had become a legendary editor within the Canadian publishing industry. Hugh Eayrs came to think of him as a "likeable ruffian – a tough fighter."[35] Eayrs had come to have more than one reason for thinking so, for within months of the return of Florence and Mabel Deeks from London in 1933, his young assistant, John Morgan Gray, found himself seated in a boardroom in the building that housed the offices of the Gage publishing firm, defending his company and the Ryerson Press against an accusation of plagiarism.

Many passages from several American school texts had found their way into a reader, published by Macmillan of Canada and edited under the supervision of Ryerson's Lorne Pierce, intended for use in Canadian schools. Across the boardroom table from Gray sat John Saul, Gage's editor-in-chief, and the manager of Nelson in Canada, Sidney Watson – long-time golf partner of Saul and Hugh Eayrs and the one to whom Saul had confided that he had sent the Deeks manuscript to England. Watson, whose firm's texts had been among those plagiarized, was normally "a stiffly polite man." But to Gray he appeared at the time "so angry that he had trouble controlling his voice." Saul had done his homework, and had marked all the offending passages. He "looked like a prosecuting counsel eager to open his case," Gray later recalled. He had prepared "a stunning indictment." The men settled the matter amicably, out of court, after Gray suggested a suitable form of compensation for the other firms.[36] For his part, Saul might well have thought that the whole business truly was one of life's more delightful ironies.

One senses that the whiff of scandal that trailed behind Saul over the Deeks affair helped add to the aura that surrounded him.

He died in June 1939, at the age of seventy, and was buried near the perimeter of Mount Pleasant Cemetery. The handsome engraved stone that marks his resting place has become softened and shaded by the stately tree and the evergreen shrub that frame it.

An elusive figure even in the grave, Frank Wise is not to be found in Mount Pleasant Cemetery. After his release from prison in 1930, he moved to Montreal, where he became a printer of fine water-colour illustrations, a binder of fine books, and a friend to those who appreciated them. In a letter written in 1952 to Lorne Pierce, publisher of the Ryerson Press, he claimed Lawrence Lande, later a distinguished book collector and benefactor of McGill University, as his protegé. Among those with whom Wise corresponded in his later years were the Queen Mother, Lady Churchill (wife of Sir Winston), and Greer Garson. Wise died in Montreal on December 19, 1960, at the age of ninety-one, remembered by his granddaughter in later years as a lovable old grammarian with failing eyesight living out his days in an old folks' home near Montreal.[37]

Hugh Eayrs died of a heart attack on April 29, 1940, ten months after John Saul. Death notices remarked, quite appropriately, on the contribution he had made to the cause of Canadian letters – as publisher of Mazo de la Roche, Hector Charlesworth, Morley Callaghan, E.J. Pratt, and Marius Barbeau. The obituaries said that Eayrs had been "essentially a man in whom social instincts were uppermost," a person with a "driving personality and impulsiveness of action."[38] Those who knew the man could read between these lines, with their discreet reference to a "precarious state of health" that made him "temperamentally unfitted to follow the orders of his physician." The fact was that Eayrs had long had an affinity for the bottle, and in the end the bottle bested him. He was interred in the Toronto Necropolis, the city's oldest non-denominational cemetery. At the time of his death he was forty-six years old.

Not far from the graves of John Saul and Florence Deeks in Mount Pleasant Cemetery lies that of Hector Charlesworth, beneath a stone marker set flush with the soil. Many years earlier, Charlesworth had attacked the Group of Seven for their devotion to the "sinister wilderness" and other young artists for their violation of "eternal standards of poetry and beauty."[39] Outspoken to the end, in late December 1945, after listening to a concert given by Duke Ellington at Massey Hall, he penned a newspaper column that dismissed the musician's jazz as a form of aesthetic corruption. His editors at the *Globe and Mail* ran it under the headline "Ellington Tests Nerves in Orgy of Cacophony." Charlesworth family memories have it that the following morning, after reading the review, Ellington telephoned Charlesworth at home and so berated him that it brought on the heart attack that killed him the next day. He was seventy-three.[40]

Herbert George Wells died less than a year after Hector Charlesworth. The prophet had reached the height of his fame and influence in the spring of 1934, when he had met separately with Joseph Stalin and Franklin D. Roosevelt to determine whether their "two brains" truly worked towards the "socialist world-state" he believed to be "the only hopeful destiny for mankind."[41] During his later years, he continued to pontificate on the idea of an Open Conspiracy and other well-worn Wellsian themes. He discarded Odette Keun and renewed his liaison with Moura Budberg. The estrangement from Rebecca West diminished in rancour until each recalled the other with genuine affection. Margaret Sanger corresponded with Wells on birth control and other matters until almost the end of his life.

Wells's place within the canon of English literature fell quickly under the modernist weight of Joyce and Eliot and Woolf. His early scientific romances continued to find a wide readership and ensured his place as one of the great founders of "science fiction." Others would continue to find inspiration in his internationalism. A certain audience existed for his later novels, but in declining numbers, for they lacked the power of imagination of those written earlier. Eventually Wells came to view himself as unappreciated by his public; the reality was probably that his public had come to know him all too well. A continuing stream of royalties from *The Outline of History* kept him in comfort, even during the blitzkrieg that blackened his mood during the Second World War he had once predicted would never come. His final book, published the year before his death, was called *Mind at the End of Its Tether*.

Among the visitors to the ailing author at his London flat in the months before he died was Sir Richard Gregory. They talked about the days under Huxley and about Sir Richard's forthcoming presidential address to the British Association for the Advancement of Science, scheduled for July 20, 1946. Sir Richard invited his "oldest and dearest friend" to attend the event, if he felt up to it. When the day arrived, Wells tried his best, but his failing heart kept him bedridden. He died in his sleep on the afternoon of August 13, 1946, five weeks short of his eightieth birthday.

Afterwards, Sir Richard wrote a letter of condolence to Wells's son George. "When I was with him as a fellow student at the Royal College of Science, South Kensington, sixty years ago," he recalled, "I became his disciple as well as his friend, my attachment to him has always been stronger than to any friend in the world."[42] He spent the next two years attempting to organize a Wells Memorial, but the initiative met with indifferent results.[43] Sir Richard passed away in 1952 at his home in Middleton-on-Sea, at the age of eighty-eight.

Florence Amelia Deeks outlived all these men, in most cases by many years, and she took her own version of her fate at the hands of a famous author, several publishers, and British justice to her grave. The history of the world this woman had dared to write remains virtually unknown, as if buried with her. Historical research and feminist scholarship have advanced well beyond the turn-of-the-century insights she had to bear on her subject.

Once, however, her achievement would have constituted a unique and important contribution to feminist history, and perhaps to feminism itself. In 1935, the American historian Mary Ritter Beard, one of the first champions of women's history, wrote: "What we now have is the instruction of young men and women in the history of men – of men's minds and manner; in not one college of this country . . . is there any comprehensive treatment of women's contributions to civilization and culture."[44] Beard did not know it, but the book she hoped for had been written almost a generation earlier and sat unread in a woman's home in Toronto. What shape might the writing of women's history have taken had this feminist outline of history, with its thorough emphasis on patriarchy, inequality, and gender, been published? What revitalizing influence might it have had on feminist historiography during the interwar years, when feminism seemed to be in retreat?

In spite of her setback at the hands of the law and the courts, Florence Deeks knew she had something to say, and at some unknown point between her final defeat at the hands of the Privy Council in 1933 and her death twenty-six years later, she undertook one final sustained exercise in the writing of history. During the eighth or ninth decade of her life, she gathered her resources and sat down to write. She did not repeat the foolishness involved with "The Highway of History," years before. This time she consulted no man and maintained a steady gaze on the story of her own sex. By the time she had finished, a neatly typed untitled manuscript, half the length of "The Web," sat on her desk. It was a concise history of women through the ages – history with the men left out. By that stage in her life, publication scarcely mattered. She gained satisfaction enough in having made the statement.

Florence's dearest friend, her sister Mabel, died in 1962 at the age of eighty-seven, and with her passing the house on Farnham Avenue stood silent. She was buried next to Florence, companion even in death. A year earlier, she had deposited with the Toronto Public Library the many papers of the sister she had so loved, encouraged, and protected. Almost everything among them dwelt on the strange case of *Deeks v. Wells*. In this way, "The Web" came to be returned to the place where Florence had given it birth. Her history of women rests there, too – another burial, unpublished, unread, and all but unknown and forgotten. Like "The Web" and its feisty author, it remains one of history's many silences. What counts is its very existence, for it tells us that Florence Deeks, like Catherine Wells, had rediscovered her own true voice and had found words once more to speak her mind.

Sources

BOOKS LIKE THIS ONE, intended for a general audience rather than specialists, risk alienating their readers if they carry that sign of scholarly authority, the footnote. Central to *The Spinster and the Prophet*, however, is the serious matter of literary theft. It is essential, therefore, to point as clearly as possible to the sources of the evidence for my claims so that those who wish to do so can weigh the likelihood of their truth for themselves.

The archival evidence in the book is drawn from four major collections of manuscripts: the Florence A. Deeks Fonds, Baldwin Room, Toronto Reference Library, Toronto; the H.G. Wells Collection, University of Illinois at Urbana-Champaign; the Macmillan Archive, British Library, London; the Macmillan of Canada Papers, William Ready Division of Archives and Research Collections, McMaster University Library, Hamilton, Ontario. In addition, I examined the papers of other key figures. These include the Gilbert Murray Papers, Bodleian Library, University of Oxford; the Sir Richard Gregory Papers, University of Sussex Library, Brighton; the Lawrence J. Burpee Papers and the Frank H. Underhill Papers, National Archives of Canada, Ottawa. Limitations of space preclude citation of some box and file numbers, but I will be pleased to provide this information to any interested reader.

Today "The Web" is no longer a publishable work. Written in the elevated style of High Victorian Romanticism, its combination of evangelical enthusiasm and moral umbrage would sit well with few contemporary readers. Since it was not an act of formal scholarship, "The Web" is not easily compared with works of history by early-twentieth-century academic historians or by recent feminist historians. Nevertheless, it merits examination as a significant historical document in its own right, one of the very first to criticize the notion of patriarchy. It therefore deserves attention from historians of women.

A similar judgment must be rendered on Florence Deeks's history of women, now in the Deeks Fonds, a much shorter book-length manuscript long surpassed by later scholarship. Written as it was in the 1930s or later, it is without the ornate style of "The Web," but it also lacks that work's freshness of moral concern. Even so, it too merits scrutiny and study, a feminist tree that once fell in a silent forest.

As part of my research, I prepared a computerized transcription of the text of "The Web" to allow searches by key words. One of the reasons for creating this electronic document was to have it and the text of *The Outline of History* examined by Drs. Ned Feder and Walter Stewart, of the National Institutes of Health in Bethesda, Maryland. Some years back, Feder and Stewart developed a computer-based technique for comparing two texts and isolating "strings" of thirty characters held in common. In their private time and at no charge, these dedicated men ran the texts of "The Web" and *The Outline* through their "plagiarism machine." Apart from passages quoted by both works, their program detected no more instances of commonality than those found by Florence Deeks or presented as evidence in court.

As the notes attest, I have relied heavily on existing biographies of H.G. Wells for my treatment of his life and relationships with others. Of these, the most thorough remains Norman and Jeanne Mackenzie, *H.G. Wells: A Biography* (New York: Simon and Schuster, 1973). Also of substantial value is David C. Smith, *H.G. Wells: Desperately Mortal* (New Haven: Yale University Press, 1986).

Michael Coren, *The Invisible Man: The Life and Liberties of H.G. Wells* (Toronto: Vintage Books, 1993), is by intent the most provocative biographical account. It is also the only account that has challenged the conventional view of *The Outline*'s near miraculous production. *H.G.: The History of Mr. Wells*, by Michael Foot (Washington, D.C.: Counterpoint, 1995), offers a useful contrast to the conservative socio-political orientation of Coren's book. An author steeped in the British socialist tradition, Foot is highly sympathetic to Wells's political views. He was also acquainted personally with several of the women (Rebecca West, Moura Budberg) in the life of his subject. Lovat Dickson, *H.G. Wells: His Turbulent Life and Times* (Toronto: Macmillan of Canada, 1969), offers the perspective of a distinguished publisher with long and intimate association with the Macmillan publishing companies in London and in Canada. Dickson also came to know Wells during his later years. The chronological focus of his book is on the period after 1900, and in some ways it provides the most penetrating psychological assessment of Wells.

No sustained history of Macmillan of Canada exists, although one is certainly merited. *The Archive of the Macmillan Company of Canada Ltd., Part I: 1905–1965*, compiled by Bruce Whiteman (Hamilton, Ont.: Archives and Research Collections, McMaster University Library, 1984), provides an overview of the company history. The unpublished doctoral dissertation by Danielle Hamelin, "Nurturing Canadian Letters: Four Studies in the Publishing and Promotion of English-Canadian Writing, 1890–1920" (University of Toronto, 1994), contains a chapter on the years of Frank Wise as president, but ends at 1920.

Surprisingly, the American branch of Macmillan, too, lacks a biographer. Interesting material on the history of the company can nevertheless be found in the works of John Tebbel, most notably the second and third volumes of his comprehensive history of American publishing, *A History of Book Publishing in the United States, Volume II: The Expansion of an Industry 1865–1919* (New York and London: R.R. Bowker, 1975), and *A History of Book Publishing in the United States, Volume III: The Golden Age Between Two Wars 1920–1940* (New York and London: R.R. Bowker, 1978).

The history of the British branch of Macmillan has been well served by Charles Morgan, in *The House of Macmillan* (London: Macmillan, 1944), and by Richard Davenport-Hines, *The*

Macmillans (London: Heinemann, 1992). Other relevant perspectives on British publishers and publishing can be found in Alistair Horne, *Macmillan 1894–1956: Volume I of the Official Biography* (London: Macmillan, 1988); Newman Flower, *Just As It Happened* (London: Cassell, 1950); and Simon Nowell-Smith, *The House of Cassell 1848–1958* (London: Cassell, 1958).

Of value in gaining perspective on Wells's view of life are of course his own autobiographical writings, most notably *Experiment in Autobiography* (New York: Macmillan, 1934), most of which deals with the period prior to the 1920s. Almost nothing is said about the writing of *The Outline of History*. Wells also intentionally omitted intimate discussions of his love affairs with women still alive at the time. This gap was filled with the publication of *H.G. Wells in Love: Postscript to An Experiment in Autobiography*, edited by G.P. Wells (London: Faber and Faber, 1984). The book consists of previously unpublished parts of Wells's autobiography. It should be supplemented by Gordon N. Ray, *H.G. Wells & Rebecca West* (New Haven: Yale University Press, 1974). The perspective Ray provides (largely that of Rebecca West) should be balanced by a reading of Anthony West, *H.G. Wells: Aspects of a Life* (New York: New American Library, 1974).

Two scholars who have written with particular sensitivity and insight on H.G. Wells's relationships with women are Ruth Brandon, "The Uses of Principle – 2: H.G.'s New Utopia," in her *The New Women and the Old Men: Love, Sex and the Woman Question* (London: Secker and Warburg, 1990), 160–207; and Patricia Stubbs, "Mr Wells's Sexual Utopia," in her *Women and Fiction: Feminism and the Novel 1880–1920* (Sussex: Harvester Press, 1979), 177–94.

In my determination to let the story of the spinster and the prophet unfold on its own terms, rather than those dictated by scholarly interests, I studiously avoided unwarranted deflection into other interesting byways. One is the history of plagiarism and literary fraud. Those who wish to situate the case of *Deeks v. Wells* within the larger context of literary theft might start by reading Thomas Mallon, *Stolen Words: Forays into the Origins and Ravages of Plagiarism* (Harmondsworth, Middlesex, England:

Penguin, 1989), and Marcel C. LaFollette, *Stealing into Print: Fraud, Plagiarism, and Misconduct in Scientific Publishing* (Berkeley, California: University of California Press, 1992).

As my choice of chapter epigraphs attests, Angus Wilson's *Anglo-Saxon Attitudes, A Novel* (London: Secker, 1956) has much to say about scholarly fraud and other forms of deceit, betrayal, and loss.

Intrinsic to the story of Florence Deeks from a scholarly per-spective is an extraordinarily rich vein of work on women's experi-ence, feminist theory and history. Had *The Spinster and the Prophet* taken the form of an academic monograph, much of this work would be more evident in the footnotes or in the text itself. Florence Deeks was a woman who occupied a singular position in her society and culture, but her situation was by no means unique. In many ways, it was emblematic of that of unmarried women of her generation who held aspirations of intellectual accomplish-ment and who lived into old age. Among the works that provide immediate access to her situation, readers might consult: Jill Ker Conway, *When Memory Speaks: Exploring the Art of Autobio-graphy* (New York: Vintage Books, 1998); Kennedy Fraser, *Orna-ment and Silence: Essays on Women's Lives from Edith Wharton to Germaine Greer* (New York: Vintage Books, 1998); Elaine Showalter, *A Literature of Their Own: British Women Novelists from Brontë to Lessing*, expanded edition (Princeton, New Jersey: Princeton University Press, 1999); Elizabeth Abbott, *A History of Celibacy* (Toronto: HarperCollins, 1999); Sandra Haldman Martz, ed., *When I Am An Old Woman I Shall Wear Purple* (Watsonville, California: Papier-Mache Press, 1991); and Tillie Olsen, *Silences* (New York: Delacorte Press/Seymour Lawrence, 1989).

One work of this sort deserves to be singled out: *Writing a Woman's Life* (New York: Ballantine, 1988), by Carolyn G. Heilbrun, which provides illuminating and at times poignant obser-vation and testimony. Heilbrun's writing includes the popular novels written under the pseudonym "Amanda Cross," featuring the detective Kate Fansler. *Sweet Death, Kind Death*, for example, while an intriguing murder mystery set in the context of a women's college, is also a meditation about women's lives in middle age and beyond. Novels, in fact, often provide the most direct access to the dignity of old age. See, for example, Penelope Lively, *Moon Tiger* (Harmondsworth, Middlesex, England: Penguin, 1988), and Margaret Laurence, *The Stone Angel* (Toronto: McClelland and Stewart, 1964). Carol Shields's *Swann: A Mystery* (Toronto: Stoddart, 1987) is a novel about one of Florence Deeks's sisters-in-spirit and the fate of her reputation at the hands of "experts."

Recent feminist history has provided part of the perspective I have brought to bear on the subject of women in history. Among many such works, a few serve as particularly good points of entry: Gerda Lerner, *The Creation of Patriarchy* (New York: Oxford University Press, 1986), *The Creation of Feminist Consciousness: From the Middle Ages to Eighteen-seventy* (New York: Oxford University Press, 1993), and *Why History Matters: Life and Thought* (New York: Oxford University Press, 1997); Bonnie S. Anderson and Judith P. Zinsser, *A History of Their Own: Women in Europe from Prehistory to the Present*, two volumes (New York: Harper and Row, 1988); Elizabeth Wayland Barber, *Women's Work: The First 20,000 Years: Women, Cloth, and Society in Early Times* (New York: W.W. Norton and Company, 1994); Jane Lewis, *Women in England 1870–1950: Sexual Divisions & Social Change* (Bloomington, Indiana: Indiana University Press, 1984); Sheila Jeffreys, *The Spinster and Her Enemies: Feminism and Sexuality, 1880–1930* (London: Pandora Press, 1985); and Sheila Bowbotham, *A Century of Women: The History of Women in Britain and the United States in the 20th Century* (Harmondsworth, Middlesex, England: Penguin Books, 1999). Such works, however, are but the tip of a very large historiographical iceberg.

Notes

ABBREVIATIONS

"Argument"	Florence A. Deeks, "Deeks versus Wells et al; The Argument," typescript of Deeks's argument before the Judicial Committee of the Privy Council, [1932], copy in DF
Brett	George Platt Brett
"Case"	Florence A. Deeks, "The Case – A Literary Tragedy," typescript, [c. 1934], copy in DF. Mostly unpaginated.
Catherine	*The Book of Catherine Wells; With an Introduction by Her Husband H.G. Wells* (London: Chatto and Windus, 1928)
"Comparison"	Florence A. Deeks, "Comparison – Appendix. Mistakes – Original in 'The Web,'" typescript, [1922], in DF
Coren	Michael Coren, *The Invisible Man: The Life and Liberties of H.G. Wells* (Toronto: Vintage Books, 1993)
Deeks	Florence Amelia Deeks
DF	Florence A. Deeks Fonds, Baldwin Room, Toronto Reference Library, Toronto, Ontario
Dickson	Lovat Dickson, *H.G. Wells: His Turbulent Life and Times* (Toronto: Macmillan of Canada, 1969)
Eayrs	Hugh Smithurst Eayrs
Experiment	H.G. Wells, *Experiment in Autobiography: Discoveries and Conclusions of a Very Ordinary Brain (Since 1866)* (New York: Macmillan, 1934)
Foot	Michael Foot, *H.G.: The History of Mr. Wells* (Washington, D.C.: Counterpoint, 1995)
"Links"	Mabel Deeks, untitled and undated account beginning, "These few 'links in a chain,'" copy in DF

MA   Macmillan Archive, British Library, London
Mackenzie   Norman and Jeanne Mackenzie, *H.G. Wells: A Biography*
                   (New York: Simon and Schuster, 1973)
Macmillan   Sir Frederick Macmillan
McLaughlin   William W. McLaughlin
MCP   Macmillan of Canada Papers, William Ready Division of
                   Archives and Research Collections, McMaster University
                   Library, Hamilton, Ontario
Outline   *The Outline of History: Being a Plain History of Life and
                   Mankind*, 2 volumes (New York: Macmillan, 1920)
"Plagiarism?"   Florence A. Deeks, "Plagiarism?" unpublished typescript,
                   [c. 1930s], copy in DF
"Proceedings"   "In the Privy Council. No. 18 of 1932. On Appeal from
                   the Appellate Division of the Supreme Court of Ontario.
                   *Florence A. Deeks (Plaintiff) – Appellant and H.G. Wells,
                   The Macmillan Company, Inc., The Macmillan Company
                   of Canada Limited, George Newnes Limited, Cassell &
                   Company, Limited (Defendants) – Respondents.* Record
                   of Proceedings," copy in DF
Saul   John Cameron Saul
Smith   David C. Smith, *H.G. Wells: Desperately Mortal* (New
                   Haven: Yale University Press, 1986)
WC   H.G. Wells Collection, University of Illinois, Urbana-
                   Champaign, Illinois
"Web"   Florence A. Deeks, "The Web of the World's Romance. By
                   Adul Weaver," typescript, [1918], in DF
Wells   Herbert George Wells
Wells in Love   *H.G. Wells in Love: Postscript to an Experiment in Auto-
                   biography*, G.P. Wells, ed. (London: Faber and Faber, 1984)
Wise   Frank Wise

PREFACE

1. Toronto: University of Toronto Press, 1986
2. Donald Jones, *Fifty Tales of Toronto* (Toronto: University of Toronto Press, 1992); Robert Fulford, "Imperial Bedrooms," *Saturday Night* (Apr. 1993), 24–6, 65
3. William Dawson LeSueur, *William Lyon Mackenzie: A Reinterpretation*, A.B. McKillop, ed. (Toronto: Macmillan of Canada, 1979)

4. Simon Schama, *Dead Certainties (Unwarranted Speculations)* (Toronto: Vintage Books, 1992), 319–20

ONE: LACE CURTAINS

1. See Morris Wolfe, ed., *A Saturday Night Scrapbook* (Toronto: New Press, 1973), ix–x.
2. Frances Fenwick Williams, "The Little People of the Cornfields," *Saturday Night* (Dec. 18, 1920), 29; "Society," 34
3. "The Bookshelf," *Saturday Night* (Dec. 18, 1920), 8
4. Hector Charlesworth, *The Canadian Scene; Sketches Political and Historical* (Toronto: Macmillan, at St. Martin's House, 1927), especially his chapter "Robert B. Angus, A Canadian Patriarch." Charlesworth wrote of Angus: "Patriarchal in years . . . patriarchal in historical experience, he was also marvellously patriarchal in appearance." (12)
5. *A Cyclopedia of Canadian Biography*, Hector Charlesworth, ed. (Toronto: Hunter-Rose, 1919), 254. See also the entry on Charlesworth in *Who's Who in Canada, 1943–44* (Toronto: International Press, 1944), 302.
6. Hector Charlesworth, "Reflections," *Saturday Night* (Dec. 18, 1920), 2
7. Consumer details are drawn from Eaton's advertisements in the Toronto *Star*, Dec. 18, 1920; the weather for Monday, Dec. 20, is taken from the Toronto *Star* of that day.

TWO: FORMATIONS

1. "How Changed the Scene," typescript by "Amelia and Louise George," DF. This *nom de plume* is derived from the middle names of Florence and Mabel Deeks and the first name of their father.
2. Undated typescript beginning "I, Florence Amelia Deeks, 140 Farnham Avenue . . . ," DF, 1
3. Directories for the city of Toronto consistently give her name as "Melinda" after she moved there in the late 1890s.
4. The detailed census records are available on microfilm at the National Archives of Canada. The census indicates that George Deeks was forty years old, but this appears to be in error. According to the headstone marking his grave in Mount Pleasant Cemetery in Toronto, he was in fact forty-one, born on Dec. 8, 1830. Biographical material and dates of birth and death have been obtained from various sources: professionally researched genealogical data provided to the author by William G. Deeks of Toronto, grandson of George S. Deeks; obituaries of George Deeks and Catherine Melinda Deeks in Toronto *Globe*, Mar. 5, 1897, and Mar. 12, 1930, respectively; clippings in University of Toronto Archives on George S. Deeks, File A73.0026/081(66); Douglas Burk Deeks, File A73-0026/081(63); Edward R. Deeks, File A73-0026/081(64); and George Campbell Deeks, File A73-0026/081(65).

5. See *Index to the 1871 Census of Ontario. Stormont, Dundas, Glengarry, Prescott, Russell*, Bruce S. Elliott, general editor (Toronto: Ontario Genealogical Society, 1987), 65.

6. Smyth Carter, *The Story of Dundas; Being a History of the County of Dundas from 1784 to 1904* (Iroquois [Ont.]: St. Lawrence News Publishing House, 1905), 162; Eleanor Wickware Morgan, *"Up the Front": A Story of Morrisburg* (Toronto: n.p., 1964), 52

7. "I, Florence," 1

8. Telephone conversation with William G. Deeks, May 19, 1997

9. Robert Gidney and W.P.J. Millar, *Inventing Secondary Education: The Rise of the High School in Nineteenth-Century Ontario* (Montreal and Kingston: McGill-Queen's University Press, 1990), 136–45

10. Gidney and Millar, *Inventing Secondary Education*, 147

11. Morgan, *"Up the Front,"* 91–2

12. Gidney and Millar, *Inventing Secondary Education*, 192–4, 250–1. For a general overview of the Victorian middle-class girl, see also Deborah Gorham, *The Victorian Girl and the Feminine Ideal* (London and Canberra: Croom Helm, 1982), 15–35.

13. Morgan, *"Up the Front,"* 98

14. Mackenzie, 9–12

15. Foot, 1–4

16. Mackenzie, 21

17. Quoted in Mackenzie, 33

18. Wells, *Tono-Bungay* (London: J.M. Dent, 1994 [1909]), 7. His description of "Bladesover House" in the first chapter is an evocative portrayal of the world of Up Park.

19. Mackenzie, 47–51

20. Quoted in Adrian Desmond, *Huxley: Evolution's High Priest* (London: Michael Joseph, 1997), 158

21. Wells quoted in Mackenzie, 59

22. *Experiment*, 231, 236

23. *Experiment*, 242

24. C.B. Sissons, *A History of Victoria College* (Toronto: University of Toronto Press, 1952), 193

25. George S. Deeks's brief career as a teacher is mentioned in Sissons, *Victoria College*, 193. I have found no other reference to it.

26. "Railroad Builder Dead," Toronto *Telegram*, May 2, 1930

27. Toronto *Globe*, Mar. 5, 1897

28. "I, Florence," 1

29. A.B. McKillop, *Matters of Mind: The University in Ontario, 1791–1951* (Toronto: University of Toronto Press for the Ontario Historical Studies Series, 1994), 130. An experiment in coeducation at Victoria in its very early years was quickly abandoned by its founder, Egerton Ryerson.

30. *Victoria College. Register of Students in Arts, 1894–96*. United Church of Canada Archives, Toronto

31. C.S. Clark, *Of Toronto the Good: The Queen City of Canada as it is* (Montreal: Toronto Publishing Company, 1898), 73–6
32. *8th Annual Calendar of the Presbyterian Ladies' College (incorporated) for the higher education of young women, 1896–7.* Women's Arts Association, Toronto.
33. *Experiment*, 298
34. *Experiment*, 353
35. *Experiment*, 299–300. See also Mackenzie, 88–98.
36. Richard Gregory quoted in Mackenzie, 97
37. *8th Annual Calendar*, 7–9
38. Toronto *Globe*, Mar. 5, 1897
39. "I, Florence," 1

THREE: LABOUR AND CONSTANCY

1. Allison Thompson, "A Worthy Place in the Art of Our Country: The Women's Art Association of Canada, 1887–1987" (unpublished M.A. thesis, Institute of Canadian Studies, Carleton University, 1989), 51–4
2. Thompson, "A Worthy Place," 53–6
3. Women's Art Association of Canada, *Annual Report, 1903*. Women's Art Association, Toronto. Box labelled "W.A.A. *Annual Reports,* 1892–1924."
4. "Historical Sketch of the Women's Art Association of Canada, prepared by Miss F. Deeks and read by Mrs. W.D. Gregory, on the occasion of the 25th Anniversary of the Association, in the New Galleries, 594 Jarvis Street." Women's Art Association of Canada, *Annual Report, 1911–1912,* 24–33.
5. Thompson, "A Worthy Place," 58–9
6. Beverly Boutilier, "Women's Rights and Duties: Sarah Anne Curzon and the Politics of Canadian History," in Beverly Boutilier and Alison Prentice, eds., *Creating Historical Memory: English-Canadian Women and the Work of History* (Vancouver: UBC Press, 1997), 51–74
7. Toronto *Globe*, Feb. 1, 1892
8. "Impressions – Woman's Art Exhibit," *Saturday Night* (Mar. 6, 1897)
9. "Studio and Gallery," *Saturday Night* (Dec. 23, 1919), 15
10. Mackenzie, 148–9
11. Coren, 57
12. Mackenzie, 265
13. Foot, 29–43
14. *Experiment*, 385
15. Quoted by Jeremy Lewis, "Introduction" to Wells, *Love and Mr. Lewisham* (London: J.M. Dent, 1993 [1900]), xxxix
16. Quoted in Ruth Brandon, *The New Women and the Old Men: Love, Sex and the Woman Question* (London: Secker and Warburg, 1990), 166–7
17. Gregory to Wells, June 15, 1900, quoted in Mackenzie, 152

18. Quoted in Brandon, *New Women and Old Men,* 167
19. See Patricia Stubbs, *Women and Fiction: Feminism and the Novel 1880–1920* (Sussex: Harvester Press, 1979), 190.
20. Wells to Elizabeth Healey, June 19, 1888, quoted in Smith, 183
21. Smith, 208
22. Mackenzie, 119
23. See reminiscences by M.M. Meyer, Berta Ruck, and Margaret Cole in J.R. Hammond, ed., *H.G. Wells: Interviews and Recollections* (London: Macmillan, 1980), 17–18, 28, 35.
24. Dorothy Richardson, *Pilgrimage, Volume II: The Tunnel/Interim* (London: Virago, 1979), 112–3
25. Gloria G. Fromm, *Dorothy Richardson: A Biography* (Urbana, Ill.: University of Illinois Press, 1977), 30–5; Coren, 55
26. Richardson, *Tunnel,* 113
27. *Experiment,* 471
28. Fromm, *Richardson,* 34, 37
29. Smith, 195
30. Beatrice Webb, quoted in Brandon, *New Women and Old Men,* 165
31. For quotations from Catherine Wells, see Smith, 197.
32. Wells quoted in Smith, 198
33. "Father Founder of Flour Mills," Toronto *Globe and Mail,* Dec. 3, 1945
34. "Campbell, Hon. Archibald," *The Canadian Who's Who* (Toronto: Musson, 1910), 34
35. Ruth Freeman and Patricia Klaus, "Blessed or Not? The New Spinster in England and the United States in the Late Nineteenth and Early Twentieth Centuries," *Journal of Family History,* Vol. 9 (winter 1984), 395. See also Susan Cotts Watkins, "Spinsters," in the same issue, 310–25; and Cécile Dauphin, "Single Women," in Geneviève Fraisse and Michelle Perrot, eds., *A History of Women, Volume IV: Emerging Feminism from Revolution to World War* (Cambridge, Mass.: Belknap Press, Harvard University Press, 1995), 427–8.
36. See, for example, George Gissing's novel, *The Odd Women* (New York: W.W. Norton, 1977). It was first published in 1893.
37. Lilian Bell, "Talks to Spinsters. II. On the Tendency toward Crabbedness," *Harper's Bazar* (Jan. 1903), 3
38. Quoted in Watkins, "Spinsters," 317
39. Freeman and Klaus, "Blessed or Not?" 395–6
40. Telephone conversation with William G. Deeks, May 19, 1997
41. Carol Christ, "Victorian Masculinity and the Angel in the House," in Martha Vicinus, ed., *A Widening Sphere: Changing Roles of Victorian Women* (Bloomington: Indiana University Press, 1980), 146–62. See also Deborah Gorham, *The Victorian Girl and the Feminine Ideal* (London and Canberra: Croom Helm, 1982).
42. Myrtle Reed, *The Spinster Book* (New York: G.P. Putnam and Sons, 1909), 206–7

43. Jane Austen, *Emma* (Boston: Riverside Press, 1957 [1816]), 65
44. Bell, "Talks to Spinsters," 4

FOUR: THE GREAT RESERVE

1. Quoted in Coren, 64
2. Smith, 208
3. Wells quoted in Ruth Brandon, *The New Women and the Old Men: Love, Sex and the Woman Question* (London: Secker and Warburg, 1990), 178–9
4. Smith, 209
5. Wells quoted in Brandon, *New Women and Old Men*, 195–6
6. For Wells's visit to Reeves, see Mackenzie, 233; Rupert Brooke and Beatrice Webb quoted in Mackenzie, 234.
7. Gloria G. Fromm, *Dorothy Richardson: A Biography* (Urbana, Ill.: University of Illinois Press, 1977), 43
8. Mackenzie, 229
9. Brandon, *New Women and Old Men*, 178
10. Mackenzie, 247
11. Brandon, *New Women and Old Men*, 184
12. Smith, 211
13. Smith, 182. The photograph in question is reproduced in Mackenzie at 111.
14. Brandon, *New Women and Old Men*, 194; *Wells in Love*, 81
15. Beatrice Webb quoted in Brandon, *New Women and Old Men*, 198
16. Wells quoted in Mackenzie, 253
17. Violet Paget quoted in Smith, 214–5
18. Flora MacDonald Denison, "Under the Pines; What Women are Doing for the Advancement of Civilization – Suffrage News," Toronto *World*, Nov. 14, 1909. Sunday Morning edition. This item is one of the few newspaper clippings to be found in the Deeks Fonds.
19. See Deborah Gorham, "Flora MacDonald Denison: Canadian Feminist," in Linda Kealey, ed., *A Not Unreasonable Claim: Women and Reform in Canada 1880s–1920s* (Toronto: Women's Press, 1979), 47–70.
20. Denison, "Under the Pines; What Women are Doing"
21. George Dangerfield, *The Strange Death of Liberal England 1910–1914* (New York: Capricorn Books, 1961), 154
22. Toronto *Globe*, Nov. 20, 1909
23. Toronto *Globe*, Nov. 22, 1909. Subsequent references to Pankhurst's speech are drawn from this source.
24. Piers Brendon, *Eminent Edwardians* (London: Penguin Books, 1979), 135
25. For another description of Mrs. Pankhurst, see Dangerfield, *Strange Death*, 150–1.
26. Emmeline Pankhurst, *My Own Story* (New York: Krause Reprint Co., 1971 [1914]), 161

27. Denison quoted in Gorham, "Flora MacDonald Denison," 62

28. Denison quoted in Gorham, "Flora MacDonald Denison," 63, 64

29. Dickson, 219

30. See *Experiment*, 546.

31. Dickson, 169

32. Mackenzie, 264

33. John Hammond, "Introduction" to Wells, *Tono-Bungay* (London: J.M. Dent, 1994 [1909]), xxxvi–xxxvii

34. Macmillan to Wells, Oct. 19, 1909, quoted in Dickson, 166

35. *Spectator*, Nov. 20, 1909; quoted in Foot, 102

36. Gregory quoted in Mackenzie, 251

37. Wells quoted in Brandon, *New Women and Old Men*, 200, 201

38. Webb quoted in Mackenzie, 257

39. Quoted in Dickson, 191–2

40. Mackenzie, 268

41. Wells, *The New Machiavelli* (London: J.M. Dent, 1994 [1911]), 146

42. Dickson, 195

43. Macmillan quoted in Dickson, 183

44. James quoted in Mackenzie, 271

FIVE: LOVES AND WARS

1. R.J. Minney, *The Edwardian Age* (London: Cassell, 1964), 79–81. For Warwick's memoirs, see Frances, Lady Warwick, *Afterthoughts* (London: Cassell, 1931).

2. Mackenzie, 273–4; Wells, *Mr. Britling Sees It Through* (New York: Macmillan, 1916), 5. In this novel, Wells's Essex estate is thinly disguised as "Matching's Easy."

3. Elizabeth von Arnim quoted in Coren, 91

4. Quoted in Mackenzie, 272

5. Quoted in Smith, 373

6. *Wells in Love*, 88–9. In *Desperately Mortal*, David C. Smith mistakenly cites (page 211 and without attribution) the incident of lovemaking on the *Times* as taking place between Wells and Amber Reeves. It is clear from Wells's own account that it was with Elizabeth von Arnim.

7. *Wells in Love*, 88–90

8. Smith, 375

9. Wells, *Marriage* (New York: A.L. Burt, 1913), 11

10. Rebecca West quoted in Foot, 120. Foot's book contains a lengthy excerpt from West's review of *Marriage*.

11. West quoted in Foot, 120

12. For a poignant depiction of Catherine's unease amidst the famous guests at Easton Glebe, see her short story "Night in the Garden," in *Catherine*, 294–9. The quotation in the text is from this story. (296, 299)

13. This is Wells's description of her. See *Wells in Love*, 94.

14. *Wells in Love*, 95

15. *Wells in Love*, 94–6
16. Wells quoted in Mackenzie, 304
17. Mackenzie, 303
18. See Barbara Wilson, ed., *Ontario and the First World War 1914–1918* (Toronto: University of Toronto Press, 1977), xvii–xix.
19. "Plagiarism?" 1
20. "Case," 1. She did not identify the acquaintance by name.
21. "Plagiarism?" 3–4
22. Flora MacDonald Denison, *War and Women* (Toronto: Canadian Suffrage Association, 1914), excerpted in Ramsay Cook and Wendy Mitchinson, eds., *The Proper Sphere: Woman's Place in Canadian Society* (Toronto: Oxford University Press, 1976), 249–51
23. Mackenzie, 298; Coren, 129–31; Dickson, 228–9. In this respect, real life came to replicate the author's art, for in 1933, the very year Wells predicted for the breakthrough in physics, the physicist Leo Szilard was to read *The World Set Free* and gain insight and inspiration for his research into nuclear physics. From that moment on, "the Bomb" was a real possibility. See Richard Rhodes, *The Making of the Atom Bomb* (New York: Simon and Schuster, 1986), 14; William Lanouette, *Genius in the Shadows: A Biography of Leo Szilard* (New York: Scribner's, 1992), 107, 134.
24. See Mackenzie, 255.
25. See Carl Rollyson, *Rebecca West: A Life* (New York: Scribner, 1996), 60–1.
26. Ruth Brandon, *The New Women and the Old Men: Love, Sex, and the Woman Question* (London: Secker and Warburg, 1990), 260
27. Description derived from a photograph of the Toronto Public Library Reading Room c. 1920. T12152, Historical Picture Collection of Special Collections, Genealogy & Maps Centre, Baldwin Room, Toronto Reference Library.
28. John Richard Green, *A Short History of the English People*, revised and enlarged, with epilogue by Alice Stopford Green (London: Macmillan, 1917). The revised version of Green's "short" history ran to 1,040 pages; the original was not much shorter.
29. On Wrong's textbooks, see Robert Bothwell, *Laying the Foundation: A Century of History at University of Toronto* (Toronto: Department of History, University of Toronto, 1991), 27; on Green's concerns, see Ernst Breisach, *Historiography: Ancient, Medieval, and Modern*, 2nd ed. (Chicago: University of Chicago Press, 1994), 271; John Kenyon, *The History Men: The Historical Profession in England Since the Renaissance* (London: Weidenfeld and Nicolson, 1983), esp. 159–63.
30. See "Proceedings," Exhibit 2: "List of Authorities Used by Plaintiff, Appellant," 396.
31. "Case," 1. This document consists of a 246-page typescript on legal-size pages. The photocopy of "Case" from which I worked often lacked page numbers.
32. In this respect, she was quite correct, as contemporary feminist scholarship on women historians demonstrates. This scholarship has uncovered

a sizable number of women, from the early modern period to the early twentieth century, who wrote about the past. Most of their writing, however, took the form of biographies or memorials of "Women Worthies." I have been unable to locate any example of a work of history by a woman historian of Deeks's generation with the ambitious scope of "Web." See, for example, Bonnie G. Smith, "The Contribution of Women to Modern Historiography in Great Britain, France, and the United States, 1750–1940," *American Historical Review*, Vol. 89 (June 1984), 709–32; Kathryn Kish Sklar, "American Female Historians in Context, 1770–1930," *Feminist Studies*, Vol. 3 (fall 1975), 171–84; Natalie Zemon Davis, "Gender and Genre: Women As Historical Writers, 1400–1820," in Patricia H. Labalme, ed., *Beyond Their Sex: Learned Women of the European Past* (New York: New York University Press, 1984), 153–82; Natalie Zemon Davis, "'Women's History' in Transition: The European Case," in Joan Wallach Scott, ed., *Feminism and History* (New York: Oxford University Press, 1996), 79–104; Beverly Boutilier and Alison Prentice, eds., *Creating Historical Memory: English-Canadian Women and the Work of History* (Vancouver: UBC Press, 1997).

33. "Case," 1
34. Victor Duruy, *General History of the World* (New York: Thomas Y. Crowell, c. 1901). Duruy had been minister of public instruction under Napoleon III and founder of the École Pratique des Hautes Études. See "Victory Duruy and Liberal Education," in Roger L. Williams, *Gaslight and Shadow: The World of Napoleon III 1851–1870* (New York: Macmillan, 1957), 187–227.
35. On Deeks's use of Green, Duruy, and other texts in "Web," see "Proceedings," 396.
36. Robert Craig Brown and Ramsay Cook, *Canada 1896–1921: A Nation Transformed* (Toronto: McClelland and Stewart, 1974), 217; Wilson, *Ontario*, xliii
37. Joseph Schull, *Ontario Since 1867* (Toronto: McClelland and Stewart for the Ontario Historical Studies Series, 1978), 218; Wilson, *Ontario*, xliv–liii; Brown and Cook, *Nation Transformed*, 219
38. "Web," 1. Pagination in the original version of "Web" numbers from 1 within each chapter. For purposes of research and analysis, I prepared an electronic transcript of the text with consecutive pagination throughout. All page references here refer to this electronic version.
39. "Web," 4–9
40. "Web," 11–12. Some of Deeks's ideas, she wrote, came from O.T. Mason, *Woman's Share in Primitive Culture* (London: Macmillan, 1895).
41. "Web," 20
42. "Web," 20–2, 26, 27
43. "Web," 72–3, 78–9, 83–4, 95–6, 120–1
44. "Web," 95, 130
45. "Web," 134

46. "Web," 164
47. "Web," 185, 196
48. "Web," 213, 214–5, 223–4
49. "Web," 239–40
50. German air raids over London began in 1915. See Samuel Hynes, *A War Imagined: The First World War and English Culture* (London: Bodley Head, 1990), 100; see also Sir Ray Lankester to Wells, Oct. 11, 1917, WC, L-55/2.
51. Wells quoted in Mackenzie, 309. See also Dickson, 262–3.
52. West quoted in Victoria Glendinning, "Introduction" to Wells, *The Passionate Friends* (London: Hogarth Press, 1986 [1913]), 3
53. Wells, *Passionate Friends*, 252
54. Foot, 157–61
55. Hynes, *A War Imagined*, 130–2; Wells quoted at 132
56. See *Toronto City Directory, 1914*.
57. "Links," 1
58. Biographical information on the sons of George S. Deeks was obtained from clippings in the University of Toronto Archives. See files on George Campbell Deeks, A73-0026/081(65); Douglas Burk Deeks, A73-0026/081(63); Edward R. Deeks, A73-0026/081(64).
59. "Web," 409, 412
60. "Links," 1

SIX: HISTORY AND HUMANITY

1. *Experiment*, 571
2. *Experiment*, 570–2
3. *Experiment*, 572
4. *Experiment*, 575–6
5. Wells, *Joan and Peter: The Story of an Education* (New York: Macmillan, 1918), 443, 450–2
6. Wells, *Joan and Peter*, 551, 563–5
7. Wells, *Joan and Peter*, 555–67, 592–3
8. "Case," 1
9. See Barbara Wilson, ed., *Ontario and the First World War 1914–1918* (Toronto: University of Toronto Press, 1977), lxiii.
10. See "Proceedings," 29.
11. "Web," 263, 264, 272, 293–5, 300–1, 311–2
12. "Web," 314–5, 322–3, 344–5, 360
13. See J.W. Burrow, *A Liberal Descent: Victorian Historians and the English Past* (Cambridge: Cambridge University Press, 1981), 1–3.
14. "Web," 402–3
15. "Web," 418–9, 450
16. "Web," 451–4
17. "Web," 475, 478–9

18. "Web," 506
19. Wells, *War and the Future: Italy, France and Britain at War* (London: Cassell, 1917), 4, 8–9, 11–3, 27–8
20. Wells, *War and the Future*, 267, 271–2, 275, 279
21. Mackenzie, 315
22. *Experiment*, 596, 598, 583–4, 586–7, 599
23. *Experiment*, 599–602; Mackenzie, 316–7; Foot, 179
24. *Experiment*, 604
25. See Gilbert Murray, J.L. Garvin, Wells, and five others to "Dear Sir," July 1918, on "League of Free Nations Association" letterhead. In the letter, the association describes itself as "a society of men and women of all parties who accept the principles laid down by President Wilson, and are resolved that out of this war we shall secure no patched up and temporary peace but the complete overthrow of the militarist system which has brought this evil upon the world." Gilbert Murray Papers, 178/fol. 127, Bodleian Library, University of Oxford.
26. For a description of the street and the Macmillan building, see *Canadian Bookseller*, June 24, 1910, 800.
27. "Proceedings," 45
28. "Proceedings," 24
29. For details on Saul and his work environment, see John Morgan Gray, *Fun Tomorrow: Learning to Be a Publisher and Much Else* (Toronto: Macmillan, 1978), 166–8.
30. "Proceedings," 46; Gray, *Fun Tomorrow*, 167
31. "Proceedings," 47

SEVEN: SHADOWS

1. Photograph entitled "Frank Wise at his desk – Macmillan's, Toronto"; in Accession number 11-1993, MCP. This accession consists of photocopies of news clippings, photographs, offprints, and typescripts concerning Wise. It was donated to the McMaster University Archives by Mrs. E.A. Milsom of Vancouver, granddaughter of Frank Wise. Unless otherwise noted, biographical information concerning Wise is drawn from this source.
2. John Tebbel, *A History of Book Publishing in the United States, Volume II: The Expansion of an Industry 1865–1919* (New York and London: R.R. Bowker, 1975), 354–5
3. Tebbel, *History of Book Publishing*, II, 354
4. Charles Morgan, *The House of Macmillan* (London: Macmillan, 1944), 164
5. Morgan, *House of Macmillan*, 163
6. Tebbel, *History of Book Publishing*, II, 355
7. John Tebbel, *A History of Book Publishing in the United States, Volume III: The Golden Age Between Two Wars 1920–1940* (New York and London: R.R. Bowker, 1978), 101–2
8. "Macmillan Company's Manager," *Canadian Bookseller*, Jan. 1906

9. See photographs in *Canadian Bookseller*, Jan. 1906; Toronto *News*, Sept. 16, 1916.
10. Wise to G.J. Heath, Feb. 27, 1906, June 9, 1906: MA, Add. Mss. 54796
11. Wise to Macmillan, June 22, 1906, July 7, 1906; Wise to G.J. Heath, Oct. 15, 1906; Macmillan New York (unsigned but, given the admonition, most likely George Brett) to Wise, Dec. 23, 1907: MA, Add. Mss. 54796
12. Wise to Macmillan, Sept. 5, 1908, MA, Add. Mss. 54796. See also Wise to Macmillan, Oct. 9, 1908, and Oct. 19, 1908: MA, Add. Mss. 54796.
13. Wise to G.J. Heath, Feb. 18, 1911, MA, Add. Mss. 54796
14. Wise to Brett, Feb. 11, 1909; Macmillan to Wise, Oct. 11, 1910: quoted in Bruce Whiteman, "The Early History of the Macmillan Company of Canada, 1905–1921," *Papers of the Bibliographical Society of Canada*, Vol. 23, 1 (1984), 70, 68
15. Whiteman, "Early History," 71–2
16. See, for example, "A Copyright Issue," Montreal *Gazette*, Aug. 14, 1911; "The Proposed Copyright Law," Toronto *Globe*, June 27, 1911; "The Canadian Book Market," Winnipeg *Telegram*, Mar. 22, 1913; "A Canadian Point of View," *Daily News* (London), Feb. 4, 1913; "Canadians Fear Magazine Menace," Chicago *Tribune*, June 12, 1914 (commentary on, and reprint of, letter to the *Times* [London]). Accession number 11-1993 of the MCP contains many clippings on these and other topics.
17. See the many clippings on the Reunion Association in MCP, Accession number 11-1993. For example: "Form Association to Bring Families to the Dominion," Montreal *Star*, May 18, 1912; "Here to Explain a Splendid Work For Immigrants . . . Frank Wise and His Propaganda," Ottawa *Free Press*, May 3, 1912; "The Empire Home Reunion Association," *Canadian News*, May 24, 1913.
18. "Labor Bureau to Help Immigrants – Head of a Well-Known Publishing House in Canada Establishes an Office – Running at a Loss," Toronto *Star*, Nov. 21, 1913
19. See Danielle Hamelin, "Nurturing Canadian Letters: Four Studies in the Publishing and Promotion of English-Canadian Writing, 1890–1920" (doctoral dissertation, Department of History, University of Toronto, 1994), 121.
20. "Macmillan Company of Canada, Buy Morang," *Publishers' Weekly* (week of June 3, 1912); Whiteman, "Early History," 72–3. Figures for annual dividends, turnover, and assets were provided by Wise himself, in a typescript career profile he prepared around the time he left Macmillan (1921). This document can be found in MCP, Accession number 11-1993.
21. Wells to Brett, [c. Oct. 20, 1918]; Brett to Wells, Nov. 8, 1918: "Proceedings," 407–9
22. Wells to Macmillan, Nov. 19, 1918; Macmillan to Wells, Nov. 22, 1918: "Proceedings," 256
23. Newnes to Wells, Nov. 13, 1918; testimony of Sir Richard Gregory and Newnes: "Proceedings," 409, 267, 318
24. Wells to Brett, [c. Nov. 30], 1918, "Proceedings," 411–2

428 NOTES TO PAGES 127–37

25. Wells to Brett, Dec. 1918, "Proceedings," 412
26. Wells to Brett, Dec. 1918, "Proceedings," 412
27. "Plagiarism?" 14. No dialogue is employed in this book unless it was written down (as in this instance) or witnessed by a participant.
28. "Plagiarism?" 14; "Proceedings," 47
29. Saul to Deeks, Jan. 31, 1919, "Proceedings," 48
30. "Plagiarism?" 15
31. "Proceedings," 48–9; "Plagiarism?" 17–8
32. "Plagiarism?" 19
33. "Plagiarism?" 19
34. See stationery in MCP, box 3, file 4.
35. Wise to R.L. Fairbarn, Canadian Northern Railway, Jan. 23, 1915, MCP, box 3, file 4; MCP, box 3, file 9
36. Wise to Sir George E. Foster, June 3, 1915, MCP box 3, file 4
37. MCP, box 5, files 5–9
38. Wise to Macmillan, Oct. 22, 1917, MCP, box 6, file 22
39. Macmillan to Wise, June 5, 1917, MCP, box 6, file 22
40. Brett to Macmillan, May 10, 1918, MA, Add. Mss. 54824
41. Wise to Brett, Jan. 10, 1919, MCP, box 3, file 2
42. Biographical material on John C. Saul is drawn from W. Stewart Wallace, *The Macmillan Dictionary of Canadian Biography*, 3rd ed., revised and enlarged (London and Toronto: Macmillan, 1963), 669; Henry James Morgan, ed., *The Canadian Men and Women of the Time*, 2nd ed. (Toronto: William Briggs, 1912), 993; Sir Charles G.D. Roberts and Arthur Leonard Tunnell, eds., *The Canadian Who's Who, Volume II: 1936–1937* (Toronto: Trans-Canada Press, 1938), 966; Hugh Morrison, "Poets Furnish Him With a Hobby," *Star Weekly*, Oct. 10, 1936.
43. For a complete list of these textbooks, see the records of the Canadian Institute for Historical Microreproductions, National Library of Canada, Ottawa.
44. Wise to Brett, Feb. 6, 1919, MCP
45. Saul to Wise, June 22, 1917, MCP
46. Saul to Wise, July 17, 1917, MCP
47. Saul to Wise, July 25, 1917, MCP
48. Saul to Wise, Feb. 3, 1918, MCP
49. Saul to Wise, Feb. 11, 1918, MCP
50. Saul to Wise, July 20, 1918, MCP
51. Saul to Wise, Aug. 20, 1918, MCP

EIGHT: OUTLINES

1. Samuel Hynes, *A War Imagined: The First World War and English Culture* (London: Bodley Head, 1990), 313
2. As work on *The Outline of History* progressed, Wells continued to revise his estimates of the final length upward, suggesting that it might total 250,000 or 300,000 words. In the first American edition, a typical full

page of print consistently contains over 400 words. Even taking into account space for illustrations, the 1,324 pages of the two volumes would contain a half-million words or more.

3. See, for example, Mackenzie, 319–21.

4. Henry S. Canby to Wells (undated but judged in the record to be July 16, 1918), "Proceedings," 406. Canby may have suggested to Wells at that time that he write a history of the Anglo-Saxon peoples. In his history of American publishing, John Tebbel speculates that Brett had suggested the project to Wells five years earlier. See Tebbel, *A History of Book Publishing in the United States, Volume III: The Golden Age Between Two Wars 1920–1940* (New York and London: R.R. Bowker, 1978), 33–4.

5. *Wells in Love*, 100–1

6. Coren, 109

7. See "Lankester, Sir Edwin Ray (1847–1929)," in *Dictionary of National Biography, 1922–1930*, J.R.H. Weaver, ed. (London: Oxford University Press, 1937), 481–3. Unless otherwise noted, biographical material on Lankester is drawn from this source. See also Ray Lankester, ed., *A Treatise on Zoology*, 8 volumes (London: Black, 1900); *Zoological Articles contributed to the "Encyclopedia Britannica"* (London: Black, 1891), 195; "Sir Ray Lankester," British Library, Add. Mss. 55219.

8. *Experiment*, 396

9. Lankester to Wells, Oct. 11, 1917; also Dec. 8, 1917: WC, L-55/2. Sir Ray was especially fond of Jane, and the feeling seems to have been mutual. His correspondence with the Wellses dates from 1901 (L-55/1, 1901–1916), but the bulk was written during the war and shortly after. Of the forty-five letters to the Wellses between 1917 and 1920 (L-55/2), most are to Jane.

10. Lankester to Wells, Sept. 23, 1918, WC, L-55/2; Lankester to Wells, Oct. 2, 1918, "Proceedings," 406

11. Lankester to Wells, Nov. 4, 1918, Nov. 8, 1918; Lankester to Jane Wells, Nov. 24, 1918: WC, L-55/2

12. "Johnston, Sir Harry Hamilton (1858–1927)," *Dictionary of National Biography, 1922–1930*, 456. Unless otherwise noted, biographical information on Johnston is from this source (456–8).

13. Sir Harry Johnston, *The Story of My Life* (London: Jonathan Cape, 1929), 489; Wells, *Joan and Peter: The Story of an Education* (New York: Macmillan, 1918), 212, 214

14. See Roland Oliver, *Sir Harry Johnston and the Scramble for Africa* (London: Chatto and Windus, 1959), 356.

15. See file "Johnston, Sir Harry Hamilton. 1916–1919," WC, J-105/1, especially Johnston to Wells, Mar. 12, 1917, and Jan. 17, 1918.

16. Johnston, *Story of My Life*, 489; letters in WC, J-105/1

17. Sir Harry Johnston, *The Gay-Dombeys: A Novel* (New York: Macmillan, 1919). A great admirer of Dickens, Sir Harry wrote his novel as a continuation of *Dombey and Sons* into modern times. Wells contributed an appreciative foreword.

18. Johnston, *Story of My Life*, 494–5
19. Words attributed to Wells in Alex. Johnston, *The Life and Times of Sir Harry Johnston* (London: Jonathan Cape, 1929), 330
20. "Murray, George Gilbert Aimé (1866–1957)," *Dictionary of National Biography, 1951–1960*, 757–61. Unless otherwise noted, biographical details on Murray are from this source.
21. See Francis West, *Gilbert Murray: A Life* (London and Canberra: Croom Helm, 1984), 179.
22. See Duncan Wilson, *Gilbert Murray OM, 1866–1957* (Oxford: Clarendon, 1987), 219, 253, 255
23. Wells to Murray, n.d., Gilbert Murray Papers, 183/fol. 43–4, Bodleian Library, University of Oxford. Archivists of the Bodleian Library estimate that this important letter was written in 1919.
24. Wells to Murray, June 15, 1919, Murray Papers, 39/fol. 139–40
25. Wells to Murray, July 22, 1919, Murray Papers, 39/fol. 203–4
26. Ernest Barker to Gilbert Murray, Nov. 28, 1918, Mar. 10, 1919, Murray Papers, 38/fol. 35 and 39/fol. 24. See "Barker, Sir Ernest (1874–1960)," *Dictionary of National Biography 1951–1960*, 62–4, for biographical details.
27. Barker to Wells, Aug. 17, 1919, WC, B-78
28. *Outline*, I, viii–ix
29. Bennett to Jane Wells, Jan. 22, 1920, in *Letters of Arnold Bennett, Volume III: 1916–1920*, James Hepburn, ed. (London: Oxford University Press, 1970), 120–1
30. *Outline*, I, viii–x
31. Mackenzie, 321
32. "Proceedings," 236–7
33. Brett to Wise, May 9, 1919, MCP
34. Wise to Brett, May 12, 1919, MCP
35. Lawrence J. Burpee to Deeks, Feb. 8, 1927, DF
36. Brett to Macmillan, June 4, 1919 (with enclosure), MA, Add. Mss. 54824
37. Macmillan to Brett, July 2, 1919, MA, Add. Mss. 54824
38. Brett to Macmillan, May 23, 1919, MA, Add. Mss. 54824; Wise to Brett, July 18, 1919, July 24, 1919: MCP
39. Brett to Wise, Sept. 24, 1919, MCP
40. Wise to Brett, [between Sept. 25 and 28, 1919]; Brett to Wise, Sept. 29, 1919: MCP
41. Brett to Macmillan, Nov. 26, 1919, MA, Add. Mss. 54824; Brett to Wise, Dec. 1, 1919, MCP. Brett may have had his own son – George P. Brett, Jr. – in mind, for the young man had recently joined the firm and had been given 250 shares in its stock. His father had already arranged for him to gain further experience (and perhaps inside information) by transferring him from the Chicago office to Toronto for several months.
42. Wise to Brett, Dec. 1, 1919, MCP
43. "Plagiarism?" 19–20
44. "Plagiarism?" 20

45. Mercer to Brett, May 19, 1920; enclosed with Brett to Macmillan, May 28, 1920, MA, Add. Mss. 54824
46. Brett to Wise, May 27, 1920; Brett to Macmillan, May 28, 1920: MA, Add. Mss. 54824
47. Brett to Wise, [June 1920]; Wise to Brett, July 3, 1920: MCP
48. Brett to Macmillan, Oct. 21, 1920; Macmillan to Wise, Oct. 28, 1920; Brett to Macmillan, Oct. 29, 1920; Brett to Macmillan, Nov. 26, 1920; Brett to Macmillan, Dec. 9, 1920: MA, Add. Mss. 54825; Macmillan to Wise, Nov. 24, 1920, MA, Add. Mss., "Canadian Letter Book: 13 Feb. 1914–May 1923"
49. Brett to Macmillan, Dec. 9, 1920, MA, Add. Mss. 54825
50. Wise to Brett, Jan. 27, 1921; Secretary [Eayrs] to Robert Johnston, of McLaughlin, Johnston, Moorhead & Macaulay, Jan. 31, 1921: MCP

NINE: DEVILS IN DETAILS

1. "Plagiarism?" 28–9; "Case," 5
2. "Plagiarism?" 29
3. "Plagiarism?" 29–30
4. See "Web," 1; and Wells, *Outline*, I, 6.
5. "Plagiarism?" 34–6; "Comparison," 1
6. "Comparison," 1–2
7. "Comparison," 3
8. "Comparison," 11; "Plagiarism?" 31
9. "Plagiarism?" 47
10. "Plagiarism?" 49–50
11. "Links," 5; Tilley, Johnston, Thomson & Parmenter to George S. Deeks, Nov. 30, 1921, DF
12. Canada, *An Act Respecting Copyrights*, 38 Vict., cap. 88 (1875), and Canada, *An Act to Amend the Copyright Act*, 63–4 Vict., cap. 25 (1900). Canadian copyright operated within the framework of acts passed by imperial statues in Westminster and the Berne Convention. In 1921, the Canadian parliament passed a new copyright bill, but it did not come into force until Jan. 1, 1924; until then, the 1875 act (as amended) remained in force. See George L. Parker, "The Canadian Author and Publisher in the Twentieth Century," in William J. Howard, ed., *Editor, Author, and Publisher* (Toronto: University of Toronto Press, 1969), 33–4; also George L. Parker, "Appendix D: A Selected List of Copyright Acts," in Parker, *The Beginnings of the Book Trade in Canada* (Toronto: University of Toronto Press, 1985), 312–3.
13. Tilley, Johnston, Thomson & Parmenter to George S. Deeks, Nov. 30, 1921, DF
14. Wells quoted in Norman and Jeanne Mackenzie, "How H.G. Harried His Publishers," *Bookseller* (May 26, 1973), 2574
15. Flower to Wells, Nov. 17, 1919, WC, C-122/3; Brett to Wells, Nov. 8, 1918, "Proceedings," 408

16. Brett to Wells, Dec. 20, 1918; Wells to Brett, [c. Jan. 19, 1919]: "Proceedings," 413–5, 417

17. Newnes to Wells, Feb. 5, 1919; Wells to Newnes, [c. May 1919]; Newnes to Wells, Aug. 14, 1919: "Proceedings," 418, 422, 424–5

18. Memorandum of Agreement between Wells and Cassell & Co., Ltd, Jan. 14, 1920, "Proceedings," 432

19. Mackenzie, 324; "Plagiarism?" 94

20. *Wells in Love*, 163–5

21. *Wells in Love*, 103; Gordon Ray, H.G. *Wells and Rebecca West* (New Haven, Ct.: Yale University Press, 1974), 99–100

22. Rebecca West, *Black Lamb and Grey Falcon: A Journey Through Yugoslavia* (New York: Penguin Books, 1999 [1941]), 54. West began this account in 1937.

23. Ray, *Wells and West*, 100–2

24. Margaret Sanger, *Margaret Sanger: An Autobiography* (New York: W.W. Norton, 1938), 268. On Anthony Comstock, see Rowland Berthoff, *An Unsettled People: Social Order and Disorder in American History* (New York: Harper and Row, 1971), 427–8.

25. Sanger, *Autobiography*, 269–70

26. Mackenzie, 331; Lawrence Lader and Milton Meltzer, *Margaret Sanger: Pioneer of Birth Control* (New York: Thomas Y. Crowell, 1969), 93–9. See also Emily Taft Douglas, *Margaret Sanger: Pioneer of the Future* (New York: Holt, Rinehart and Winston, 1970), 142; Madeline Gray, *Margaret Sanger: A Biography of the Champion of Birth Control* (New York: Richard Marek, 1979), 180.

27. Mackenzie, 330

28. Gray, *Sanger*, 181

29. Ray, *Wells and West*, 117

30. Cornelia Otis Skinner and Emily Kimbrough, *Our Hearts Were Young and Gay* (New York: Dodd, Mead, 1942), 113–27

31. Skinner, *Our Hearts*, 120–3

32. Webb quoted in Mackenzie, 335

33. Unidentified and undated testimonial beginning, "As Sir Richard Gregory celebrated his 85th birthday . . . ," Sir Richard Gregory Papers, University of Sussex, Brighton, box 1, file 7

34. This and other biographical details have been drawn from "Gregory, Sir Richard Arman, baronet (1864–1952)," *Dictionary of National Biography 1951–1960* (London: Oxford University Press, 1971), 433–4; W.H.G. Armytage, *Sir Richard Gregory: His Life and Work* (London: Macmillan, 1957).

35. Gregory to Wells, Oct. 31, 1918, "Proceedings," 407–8; Sir Richard Gregory Papers, University of Sussex, Brighton, box 12, file 4

36. Untitled and undated handwritten memorandum from Deeks to R.S. Robertson, DF. Henceforth cited as "memorandum to Robertson." See also Deeks, "Case," 6.

37. This account and that of the following four paragraphs are drawn from "Plagiarism?" 53–5.
38. Robert Bothwell, *Laying the Foundation: A Century of History at University of Toronto* (Toronto: Department of History, University of Toronto, 1991), 47–8, 58
39. Wrong to Falconer, Jan. 13, 1926, University of Toronto Archives, Office of the President, RSIN 0002, box 97
40. Deeks, memorandum to Robertson, 1
41. Deeks, memorandum to Robertson, 1
42. Deeks, memorandum to Robertson, 2
43. Deeks, memorandum to Robertson, 2. While Wallace had not yet published a book with Macmillan of Canada, his relationship to the firm and its editors was a close one for many years. Eventually he became editor of *The Macmillan Dictionary of Canadian Biography* (Toronto: Macmillan, 1963).
44. Johnston to Catherine Wells, Mar. 15, 1923, WC, J-105/2
45. Ellen Chesler, *Woman of Valor: Margaret Sanger and the Birth Control Movement in America* (New York: Simon and Schuster, 1992), 188–9
46. *Wells in Love*, 104, 136. The description of Gatternigg is from contemporary newspapers.
47. Mackenzie, 335, 338–9
48. Mackenzie, 340; Ray, *Wells and West*, 131
49. Ray, *Wells and West*, 137–8
50. *Wells in Love*, 105
51. *Wells in Love*, 105–6; Ray, *Wells and West*, 139–40
52. Ray, *Wells and West*, 142
53. Ray, *Wells and West*, 138. Jane's presence is also claimed in Mackenzie, 340, although Gatternigg is not identified by name. Anthony West asserts that Jane Wells remained at Easton Glebe during the crisis with Gatternigg but provides no documentary evidence for the claim. See Anthony West, *H.G. Wells: Aspects of a Life* (New York: New American Library, 1984), 98–9.
54. Wrong to Deeks, Apr. 5, 1925, "Reports of experts: Deeks correspondence," DF
55. Scribner to Deeks, July 16, 1925; Houghton Mifflin (H.R.G.) to Deeks, July 21, 1925; Ginn and Company (E.N. Stevens) to Deeks, Aug. 12, 1925, Aug. 25, 1925: DF
56. Doubleday, Page & Company (Beecher Stowe) to Deeks, July 7, 1925; Little, Brown & Co. (H.T. Jenkins) to Deeks, Sept. 18, 1925: DF

TEN: ACCUSATIONS

1. Eayrs to Williams, Feb. 10, 1921, MCP
2. See David Young, "The Macmillan Company of Canada in the 1930s," *Journal of Canadian Studies*, Vol. 30 (autumn 1995), 119.

3. John Morgan Gray, *Fun Tomorrow: Learning to Be a Publisher* (Toronto: Macmillan of Canada, 1978), 157, 161; Eayrs to Lisgar L. Lang, Nov. 7, 1924, MCP

4. Eayrs to R.J. Fetherton, July 31, 1924, MCP

5. Eayrs to C. Whittaker, July 21, 1921, MCP, box 14, file 4; filed as "Executive Correspondence"

6. "Toronto Writer Asks Wells for Big Sum; Claims 'Outline of History' Contains Part of Her Unpublished Work," Toronto *Star*, Oct. 15, 1925; "Authoress Here Sues H.G. Wells for $500,000; Claims Outline of History Contains Part of Unpublished Work by Miss Florence A. Deeks," Toronto *Telegram*, Oct. 15, 1925

7. See Augustus Bridle, *The Story of the Club* (Toronto: Arts and Letters Club, 1945), 22-38

8. Eayrs to Brett, Oct. 15, 1925, MCP

9. "Miss Deeks' Suit Over Wells' Book Causes a Big Stir," Toronto *Star*, Oct. 16, 1925

10. Christopher Moore, *The Law Society of Upper Canada and Ontario's Lawyers, 1797-1997* (Toronto: University of Toronto Press, 1997), 156, 204

11. Tilley, Johnston, Thomson & Parmenter to Macmillan Company of Canada Ltd., Oct. 15, 1925, MCP

12. Undated statement signed by Millership and Eayrs, related to a letter from Wise to Eayrs, Apr. 12, 1921, MCP

13. Eayrs to Brett, Oct. 16, 1925, MCP

14. Eayrs to Macmillan, Oct. 16, 1925, MCP. I have uncovered no evidence to suggest that Wise was in contact with Deeks. Shortly after the writ was obtained, however, he made contact with her lawyer R.H. Parmenter to offer him, in her words, "any information in his power with regard to our case." "Case," DF.

15. Quoted in McLaughlin, Johnston, Moorhead & Macaulay (R.L. Johnston) to Eayrs, Oct. 23, 1925, MCP

16. Eayrs to Macmillan, Oct. 19, 1925, MCP

17. Brett to Eayrs, Oct. 19, 1925, MCP

18. Brett to Wells, Oct. 28, 1925, Oct. 20, 1925: MCP

19. "Wells Knows Nothing About Deeks Claim; Only a Newspaper Story Is Author's Message Left with Secretary," Toronto *Telegram*, Oct. 17, 1925; also "Miss Deeks' Claim Is News to Wells and Cassels Firm," Toronto *Star*, Oct. 17, 1925

20. Biographical details on Burpee have been drawn from entries in *The Canadian Who's Who* (Toronto: Musson, 1910), 30-1; *Who's Who in Canada, 1923-24* (Toronto: International Press, 1924), 332; *The Macmillan Dictionary of Canadian Biography*, 3rd edition, revised and enlarged, W. Stewart Wallace, ed. (Toronto: Macmillan of Canada, 1963), 95; also from W.S. Wallace, "Lawrence Johnston Burpee (1873-1946)," *Canadian Historical Review*, Vol. 27, no. 4 (Dec. 1946),

462; Pelham Edgar, "Lawrence J. Burpee (1873–1946)," *Proceedings and Transactions of the Royal Society of Canada*, 3rd series, Vol. 41 (Ottawa: Royal Society of Canada, 1947), 115–8.

21. "Mr. Lawrence J. Burpee's Report," Jan. 11, 1926, DF, 2

22. "Burpee's Report," 3–4

23. Biographical details on Sir Bertram Windle have been drawn from entries in *Who Was Who, Volume III: 1929–30* (London: Adam and Charles Black, 1940), 1474; *Who's Who in Canada, 1923–24* (Toronto: International, Ltd., 1924), 196.

24. "Sir Bertram Windle Passes Away After Short Illness," unidentified newspaper clipping in DF. Almost half a century later, he merited inclusion in the third edition of *The Macmillan Dictionary of Canadian Biography* in 1963.

25. *Outline*, I, 605; II, 148ff, 492–3

26. Sir Bertram Windle, "The Web and The Outline of History," [c. spring/summer 1926], DF, 1

27. Windle, "Web and Outline," 2

28. Windle, "Web and Outline," 6

29. Windle, "Web and Outline," 6–7. Windle provided only a close paraphrase of the passage from Deeks; I have substituted for it the actual passage from "Web." The variant spellings of "Amphictyonies" and "Amphictyonic" are as they appear in the originals.

30. Windle, "Web and Outline," 3, 18

31. Windle, "Web and Outline," 9–10

32. Windle to Deeks, Nov. 22, 1926, DF

33. Windle to Deeks, Apr. 13, 1927, DF, attached to "The Web and The Outline of History." Hector Charlesworth characterized Sir Bertram as a scholar whose gentle nature caused him, in a moment of weakness, to undertake his report. See Charlesworth, *I'm Telling You: Being the Further Candid Chronicles of Hector Charlesworth* (Toronto: Macmillan Company of Canada, 1937), 319.

34. "Plagiarism?"

35. Wells to Canby, June 12, 1924, WC. See also Henry Seidel Canby, *American Memoir* (Boston: Houghton Mifflin, 1947), 253–7.

36. Ogden to Deeks, May 27, 1926, DF (marked "Private"). See also Wells to Canby, June 12, 1924, and July 3, 1924: WC.

37. Canby to Deeks, Apr. 6, 1926, DF

38. Ogden to Deeks (marked "Private"), May 27, 1926, DF

39. Ogden to Deeks (marked "Private"), May 27, 1926, DF

40. I.A. Richards, "A Report Upon Certain Resemblances Between The Outline of History and The Web," [c. June 1926], DF, 38–40

41. Richards, "Certain Resemblances," 40–1

42. Richards, "Certain Resemblances," 41

43. Richards, "Certain Resemblances," 42

44. Richards, "Certain Resemblances," 42–6

45. Richards, "Certain Resemblances," 46, 48

46. Leach, Ogden, Richards, and Canby to Wells, June 26, 1926; Ogden to Wells, June 26, 1926: WC. A copy of the former can also be found in DF, accompanied by a handwritten note: "June 26 – Copy. Mr. Wells does not know we have this."
47. Ogden to Wells, Sept. 16, 1926 (marked "Private and Confidential"), WC
48. Barnes to Deeks, Nov. 2, 1926, Dec. 18, 1926: DF
49. Barnes to Deeks, Dec. 18, 1926, Dec. 31, 1926, Jan. 21, 1927: DF. On Dec. 31, 1926, he wrote to Deeks: "I did not want you to assume from what I said that I am a personal friend of Wells or have any personal relations with him. What I meant was that I am so engaged in a deadly battle with the more conservative and reactionary group of American historians that I should not want to come out personally as a critic of Mr. Wells who has endeared himself to the more progressive of American historians, upon whom I have to rely for support." By 1928, with the case well under way, Barnes insisted to Deeks that his correspondence with her remain confidential and unconnected to her case. Barnes to Deeks, Apr. 27, 1928, DF.

ELEVEN: INVESTIGATIONS

1. "Case," DF
2. Johnston, Grant, Dods & Macdonald (P.E.F. Smily) to Deeks, June 6, 1928, Nov. 21, 1928, Dec. 10, 1928: DF. Such expenses included $500 in June 1928 to retain counsel in England; the same amount for the same purpose in November; $100 in December to cover legal expenses in New York and to retain counsel there for the examination of witnesses from Macmillan, such as Brett.
3. Wells to West, [autumn 1923], quoted in Gordon N. Ray, *H.G. Wells and Rebecca West* (New Haven, Ct.: Yale University Press, 1974), 146; Mackenzie, 342
4. *Wells in Love*, 124
5. *Wells in Love*, 125; Mackenzie, 342
6. *Wells in Love*, 125
7. *Wells in Love*, 116, 128–9; Mackenzie, 343. The most sustained secondary account of the stormy relationship between Odette Keun and Wells is in Anthony West, *H.G. Wells: Aspects of a Life* (New York: New American Library, 1984), 107–12ff.
8. Wells, *The World of William Clissold: A Novel at a New Angle*, 2 volumes (New York: George H. Doran, 1926), II, 494, 541
9. Wells, *Clissold*, II, 385–7, 397–8, 468, 477–80, 494–5, 524, 533
10. Wells, *Clissold*, II, 388, 408, 475–6, 500–1, 537, 538–9
11. Mackenzie, 345
12. Eayrs to Macmillan, Sept. 8, 1927; Eayrs to Brett, Sept. 14, 1927; Brett to Eayrs, Sept. 16, 1927; Eayrs to Brett, Sept. 16, 1927: MCP
13. Wells, "Memorandum of the Case of The Web," attached to letter of Wells to Brett, Oct. 29, 1925, "Proceedings," 455

14. Macmillan to Eayrs, Sept. 23, 1927, MCP; Fiske to Wells, Sept. 26, 1927, WC. In several instances, copies of correspondence from Wells to his solicitors, mentioned in the return correspondence, appear not to have been kept. I have been unable to locate Wells letters of Sept. 23, 1927, and Jan. 1, 1928, in the otherwise extensive WC. (See Fiske to Wells, Sept. 26, 1927, and Jan. 5, 1928.)

15. Eayrs to Brett, Sept. 16, 1927; Brett to Eayrs, Sept. 20, 1927: MCP

16. Brett to Eayrs, Sept. 28, 1927, MCP. MacIver's "Confidential Memorandum," unsigned but acknowledged in Brett's letter, is attached to it.

17. Eayrs to Brett, Sept. 30, 1927, MCP

18. Eayrs to McLaughlin, Sept. 30, 1927, MCP. Emphasis in original.

19. Brett to Eayrs, Sept. 30, 1927, MCP

20. Eayrs to McLaughlin, Oct. 1, 1927, MCP

21. Eayrs to Brett, Oct. 5, 1927, MCP

22. Wrong to Falconer, Jan. 13, 1926, University of Toronto Archives, Office of the President, RSIN 0002, box 97. In the same collection see also Wrong to Falconer, Jan. 7, 1926.

23. Mackenzie, 345; Dickson, 294; Coren, 183

24. Mackenzie, 345

25. The main forum for Belloc's criticism of *Outline* is in some dispute. Mackenzie (348) asserts that it was the Roman Catholic weekly the *Universe*; Coren (161–2) claims it was the *London Mercury* and the *Dublin Review*.

26. See Joseph Pearce, *Wisdom and Experience: A Life of G.K. Chesterton* (London: Hodder and Stoughton, 1996), 303–11.

27. Quoted in Coren, 165

28. Coren, 163–9

29. Mackenzie, 349

30. Wells, *Clissold*, II, 485–6

31. See Wells, *Clissold*, II, 440, 486.

32. Quoted in Mackenzie, 351

33. Quoted in Mackenzie, 351

34. *Catherine*, 36–7

35. *Catherine*, 40

36. Mackenzie, 353

37. *Catherine*, 35

38. *Catherine*, 6. For example, Lovat Dickson: "His preface goes as far as we need to follow in understanding what troubled these two lives and yet held them together for over thirty years." Dickson, 295. An exception is Michael Foot, who devotes a brief paragraph to the way Catherine's poems "expressed the anguish he had caused her." Foot, 213.

39. Hitchcock to Eayrs, Oct. 6, 1927; Eayrs to Hitchcock, Oct. 3, 1927: MCP

40. McCormick to Windle, Oct. 6, 1927; Hitchcock to Eayrs, Oct. 11, 1927: MCP

41. Windle to McCormick, Oct. 8, 1927, MCP (marked "Private and Confidential")

42. Eayrs to Hitchcock, Oct. 13, 1927; Hitchcock to Eayrs, Oct. 11, 1927: MCP

43. Eayrs to McLaughlin, Oct. 21, 1927; Eayrs to Brett, Oct. 10, 1927: MCP

44. Brett to Eayrs, Oct. 24, 1927, MCP

TWELVE: DELAYS AND DISCOVERIES

1. Eayrs to Brett, Oct. 12, 1927, MCP
2. "Argument," 15
3. Eayrs to Brett, Oct. 12, 1927, MCP
4. Brett to Wells, Apr. 13, 1928, MCP
5. Eayrs to Brett, Oct. 19, 1928, MCP
6. Eayrs to Saul, Nov. 4, 1928, MCP. The Saul memorandum, entitled "Deeks vs. Wells. Memorandum relative to the correspondence and conversation of Mr. J.H. [sic] Saul, the editor of The Macmillan Company of Canada with Miss Florence Deeks in reference to the manuscript 'The Web,'" was attached to McLaughlin to Eayrs, Dec. 21, 1928, MCP.
7. See Peter Novick, *That Noble Dream: The "Objectivity Question" and the American Historical Profession* (Cambridge, Eng.: Cambridge University Press, 1988), 214–9. See also Ernst A. Breisach, *American Progressive History: An Experiment in Modernization* (Chicago: University of Chicago Press, 1993).
8. Barnes to Deeks, Jan. 21, 1927, DF; Keenleyside to Eayrs, Apr. 4, 1928, MCP; Barnes to Deeks, Apr. 27, 1927, DF; Gedge, Fiske & Gedge to Wells, Apr. 11, 1928, WC
9. Hitchcock to Eayrs, Apr. 11, 1928; Eayrs to Hitchcock, Apr. 13, 1928; Hitchcock to Eayrs, July 10, 1928: MCP
10. McLaughlin to Eayrs, Jan. 24, 1928; Eayrs to Hitchcock, Jan. 26, 1928: MCP
11. McLaughlin to Eayrs, Feb. 24, 1928, MCP
12. Eayrs to Macmillan, Feb. 25, 1928, MCP
13. Gedge, Fiske & Gedge (W. Sanders Fiske) to Wells, Feb. 28, 1928, WC
14. Fiske to Wells, Mar. 12, 1928, WC
15. Wells to Brett, Mar. 14, 1928, enclosed with McLaughlin to Eayrs, Apr. 12, 1928, MCP.
16. Gedge, Fiske & Gedge to Macmillan and Company, Toronto, Apr. 25, 1928, MCP
17. McLaughlin to Macmillan New York, Office of the President ("Attention Mr. Hitchcock"), Apr. 10, 1928, MCP
18. Eayrs to Brett, Apr. 12, 1928, with which is enclosed Wells to Brett, Mar. 14, 1928, MCP; Johnston, Grant, Dods & Macdonald to Deeks, May 28, 1928, June 19, 1928: DF
19. "Plagiarism?" 92
20. Fiske to Wells, July 24, 1928, WC; Johnston, Grant, Dods & Macdonald (P.E.F. Smily) to Deeks, Sept. 28, 1928, DF

21. "Apparently it [*Outline*] is a very bulky document, being completely written by Mr. Wells, and is valued by Mr. Wells at $100,000. Mr. Wells was mortally afraid that souvenir hunters might remove pages from time to time as souvenirs, and Mr. Elliott, therefore, arranged to have the document sealed by the Court only to be opened in the presence of Mr. Wells's solicitor." McLaughlin to Hitchcock, Nov. 3, 1928, MCP.
22. "Case," 17
23. "Links," 6–7. Walter Arthur Copinger (1847–1910) published *The Law of Copyright, in Works of Literature and Art* in 1870. In an 11th edition, it exists as *Copinger and Skene James on Copyright, Including International Copyright* (London: Sweet and Maxwell, 1971).
24. "Case," 17
25. "Links," 8–9
26. Eayrs to Macmillan, Nov. 21, 1927; Eayrs to Brett, Nov. 21, 1927; Brett to Eayrs, Nov. 23, 1927; Eayrs to Brett, Nov. 25, 1927: MCP
27. Eayrs to Brett, May 14, 1928, MCP
28. "Case," 15
29. "Proceedings," 22–5. Throughout the trial transcript, the name Macmillan is misspelled as "McMillan." I have corrected this and other similar minor errors.
30. "Proceedings," 26
31. "Proceedings," 26–7
32. "Proceedings," 27–8
33. Eayrs to Brett, Oct. 19, 1928, Nov. 3, 1928; Eayrs to Macmillan, Nov. 26, 1928: MCP
34. Smily to Deeks, Nov. 21, 1928, Dec. 10, 1928: DF
35. Grant to Deeks, Jan. 24, 1929, DF
36. Eayrs to Macmillan, Feb. 14, 1929, MCP
37. Untitled and undated handwritten memorandum from Deeks to R.S. Robertson, DF
38. Elliott, Hume, McKague, & Anger to McLaughlin, Johnston, Moorhead & Macaulay, Apr. 23, 1929; Brett to Eayrs, Apr. 30, 1929; McLaughlin to Eayrs, May 1, 1929: MCP
39. "Plagiarism?" 95
40. "Plagiarism?" 95; "Case"
41. "Plagiarism?" 96; "Case." For the Law Society Hall location, see Fiske to Wells, June 13, 1929, WC.
42. "Case"
43. "Case"; *Experiment*, 620
44. Murray to Wells, June 21, 1929, July 13, 1929; Wells to Murray, July 16, 1929: WC
45. "Plagiarism?" 97–103; "Case"
46. "Case"
47. McLaughlin spells the name "Durant," but it is clear that Laura Durand is the person in question.
48. McLaughlin to Eayrs, Sept. 14, 1929, MCP

49. McLaughlin to Eayrs, Sept. 14, 1929; Eayrs to McLaughlin, Sept. 17, 1929: MCP
50. Eayrs to Brett, Oct. 7, 1929, MCP
51. McLaughlin to Eayrs, Oct. 4, 1929; Eayrs to Brett, Oct. 7, 1929; Brett to Eayrs, Oct. 9, 1929; Eayrs to Brett, Oct. 11, 1929: MCP
52. Eayrs to McLaughlin, Oct. 31, 1929; Eayrs to Brett, Oct. 22, 1929; Brett to Eayrs, Oct. 23, 1929; Eayrs to McLaughlin, Oct. 31, 1929: MCP; also Fiske to Mrs. [G.P.] Wells, Nov. 18, 1929; Elliott to Gedge, Fiske & Gedge, Dec. 19, 1929: WC
53. Eayrs to Macmillan, Mar. 10, 1930, MCP
54. Elliott to Gedge, Fiske & Gedge, Mar. 11, 1930, WC
55. Brett to Wells, Mar. 17, 1930, WC; Maurice H. Macmillan to Brett, Apr. 11, 1930, May 16, 1930: MA; unknown member of parliament to J. Ramsay MacDonald, Apr. 15, 1930, copy in Sir Richard Gregory Papers, University of Sussex, Brighton
56. See "Railroad Builder Dead," Toronto *Telegram*, May 2, 1930; "Pioneer Engineer George Deeks Dead; Noted Railway Builder Requested He Be Buried Without Publicity," Toronto *Star*, May 2, 1930; Toronto *Globe*, May 3, 1930.
57. Biographical details derived from clippings in University of Toronto Archives. See files on George Campbell Deeks, A73-0026/081(65); Douglas Burk Deeks, A73-0026/081(63); Edward R. Deeks, A73-0026/081(64).

THIRTEEN: ENTER KING DAVID, AND SO ON

1. The term "bencher" is used by the Law Society of Upper Canada to designate members of its governing body; in use since the founding of the Law Society in 1797, it was borrowed from the English Inns of Court, "which once reserved benches in their dining-halls for their governing members." See Christopher Moore, *The Law Society of Upper Canada and Ontario's Lawyers 1797–1997* (Toronto: University of Toronto Press, 1997), 343; Robert L. Gowe, "Osgoode Hall, Century Old Mystery," Toronto *Telegram*, Sept. 12, 1931.
2. See George A. Johnston, Q.C., *Osgoode Hall Lore* (Toronto: Law Society of Upper Canada, 1955), esp. 7–11.
3. Biographical details are drawn from records of the Ontario Bar Biographical Research Project, in the Archives of the Law Society of Upper Canada, Osgoode Hall, Toronto.
4. Randall White, *Too Good to Be True: Toronto in the 1920s* (Toronto and Oxford: Dundurn Press, 1993), 30, 61, 159; see also Peter Oliver, "The New Order: W.E. Raney and the Politics of 'Uplift,'" in Oliver, *Public and Private Persons: The Ontario Political Culture 1914–1934* (Toronto and Vancouver: Clarke, Irwin, 1975), 65–90.
5. "Proceedings," 17–20
6. "Proceedings," 21

7. "Proceedings," 42–4
8. "Proceedings," 44–50
9. "Proceedings," 58
10. "Proceedings," 59–60
11. "Proceedings," 63
12. "Proceedings," 63
13. "Proceedings," 64–7
14. "Proceedings," 68
15. "Proceedings," 70–1
16. "Proceedings," 71
17. "Proceedings," 74
18. "Proceedings," 75–6
19. "Proceedings," 77
20. "Proceedings," 78–9
21. "Proceedings," 282
22. "Proceedings," 83–5
23. "Proceedings," 95–6
24. "Proceedings," 97
25. "Proceedings," 98
26. Biographical information on William A. Irwin is drawn from the biographical files collection of the United Church of Canada Archives, Victoria University in the University of Toronto.
27. "Proceedings," 98
28. "Proceedings," 99
29. "Proceedings," 100–1
30. "Proceedings," 101–2
31. "Proceedings," 102
32. "Proceedings," 104–5
33. "Proceedings," 105–6
34. "Proceedings," 107–10
35. Toronto *Star*, June 3, 1930
36. Eayrs to Macmillan, June 3, 1930, MCP
37. "Proceedings," 111–3
38. "Proceedings," 115
39. "Proceedings," 116–7
40. "Proceedings," 117–8
41. "Proceedings," 118–9
42. "Proceedings," 121–2
43. "Proceedings," 123
44. "Proceedings," 124–5
45. "Proceedings," 126
46. "Proceedings," 128–9
47. "Proceedings," 133
48. "Proceedings," 135
49. "Proceedings," 142–4
50. "Proceedings," 144

51. "Proceedings," 144
52. "Proceedings," 145
53. "Proceedings," 147–56
54. "Proceedings," 156–8
55. Hector Charlesworth, *I'm Telling You: Being the Further Candid Chronicles of Hector Charlesworth* (Toronto: Macmillan of Canada, 1937), 229–30

FOURTEEN: RIPOSTES

1. At the bottom of the first page of Burpee's testimony in her copy of "Proceedings," Florence wrote: "Mr. Burpee was ill at this time but made a special effort to come to the court to testify." (158)
2. "Proceedings," 158–9
3. "Proceedings," 159
4. "Proceedings," 160
5. "Proceedings," 161–2
6. "Proceedings," 163–8
7. "Proceedings," 169
8. "Proceedings," 169–70
9. "Proceedings," 170–1
10. "Proceedings," 173–4
11. "Proceedings," 175–9. The common date of 800 AD as the origin of the Holy Roman Empire came from the following passage in James Bryce's book *The Holy Roman Empire* (new edition, enlarged and revised, New York: Macmillan, 1904): "The Holy Roman Empire, taking the name in the sense which it commonly bore in later centuries, as denoting the sovereignty of Germany and Italy vested in a Germanic prince, is the creation of Otto the Great. Substantially, it is true, as well as technically, it was a prolongation of the Empire of Charles; and it rested . . . upon ideas essentially the same as those which brought about the coronation of A.D. 800." (p. 80) The passage begins with the phrase "Holy Roman Empire" and ends with the date 800 AD, but the direct relationship between the two is contradicted by the statement that the empire was "the creation of Otto the Great." That Bryce had 962 AD, the date of the crowning of Otto in the church of St. John Lateran by John XII, in mind is clearly indicated on the final page of the relevant chapter. In this respect, Wells and Deeks were equally sloppy in their initial research.
12. "Proceedings," 179. For details on Brett, Innis, and Cochrane, see A.B. McKillop, *Matters of Mind: The University in Ontario, 1791–1951* (Toronto: University of Toronto Press for the Ontario Historical Studies Series, 1994).
13. "Proceedings," 180
14. "Proceedings," 181
15. "Proceedings," 182–3
16. "Proceedings," 184

17. "Proceedings," 185. See also "Says Wells Hadn't Time Without Use of 'The Web' – Prof. G.S. Brett Testifies Nine Months Impossible for 'Outline' Without Access to Miss Deek's [sic] Work," Toronto *Telegram*, June 5, 1930; Hector Charlesworth, *I'm Telling You: Being the Further Candid Chronicles of Hector Charlesworth* (Toronto: Macmillan of Canada, 1937), 331.
18. "Proceedings," 186
19. "Proceedings," 186–90
20. W.A. Irwin, "With What Judgment You Judge: A Study in Judicial Efficiency" (1956), 108, copy in DF
21. "Proceedings," 254–7
22. "Proceedings," 260
23. "Proceedings," 266
24. "Proceedings," 260
25. "Proceedings," 261
26. "Proceedings," 261–2
27. "Proceedings," 193–4
28. "Proceedings," 196–7, 199–203
29. "Proceedings," 205
30. "Proceedings," 206, 208–9, 210–3
31. "Proceedings," 215–6
32. "Proceedings," 225–6
33. "Proceedings," 239
34. "Proceedings," 239–40
35. "Proceedings," 240
36. "Proceedings," 242–5, 248
37. "Proceedings," 249–50
38. "Proceedings," 250. Wells's testimony concerning the date he first heard of Deeks and her manuscript is at page 235. In the margin of this page in Deeks's copy of "Proceedings," she had written: "Perjury."
39. "Proceedings," 252
40. "Proceedings," 266–9
41. Wise to Gregory, Dec. 20, 1917, Sir Richard Gregory Papers, University of Sussex, Brighton, Vol. 3, file 9
42. "Wells Places Resemblance to a Common Obvious Idea; Author's Testimony Taken in England Is Read at Trial Here," Toronto *Star*, June 5, 1930
43. "Proceedings," 269–70
44. "Proceedings," 271
45. "Proceedings," 271
46. "Case"
47. See Archives of Ontario, Toronto: Supreme Court of Ontario Criminal Indictment file RG 22-392-0-9386. See also the entry for Wise in the Convict Register and Description Book, Kingston Penitentiary, in the Correctional Service of Canada Museum, Collins Bay, Ontario.
48. "Proceedings," 272
49. "Proceedings," 275–6

50. "Proceedings," 276
51. "Proceedings," 277–8
52. "Proceedings," 279–80
53. "Proceedings," 280–2
54. "Proceedings," 282
55. Irwin, "With What Judgment," 24
56. Irwin, "With What Judgment," 26–7
57. "Proceedings," 284–5
58. "Proceedings," 286–7
59. Irwin, "With What Judgment," 23–4
60. "Proceedings," 288
61. "Proceedings," 288–9
62. For biographical details and an account of this phase of the academic career of Frank Underhill, see McKillop, *Matters of Mind*, 377–401.
63. "Proceedings," 290
64. "Proceedings," 290
65. "Proceedings," 291–3
66. "Proceedings," 293
67. "Proceedings," 294
68. "Proceedings," 295–9
69. "Proceedings," 301
70. This statement is not as wildly speculative as it may seem. The Frank H. Underhill Library of the Department of History, Carleton University, Ottawa, had its beginnings with Underhill's bequest of his personal library to the department. It holds the copy of *The Outline of History* (New York edition, 1920) Underhill used to prepare his testimony. His habit was to underline key passages in his books, and to make marginal annotations and write key page numbers (and passing thoughts) on their inside covers. I have carefully examined the degree of such annotation, which is slight given the task at hand. It is no greater, and perhaps less extensive, than that in other books in his personal library (for example, Graham Wallas, *The Great Society*).
    Underhill did take some notes and submitted them to the office of counsel to Macmillan of Canada. At trial, he had a memorandum at his disposal, prepared by McLaughlin's law firm ("Proceedings," 302). Neither MCP nor the Frank H. Underhill Papers in the National Archives of Canada contain any written memorandum that might have served as the basis of his testimony.
71. Underhill's outspoken views would soon make him a figure central to the history of academic freedom in Canada. See McKillop, *Matters of Mind*, 363–401, 541–3.
72. "Proceedings," 303–4
73. "Proceedings," 305
74. "Proceedings," 305–6
75. "Proceedings," 306–7
76. "Proceedings," 306–7

77. "Proceedings," 308–9
78. "Proceedings," 310
79. "Proceedings," 311–2
80. "Proceedings," 314–5
81. "Proceedings," 317. For an overview of the attitudes of Underhill and other male Canadian historians towards women in the historical profession, see Donald Wright, "Gender and the Professionalization of History in English Canada before 1960," *Canadian Historical Review*, Vol. 81, no. 1 (March 2000), 29–66.

FIFTEEN: JUSTICE

1. McLaughlin to Eayrs, June 7, 1930, MCP
2. McLaughlin to Eayrs, June 13, 1930, MCP
3. McLaughlin to Eayrs, June 27, 1930, MCP
4. "Links," 13
5. Eayrs to Macmillan, Sept. 13, 1930; Eayrs to Jennings, Sept. 15, 1930; Eayrs to Macmillan, June 6, 1930: MCP
6. Eayrs to Brett, Sept. 17, 1930, MCP
7. "Links," 13
8. "Reasons for Judgment of the Honourable Mr. Justice Raney," Sept. 27, 1930, "Proceedings," 368
9. "Proceedings," 369–70
10. "Proceedings," 370–75
11. "Proceedings," 376
12. "Case," 170
13. "Case," 172–3. Counsel for Deeks registered the appeal on Oct. 6, 1930, on the grounds that "the judgement was contrary to law and evidence and the weight of evidence." Ten reasons were given (180). The notice of appeal is in "Proceedings," 377–8.
14. Fiske to Wells, Sept. 22, 1930, Oct. 1, 1930: WC
15. Fiske to Wells, Oct. 10, 1930, Oct. 13, 1930: WC; "Five Years' Litigation Against Wells Fails; Miss Deeks' Action for $500,000 is Dismissed in Judgment. Sees No Plagiarism. Suit Should Never Have Been Brought, Justice Raney Declares," Toronto *Mail and Empire*, Sept. 29, 1930. In his Oct. 10 letter, Fiske misrepresented the association's name: Burpee had been secretary of the Canadian Authors' Association.
16. Eayrs to A. Klugh, Oct. 13, 1930; Eayrs to Brett, Oct. 13, 1930: MCP; Fiske to Wells, Oct. 28, 1930, WC
17. Eayrs to McLaughlin, Nov. 19, 1930; McLaughlin to Eayrs, Nov. 24, 1930; Brett to Eayrs, Nov. 21, 1930; Eayrs to Brett, Dec. 10, 1930: MCP
18. McLaughlin to Eayrs, Feb. 24, 1931; McLaughlin to George P. Brett, Jr., Mar. 10, 1931, Apr. 2, 1931: MCP. Henceforth, Eayrs's correspondence with the New York branch of Macmillan was usually with Brett, Jr.
19. "Contractor Leaves $842,609; Widow, Sons, Sisters Share; Sons of George S. Deeks Come Into Inheritance at Age of 24; Further $5,000

Annuity at 30, Provision for $12,000 a Year for Widow," Toronto *Telegram*, June 17, 1930

20. Mabel Deeks wrote letters from London, England, to relatives at home in Toronto. Some of these will be cited towards the conclusion of this chapter.

21. "Case," 180

22. "Case," 180

23. "Links," 13

24. "Case," 180

25. Biographical details have been drawn from the Ontario Bar Biographical Research Project of the Law Society of Upper Canada. See also Hilary Bates Neary, "William Renwick Riddell: Judge, Ontario Publicist and Man of Letters," *Law Society of Upper Canada Gazette*, Vol. XI, 3 (Sept. 1977), 144-74.

26. Quoted in Cecilia Morgan, " 'An Embarrassingly and Severely Masculine Atmosphere': Women, Gender and the Legal Profession at Osgoode Hall, 1920s-1960s," *Canadian Journal of Law and Society*, Vol. 11, 2 (fall 1996), 31. See also Christopher Moore, *The Law Society of Upper Canada and Ontario's Lawyers, 1797-1997* (Toronto: University of Toronto Press, 1997), 202.

27. See Valerie Knowles, *First Person: A Biography of Cairine Wilson, Canada's First Woman Senator* (Toronto: Dundurn Press, 1988), for details concerning the "Persons Case."

28. "Argument," 115. A note in Deeks's handwriting on the cover of this document reads: "Before the Appellate Division of the Supreme Court of Ontario." The text of the lengthy document indicates, however, that it was revised for oral presentation to the Judicial Committee of the Privy Council.

29. "Links," 14; "Case," 181

30. "Argument," 89

31. "Argument," 2, 24, 30-1, 55, 70, 73, 83, 109, 114

32. "Case," 181. I have made minor changes in punctuation in the transcription of these exchanges.

33. "Argument," 100-3

34. "Argument," 104-7

35. "Argument," 107-11

36. "Argument," 111

37. "Argument," 111. Putman's letter to Deeks was dated Jan. 30, 1931.

38. "Argument," 112-3

39. Eayrs to Macmillan, May 15, 1931, MCP; Ogden to Wells, June 30, 1931, WC

40. "Proceedings," 380-92

41. "Case," 190

42. Eayrs to Macmillan, Aug. 27, 1931; Eayrs to Brett, Sept. 2, 1931: MCP

43. Fiske to Wells, Sept. 3, 1931, WC. Wells recorded his reply in his own script at the bottom of this letter.

44. Fiske to Mrs. [G.P.] Wells, Sept. 16, 1931, WC; Eayrs to McLaughlin, Oct. 13, 1931; McLaughlin to Eayrs, Oct. 15, 1931: MCP
45. Brett, Jr., to Eayrs, Oct. 19, 1931, MCP
46. "Case," 191; Eayrs to Macmillan, MCP
47. McLaughlin to Eayrs, Oct. 29, 1931; Eayrs to Brett, Jr., Nov. 10, 1931: MCP
48. Spry to Eayrs, Dec. 16, 1931; Eayrs to Spry, Dec. 17, 1931; Eayrs to McLaughlin, Dec. 17, 1931; McLaughlin to Eayrs, Dec. 21, 1931; Eayrs to Spry, Dec. 22, 1931: MCP
49. McLaughlin to Eayrs, Feb. 5, 1932; Eayrs to Brett, Jr., Feb. 19, 1932: MCP
50. McLaughlin to Eayrs, Feb. 20, 1932, Feb. 27, 1932: MCP
51. Elliott, Hume, McKague & Anger to Gedge, Fiske & Gedge, Feb. 25, 1932; Fiske to Mrs. [G.P.] Wells, Mar. 9, 1932: WC

SIXTEEN: LANCASTER GATE

1. "Case," 192–3
2. "A *barrister* was entitled to plead cases at the bar of the superior courts of common law. An *attorney* was entitled to represent others in court business, but not to plead cases. '*Counsel*' and '*solicitor*' were equivalents of 'barrister' and 'attorney' in the court of Chancery." Christopher Moore, *The Law Society of Upper Canada and Ontario's Lawyers 1797–1997* (Toronto: University of Toronto Press, 1997), 344.
3. "Case," 194
4. "Case," 195. See also David M. Walker, *The Oxford Companion to Law* (New York: Oxford University Press, 1980), 672–3; Coen G. Pierson, *Canada and the Privy Council* (London: Stevens & Sons, 1960).
5. "Case," 197–8
6. "Case," 195
7. "Case," 202–3
8. "Case," 205–6
9. "Case," 206–8
10. See Daniel Macmillan to Eayrs, Nov. 10, 1931; Eayrs to Daniel Macmillan, Nov. 10, 1931; Eayrs to Arthur Macmillan, Nov. 10, 1931; Eayrs to Brett, Jr., Nov. 10, 1931; Brett, Jr., to Eayrs, Nov. 12, 1931; Arthur Macmillan to Eayrs, Nov. 23, 1931: MCP
11. "Case," 211–2
12. "Case," 212
13. "Case," 212–3
14. Mabel Deeks to "Dear Charlie and Everyone," Nov. 5, 1932, DF
15. Mabel Deeks to Jessica [?], Nov. 24, 1932, DF. This correspondence appears to have been with a niece.
16. Mabel Deeks, letter fragment beginning: "Here is a copy of a letter we got this morning." DF. The document is marked with a tag saying

"1933," but internal evidence ("I think we will try to run down to Brighton on Saturday") suggests that it was written on approximately Dec. 20, 1932.

17. Decidedly unconventional as well: among his several books (usually self-published) are *Harwood's Easy Lessons on Astrology: Giving Detailed Instructions on How to Cast and Read a Horoscope* (Brighton: P.J. Harwood, 1932); *The Re-Organization of the State, in Relation to the Present Crisis* (Brighton: P.J. Harwood, 1932); *When the War Will End: An Astrological Almanac* (Brighton: P.J. Harwood, 1941); and *When Will Peace Come?* (Brighton: P.J. Harwood, 1945). Independent of the question of whether his book on the solar system had come to be used by Wells, it seems clear that Harwood saw himself as fulfilling a prophetic, even "Wellsian" role.

18. See *Bulletin and Scots Pictorial*, Oct. 19, 1932; *Daily Herald*, Nov. 1, 1932; *Daily Mirror*, Nov. 2, 1932.

19. Mabel Deeks to "Annie & all," Dec. 5, 1932, DF

20. Wells to Gedge, Oct. 19, 1932, Nov. 4, 1932: WC; Macmillan to Eayrs [telegram], Nov. 3, 1932, MCP

21. Kennedy to Wells, Nov. 6, 1932; Wells to Kennedy, Nov. 8, 1932: WC

22. Kennedy to Wells, Nov. 8, 1932; Wells to Kennedy, Dec. 5, 1932: WC

23. Elliott, Hume, McKague & Anger to Gedge, Fiske & Gedge, Dec. 21, 1932, WC

24. McLaughlin to Eayrs, Dec. 27, 1932, MCP

25. Eayrs to Brett, Jr., Dec. 28, 1932, MCP

26. Eayrs to Brett, Jr., Jan. 5, 1933; Brett, Jr., to Eayrs, Jan. 30, 1933: MCP

27. Paragraphs concerning the Privy Council decision are drawn from *Dominion Law Reports*: [1933] 1 D.L.R., 353–9.

28. "Case," 230

29. "Case," 230

30. Mabel Deeks to "Dear Ann," [between Dec. 5 and 20, 1932], Aug. 26, 1933, DF

31. Mabel Deeks to "Charlie & all," Feb. 15, 1933, DF

32. Mabel Deeks to: "Dear Ann & all," [Jan. 1933]; "Dear Everyone," [Jan. 1933]; "Dear Ann & all," Feb. 2, 1933; "Dear Ann & everyone," Mar. 8, 1933; "Dear Ann & all," Mar. 21, 1933: DF

33. Mabel Deeks to "Dear Ann and all," Mar. 21, 1933, DF

34. "Case," 233–7

35. "Case," 237. The text of the letter is reproduced in this source.

36. Neish to Deeks, Apr. 10, 1933; Deeks to Neish, Apr. 12, 1933: DF

37. Eayrs to Brett, Jr., Apr. 13, 1933, May 6, 1933; Eayrs to McLaughlin, Apr. 13, 1933: MCP

38. The above account of Deeks and Buckingham Palace is drawn from "Case," 239–40.

39. The text of this letter of personal petition to the King is reproduced in "Case," 242–3.

40. "Case," 243–4
41. "Case," 244–5

SEVENTEEN: VOICES

1. William G. Deeks to the author, Dec. 16, 1998. Professor Campbell R. Harvey, of Fuqua School of Business, Duke University, has calculated that $1,000,000 Canadian in 1920 equalled $7,958,874 in October 1996. See Marianne P.F. Stevens, "Dollars and Change: The Effect of Rockefeller Foundation Funding on Canadian Medical Education at the University of Toronto, McGill University, and Dalhousie University" (unpublished doctoral thesis, Institute for the History and Philosophy of Science and Technology, University of Toronto, 1999), 154, n3.
2. Marquis to Deeks, May 7, 1934, DF
3. Draft copies of these manuscripts exist in DF.
4. Robinson to Deeks, Sept. 11, 1935; Ashley to Deeks, Sept. 22, 1935; Barker to Deeks, Sept. 24, 1935: DF
5. "Links," 25
6. See "Deeks-Featherstonhaugh," Toronto *Telegram*, Sept. 27, 1930.
7. Mary G. Mason, "The Other Voice: Autobiographies of Women Writers," in James Olney, ed., *Autobiography: Essays Theoretical and Critical* (Princeton: Princeton University Press, 1980), 210. See also Sidonie Smith, *A Poetics of Women's Autobiography: Marginality and the Fictions of Self-Representation* (Bloomington and Indianapolis: Indiana University Press, 1987), 9–18; Jill Ker Conway, *When Memory Speaks: Exploring the Art of Autobiography* (New York: Vintage Books, 1999).
8. *Experiment*, 619–20
9. Secretary to Wells to John A. Gedge, July 6, 1933, WC
10. McLaughlin to Eayrs, Sept. 13, 1937; Eayrs to McLaughlin, Sept. 13, 1937; Eayrs to Charlesworth, Sept. 14, 1937: MCP
11. Hector Charlesworth, *I'm Telling You: Being the Further Candid Chronicles of Hector Charlesworth* (Toronto: Macmillan of Canada, 1937), 294–339
12. Guillet to Wells, Feb. 1, 1945, WC. See also J.V. McAree, "Extraordinary Suit Begun in Toronto," Toronto *Globe and Mail*, Jan. 31, 1945; and McAree, "All Courts Wrong, Suggest Professor," Toronto *Globe and Mail*, Apr. 3, 1945.
13. Guillet to Wells, Apr. 10, 1945, June 9, 1945, Nov. 9, 1945, June 9, 1946, WC. Guillet later circulated a typescript of his account of the Deeks trial: "Much Ado About Nothing: A Study of the Evidence in the Literary Piracy Case of Florence A. Deeks, Toronto, versus Herbert G. Wells, England, 1925–1932," "Famous Canadian Trials," Vol. XIX (1945), 46; copy in DF.
14. Channing Pollock, "The Plagiarism Racket," *American Mercury* (May 1945), 613–9

15. Greg Gatenby, *Toronto: A Literary Guide* (Toronto: McArthur & Company, 1999), 373–4

16. Donald Jones, *Fifty Tales of Toronto* (Toronto: University of Toronto Press, 1992), 233–7

17. In 1933, influenced by the "moral rearmament" crusade of the Oxford Group, Wise wrote a letter to Sir Frederick Macmillan in order to make restitution for past misdeeds. Among other matters, he referred in it to "an accumulation of . . . unaccounted-for expense moneys" that he estimated to "run to some $300." He asked for forgiveness, but did not enclose a cheque. The original is in the Macmillan corporate archive at the University of Reading, England. A copy was forwarded on April 19, 1996, by John Handford, archivist and librarian of Macmillan Publishers Ltd., to Carl Spadoni, research collections librarian in the William Ready Division of Archives and Research Collections, Mills Memorial Library, McMaster University.

18. Fourteen years earlier, the eminent physician Sir William Osler sailed from North America for England on the *Campania* on July 16, 1904, and was well settled into Oxford by July 23. See Michael Bliss, *William Osler: A Life in Medicine* (Toronto: University of Toronto Press, 1999), 313.

19. Gregory to Wells, Oct. 31, 1918, "Proceedings," 407–8. See also Gregory's testimony during his evidence on commission: "Proceedings," 266–9.

20. Wells, "Introduction" to *Catherine*, 4–5

21. Catherine Wells, "The Draught of Oblivion," *Catherine*, 202–17

22. Catherine Wells, "In a Walled Garden," *Catherine*, 218–36

23. Catherine Wells, "Two Love Songs," *Catherine*, 284

24. Wells, "Introduction" to *Catherine*, 5

25. In a thorough survey of Wells's relations with women, particularly as reflected in his fiction, Robert Wallwork states: "Wells fashioned his own identity by repudiating and disparaging the qualities in himself which he viewed as 'feminine' – weakness, egotism, passion. His abhorrence of the feminine was reflected in his depictions of women as shallow and egotistical philistines intent on sabotaging masculine efforts." Robert Wallwork, "'The Besetting of Sex': Feminism, Masculinism, and the Woman Question in H.G. Wells, 1900–1914" (M.A. research essay, Carleton University, 1995), 5. See also Patricia Stubbs, "Mr. Wells's Sexual Utopia," chapter eleven of Patricia Stubbs, *Women and Fiction: Feminism and the Novel 1880–1920* (Sussex: Harvester Press, 1979), 177–94. In her book *The New Women and the Old Men: Love, Sex and the Woman Question* (London: Secker and Warburg, 1990), Ruth Brandon writes: "Jane purposed to keep H.G. Having caught her amazing husband, she was not about to let him slip away. If that involved subordinating her life to his – and he made it abundantly clear that those were the only terms upon which he would stay with any woman – that was a price worth paying." (204)

26. Ingvald Raknem, "Part VI: Originality or Plagiarism," in *H.G. Wells and His Critics* (London: George Allen & Unwin, 1962), 337–421, esp. 338–9, 421

27. This rendering of the myth is drawn from Timmen L. Cermak, M.D., "A New Look at Narcissus and Echo," in *Diagnosing and Treating Co-Dependence: A Guide for Professionals Who Work With Chemical Dependents, Their Spouses and Children* (Minneapolis: Johnson Institute Books, 1986), ix–x.

28. E. Nisbet, "The Centenary of H.G. Wells," unpaginated typescript in H.G. Wells Collection, Bromley Central Library. This four-page document is the text of an address Nisbet gave at the 1966 centenary celebrations of Wells's birth, held in Bromley. See also a similar address prepared by Nisbet, "H.G. Wells as the Young Writer," in the same location.

29. Mrs. C.A. Dawson-Scott, "As I Know Them; Some Famous Authors of To-day; H.G. Wells – Bernard Shaw – H. de Vere Stacpoole," *Strand Magazine* (July–Dec. 1923), 390; copy in Wells Collection, Bromley

30. For evidence of Catherine Wells's involvement in all aspects of her husband's affairs of publication except the actual writing, see the many letters from her to Macmillan in MA, Add. Mss. 54945.

31. Wells's tendency to "harry" his publishers about royalties and sales often worked to his financial detriment. "My reputation," he once said, "is out of all proportion greater than my book sales." See Norman and Jeanne Mackenzie, "How H.G. Harried His Publishers," *The Bookseller* (May 26, 1973), 2547–77; for details on Wells's finances, see Mackenzie, 289, 311.

32. See Thomas Mallon, *Stolen Words: Forays into the Origins and Ravages of Plagiarism* (New York: Penguin Books, 1989), 1–88.

33. See Lawrence J. Burpee to Deeks, Feb. 8, 1927, DF.

34. In a letter to Wise, Macmillan expressed surprise at Saul's departure. "This is the first we have heard of it, . . . and I think it would have been just as well if you had let us hear about it before." Macmillan to Wise, Mar. 12, 1919, MA, Add. Mss. 54282: "Canadian Letter Book, 13 Feb. 1914–5 May 1923."

35. See John Morgan Gray, *Fun Tomorrow: Learning to Be a Publisher and Much Else* (Toronto: Macmillan of Canada, 1978), 169.

36. Gray, *Fun Tomorrow*, 165–71

37. Wise to Pierce, Apr. 30, 1952, Lorne Pierce Papers, Queen's University Archives, Kingston, Ontario; "Olive Rubens, "Hobbies Make Life and People Interesting," Sherbrooke *Daily Record*, Mar. 21, 1959

38. William Tyrell, "To a Young Bookseller," *Quill & Quire* (May 1940), 26; "Hugh S. Eayrs, Publisher, Dies After Seizure," Toronto *Globe and Mail*, April 30, 1940

39. Paul H. Walton, "Beauty My Mistress: Hector Charlesworth as Art Critic," *Journal of Canadian Art History*, Vol. XV, 1 (1992), 95–8

40. Walton, "Beauty My Mistress," 99–100, 105. The Toronto *Globe and Mail* review ran on December 28, 1945.

41. Mackenzie, 378–9
42. Gregory to George Philip Wells, [1946], Sir Richard Gregory Papers, University of Sussex, Brighton
43. W.H.G. Armytage, *Sir Richard Gregory: His Life and Work* (London: Macmillan, 1957), 206–13
44. Quoted in Nancy F. Cott, ed., *A Woman Making History: Mary Ritter Beard Through Her Letters* (New Haven and London: Yale University Press, 1991), 15

Acknowledgments

Rₑₐᴅᴇʀꜱ ᴏꜰ ᴛʜɪꜱ ʙᴏᴏᴋ will understandably be wary of authors who provide lengthy lists of the names of helpful people. The fact remains that a number of institutions and individuals proved instrumental in bringing *The Spinster and the Prophet* to publication. None conducted research for the work, but I owe them many debts.

I am grateful to the Faculty of Graduate Studies and Research, Carleton University, Ottawa, using funds from the Canada Council for the Arts, for grants facilitating research in the United States and England. Receipt of a Research Achievement Award from Carleton University for the academic year 1996/97 made possible much of the research and the writing of early chapters. I also acknowledge with thanks the award of a sabbatical leave in 1997/98.

The following people have my gratitude for help they provided: Harold Averill, assistant university archivist, University of Toronto Archives, Toronto; Tom Belton, senior archivist, justice portfolio, Archives of Ontario, Toronto; Elise Brunet, curator, Archives of the Law Society of Upper Canada, Toronto; Jeanette Bosschart, reference librarian, the Law Society of Upper Canada, Toronto; Mary Burkee, Rare Book and Special Collections Library, University of Illinois at Urbana-Champaign; Jacqueline Carter, Humanities Reference Service, British Library, London; Lynn Cumine, past president, Women's Art Association of Canada, Toronto; Simon Finch, local studies librarian, Central Library,

Bromley, England; Roy Gainsburg, St. Martin's House, New York; John Honsberger, Raymond & Honsberger, a director of the Osgoode Society for Canadian Legal History, Toronto; Elizabeth Inglis, Manuscripts Section, University of Sussex Library, Brighton, England; Shayna Keces, Reference Department, Ottawa Public Library; Susan Lewthwaite, research coordinator, Archives of the Law Society of Upper Canada, Toronto; Gene Rinkel, curator of special collections, Rare Book and Special Collections Library, University of Illinois at Urbana-Champaign; Mary Rae Schantz, manuscripts librarian, Baldwin Room, Toronto Reference Library; Carl Spadoni, research collections librarian, Mills Memorial Library, McMaster University, Hamilton, Ontario; Bruce Whiteman, head librarian, William Andrews Clark Memorial Library, University of California at Los Angeles; and Ken Wilson, archivist, United Church Archives and Victoria University Archives, Toronto.

I also owe much to anonymous employees of the British Library, London; the Bodleian Library, Oxford; the Bromley Central Library, Bromley, England; the University of Sussex Library, Brighton, England; the City of Westminster Public Library, London; the National Library of Canada, Ottawa; the National Archives of Canada, Ottawa; the Carleton University Library, Ottawa; the University of Ottawa Library; the Canadian Corrections Museum, Portsmouth, Ontario; and the Toronto Reference Library.

An outline of my general argument was presented in 1997 to the annual conferences of the British Association of Canadian Studies in Swansea, Wales, and the Canadian Historical Association in St. John's, Newfoundland. Other invitations to speak resulted in the presentation of an expanded version of the story in October 1998 to the Ottawa Historical Association at Carleton University and (as the keynote address) to the Tri-University History Graduate Student Colloquium (University of Waterloo, Wilfrid Laurier University and University of Guelph) at the University of Waterloo. I am grateful to the organizers of these events, in particular Carter Elwood of Carleton University and Geoffrey Hayes of the University of Waterloo, for affording me the opportunity to share the story of Deeks and Wells with others.

Many friends and colleagues provided great support during the years in which I pursued this small footnote to history. For their invaluable advice and encouragement, I wish to thank the following people, with very different perspectives, who took time from their busy schedules to read an early (and more lengthy) version of the manuscript in a critical vein: Sandra Campbell, Phillip Cercone, Modris Eksteins, Gaye Facer, Martin Friedland, Gerald Hallowell, Bill Hanna, Bill Harnum, John Kendle, Judith Kendle, Duncan McDowall, and Melissa Pitts. Their enthusiasm for the project and their critical observations were much-welcome acts of genuine collegiality and intellectual exchange. Janet B. Friskney brought to bear her detailed knowledge of the history of Canadian publishing in the reading of certain chapters. George L. Parker provided invaluable information about the baroque mysteries of international copyright. Matthew Skelton, who is completing his doctoral dissertation at the University of Oxford on the relations of H.G. Wells with his publishers, shared with me his own insights and perspectives on Wells and the making of *The Outline of History*. Erin Adamo helped me check quotations. I am deeply grateful to all of these colleagues and friends.

When *The Spinster and the Prophet* was almost at the production stage, David C. Smith, biographer of Wells as author of *H.G. Wells: Desperately Mortal*, kindly agreed to answer a number of queries and to read the manuscript. It is a measure of his generosity of spirit that at short notice he was willing to provide a detailed assessment of it.

At a time when I possessed more enthusiasm than knowledge about the story of Deeks and Wells, several people provided just the right note of encouragement. Robert Fulford kindly responded to several queries I made of him very early on and became, in a sense, the "godfather" of the project. One of the questions I asked him was for more information about a "plagiarism machine" he had once mentioned in a column in the *Globe and Mail*. This led to my communication with two American scientists, Dr. Ned Feder and Dr. Walter Stewart, of the National Institutes of Health in Bethesda, Maryland. I am grateful to them for the interest they showed and for the laborious work they subsequently undertook on my behalf. (See "Sources.") Elizabeth Jonkel helped create the electronic version of "The Web."

Glenn Macinnes and Barbara Macinnes of Ottawa have taken an extraordinary interest in the story of Miss Deeks and Mr. Wells, and have encouraged others also to do so. William G. Deeks, son of George Campbell Deeks, kindly provided me with genealogical material on the Deeks family and with his recollections of Florence Deeks and others dear to her. Similarly, Mrs. Elizabeth A. Milsom, grand-daughter of Frank Wise, generously shared fond memories of him during his latter years. Professor James Eayrs, of Toronto, shared his memories of Hugh Eayrs, his stepfather. I thank each of these people for their interest and their willingness to help.

I am greatly indebted to Susan Kent Davidson — friend, editor, strategist, accomplice. During the hectic months during which much of the book was drafted, for the most part in a small log cabin in the Haute Gatineau, Susan in Toronto read each chapter. Her many electronic messages of enthusiasm, encouragement and advice proved invaluable. She is truly the midwife responsible for the birth of this book. Her unbridled enthusiasm for the story helped find it a home, and her enthusiasm has proved to be infectious.

That "home" is Macfarlane Walter & Ross, the book's publisher. In an act of faith, Jan Walter, its president and my editor, welcomed the book when it was only half-written, and I am profoundly grateful for the gentle but firm ways in which she has helped nurture and shape it. I have also been very pleased to work once again with Peter Oliver, editor-in-chief of the Osgoode Society – pleased that he proved willing to sponsor a work by an author who once took fifteen years to produce a book commissioned under his editorship. My copy editor, Barbara Czarnecki, practises her craft with peerless skill and has constantly reminded me by example of the many ways in which the best copy editors are an author's saving grace.

For reasons entirely unrelated to publishing, I owe much to the founding (and only) members of the Other Side Society, a small but very special group dedicated to surviving life's many vicissitudes, and with a smile. To Patricia Kelly, Roxanne Proulx, Morina Reece, and Beverley Webster I offer my enduring gratitude.

My parents have been unflagging sources of encouragement. My father, George, will probably be pleased to discover that his academic son has written a book that can be found in an ordinary bookstore. My mother, Jeannie, did not live to see *The Spinster and the Prophet* in print, but even during her final illness she maintained a steady interest in the story of Miss Deeks. This book is dedicated to her, in loving memory.

My deepest gratitude is to my partner and my son, Pauline and Hamish, who have witnessed the word "Deeks" becoming a verb around our home. I have spent much of my time "Deeksing" over the past five years, and they have unfailingly encouraged me to keep doing so. Pauline's years of experience in publishing led her to spot many weaknesses in the drafts of the book, and Hamish once again allowed his father to spend time away from responsibilities of fatherhood. I cannot thank them enough for the good humour and understanding they have shown in allowing me to spend time with the lady who so unexpectedly came to be the other woman in my life.

Credits and Permissions

ILLUSTRATION CREDITS

H.G. Wells (*Experiment in Autobiography*, Macmillan Inc., 1934, p 385): A7 (section A, page 7), top

Law Society of Upper Canada Archives: A8, bottom, P562; B5, bottom, P420

Toronto Reference Library: A1, top; A3, bottom, T12152; A7; A8, top (*Toronto Daily Star*, June 4, 1930); B5, top, T12025; B6-7; B8 (*Bulletin & Scots Pictorial* [Glasgow], October 19, 1932)

University of Illinois Library at Urbana-Champaign: A3, top; A4, bottom; A5; B1; B2, both; B3, both

Violet Keene (frontispiece of Hector Charlesworth, *I'm Telling You*, Macmillan of Canada, 1937): A6, top left

William G. Deeks: A2, both

William Ready Division of Archives and Research Collections, McMaster University Library, Hamilton, Ontario: A6, bottom; B4, top left, bottom left

Women's Art Association of Canada: A1, bottom

PERMISSIONS

The author wishes to thank the following copyright holders for their kind permission to quote or reproduce their materials.

A.P. Watt Ltd on behalf of The Literary Executors of the Estate of H.G. Wells: quotations from Wells's published works and correspondence; drawing by Wells (A4, top); quotations from published works of Catherine Wells

A.P. Watt Ltd on behalf of The Trustees of G.P. Wells deceased; illustrations A6, top right; A7

Curtis Brown on behalf of Angus Wilson: quotations from *Anglo-Saxon Attitudes*, copyright © 1956 by Angus Wilson

Macmillan Archive at the British Library: correspondence of Sir Frederick Macmillan

Macmillan Canada, an imprint of CDG Books Canada Inc.: correspondence from the Macmillan of Canada Papers, William Ready Division of Archives and Research Collections, McMaster University Library, Hamilton, Ontario; Macmillan of Canada logbook, the Deeks Fonds, Baldwin Room, Toronto Public Library

Mr. Alexander Murray, of University College, Oxford: letters of Gilbert Murray

Trustees of the Will of Mrs Bernard Shaw: correspondence of Charlotte Shaw

William G. Deeks: family photographs and works of Florence and Mabel Deeks, from the Deeks Fonds, Baldwin Room, Toronto Reference Library

Every reasonable effort has been made to locate and acknowledge the owners of copyright in texts and images reproduced in this volume. The author and the publishers would welcome any information regarding errors or omissions.

Index